LENS ⬡N LIFE

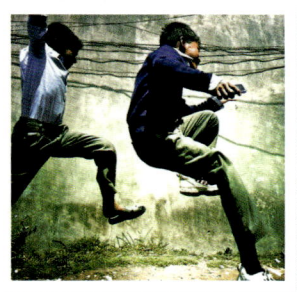 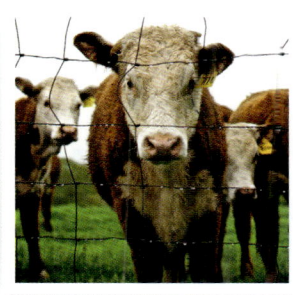 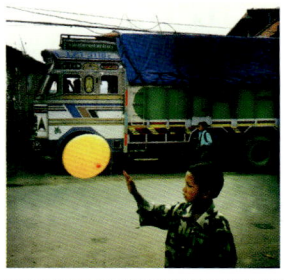

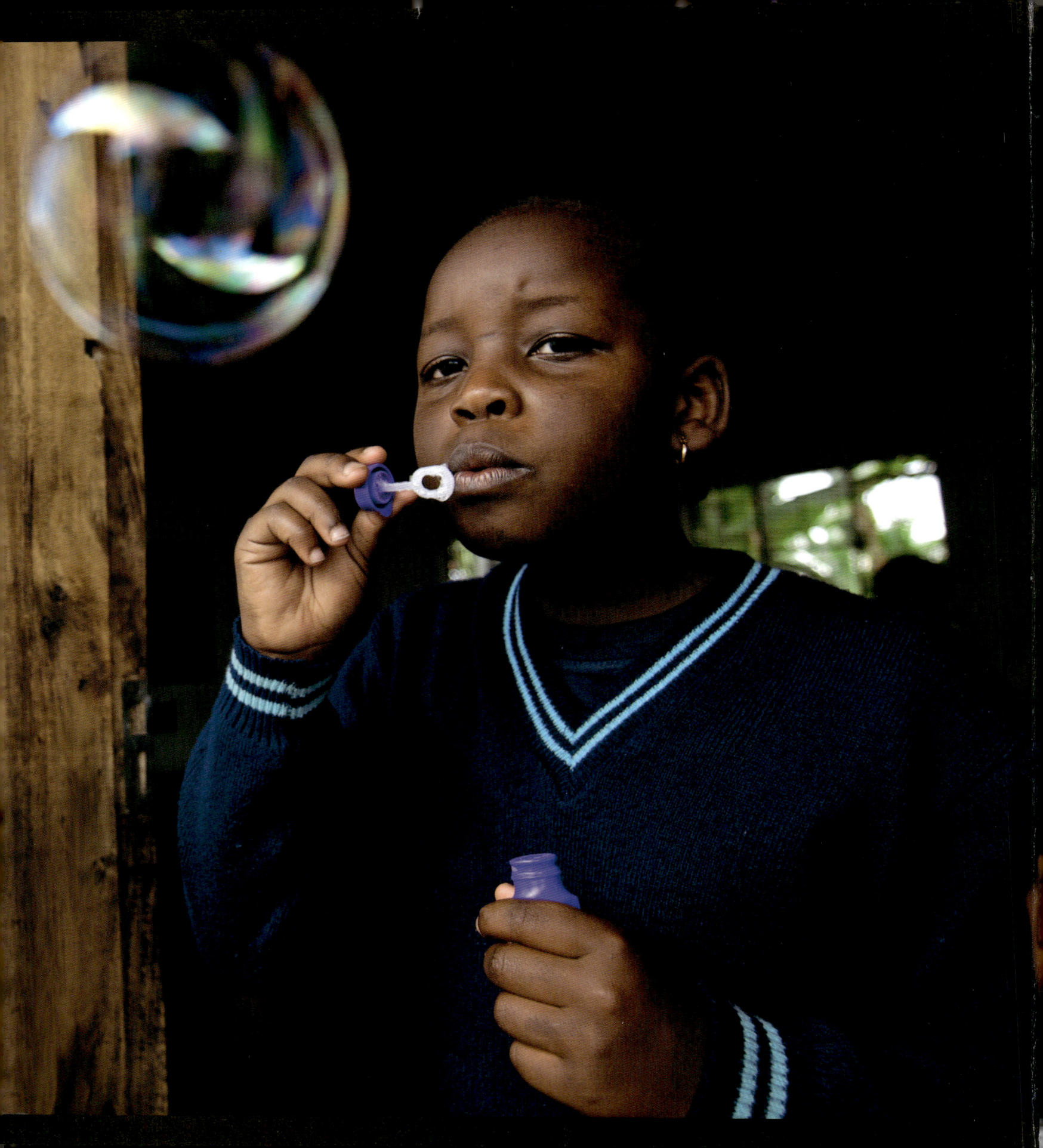

LENS ON LIFE

DOCUMENTING YOUR WORLD THROUGH PHOTOGRAPHY

STEPHANIE CALABRESE ROBERTS

ILEX

First published in the UK in 2012 by

I L E X

210 High Street
Lewes
East Sussex BN7 2NS
www.ilex-press.com
Copyright © 2012 The Ilex Press Limited

Publisher: Alastair Campbell
Associate Publisher: Adam Juniper
Creative Director: James Hollywell
Managing Editor: Natalia Price-Cabrera
Editor: Carey Jones
Editor: Tara Gallagher
Specialist Editor: Frank Gallaugher
Senior Designer: Kate Haynes
Design: JC Lanaway
Picture Manager: Katie Greenwood
Colour Origination: Ivy Press Reprographics

British Library Cataloguing-in-Publication Data
A catalogue record for this book is available from the British Library.

ISBN: 978-1-908150-34-9

Printed and bound in China
10 9 8 7 6 5 4 3 2 1

All photographs in this book are copyright Stephanie Calabrese Roberts unless otherwise noted. Photographs featured in the contributing photographers' sections are copyright to featured photographers Elliott Erwitt, Elizabeth Fleming, Sion Fullana, Ed Kashi, Jen Lemen, John Loengard, Beth Rooney, and Rick Smolan.

About the cover photograph: Koseli School students generate motion and serve as subjects for their fellow classmates shooting with iPhone cameras on the streets of Kathmandu, Nepal on April 15, 2011. These two boys are among eight students participating in the first Lens on Life photography program. Learn more about Koseli School on page 166 in Chapter 4: Push Through Boundaries and Let Your Subject Guide You.

Contents

Documentary photography holds the power to capture moments of historical significance; to reveal what's hidden; to broaden our exposure to people, places, and experiences beyond our reach; to shape (or shatter) our perceptions; and to offer an authentic view of humanity. Think of this book as a companion on your journey to capturing life as it unfolds.

Broaden your concept of documentary photography and get inspired by going behind the lenses of a diverse collection of documentary photographers including: Beth Rooney, Sion Fullana, Ed Kashi, John Loengard, Elizabeth Fleming, Rick Smolan, and Elliott Erwitt. Trace their paths to photography. Hear about their inspirations and find out what makes their visions unique. Explore and learn from their approaches.

Thoughts on Documentary Photography & the Intent of this Book

Life in the present moment is the canvas of the documentary photographer. Life, rich with intrigue, complex textures, layers of story, mixed emotions, spontaneous gestures, brilliant light to warm our souls, and sultry shadows that send us deep into the depths of our imaginations . . . this is our focus. Viewing the world through the magic window that is our lens, documentary photographers are curious beings. We ask questions, explore possibilities, push boundaries, and seek answers by studying and dissecting the complexity of life with intense scrutiny and great anticipation. We seek to discover and expose moments of truth in our photographs to say something about who we are as diverse characters performing our unrehearsed acts on this stage called life.

While photography is about exposing what we see, there's so much more going on beneath the surface. There's a complicated concoction of thoughts and feelings that drive the impulse to lift a camera to our eyes, to compose the raw material of what's present, and to wait patiently for the proper moment of capture,

when time and space sync and align. We as documentary photographers most often play the role of observers, attempting to minimize our influence on the subject in focus, yet I believe in each of the images we create we subconsciously infuse a bit of ourselves.

Whether you're an avid mobile shooter, an eager amateur photographer, or a seasoned professional with a desire to explore the path of documentary photography, this book is intended to be your trusted companion—a source of inspiration and a guide on your journey. You don't have to visit faraway lands, witness newsworthy events, expose exotic strangers within an urban streetscape, or carry expensive camera gear to practice the art of documentary photography. You can practice it every day with a camera that's small enough to fit in your pocket.

Before we get started, I'll assume you are comfortable using the camera of your choice, whether it's a basic point-and-shoot, a high-end digital SLR, or the camera on your mobile phone. Becoming proficient with your camera is particularly important

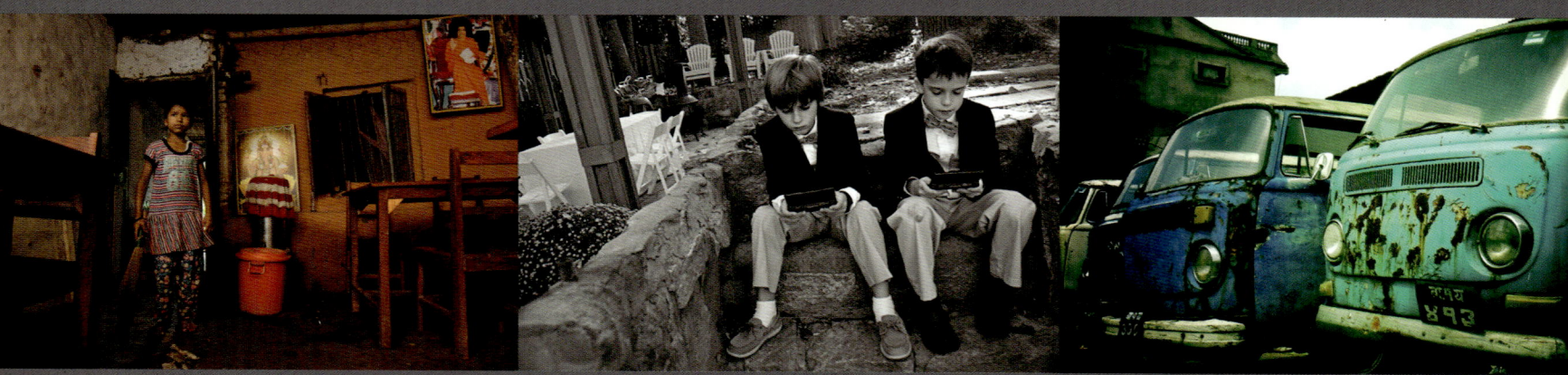

in the art of documentary photography because you must direct
your eyes and focus more on your subject and less on your camera.
While this book is not intended to teach you the technical aspects
of photography, I do highlight camera settings beside select images
throughout the book to expose my decisions related to focal
length, ISO, aperture, and shutter speed settings in a variety of
shooting environments. That said, know that there is no magic
formula or set of rules for creating an image.

I hope the secrets revealed in this book will inspire you to
document your world every day and to express your unique vision
in ways that challenge and thrill you.

Share your journey.

Looking forward,

Stephanie

Stephanie Calabrese Roberts

IN THIS BOOK WE WILL

- Broaden your perspective of documentary photography.
- Go behind the lens with some of the world's most talented documentary photographers to learn from their experience and viewpoint.
- Challenge you to stretch your creative boundaries, shoot in new ways, and take steps toward uncovering your unique visual voice.
- Explore image-processing techniques and examples to help you evaluate and enhance your documentary images.
- Help you define and plan the execution of a documentary project.
- Encourage you to explore beyond your boundaries and go someplace you've never been.
- Reveal examples and stories behind the creation of several documentary projects to help you open your mind and let your subject guide you.

PHOTOGRAPHS IN THIS BOOK

Unless otherwise credited to another photographer, Stephanie Calabrese Roberts created the photographs in this book using three cameras: a Nikon D3s, a Nikon D90, and an iPhone 4. Her lenses include: 50mm f/1.4, 14–24mm f/2.8, and 24–70mm f/2.8. For image processing, she used Aperture on an iMac and a variety of photography apps on her iPhone including Hipstamatic, Cameramatic, Photo fx, Instagram, and Photoshop Express.

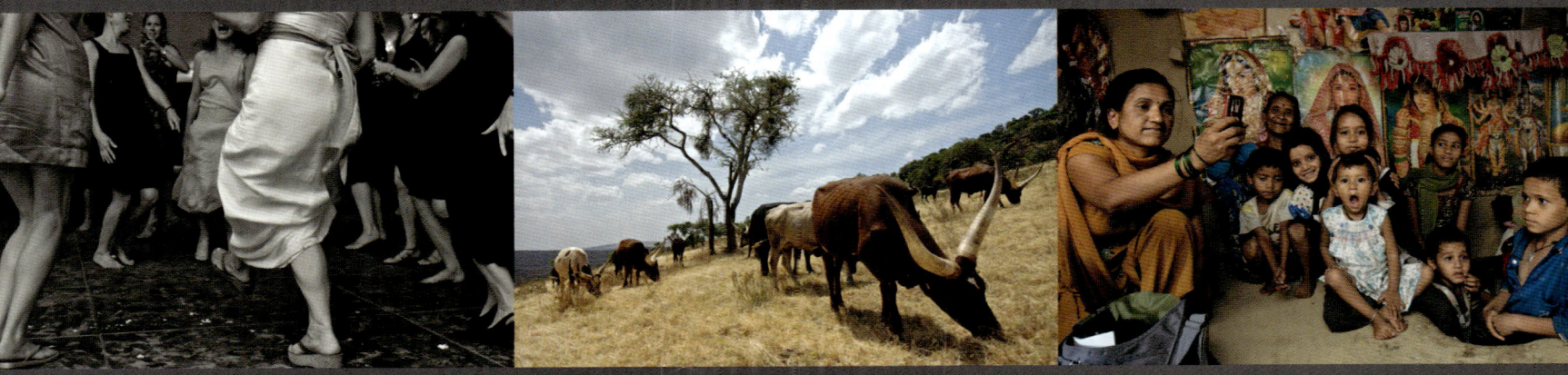

The Secret of How Photography Found Me

For as long as I can remember, I've been drawn to documentary photography. As a child, I'd pore over stacks of well-worn *National Geographic* and *Life* magazines in the library at my small elementary school in Saddle Brook, New Jersey. Ignoring the words and embedding myself within rich images of colorful people in big cities and faraway lands, I'd step away from the predictability of my day-to-day existence and wander through the intriguing stories found in these still images. "I want to see this in real life," I'd think. "I want to be the one making these pictures."

The Christmas I was seven years old, Santa Claus left a Kodak camera, a cartridge of film, and a handful of flashcubes in my stocking. I can't recall if this gift was "on the list," but I do know that all of the other gifts I received that Christmas have faded from my memory. I lifted the plastic camera to my eye and composed a view of my brother in his pajamas, reaching for gifts beneath our Frazier Fur laden with opaque, colored bulbs, mismatched ornaments, and too much tinsel. It was love at first "click." The notion that I had just preserved a moment in time using a simple, handheld device moved me. I felt very grateful to hold that magic in my hands.

BELOW Self-portrait somewhere between Ngorongoro Crater and Arusha, Tanzania.

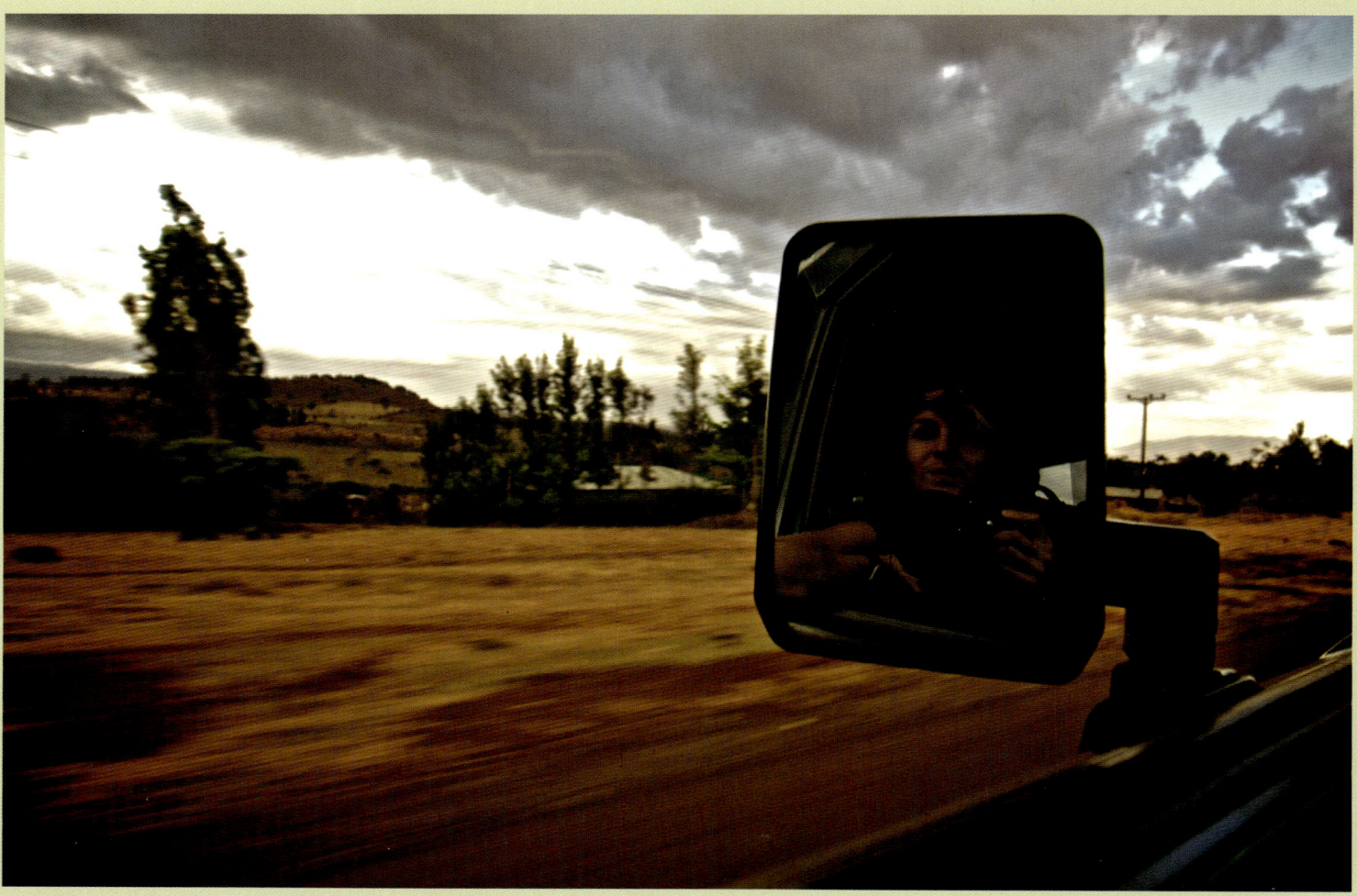

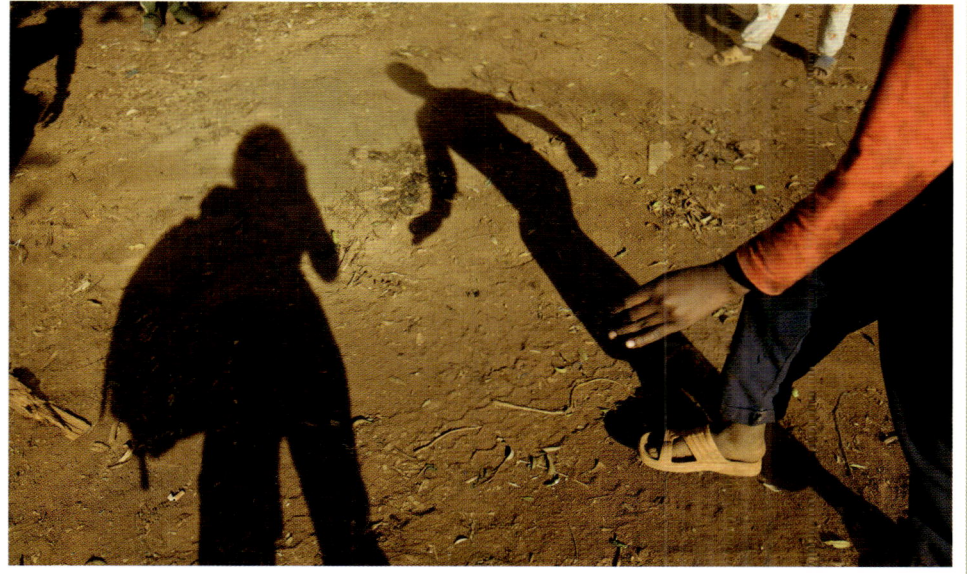

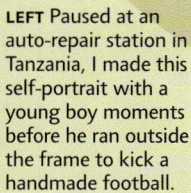

LEFT Paused at an auto-repair station in Tanzania, I made this self-portrait with a young boy moments before he ran outside the frame to kick a handmade football.

Eager for action beyond the confines of my fenced-in backyard, when I returned to my second-grade classroom after the holiday break in January 1976, my camera came too. Carefully tethering the magic device to my wrist, I assigned myself the job of photographing my classmates during our lunch hour until my exposures ran out. While my classmates scrambled around the blacktop in kickball formation and kicked up dust on the playground, I distanced myself just enough to study their movements and expressions. I'd run along beside them or lie down on the ground looking up at them as they dangled from the monkey bars, then watch compositions magically form within the small rectangular viewfinder, making my "clicks" when elements aligned into their correct positions. I didn't know the word "composition" at the time; something inside just instinctively told me when to click. Because the film cartridge in my camera was limited to 12 or 24 exposures, I learned to savor the shooting experience—to wait patiently and to be selective in the choice of my moment.

With a camera in my hand (or swinging from my wrist), I felt important and even more comfortable among my friends—I connected with my subjects unobtrusively while consciously inserting some space. There was something about this newfound distance that appealed to me. I was no longer limited to mindless play during recess, because shooting gave me interesting things to think about . . . something *to do*. On the days I brought my camera to school, I remember rushing home and placing my cartridge in the pre-addressed envelope and badgering my mother to mail it in right away. I'd check the mailbox constantly during the painful wait for the arrival of my package, and burst with excitement when I finally got the chance to carefully slip my 3 × 5 prints with their rounded corners out of the envelope and into my clean hands. Magic. I studied each image repeatedly, made mental notes on what worked and what didn't, and steadily saved my allowance to buy the next 24 exposures. I had found my place in this world, and it was happily hidden behind a camera.

I didn't realize it at the time, but it would take 32 years and a path through several careers and artistic pursuits before I made a conscious effort to rekindle my passion for photography and submit to it as my primary focus and profession—to reconfigure my life around it. I often wonder why it took so many years. So many detours, stops, and starts. Perhaps I just needed time to live, to learn how to see, and to have something to say—to build confidence in my vision. *To let it find me.*

If you're holding this book in your hands, you must feel a tug in your heart toward documentary photography—to explore, study, capture, and share an honest view of your world. But I must offer you a word of caution. Don't choose documentary photography as your profession if you think it might lead you to fame, a steady paycheck, or a predictable path through the remainder of your life. It will likely give you none of those things. It will raise questions and make you feel unsteady. It will challenge your long-standing assumptions, demand courage, and push you to break down boundaries you didn't even know existed. The drive of your curiosity and pursuit of elusive magic moments could lead you down narrow paths, winding roads, and steep hills toward people and experiences that could change you in ways you never expected—but the view will be quite spectacular. Follow the path of documentary photography because it fuels your passion for life. *Let it find you.*

1
GET INSIDE THE MIND OF A
DOCUMENTARY
PHOTOGRAPHER

Documentary photography can be defined, approached, and practiced in endless ways, but it works best when it unfolds in a way that's unique to you. When I first began thinking about this book and the idea of sharing my personal thoughts, experiences, and techniques, I felt it critical to include insight and perspective from a diverse collection of documentary photographers I respect and admire. This sent me on a path to see if I could uncover and illuminate secrets from them—to get inside the mind of each photographer and broaden the reader's view and approach to documentary photography.

"I don't have any photography secrets," cautioned Elliott Erwitt in our initial email exchange. Reading these words from one of the greatest documentary photographers of our time made me smile and question what my mission might yield. We know most photographers by way of their images—the view they compose, capture, and choose to share with the world. Clearly, the evidence of remarkable photographers is made visible in his/her images. It doesn't really matter when they first discovered photography, what type of equipment they use, where they find inspiration, or how they approach the art of making images. Perhaps there are no real secrets, I mused. Yet, I was curious to find out more, and to compare and contrast their thoughts and experiences with my own.

During each interview, I asked questions like: "When and how did you first discover photography? What inspires you to pick up a camera and make an image? What goes through your mind before you begin shooting? How would you articulate your vision? What have you learned from your failures and successes?" I don't know if their answers revealed in this chapter are best defined as secrets, but I do know their stories and perspectives are quite fascinating, and I'm more convinced than ever that there is no one way to look at life.

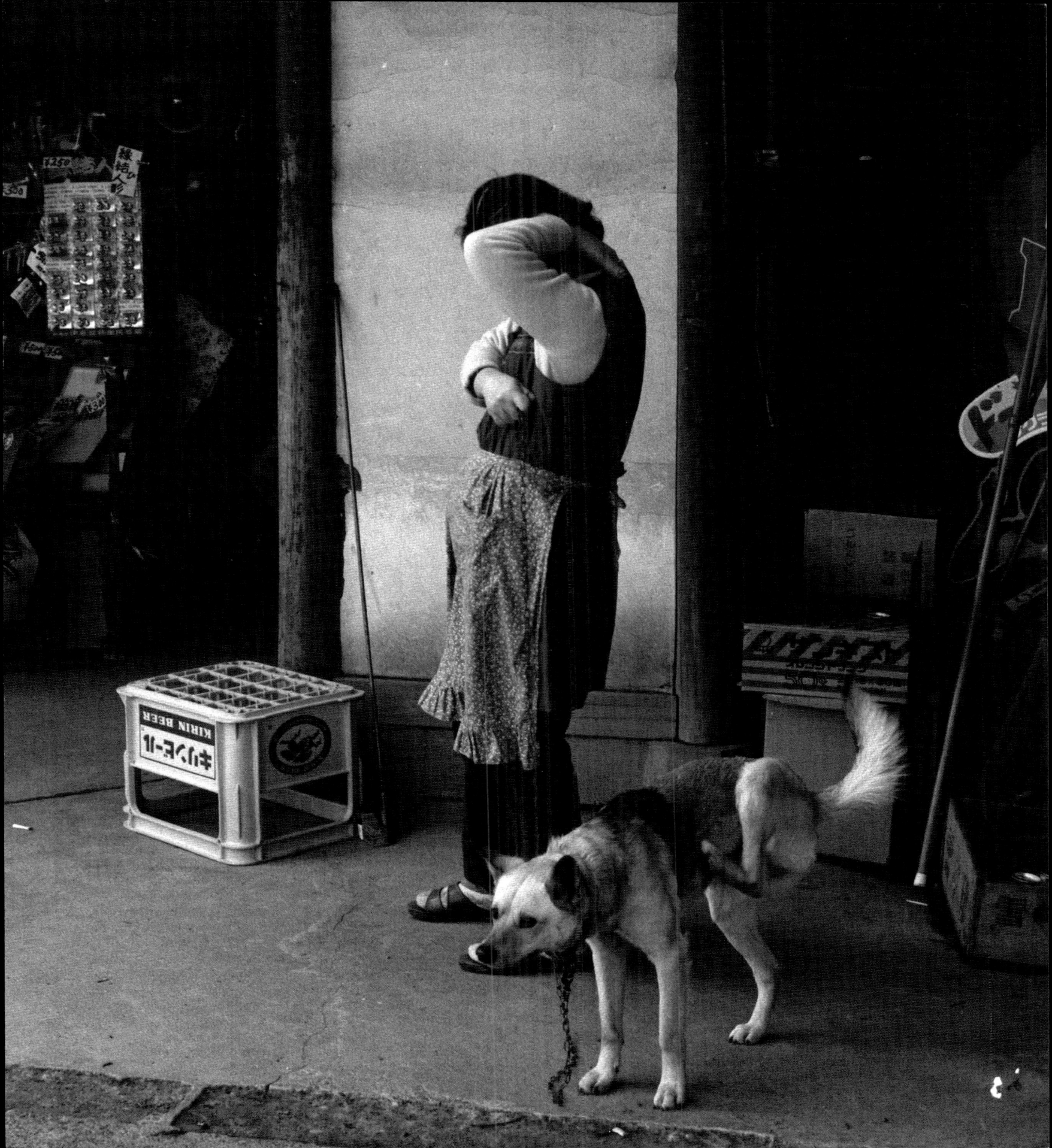

Beth Rooney

www.bethrooney.com

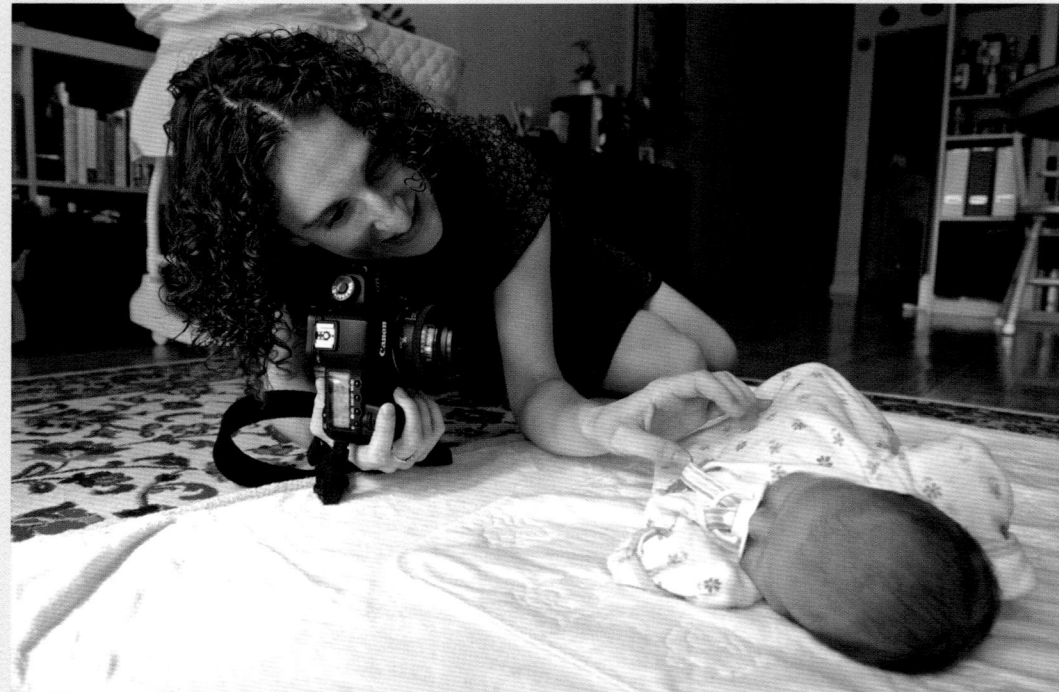

Portrait of Beth Rooney by Stephanie Calabrese Roberts

LEFT: Beth Rooney focuses on her new subject, daughter Rose.

"Documentary photography is a way for me to explore a situation that I'm curious about. Like everything else in my life, I don't have just one focus. Documentary doesn't have to be about heavy subject matter. It can be about whatever you're experiencing."

PATH TO PHOTOGRAPHY

Beth Rooney first began to make photographs as a child, during a family vacation in Yellowstone National Park. Although she doesn't remember how old she was or the specs of her first camera, she found that using the device was an easy way to document the overwhelming beauty she saw and the intense feelings she had about that experience. It wasn't until high school when Beth took a photography class (prompted by her cousin's interest in photography) that she reconnected with photography as a way of exploring and processing her experiences with the world. A curious generalist, Beth was (and still is) fascinated by most things, and didn't feel a pull toward a specific academic pursuit or career path when she began thinking about college. She felt that photography might be a path to integrate her diverse interests, which spanned history, sociology, and communication. She was drawn less to the art of photography, and more to the medium's ability to stimulate her mind and integrate her broad intellectual interests. Beth eventually settled on a rigorous photojournalism program at Ohio University, led at the time by Larry Nighswander, a former *National Geographic* editor.

Shortly after her freshman year at Ohio University, Beth remembers making a conscious decision to choose photography, following a pointed conversation she had with Marcy Nighswander, one of her professors. "[Marcy] told me to commit to the program or get out of it because you can't be on the fence about photography. If you want to do it as a job, you really have to want to do it as a job. You can't kind of like photography. You have to really focus on it and learn how to run a business if you're going to freelance. It was the kick in the pants I needed." That conversation led Beth to narrow her focus on photography as a career path, while broadening her interest in interdisciplinary subjects like global studies, history, and sociology and their influences on poverty and social justice throughout the world. After college, she traveled to Paranagua, Brazil on a photojournalism grant, and later interned with documentary photographer and filmmaker Lauren Greenfield in Los Angeles before venturing out on her own as a freelance photographer in the Chicago area.

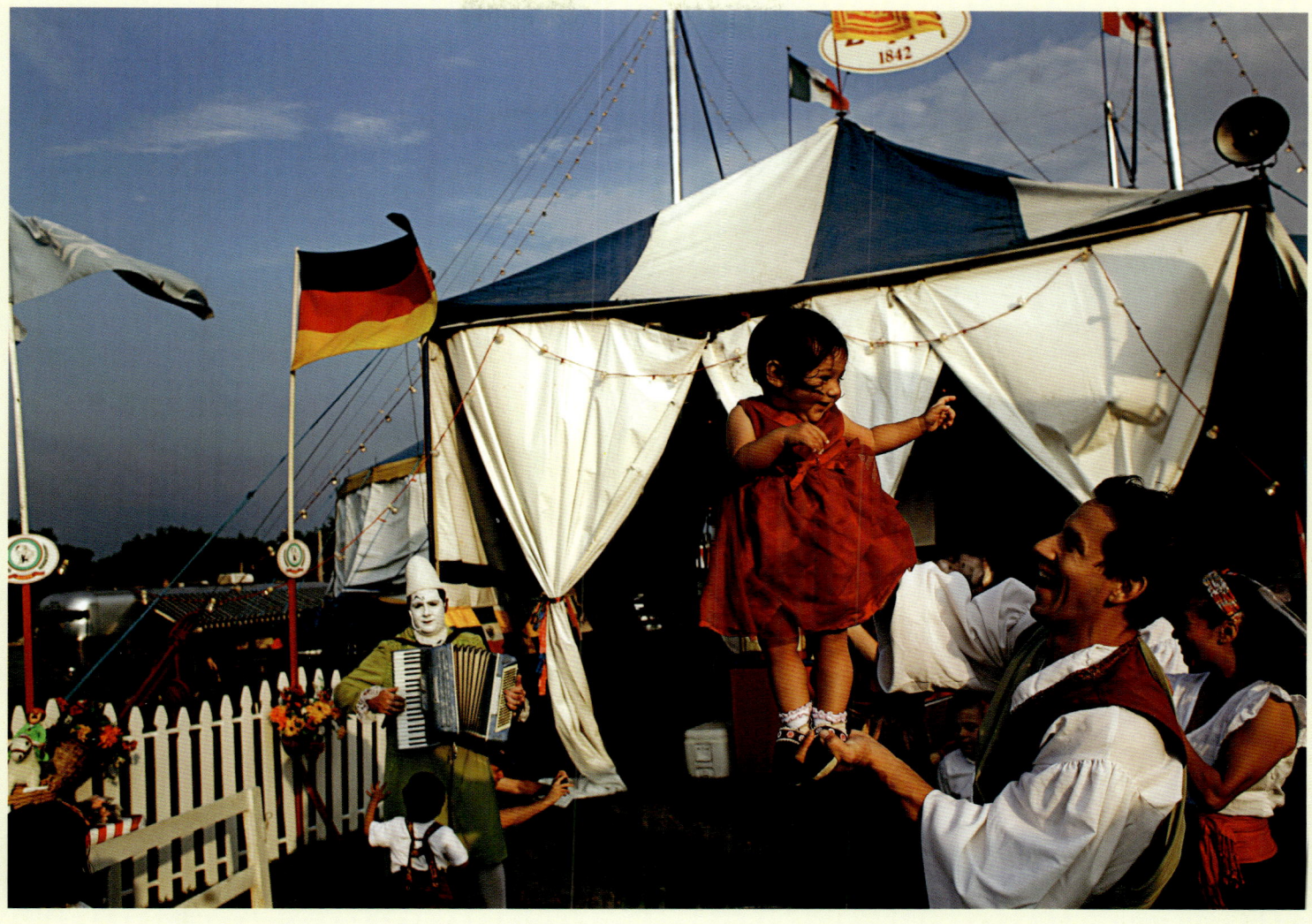

About the Series

"Zoppé, an Italian Family Circus, has been entertaining crowds around the world since 1842. Unlike most contemporary circuses, which feature unrelated individual acts, performances of the Zoppé Family circus tell a story, starring Nino the Clown and Tosca the equestrian ballerina. Nino and Tosca's tale includes acrobats, juggling, dogs, horses, audience participation, and even more clowns. With a cast that changes from city to city, the Zoppé troupe focuses on emotional connections with the audience and works to preserve the dying art of family circus. As Nino Zoppé explains, 'To me, the word circus means family.'"

BETH ROONEY

ABOVE: Carlo Gentile holds Giulia, two, in front of the tent at the Zoppé Family Circus in Addison, Illinois.

BEHIND THE IMAGE

"Carlo's daughter is two years old, and she can already stand on her dad's hand. It just shows the circus performers are so much more relaxed with their kids — the kids are allowed to do all kinds of stunts, and they're totally capable of it. This beautiful moment between father and daughter shows the genuine love they have for each other and the unique intergenerational family appeal of this circus."

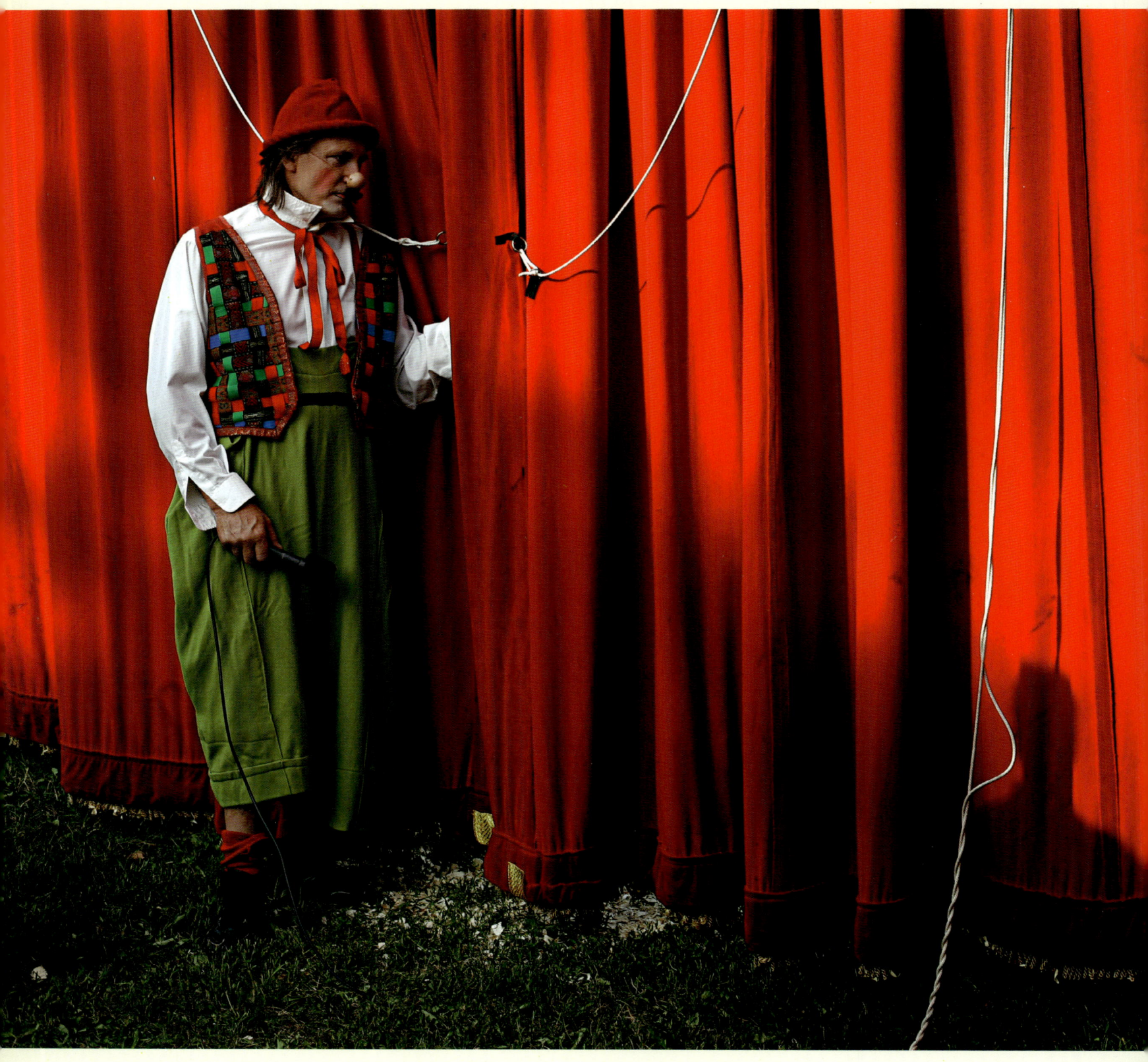

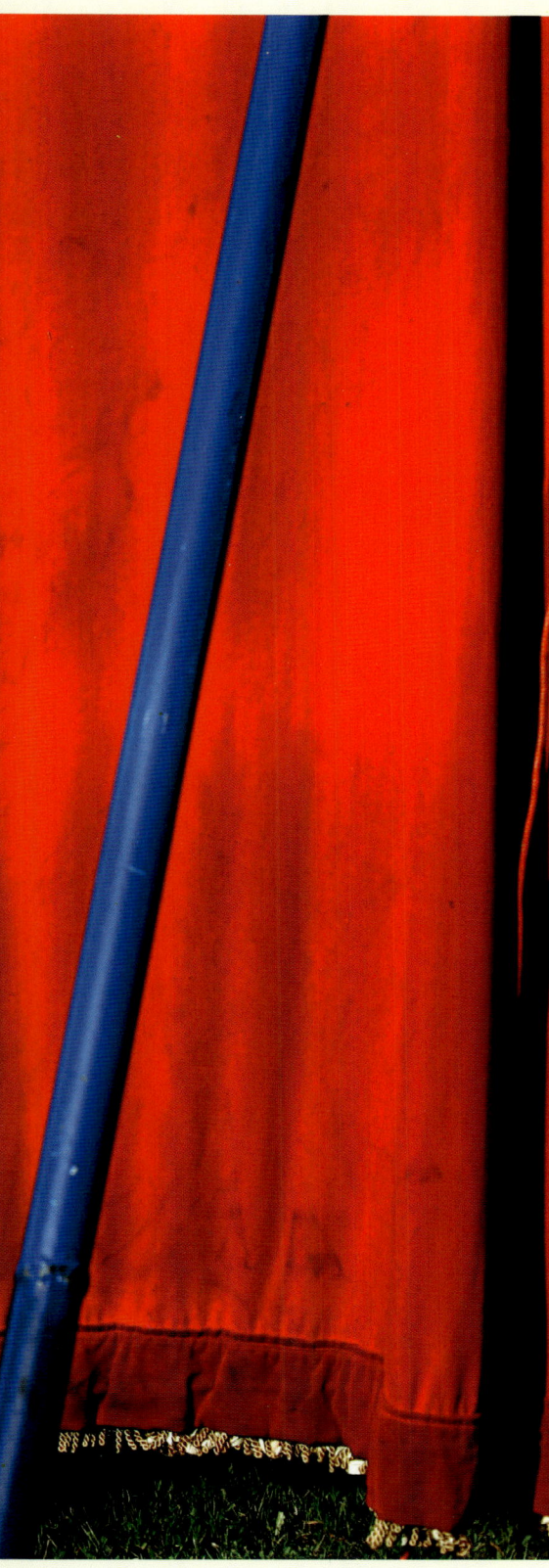

INSPIRATION

"For me, photography is not the only thing I focus on. I love it. It's my job. I can't imagine doing anything else. It's how I get through the world, but there's so much more." Beth's wide range of interests and creative pursuits include reading, traveling, cooking, gardening, sewing, and crafting. "If I get too focused on one thing, I find that I lose perspective."

Beyond her professional photography assignments for clients like the *Chicago Tribune*, *The New York Times*, *Time*, *FaderMagazine*, and *Saveur*, Beth might work on three to four personal projects each year. Ideas for projects often come serendipitously while Beth is reading a thought-provoking book on a topic like psychology, or scanning an intriguing article in a local newspaper. In fact, Beth first discovered the Zoppé Family Circus while flipping through *Time Out Chicago* in 2007. "I was looking for something to do for the weekend and saw this little blurb about an Italian family circus being in town and I thought, 'That sounds kind of interesting. Maybe I'll go see what it's all about.'"

Intrigued by the opportunity to create a visual record of an experience she hadn't seen before and to meet some fascinating new people, Beth showed up to the circus tent on a Thursday night and explained that she wanted to hang out and photograph the Zoppé family's shows during their stay in Chicago. "When I approached the family, I was honest. I told them I was a freelance photographer and that I wanted to photograph them as a personal project with the possibility of publication at a later date." Open to Beth's curiosity and sincerity, the Zoppé family welcomed Beth that night and a connection began.

APPROACH

Beth remains open to the organic evolution of her documentary projects. "I didn't really have a vision when I started the project—only an interest to show the day-to-day banal and magical moments of living life in a circus." When Beth first began shooting the Zoppé family, she initially turned her lens toward the performances, particularly the children under the tent, studying their acts and interactions with the crowd. Drawn to the simplicity of the Zoppé's classic act, unencumbered by the bells and whistles of larger, better-known circuses, Beth was able to focus more on the raw emotions and gestures of the performers rather than the production. The first few times Beth showed up to shoot, she didn't get behind the scenes. After each shoot, she brought prints or disks of images to give to her subjects as a gesture of thanks. "I wanted them to know that I wasn't there to just take from them. I was interested in sharing with them."

As her study continued, Beth knew that she wanted to shoot beyond the performances and integrate a deeper view of what life was like for the Zoppé family behind the curtain. But the family was hesitant at first. "It's not that they didn't want me there, but it was still a guarded situation. [In the beginning], we were all trying to figure out where that boundary was. I had to be patient and wait for them to slowly let me in, to trust me, and to decide if they wanted me in their life." It took time. Beth frequently spent eight hours a day with the Zoppés during their stay that first season.

Beyond the first year of the project, as Beth's friendship with the Zoppés grew, circus members invited her behind the curtain and into their homes, sharing meals and their way of life with her. "When I came for dinner, they knew I'd take pictures, but I was respectful and made a point not to shoot the entire night.

BEHIND THE IMAGE

Giovanni is the son of the Zoppés' late patriarch. He's the slapstick comedian and circus announcer, yet he's also in charge of the business. He's always a little more on edge because he's checking the crowd to see if they've sold enough tickets before each show. You'd never assume that he was the serious businessman behind the curtain. It's a view you don't see when you're out in the audience."

LEFT: Giovanni peeks out at the crowd before a show.

I enjoy talking to the people I'm working with, as it gives me a better sense of who they are and how they should be represented. Documentary work is successful when the photographer can accurately read and understand the people she is shooting."

Beth has always been very curious, open, and outgoing, though admits she doesn't like being the center of attention. She feels that her camera gives her a good excuse to meet and engage with new people—she calls it "a jumping-off point." Beth also feels that her broad range of interests and thirst for knowledge help her feel more at ease putting down the camera to engage in diverse conversations with any of her subjects, from outspoken drag queens to conservative Midwestern farmers. She believes that it's important for photographers to be tolerant,

and to hold back on judgment if a subject says or does something that's not in sync with their own personal beliefs and perspectives. In her mind, her role is to document the individual, the experience, and the space as she sees it, and not to judge it or try to change the opinions of her subject—in other words, to just "let it be."

VISION

Beth's subject matter is varied—everything from awkward adolescents making their way through middle school to hopeful African refugees rebuilding their lives in challenged low-income neighborhoods—but the common aim that runs through her work is to simply make "pictures of moments that don't hurt." Beth's photography is not politically motivated, nor is she looking to evoke pity on behalf of her subjects or to sensationalize their challenging

BEHIND THE IMAGE

"Every time I was there to photograph Carla, she tried to hide her cigarette. She'd say, 'I don't want pictures of me smoking.' I'd say, 'But Carla, you smoke.' When I finally got one of her smoking, she said, 'I knew you were going to get it, and that's fine. That's what I need to do. If I'm embarrassed, I should stop.' There's a lot going on in this frame but Carla's almost desperate drag on her cigarette before she rushed off to prepare the dogs for the performance defined the moment."

BELOW: Carla Zoppé has a cigarette before the first show in Des Plaines, Illinois. Carla used to perform equestrian tricks, but now participates in her husband's act.

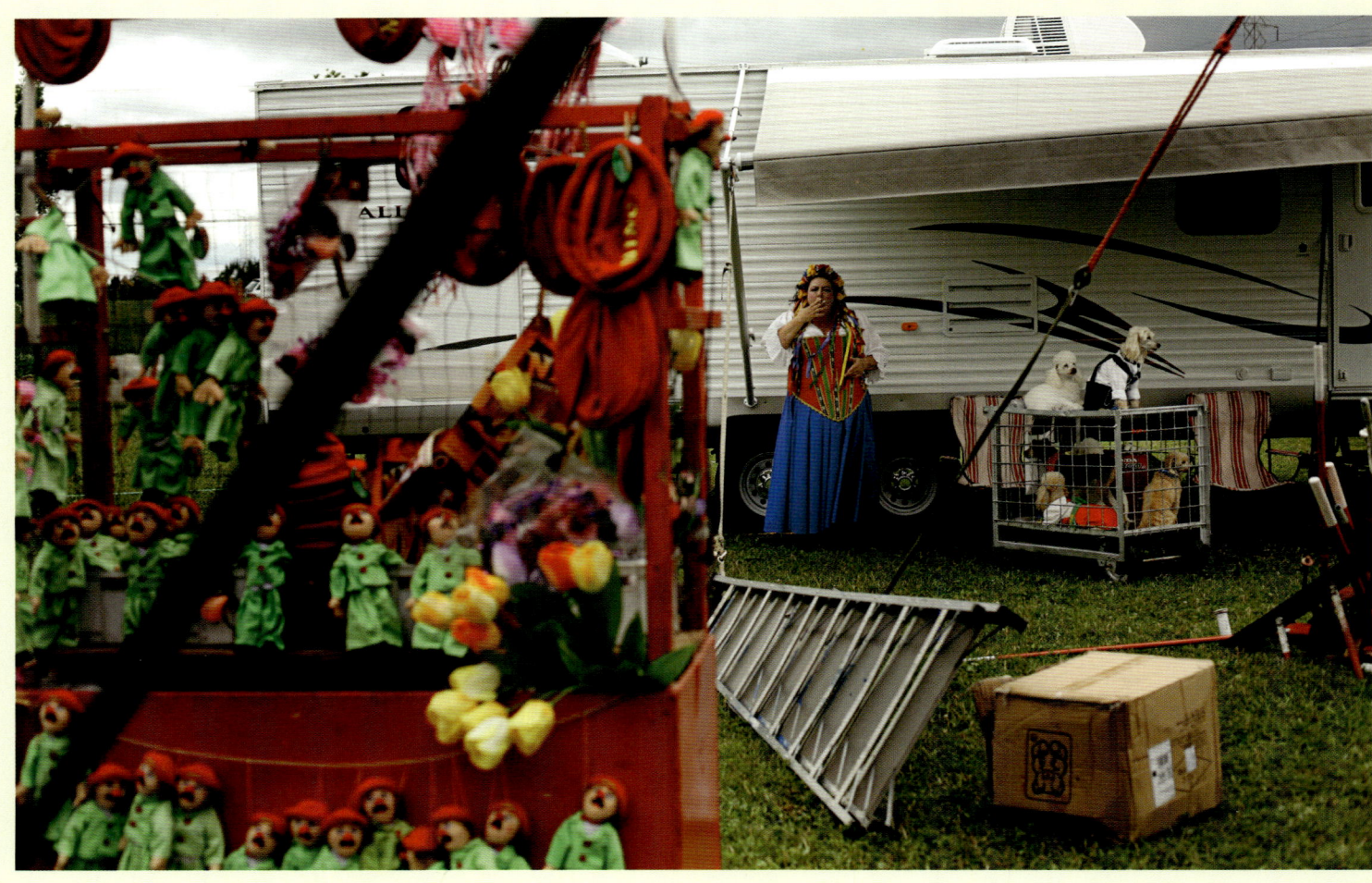

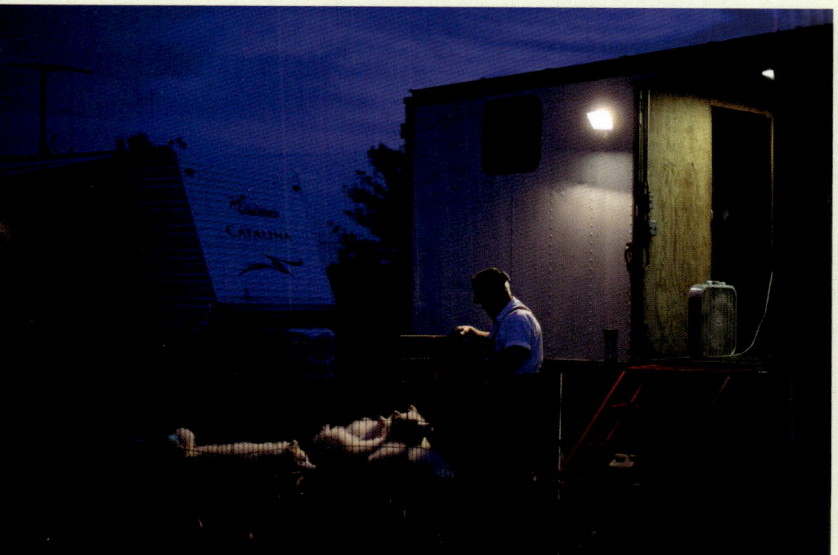

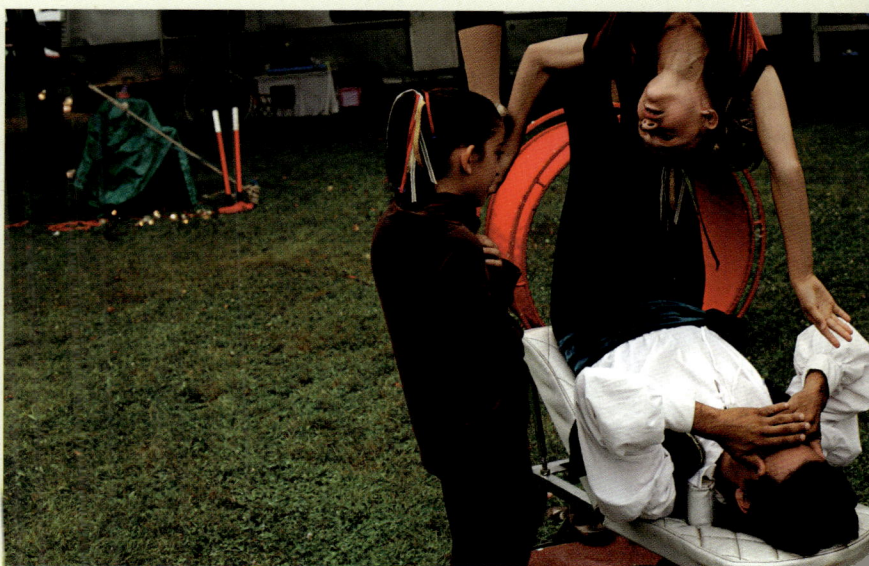

BEHIND THE IMAGE

"Rudy has always been more reserved and distant with me. He and his wife, Carla, have a dog trick performance where the dogs run obstacle courses and do cute little dances. Rudy's much more comfortable with his dogs than he is with people. Most of the performers love to be photographed, but there are times when I have to pull back from that and wonder, 'Is this who you really are? Or is this just part of your performance?' This felt like an honest moment."

ABOVE: Rudy Heinen puts his performing canines back in the pen after their final performance of the night. Rudy is married to Carla Zoppé, the eldest of the Zoppé siblings.

situations. Instead she seeks to connect viewers with diverse individuals and their situations through relatable moments. "If people can connect with my subjects by finding something that they can relate to or if they can see a little bit of themselves in the story or situation, they're more likely to have a reaction. I'm not looking to evoke a positive or a negative reaction—just a reaction."

BEHIND THE IMAGE

"This moment was so foreign and funny to me. These sisters were having a conversation while one of them was bent over her father's legs like a pretzel and flipped several times with his feet. The kids start practicing tricks like this when they're five or six years old. Their agility is mind-boggling, but what defines the moment for me is the juxtaposition of a typical sister-to-sister conversation in the context of such a bizarre setting—bizarre for me, but normal for them."

"I usually don't go into a shoot thinking that I'm going to prove something or disprove something. I just go in, see what the situation is, and form an idea of where I want the story line to be—more like touchpoints than an actual path or a mission statement to guide my work. I don't try to persuade or dissuade someone of a stereotype. I don't go into it thinking that. I'm just curious." Armed with questions, Beth discovers the answers by studying her subjects and their interactions, talking with them, and remaining careful to not let herself get hooked into a single situation or conversation for too long lest she miss something happening on the periphery of the scene.

EQUIPMENT

Beth travels lightly when she's working on a documentary assignment, using one digital SLR (a Canon 5D Mark II) and a set of fixed lenses: 28mm, 35mm (currently her favorite lens), 50mm, and 85mm. While Beth does use a zoom lens for client assignments to minimize lens changes in time-sensitive or high-stress situations, she avoids it for personal projects to minimize the intimidation factor with her subjects. Beth has chosen to work exclusively with natural light on the Zoppé family "Behind the Curtain" project thus far. "If I'm shooting in someone's home, the last thing I want to do is fire a flash a bunch of times and have a huge lens in their face. I don't even bring a camera bag. I have a few big purses (so I can) just throw stuff in and pull stuff out. For personal work I just try and minimize that professional look and make it casual so people are more comfortable."

"All documentary work is about give and take, and building a relationship with the people you are trying to photograph."

PROCESSING

Beth enjoys shooting much more than image processing. When she's completed a shoot, Beth does a quick, rough edit to see what she's captured, and categorizes and tags images using Photo Mechanic on a big screen desktop iMac in the hallway office space just outside her newborn's nursery on the second floor of her apartment. Beth then performs minimal image adjustments to tweak brightness, contrast, color, and/or white balance "to try to get [the image] to look the way I saw it" using Adobe Photoshop. "I really don't like doing Photoshop stuff and I don't like sitting at the computer. Documentary work is inherently more outside the home. That's why my office space is pretty small. I don't want to spend too much time here."

When you are shooting a story over an extended period of time, Beth suggests that it's important to think about visual continuity and how image processing can support that. When the setting, seasons, or time of day changes in a long-term project, you might have a totally different visual situation in each of your image sequences. It's important to find a way to tie all the images together—to make sure they flow, even though years may separate one image sequence from another. You might fall in love with an image, but visually it just may not fit with the series. Consider ways to connect images shot over time in a single series with a consistent color palette or monochrome processing to avoid visual disconnects in the series.

A SECRET

Consider how your own life might mirror your subject's.
Spending time with the Zoppé family behind the curtain, Beth discovered that some aspects of their life mirrored her own. "Despite their ups and downs, the Zoppés love the path they've chosen in life and find joy in working hard and putting on a great show every night. They don't have a lot of financial stability or predictability, but they make it work, and try not to worry too much. Instead, they focus on performing well, booking lots of shows, and hoping for the best. As a freelance photographer, I can relate to that mindset. It was good for me to see. I'm never sure how much work I'll have, so I just work hard at doing what I love, booking as many shoots as I can . . . and hoping for the best."

BEHIND THE IMAGE

🔴 "Tosca, one of the daughters of the original Zoppés, is very religious, so she always prays before she goes into the ring. After following the Zoppés for four years, I was finally able to get close enough to Tosca to capture this very personal, quiet moment."

RIGHT: Tosca Zoppé says a quick prayer before entering the ring to perform.

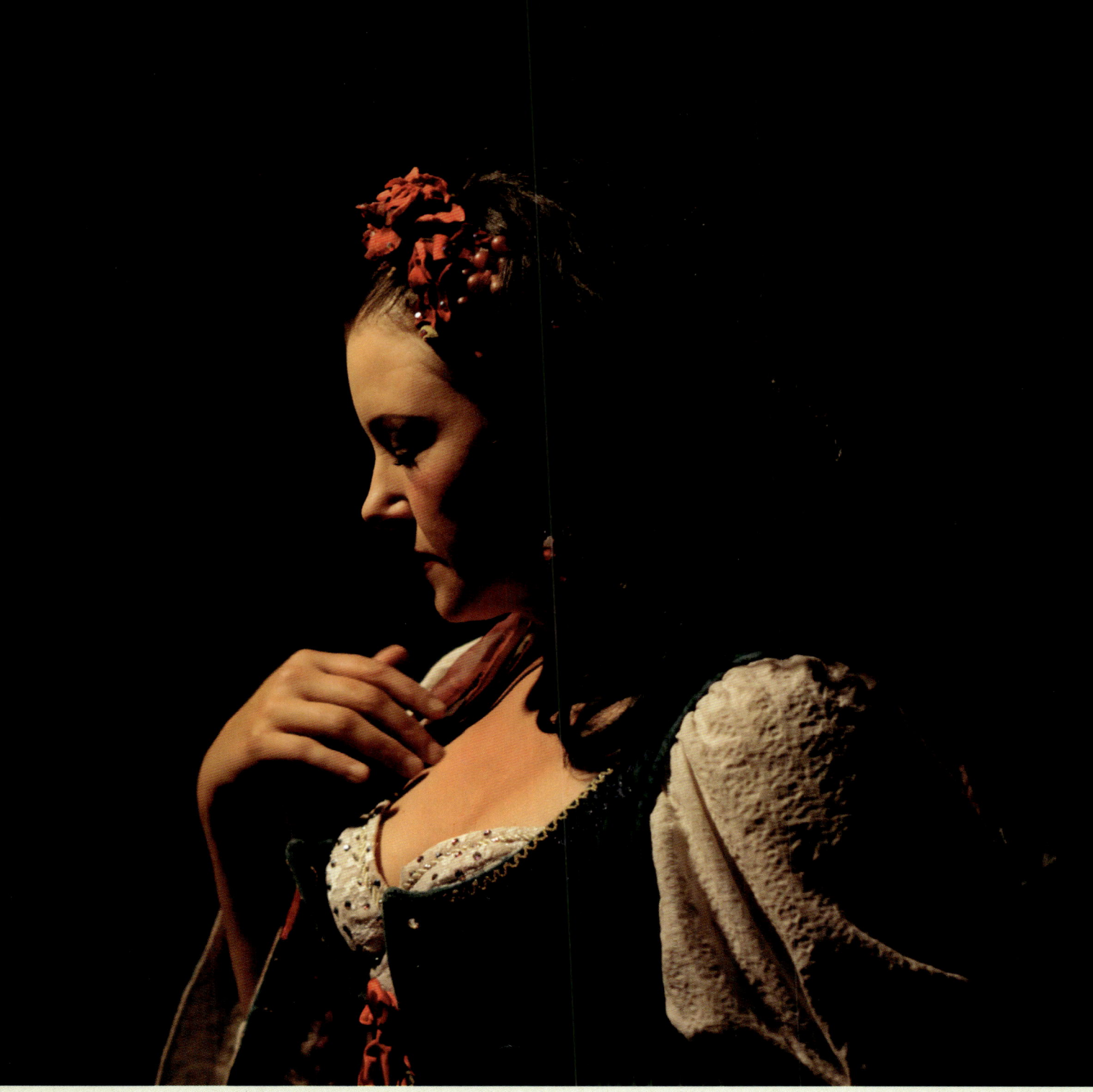

Sion Fullana

www.sionfullana.com

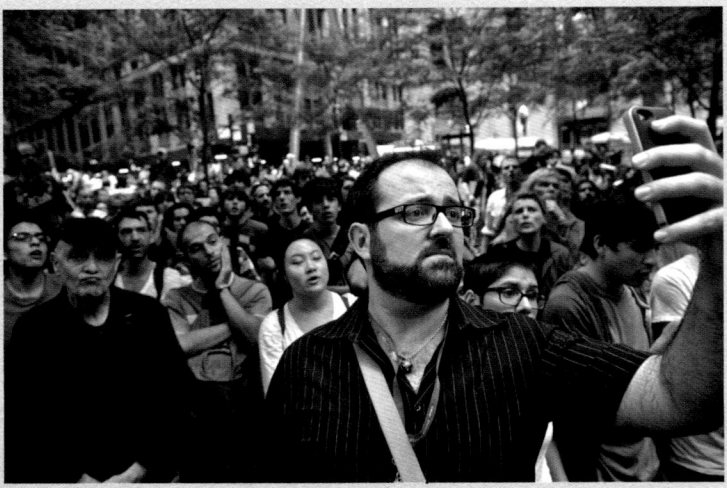

Portrait of Sion Fullana by Stephanie Calabrese Roberts

"When I really go into [my shooting], it's kind of like entering a trance. I have to stop and make myself aware and then the moments come to me when my logical thought disappears and I become open to life around me. I either find it or I don't. But if I go explicitly searching, I may not find anything."

LEFT: Sion shoots with his iPhone at the Occupy Wall Street protest in Zucotti Park (dubbed "Liberty Square") in New York City, September 2011.

PATH TO PHOTOGRAPHY

Sion Fullana grew up in an upper-middle class family in Majorca, a small island off the coast of Spain. He discovered his voice (literally) at a very young age. "My mom always says that I didn't take a step until I was two, but at nine months, I was speaking fluently all the time. She tells a funny story that one day she had me in the store, and I was in the baby cart. I think I started singing or talking and the retail person asked, 'Who is talking?' They didn't see anyone. And it was me there . . . a baby." By the time he turned eight, Sion was fascinated with comic books and fantasies, and began to express himself creatively by writing his own stories and poems throughout his teenage years.

While pursuing his journalism degree at Universitat Autónoma of Barcelona, Sion grew more interested in film as a method of storytelling and went on to attend a Robert McKee screenwriting workshop in Barcelona. Sion visited Cuba with his family while in college, and later, after graduation, he returned to the country to pursue a two-year graduate degree in film directing at The International

Film and TV School (EICTV) in San Antonio de los Baños. There he became intrigued with documentary, and though he lacked confidence in his photography skills, Sion began to experiment with street photography when he returned to Spain.

In 2005, while living in Barcelona and on the hunt for a journalism job, Sion started a blog and began sharing his photographs, personal stories, and perspectives on social justice issues with friends and family. "Sometimes if I wanted to tell a story about a gay-related issue or racism, I would go through everything I had in my [photo] library, pull an image, and write. Or sometimes I would stare at a photo for a while and think, and I would type a one-page story in ten minutes before bed." Sion enjoyed shooting images, but didn't take them seriously. He considered himself a reporter and a writer, not a photographer. "I never studied photography, so that made me a little self-conscious. At first, I had a hard time learning to use the camera. But on the other hand, I studied journalism, read comics all my life, and I studied film directing. I had the idea

of the composition and storytelling, so that kind of helped."

Around this time, Sion met Anton, a creative New Yorker in the comic book business, while he was vacationing in Spain. The spontaneous introduction was an instant connection that led to a 14-month long-distance relationship. Following several visits to Anton in New York City, Sion fell in love. "Through that year, we were deciding what to do. The job market in Spain was bad, so I didn't have much to lose. I thought, 'What are we doing?' and said to Anton, 'I'll come to New York and we'll give it a try.' Once I got to New York in March 2006, everything changed."

BEHIND THE IMAGE

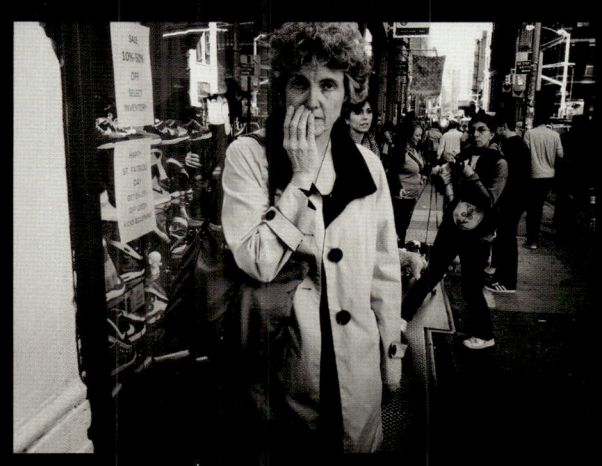

"I turned around the corner and I had the iPhone ready. When I saw that gesture, I shot. The sad thing is that the strong eye contact is an illusion. She probably saw my eyes, but I didn't see hers because I was seeing the image. You have it there but you didn't have it in life."

RIGHT: *The Woman Who Looked at Me.*

BEHIND THE IMAGE

Sion loves shooting in the rain and shot this image at East River Park in New York City. An Italian photo blogger featured Sion's work, including this image, and compared it to Elliott Erwitt's classic photograph of a silhouetted man leaping with an umbrella in the foreground of the Eiffel Tower in Paris. "The funny thing is I love that photo by master Erwitt, and yet when I shot mine I had never seen his before. I guess it was all a matter of a certain intuition."

LEFT: *The Man Who Dreamed*

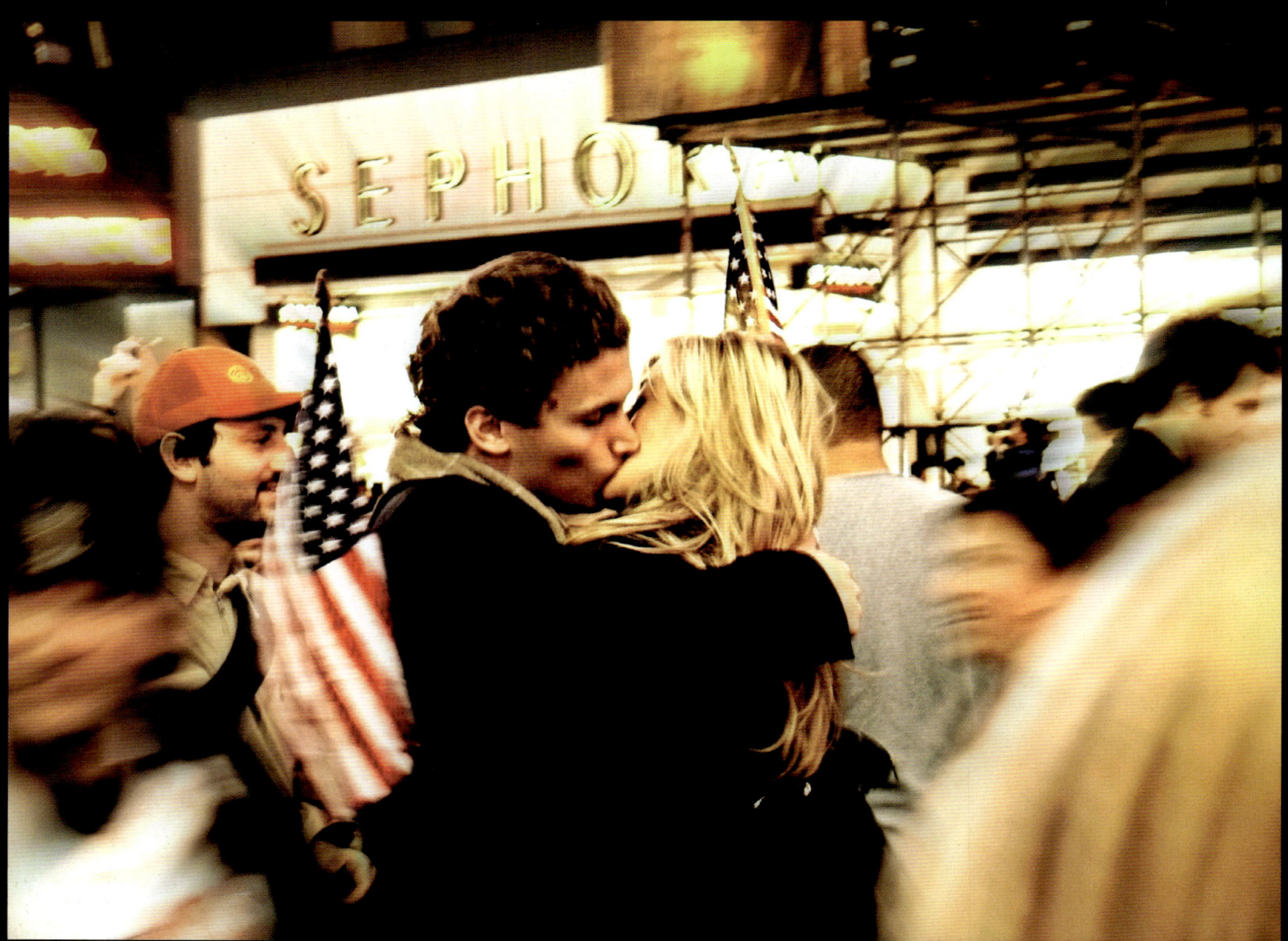

ABOVE: *The Kiss.*

INSPIRATION

Inspired by his new home in New York's West Village and fortunate to have time on his hands, Sion started exploring the streets of Manhattan and taking pictures of strangers. After pushing the limits of his digital point-and-shoot camera, Sion began to experiment with a bridge camera—one with manual settings and a zoom lens. Hesitant (and uninspired) to learn the technical aspects of photography, Sion remained focused on his subjects and honed his instincts for anticipating and capturing documentary moments on the street. While he enjoyed shooting, Sion didn't process and share many of his images at that time because the steps required seemed arduous and time-consuming. He didn't want to sit in front of a computer. He just wanted to roam the streets in search of stories.

Sion's passion for photography surged when Anton gave him an iPhone 3G for his birthday in July 2008. Suddenly, the once time-consuming and clumsy process for processing and sharing digital photographs was eliminated by the power of this hand-held device and a modest set of early photography apps. The simplicity of the camera, the creativity made possible by the apps, and the ability to instantly publish his images to his Flickr account straight from the iPhone inspired Sion, and he began to share his street photographs with a steadily increasing online audience of fans in Flickr and Twitter. Then, something magical happened.

On November 5, 2008, on the night of President Obama's historic election victory, Sion positioned himself in the center of a massive victory celebration in Times Square. Armed with a camera, he noticed a beautiful couple kissing and quickly "snatched" a photo from a distance

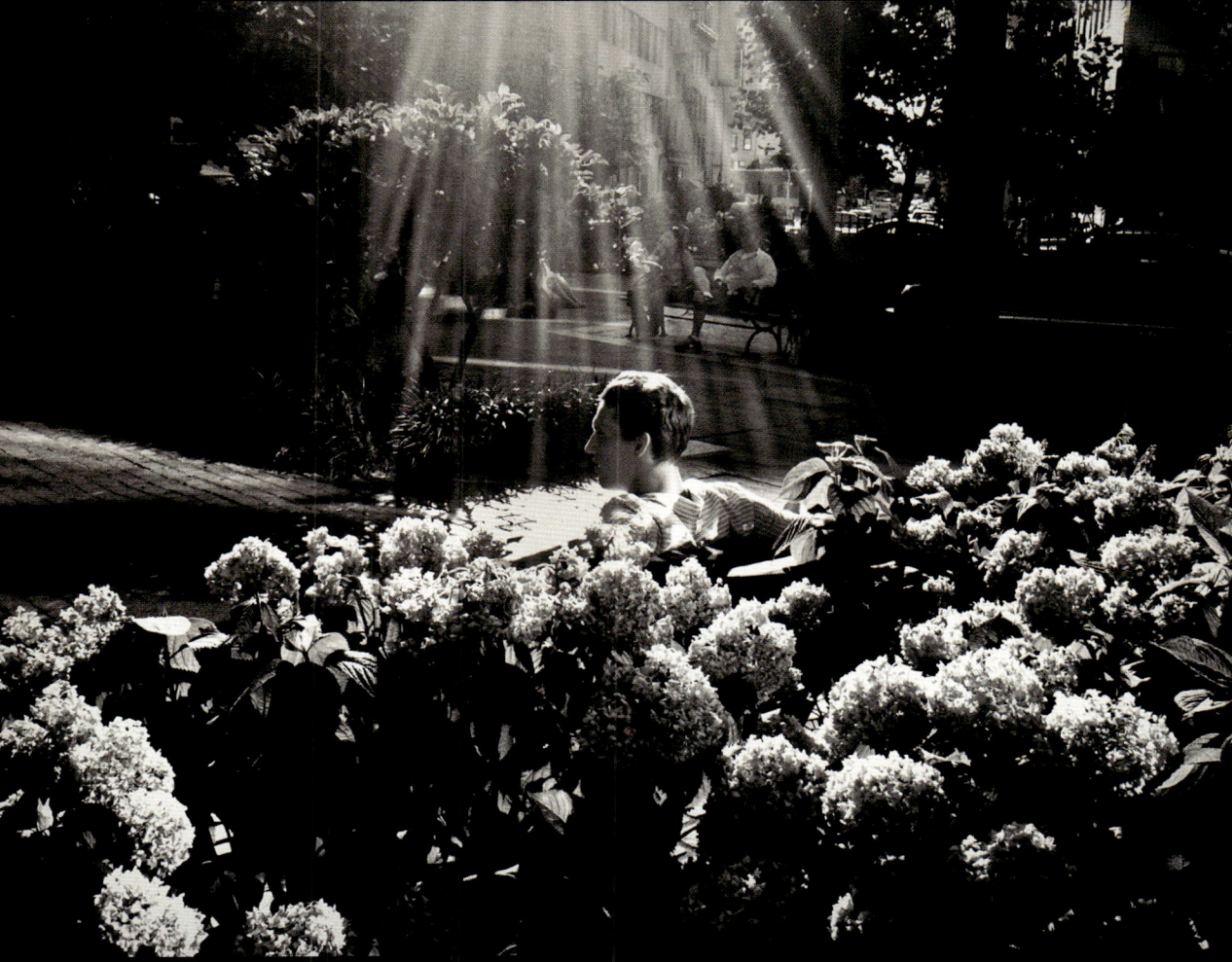

BEHIND THE IMAGE

"This is the little park on Greenwich Avenue and 8th Avenue. Sometimes if I see the rays of light, I may wait five minutes for someone to walk into the spot. That's one of my favorite aspects of shooting with the iPhone, the way it captures the light."

RIGHT: *Beauty Among the Flowers.*

"So when I see the photo on the screen I was like, 'Damn!' Being that it was a historic night, and that [the] kiss [took place] in Times Square, I was thinking, 'This has iconic potential.' If it was me, I would like to have this [photograph]." So Sion decided to approach the couple—something he typically does not do.

"When I approached them, I asked, 'Do you mind if I take your portrait?' They posed for me, and I took the portrait. When I noticed they were nice I said, 'Oh, by the way, when you were kissing before, I took a great photo of you guys,' and I showed them, and they were fascinated." As it turned out, the woman was a

French art curator living between Paris and New York. Sion exchanged email addresses with the young couple so he could share his photographs with them, and uploaded and tagged "The Kiss" as well as 15–20 of his favorite images from the celebration that night to his Flickr account when he arrived home around 3:00 a.m. When Sion woke up later that morning, he was amazed to see that "The Kiss" had already attracted thousands of views and comments.

Two weeks later, Sion discovered that www.NBCNewYork.com had featured an article by reporter Elizabeth Bougerol entitled "NYC News Highlights: Yes We Can Edition." The

article contained a link to Sion's photograph, captioned as "The New Kiss, a recreating of Alfred Eisenstaedt's iconic image of a Times Square lip lock amid celebrations at the end of WWII, originally published in *Life* magazine." A few days later, Bougerol referenced the image again in another article, "World's Most Famous Kisser Back for Vet's Day." Sion had been discovered by the mainstream media not for his writing, but for his photography. "For the first time I really thought maybe I have something. Maybe I'm on to something here." Since its initial posting, "The Kiss" has been viewed nearly 50,000 times on Flickr.

BEHIND THE IMAGE

"I was attracted to this metal wall and how the light was hitting it beautifully, and I decided to wait. I was seeing characters. I had a few brave little souls there. Then all of a sudden, I see this homeless man, with this giant fur blanket, and hair and the beard. He was like a mighty character. To me, this is not a sad person, it's a beautiful soul."

BELOW: *There is No Better Fantasy than Real Life.*

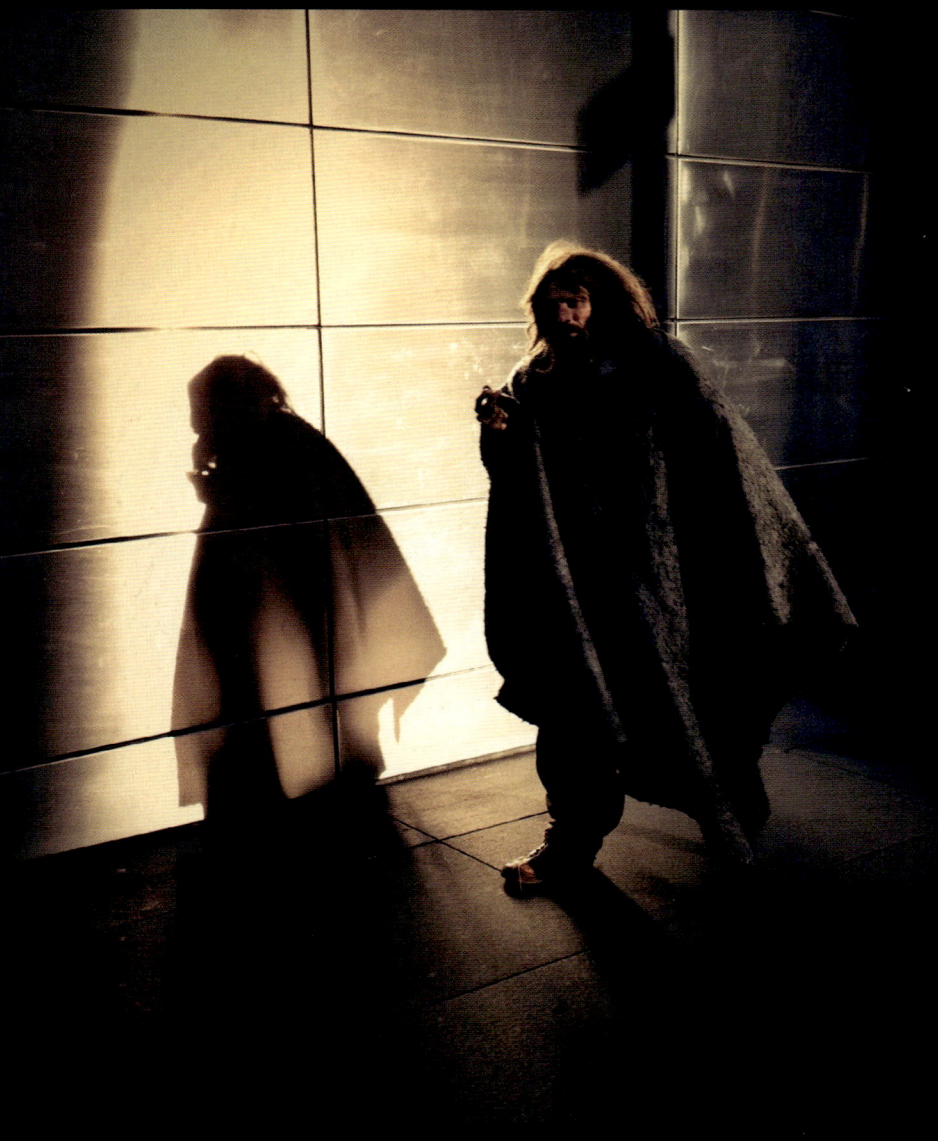

APPROACH

Watching Sion move swiftly and confidently through a crowd of agitated people at the Occupy Wall Street Protest in an area dubbed Liberty Square on September 24, 2011, I can see that Sion immerses himself in the moment with intense curiosity. A press badge swinging across his chest, he holds his iPhone out in one hand to scan and capture compositions as they evolve in his viewfinder. I follow his alert eyes beneath a furrowed brow dart quickly to follow the action unfolding around him. He's fully present, quiet, and shows no discomfort in the setting. He makes his images, processes his favorites, taps out detailed captions and personal perspectives, and blasts them from his iPhone to an audience of nearly 100,000 followers worldwide. A street photographer in New York City—he is the media.

Sion prefers to shoot his documentary street photography with his iPhone because "it's faster and easier. When I have the iPhone, I rely more on the storytelling and the composition because I [can] forget about technique. I know how to get what I want mostly. With other digital cameras, I constantly have to change stuff, so it's harder." While Sion's iPhone is always with him, if he brings another camera to a shoot, he ends up using one or the other (versus both), "mostly because the mindset (to use each camera) is so different."

While Sion does shoot prearranged portrait assignments for his clients, he prefers to shoot candid portraits on the street. He rarely speaks with his subjects before making an image in a public setting because he feels that the images are more authentic representations when his presence isn't known. "If I get to interact with the person and create a connection immediately and they can trust me, I may get something real. If not, I'll get something very guarded. That's why I like candid better. Because in the candid, there's no filter. There's no shield up." But before you begin exploring street photography and the art of the candid portrait, Sion recommends that you consult and follow the laws that govern photojournalism in your country.

VISION

Sion follows his instincts—the impulses of his heart more than his head. While his images are documentary by nature, his style is cinematic and seems to portray his subjects as complex characters in one-frame scenes on the stage of life. Though his characters are strangers, and he rarely shares verbal or physical connections with them, you can feel his warmth, respect, and fascination for his subjects. He transforms a pretty girl on the subway into a fashion model and a homeless man into a superhero. He exposes vulnerability in a tender way that connects us with these subjects, regardless of the setting. We don't know his subjects, but we see something familiar—perhaps a reflection of ourselves.

EQUIPMENT

When shooting for a client assignment, Sion shoots with a Canon digital SLR or a point-and-shoot, while for his personal street photography he uses his iPhone camera 95 percent of the time. When shooting with his iPhone, Sion shoots using the camera within his app of choice for the given situation. He lets the mood of the scene, the context of the experience, and the character dictate what shooting and processing style work best for the image. Some of his favorite apps include Snapseed, Monochromia, Cross Process, Cameramatic, and Camera +. He publishes and shares his images using Instagram and Flickr.

"Some people shoot all afternoon. They don't even look at the images, and then when they get home, they look at everything they took and delete. I cannot do that. I need to know immediately if what I'm taking is good, [has] potential, or [is] not [good]. So I shoot, and if I shoot something, and I think, 'No, I don't like it,' I'll delete. If I like it enough, I'll keep [it]. If I love it, I start processing on the go. Even if I'm crossing the street, I'm processing and doing stuff, and maybe sharing it. So it becomes a particular passion bordering on obsession, I guess."

BELOW: *Are You Asleep?* Zucotti Park known as "Liberty Square" by Occupy Wall Street Protestors, New York City, September 2011.

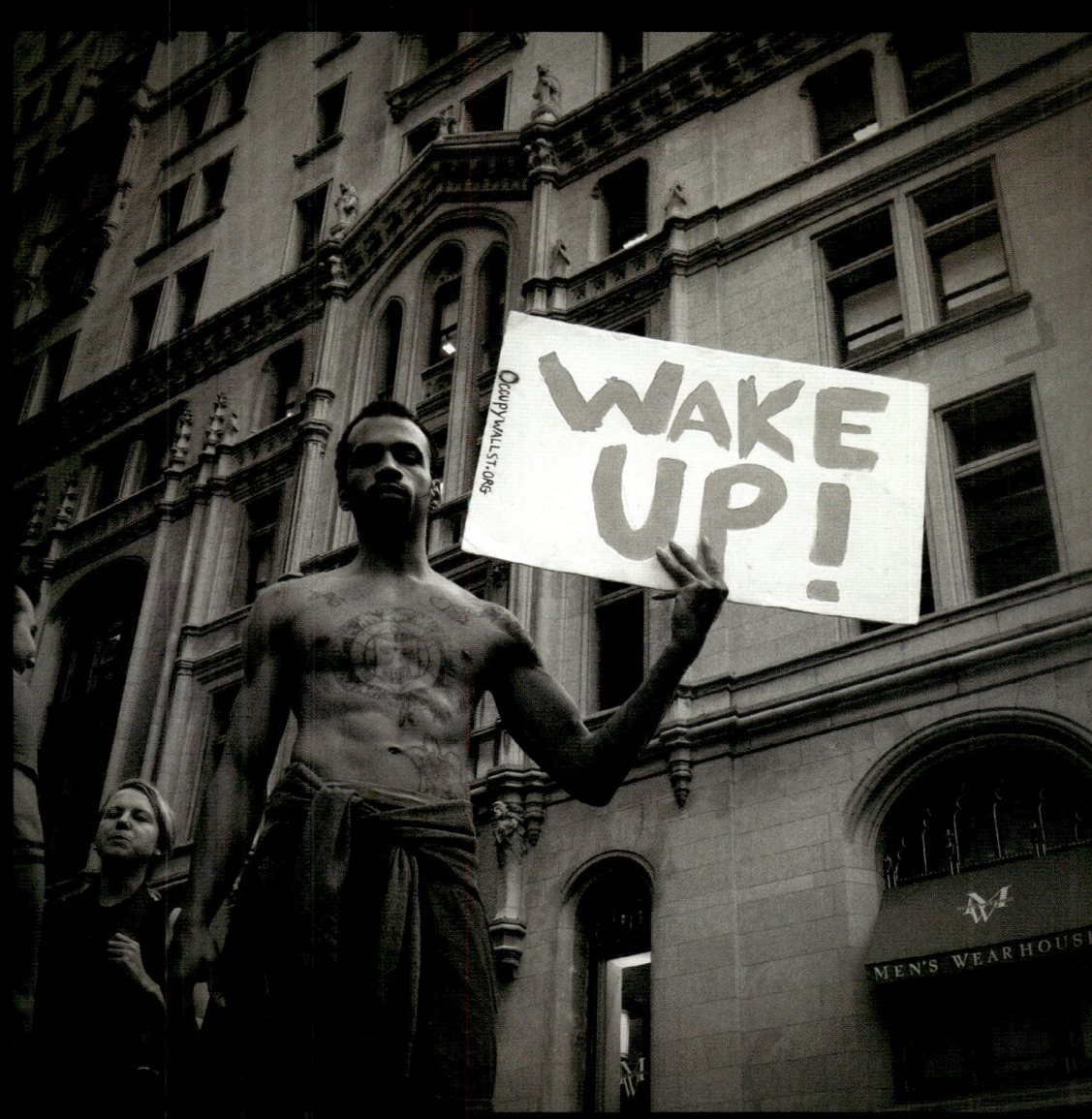

BEHIND THE IMAGE

🔴 "They bark once. They get their owners to let them get close to one another, and they stare at each other for a while. They might have been both male, one of them neutered, I overheard. And then they parted ways. It was nice . . . to see a policeman of the K-9 division, on the left, let a working dog be a real dog for once."

BEHIND THE IMAGE

🔴 "We rarely take buses. This one is my filmmaker-type approach, because she was so fabulous. You don't even appreciate it with the lack of color, but the dress and the jewelry were sparkling, and the sunglasses were sparkling. I saw her looking at the phone kind of sadly the whole time, and I made up a story about her waiting for a text that didn't come."

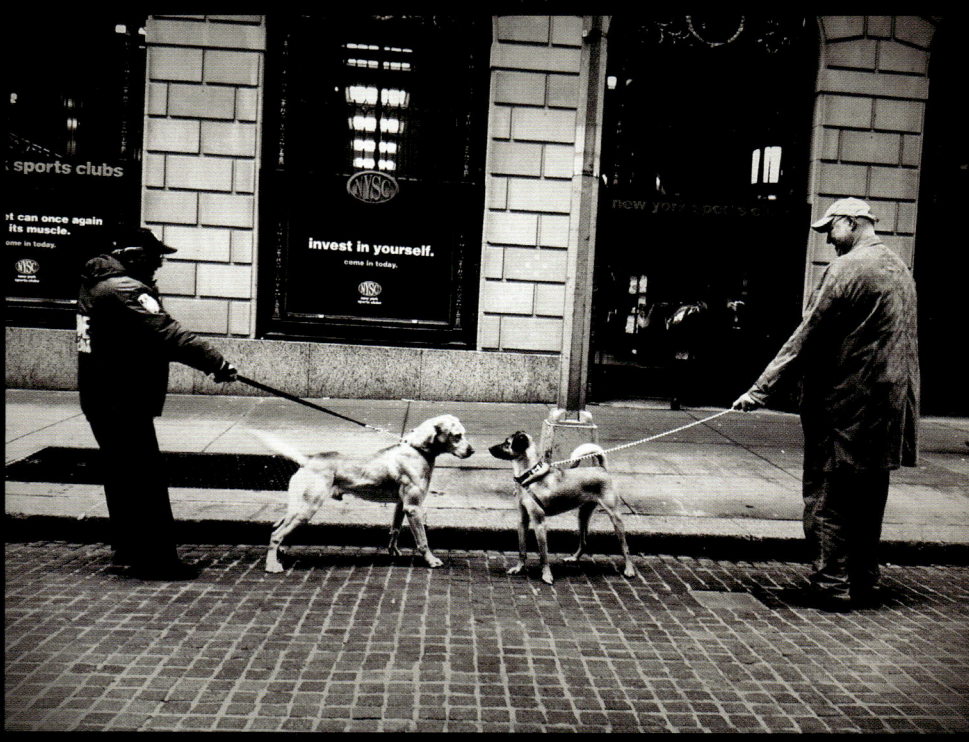

BELOW: *Waiting for a Text that Doesn't Come.*

ABOVE: *The Dogs' Standoff.*

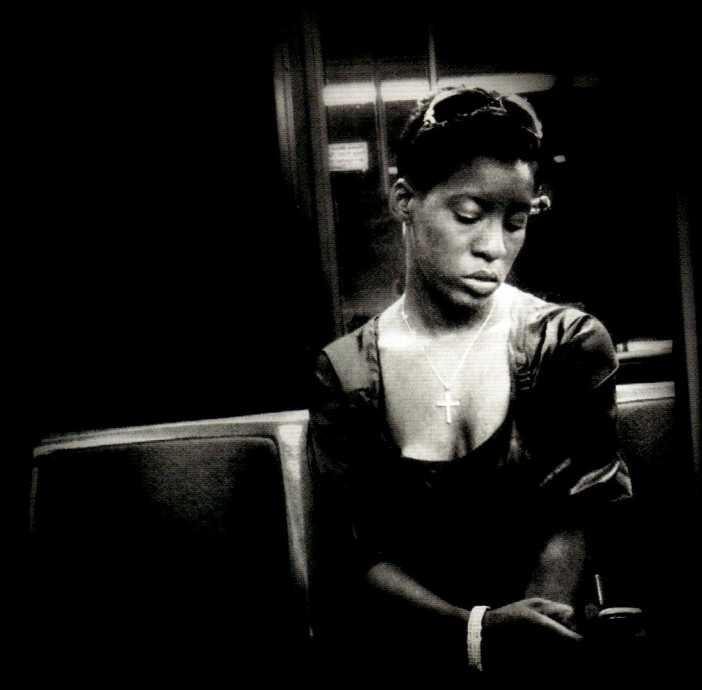

WRITING

Sion struggled with having to keep his sexual orientation a secret from his loved ones for many years. At age 26 he finally felt ready to move past this fear of rejection and came out to his family and friends. This became a liberating experience that lifted his outlook on life. Because Sion feels compelled to express his optimism and empathy for humanity, he frequently and openly shares his thoughts and feelings about visual experiences in the form of heartfelt captions (tapped out on his iPhone) below his photographs.

While his native language is Spanish, Sion has always loved the English language even though he finds it more challenging to express himself in exactly the right way. "It's harder because I know that I might not be able to trick the language into what I want to tell. Photography is a universal way to tell my story. Some people say, 'Oh, you should let the photo speak for itself.' To me, (the writing) is an enriching experience, too." Sion believes that his captions help direct the viewer to interpret the photograph the way he intends it to be viewed.

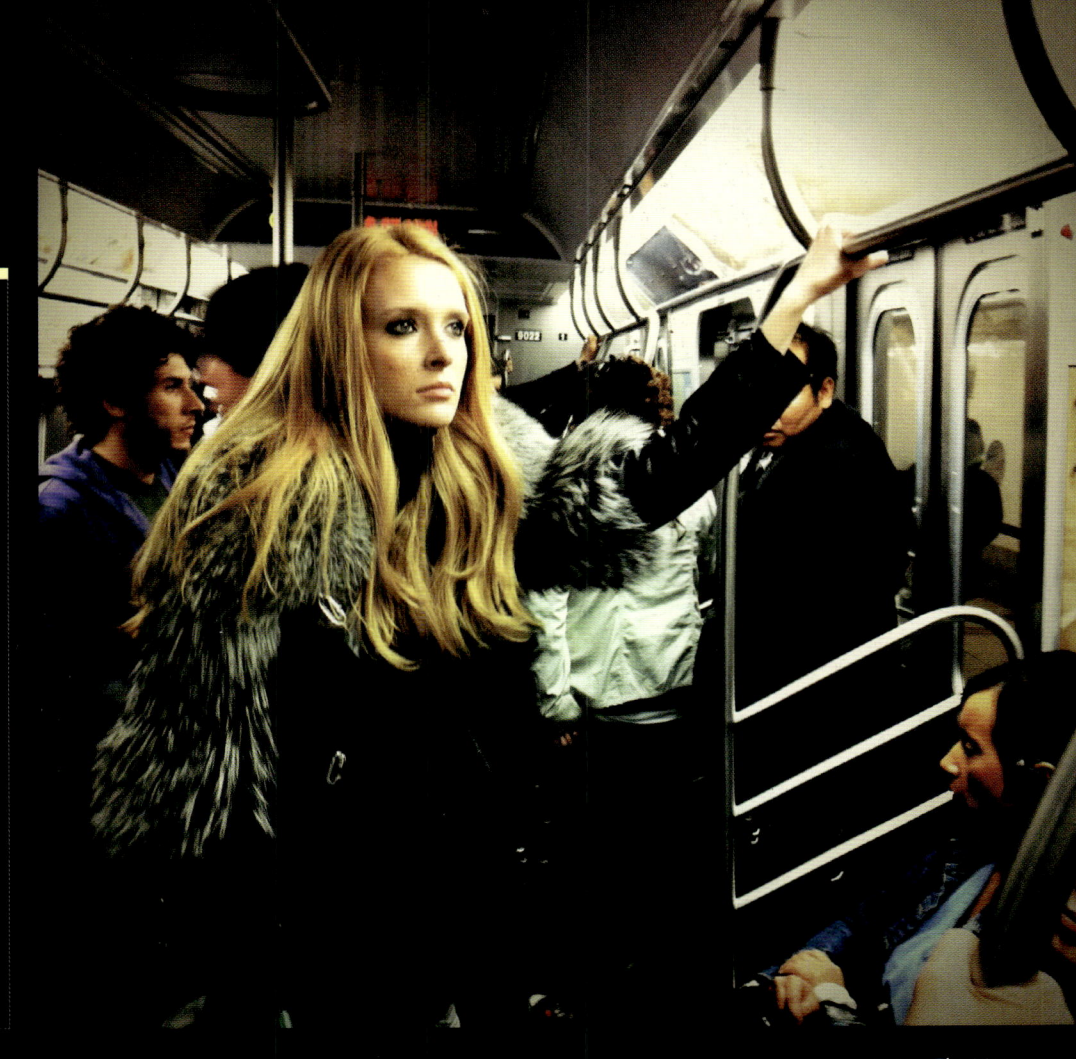

A SECRET

Focus on the moment by minimizing the complexity and size of your equipment. Documenting life through a viewfinder in search of interesting moments requires you to be fully present—following your subject and composing the moment rather than fumbling with the settings on your camera. Choose a camera that feels comfortable in your hand(s) and shoot with it daily to become familiar with its capabilities and limitations. While a high-end digital SLR does give you the flexibility of fine-tuned control over settings such as ISO, white balance, aperture, shutter speed, and exposure to capture the image in your mind's eye, it demands more time and thought to control during the shooting process. Find a simple-to-use camera that fits in your pocket, backpack, or purse and shift your focus on the moment.

ABOVE: *The Most Beautiful Rider*, subway car, New York City, March 2011.

"[My subjects] are like characters. When I capture them, their soul becomes a part of me. They're not strangers anymore. I

Ed Kashi

www.edkashi.com

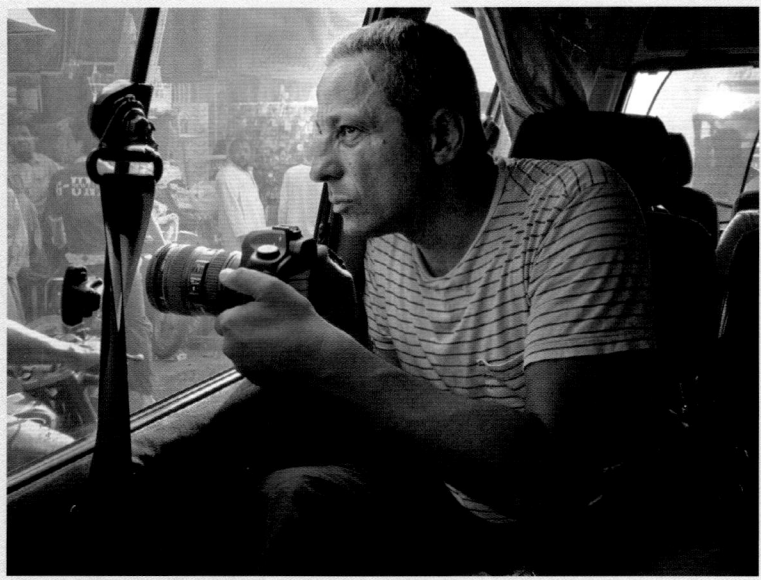

Portrait of Ed Kashi by VII Photo

"With documentary work and journalism in general I feel that we've got to present solutions; it's not good enough anymore to just show the problems."

PATH TO PHOTOGRAPHY

Initially drawn to writing and storytelling during his teenage years, Ed Kashi discovered his passion for photography around age 18 while he was a student at Syracuse University. He remembers being moved by the black-and-white images of Mary Ellen Mark in "WARD 81," a 36-day documentary of women patients in the maximum-security section of the Oregon State Hospital. He recalls studying the intimate moments of raw humanity depicted in the images, and thinking, "'This is what I want to do.' I think I've always been drawn to being around people who are troubled or who are going through rough times. So [social documentary] has always been a very natural pull for me." His photography and interest in the craft of making images suddenly had a higher purpose in that it became a way for Ed to engage in and explore social issues, and by extension, to experience the world.

Ed went on to become an award-winning photojournalist, filmmaker, and educator dedicated to documenting defining global social and political issues and their impact on the human condition. He is a member of VII Photo Agency, has produced six photography books, and often blends his still photography and filmmaking skills to produce digital media documentaries including the *Iraqi Kurdistan Flipbook* with MediaStorm, "Aging in America: The Years Ahead" (an eight-year personal project), and "Denied: The Crisis of America's Uninsured," a project produced by Talking Eyes Media, a non-profit organization Ed and his wife, writer/filmmaker Julie Winokur, founded in 2002.

Ed is most inspired and awed by the lives of the people he documents all over the world— people often found in extremely difficult, harsh, unjust, and often dire circumstances—and he makes images with a passion for social justice and positive change. "I feel enriched by [these experiences], but I feel sort of scarred by them too. It doesn't wash off of me. I'm just imbued with all of these feelings, these thoughts, these experiences, and the pain. I think in some ways it makes me more strident at times or frustrated with things I see every day when I'm back home in America. In makes me worry about the world and the state of humanity, [yet I] see the wonderment of how amazing human beings can be—the heroic and small things that people do that make us get through the day and survive, both as individuals and as a species. I feel so humbled by doing this work because the truth is [we photographers] are not that important. I think the work we do can be very important and has a wonderful role, and at the end of the day, it's worthy. I like to believe that we can have a positive impact, but in truth, we're specks in the sand. I can't tell how many times I've shown up somewhere in the world and said, 'I work with *National Geographic*,' and they look at me and say, 'What's that?' There has got to be a greater ambition or purpose to our work."

Ed maintains an even 50–50 balance between commissioned client work and personal projects or proposals he submits to publishers including *National Geographic* as well as NGOs and non-profit organizations. He finds that much of his client-commissioned work springs out of his personal projects, the work he is most passionate about. An example of this includes the personal documentary work he's done on the topic of aging for the past fifteen years and a recent commission he was awarded from a pharmaceutical company to enlist his talent and storytelling skills for a campaign on that same topic.

BELOW: A young boy carries a freshly roasted goat carcass through plumes of smoke at the Trans Amadi Slaughterhouse in the Niger Delta.

BEHIND THE IMAGE

Ed cites this image from his Niger Delta work (a project that began as a personal project and evolved into one supported by *National Geographic*) as a great example of a strong collaboration with his local contact. After conveying what he hoped to capture—a sense of the rawness and intensity of life in the region—his local contact suggested they visit the Trans Amadi Slaughterhouse. When they arrived, security guards refused to let Ed take photographs and insisted that he obtain permission. Several weeks later, they returned with permission and were permitted to witness the slaughter. "I had no idea what to expect. It was truly a scene of [horrific] slaughter. There was this large 100-foot square cement slab and you just have dozens and dozens of animals being killed simultaneously around each other amid their feces, urine, and blood. In the area where I took this picture, they burn the carcasses on fires fueled by old tires to remove the hair and prepare the animals to be butchered. It was all just so raw. It's one of those scenes where you're overwhelmed by the possibilities and think to yourself, 'This is amazing. Keep it together.'

One beautiful thing that happened when this image was published in *National Geographic* [was that] subsequently a woman in upstate New York contacted me for a print and we reluctantly gave her a low-quality print. A few months later she contacted us and said through her local church she had contacted a church in Port Harcourt, Nigeria, found this 14-year-old boy, and was now paying for him to go to school."

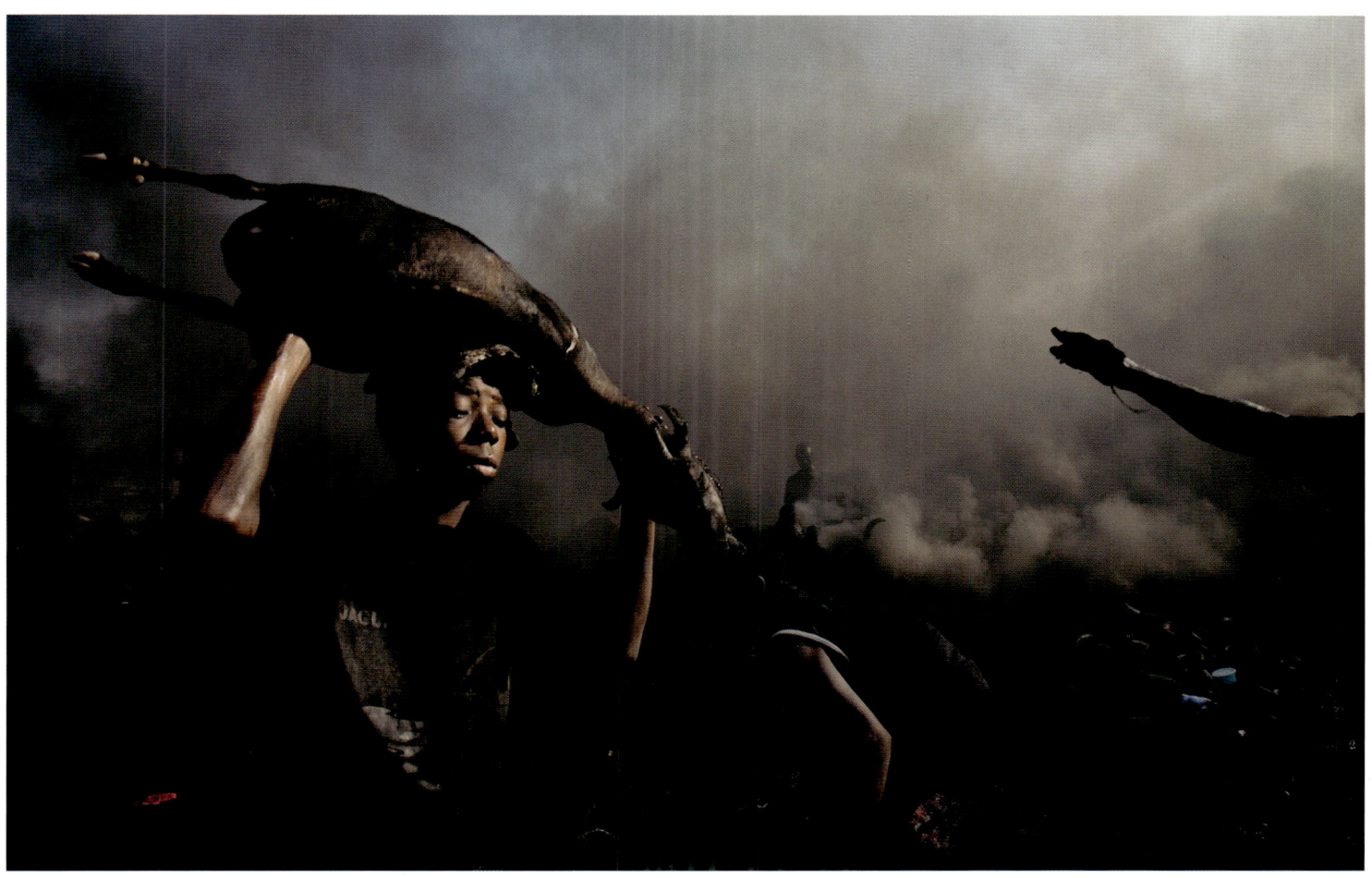

APPROACH

Ed finds that much of his role as a documentary photographer requires extensive collaboration and problem solving skills practiced on the fly. "How do I get there and back safely? What are the risks? Where do I need to be so I'm in the right place at the right time? For my geopolitical or cultural work, I'm always looking at logistics, contingencies, and backup plans. I'm looking for strong collaborators and a great fixer (or local contact), someone who will understand what I'm trying to do, support it with energy, spirit, and enthusiasm, and know the right people and the right places that I've got to go to get the pictures I need to make." When working on international still photography projects, Ed primarily works alone, with support from a fixer or an assigned writer/reporter. For film or multimedia projects, he might travel with a second videographer, an audio specialist, and/or a still photographer.

Cultivating a collaborative relationship with his subjects is a priority for Ed, particularly in

BEHIND THE IMAGE

Ed spent two weeks in Da Nang, Vietnam in 2010 working on a project about Agent Orange for the Vietnam Reporting Project. While Agent Orange was a concern tied to the Vietnam War 40 years ago, what most people don't know is that dioxin, the active chemical in Agent Orange, is passed down genetically. Today, more than 150,000 Vietnamese are living with the resultant impact so there are still people being born with deformities, learning disabilities, and physical and psychological problems. Ed became inspired by the opportunity to educate people around the world about the lingering after effects of war and the unseen impact of Agent Orange on children in Vietnam. "I decided that I would focus on two families: one who's not getting support for their children affected by Agent Orange and Ly's family, who is getting support from an American-based charity, Children of Vietnam, based in North Carolina." Ed had been shooting video in and around Ly's home that day. "I come inside and boom! I see this perfect moment. I gesture to her with my hands, 'Just wait, stay, stay there, and don't move.' I made a sequence of a few images before the moment passed but I knew inside 'something special just happened.' It doesn't happen very often."

his social documentary work because of the sensitivity required in portraying these stories visually. "If you really want to do [social documentary], not just very well, but also on an ethical level, do it with a sense of responsibility. Because you need to get into people's lives in a very intimate way, quite often you need to capture people in vulnerable, very compromised situations—moments in their lives [in which] the average person would never want to be seen, let alone be photographed. It requires sensitivity and a level of responsibility, so I

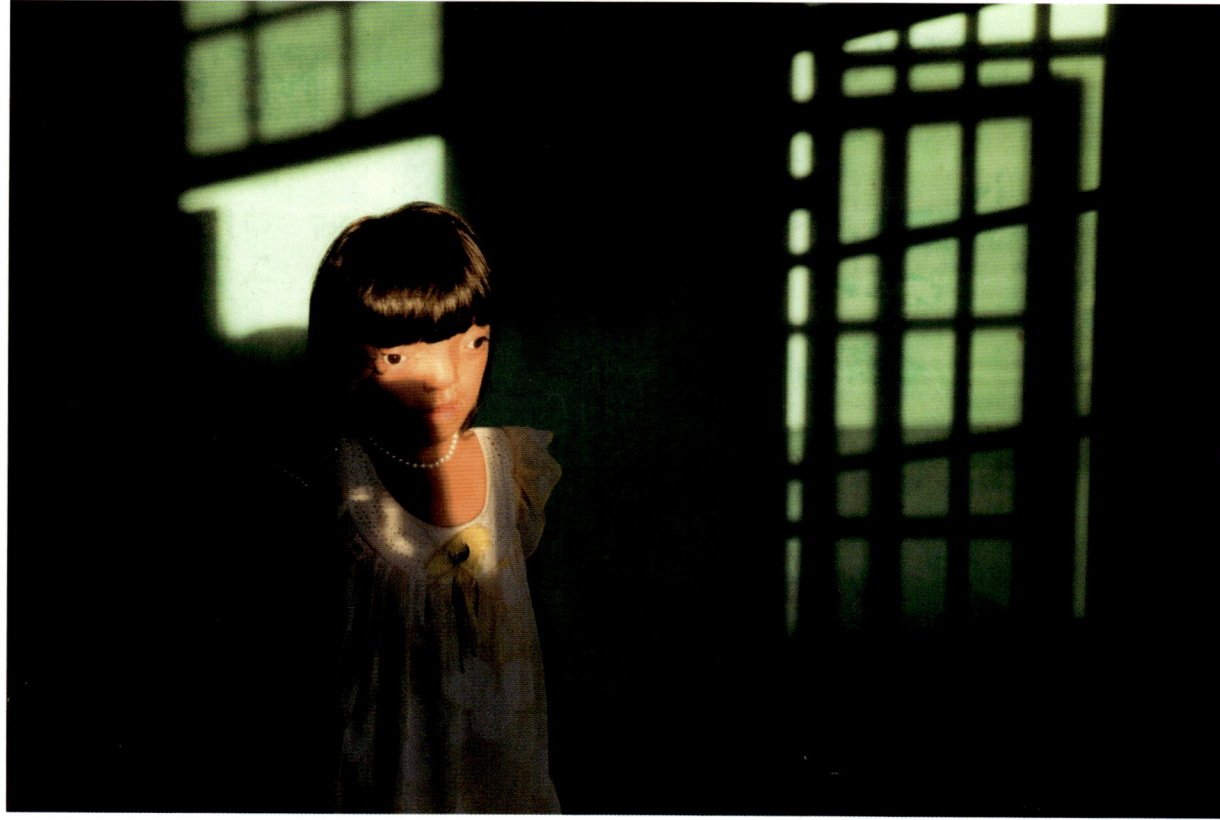

LEFT: Nguyen Thi Ly, age nine, who suffers from Agent Orange disabilities, in her home in Ngu Hanh Son district of Da Nang, Vietnam.

RIGHT: Throughout Iraqi Kurdistan, students are finally studying Kurdish history, which was forbidden under Iraqi rule. It is the only place in Kurdistan where classes are held in Kurdish. Without the money to print their own textbooks, students are forced to make do with what the Iraqis left behind, sometimes filling up notebooks and erasing them to be used again. These students are in a classroom of a bombed-out school in Penjwin, Iraq, near the border with Iran.

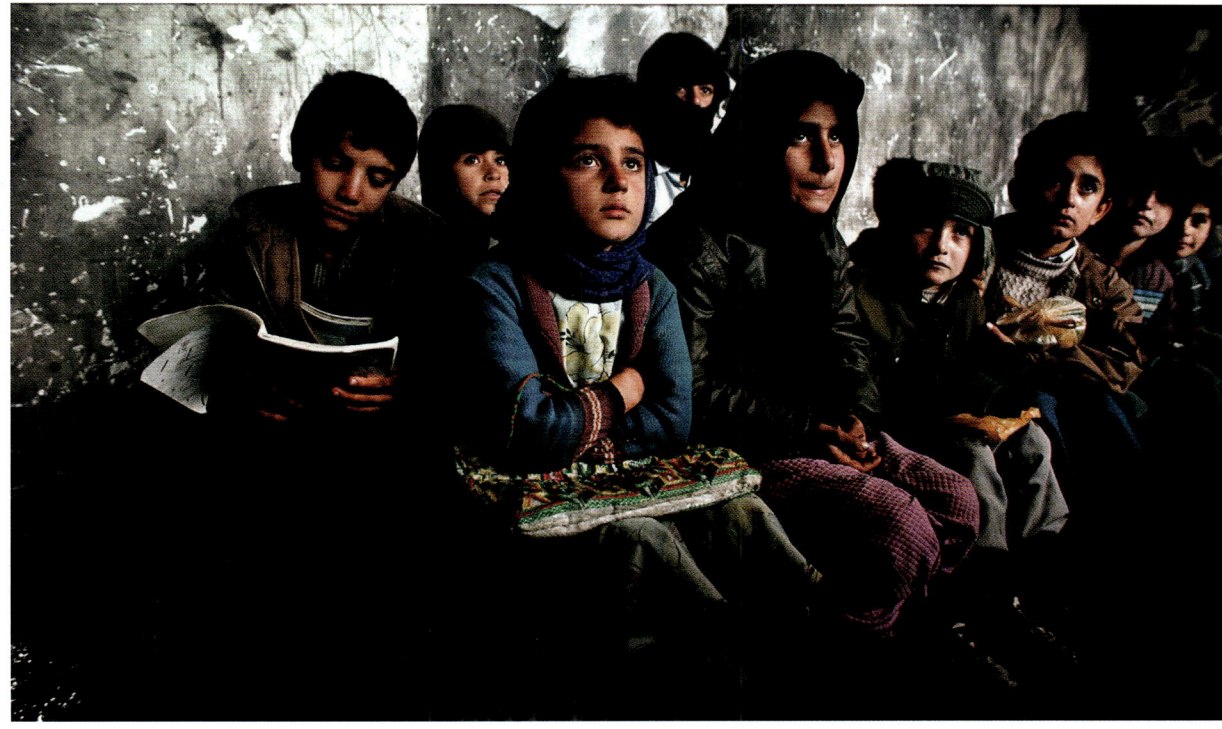

approach subjects with dignity and respect that I hope translates for them. It doesn't always work that way. Boy, there are lots of times when nobody's happy, and that's the truth. I'm trying to inveigle my way into someone's life. It might not even be a controversial subject, but they're just not happy about it, and I'm trying to convince them that it'll basically be okay. So it's really important to be very clear about who you are, to explain your purpose and mission, and share how it will be used because in essence I've come to see these [projects] as collaborations with my subjects."

EQUIPMENT

For still photography projects, Ed travels very lightly. "I have one camera, a Canon 5D Mark II, and I mostly work with a 24–105mm lens. I literally just have one camera and lens, and then I have a belt with my CF cards, a flash, my Filofax, cell phone, caption book, and extra batteries." Ed shoots still photographs and video with this camera and single lens. "That one lens just gives me everything I need. Well, it doesn't stave off the loneliness in hotel rooms."

BEHIND THE IMAGE

This image was part of Ed's project on the Kurds, the first story he proposed to *National Geographic* in 1991, an idea that led to a 26-week contract. "We were in Penjwin, a small town in Iraq on the border with Iran. It's one of 4,000 towns or villages that Saddam Hussein destroyed in his 15-year genocidal campaign against the Kurds in Iraq. This was right after the first Gulf War, after 'Operation Provide Comfort' had been established in northern Iraq above the 36th Parallel, which allowed the Kurds who had fled to Turkey and Iran to return. But what they returned to was this landscape of destruction. No water. No electricity. Every building had been destroyed. It was this incredible moment for the Kurds where they could now, in relative safety under the protection of the allied forces, go back to their homes and try to begin to rebuild. I spent a few days there and came upon the scene at this school. It was incredible to see the spirit and determination of these kids and the fact that they could now learn in Kurdish. There were literally holes in the ceilings and pieces of cement dangling from rebar, and yet they were just soldiering on. It was one of many eye-opening experiences from that project which inspired and amazed me.

This project was my first opportunity to be a voice for the voiceless and to have a chance to make a difference for people. I say with humility and understanding that I'm irrelevant in the big picture of things, but in this situation, in this moment in history, I felt that I could serve some little purpose in telling the story of the Kurds, particularly to Americans. When soldiers learned that I was an American journalist, they would have these huge smiles on their faces and they would say, 'Serchava.' In Kurdish, it means 'you are in my eyes.' It brought me to tears. I felt overwhelmed to have been given that level of trust, faith, and responsibility to tell someone's story."

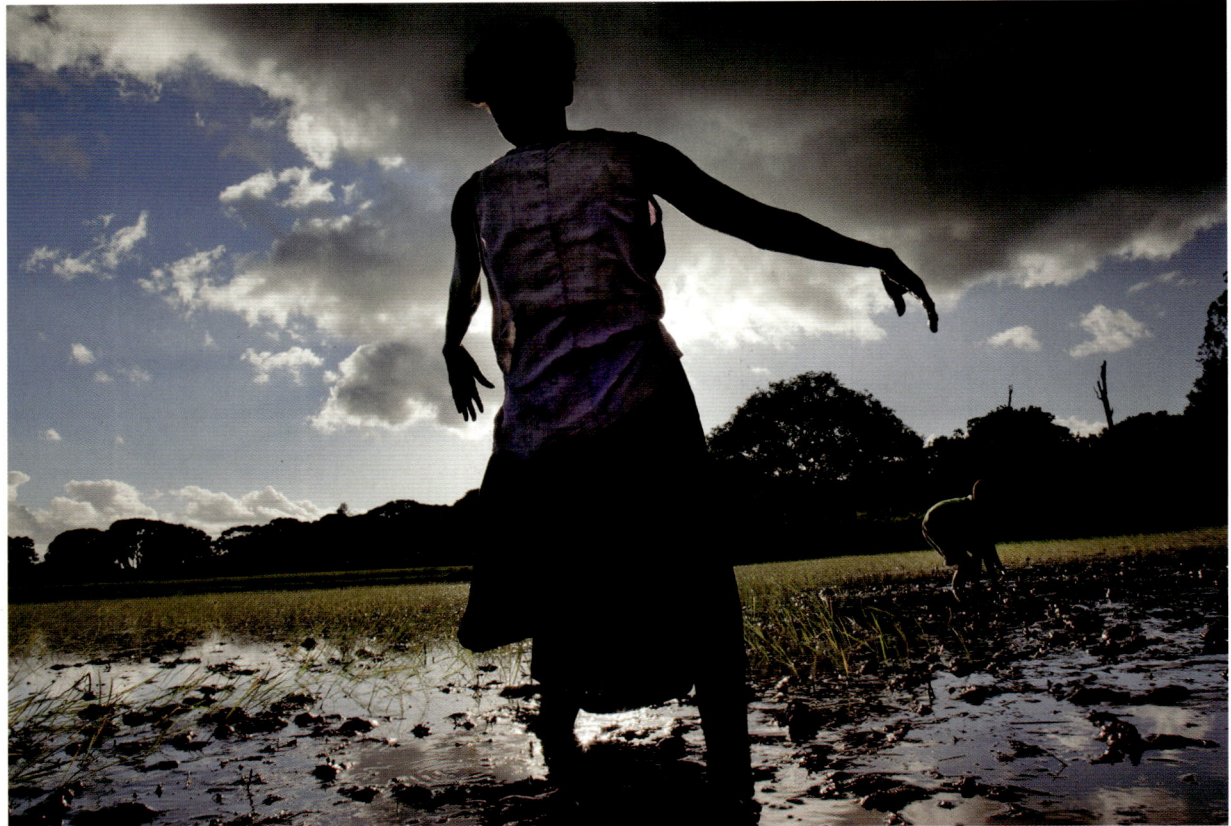

RIGHT: Local people plant rice in flooded fields. For the Malagasy of Madagascar, rice represents life, an essential and sacred part of one's daily nutrition.

CULTIVATING CONNECTION

Cultivating a strong connection with your subject, particularly when you are working on an in-depth or sensitive story, is an important aspect of documentary photography. Ed often finds himself in this position with his social justice work and shares this advice:

- Be respectful, trustworthy, and aware of how you navigate the world—how you behave and move—so people feel comfortable in your presence.

- Do your homework about the subject so that when you speak to people, you are speaking in a knowledgeable way. People will be touched or impressed by how much you might already know about their history or their country, or the specific issue you are dealing with, because your knowledge demonstrates that you care. They are more apt to be open with you and share more.

- Meet your subject where they are and lose your inhibitions. If your subject is standing in the muck of a rice field, take off your shoes, roll up your pants, and get in the muck.

- Clearly define and communicate your purpose for the project. Think beyond the art and science of making photographs of interesting subjects and stories and use your skill to improve the lives of others.

BEHIND THE IMAGE

Ed received the prestigious Prix Pictet Photography Prize in 2010, and through this award received a commission from the Geneva-based private bank Pictet & Cie to undertake a field trip to Madagascar, a region where the bank is supporting a sustainability project under the theme of "Earth." Ed worked in partnership with Azafady, a UK-based charity, to document one area of southeastern Madagascar's fragile ties to the land and Azafady's efforts to promote sustainable development to improve the lives of the people and how the land's natural resources are used.

Two hours after Ed's two-and-a-half-day journey to Madagascar, he and his Azafady contacts drove out an hour or so beyond the town to visit people working in rice fields. "Madagascar is one of the most beautiful places I've ever been, and I don't tend to go to beautiful places or look for beautiful things. It was lovely. I took my shoes and socks off, rolled up my pants, and got into the muck with them. Of course they're all laughing at me, the silly foreigner. As I'm in the mud up to my knees clopping around, this woman started to dance. It was a surprising moment that I fortunately captured. It was also actually really lovely to be in a place where people were happy to be photographed, and I didn't have to look for the hardness of life."

"What's interesting is the experiential nature of photography. It's not just that I get to make these photographs of these situations, but I get to be in the situations. I get to feel them and smell them, and experience them in a visceral way, [a] real and first-hand way . . . so that is the great appeal."

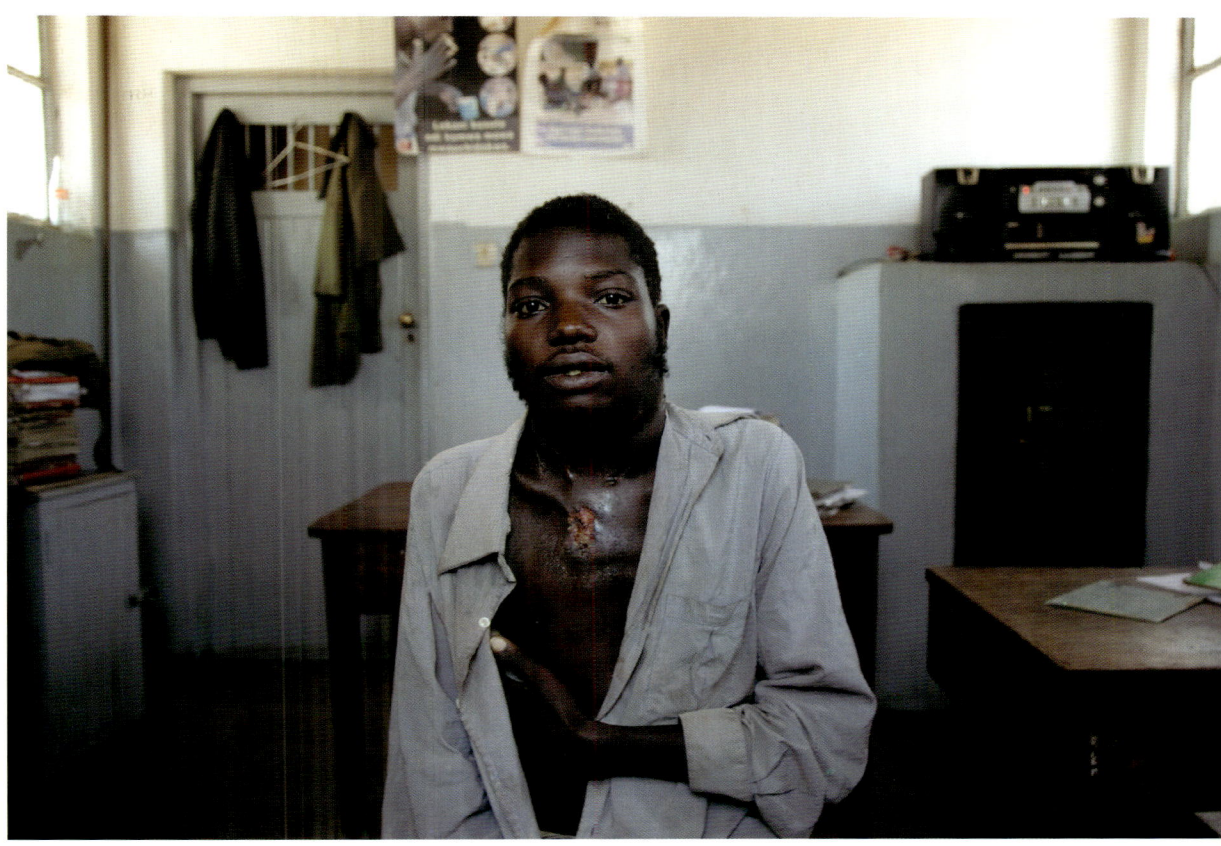

A SECRET
Reveal the truth responsibly and seek positive change.

Some of the most powerful aspects of documentary photography include its capacity to reveal unseen or ignored social injustices and its potential to inspire awareness, dialog, action, and positive change. While the path of social documentary can be intense, intellectually complex, physically demanding, and emotionally draining, the call to photograph and share stories on behalf of people in difficult and often dire circumstances is a special blessing, and often spiritually moving. Be courageous and reveal the truth with dignity and respect for your subjects, and the intent of making a positive impact in their lives.

"I do feel as a journalist, on so many projects I've worked on, that I am not objective. There is a problem here and we need to address it. You can show both sides, but that's not the point. The point is we need to wake up to this problem and deal with it. So it's very exciting when I can work with NGOs or advocacy organizations where we're on the same page and there's a purpose. The purpose is not to point fingers and place blame, the purpose is to forment action through illumination and education, and not just to communicate to the public, but to communicate to people who are in a position to change things."

BEHIND THE IMAGE
"I worked on this project in Malawi with the Open Society Foundations (OSF) and we were looking at pretrial detention, what happens to people who are arrested but not yet charged and not given legal representation. This young man, Benson, was put in this detention facility and held for nearly two and half years with no due process. He was living in abject conditions, which lead to scabies and this gaping wound in his chest. He'd lost weight, and was incredibly unhealthy. OSF wanted us to tell the story of these prisoners and the devastating impact on their families and the community when someone is detained without trial for lengthy periods of time. We did another subject besides Benson who was a young farmer. His fields died because he wasn't there to tend them, and his wife and baby were left alone, and their bike was stolen, and she had to walk 50 kilometers to visit him and bring him food in the detention center."

ABOVE: Benson Sango, 21, who has been held in Maula Prison for 28 months without seeing a lawyer or having a trial, is interviewed on August 19, 2010 in Lilongwe, Malawi.

John Loengard

www.johnloengard.com

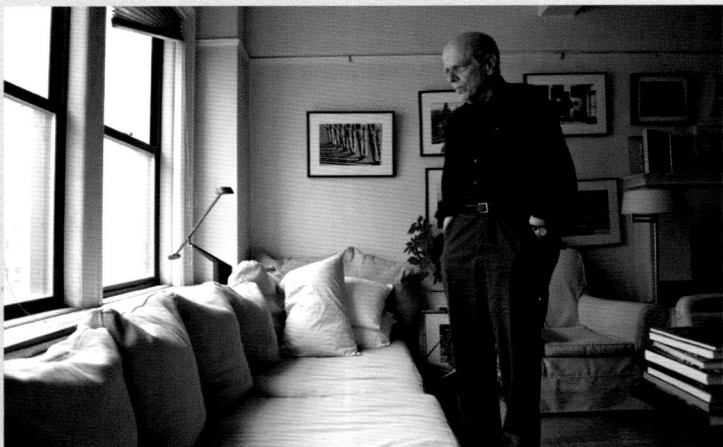

Portrait of John Loengard by Stephanie Calabrese Roberts

"If you feel you have to take risks to take a good picture, forget it. You should be able to take good pictures of ordinary things. In fact, they will be better pictures because making the everyday interesting is photography's greatest challenge."

LEFT: Though John rarely spends time in his living room, I asked him to step into the light streaming through the window overlooking Central Park. He mentioned that his wife had the sofa made during a time when she taught fourth graders.

PATH TO PHOTOGRAPHY

"I remember, when I was 12, having a conversation with my mother. Her father had gone to Yale, and she wanted to inject the notion in me that I should go to Yale and possibly be a writer. She wanted to plant the idea that I might do something in the arts."

John Loengard discovered the camera in 1945, at age 11. His father, an engineer, liked cameras and knew about photography though, says John, his technique never advanced beyond his asking subjects to stand ten feet away and smile. Just after World War II ended, John's father bought a new camera, a Kodak Rangefinder 35, to replace his 1935 pre-war Retina camera. He taught young John how to develop film in a bathroom-turned-darkroom in their home in New York City's upper East Side.

As a child, John didn't consider himself creative. "I couldn't draw. There was one guy in our class, Terry Stern, who went into advertising who could draw Japanese fighter planes and that sort of thing wonderfully. I greatly admired that skill—of which I had none. My drawings were clumsy doodles. That was why being able to take a picture with a camera seemed wonderful." John remembers. "And watching

an image emerge onto paper in the developer was magic."

John continued to make photographs in his spare time as a hobby during his freshman year at Exeter (a prestigious school then known for sending as many as eighty of its graduates on to Harvard in a year) but he remembers feeling frustrated by a lack of inspiring subject matter. "I got tired of taking pictures of buildings or clouds." During his sophomore year, someone on the school's semi-weekly newspaper asked him to take a picture of the varsity football captain. "I discovered that when working for the newspaper, I could walk onto the field and go up to the big man on campus and say, 'Would you punt a ball for me?' Suddenly I had access to people, and a reason for the people to want me to be taking their picture."

The youngest of three children in an upper-middle class family, John took the educational path that was expected of him and followed the footsteps of his older brother to Harvard, a choice he never had to think about. All he cared about was taking pictures, and he found his place as a photographer for the *Harvard Crimson*, the school newspaper, and for Harvard's alumni magazine. "Some alumni

magazines at that time were emulating *Life* magazine and doing picture stories to show current college life to graduates. The Harvard Alumni Bulletin used a number of noted professionals from the Black Star picture agency in New York, and it paid money. They paid me and at some point during college I realized that I might earn my living taking pictures."

In 1956, during his senior year at Harvard, the Boston bureau chief of *Life* magazine, Will Jarvis, contacted John and gave him his first assignment. By the time John graduated from Harvard, he thought that the style of photography that he wanted to develop would be somewhere between the flat plane compositions of Henri Cartier-Bresson and W. Eugene Smith's deep focused pictures—two photographers he greatly admired. He spent six or seven years "trying to learn how to photograph people's faces horizontally with a 35mm camera—how to cut the face in ways that weren't disturbing or annoying, [but] in fact were satisfying." John continued to shoot assignments for *Life* magazine, but admits that for nearly ten years, "I wasn't particularly happy with my results. I had not developed my style. It's as simple as that."

INSPIRATION

Three years after John had become a staff photographer for *Life* magazine in 1961, he remembers discovering a glimpse of his photographic style. "I had gone to cover a quiet coup by some generals in Brazil. I was seated in a café on the Copacabana Beach in Rio de Janeiro on a cloudy day with nothing to do, when a lone middle-aged man came walking along the shore in my direction and—very unusual for me—I walked over to photograph him. The scene in the camera was a little corny. It was not dramatic. It was not news. But it felt very, very clear, as if everything related to one point. When I saw a print in New York I said to myself, 'That's your style!' Surprisingly, it was. The style is not something I can impose on a subject. I only look for a point where the camera can most vividly record the depth of the scene and from there I try to organize the picture, keeping background as important as foreground in such a way that the abstract shapes in the picture balance themselves on the surface of the print. I found I could repeat the effect and explore it and I have done so ever since."

Throughout John's career as a documentary photographer, he's found inspiration in studying and portraying subjects "as they are, not as they are expected to be." He has photographed many famous individuals. John skillfully portrays his subjects (both the famous and not-so-famous) in intriguing ways, exposing a whisper of vulnerability in the subject's expression or gesture we likely wouldn't have otherwise noticed. He shows something unfamiliar, off-center, possibly a bit awkward, in a tender way that makes us curious about the moment, feeling a connection with his subject as a fellow human. While most of his images place primary emphasis on spontaneity, his sensitivity to background elements and curious shapes (both natural and human) in the subjects' setting contribute to the rhythm and balance of the moment.

APPROACH

Journalism opened doors for John, giving him access to a wealth of subjects who seemed worthy of documentation. "Some photographers stand on the street corner and watch hundreds of people in the city pass by (I've certainly done that). People walk along, talking and moving in their own special ways. You select from a field of subjects. What working for a newspaper or a magazine gives you is that, rather than being in the street, you can go into houses where people are doing things. They stand around or laugh or whatever, and let you watch not because you are a friend or a great photographer. They do so because they think some publication notices them, and we all like to be noticed. They are happy to be your subjects."

BELOW: Man in Rio.

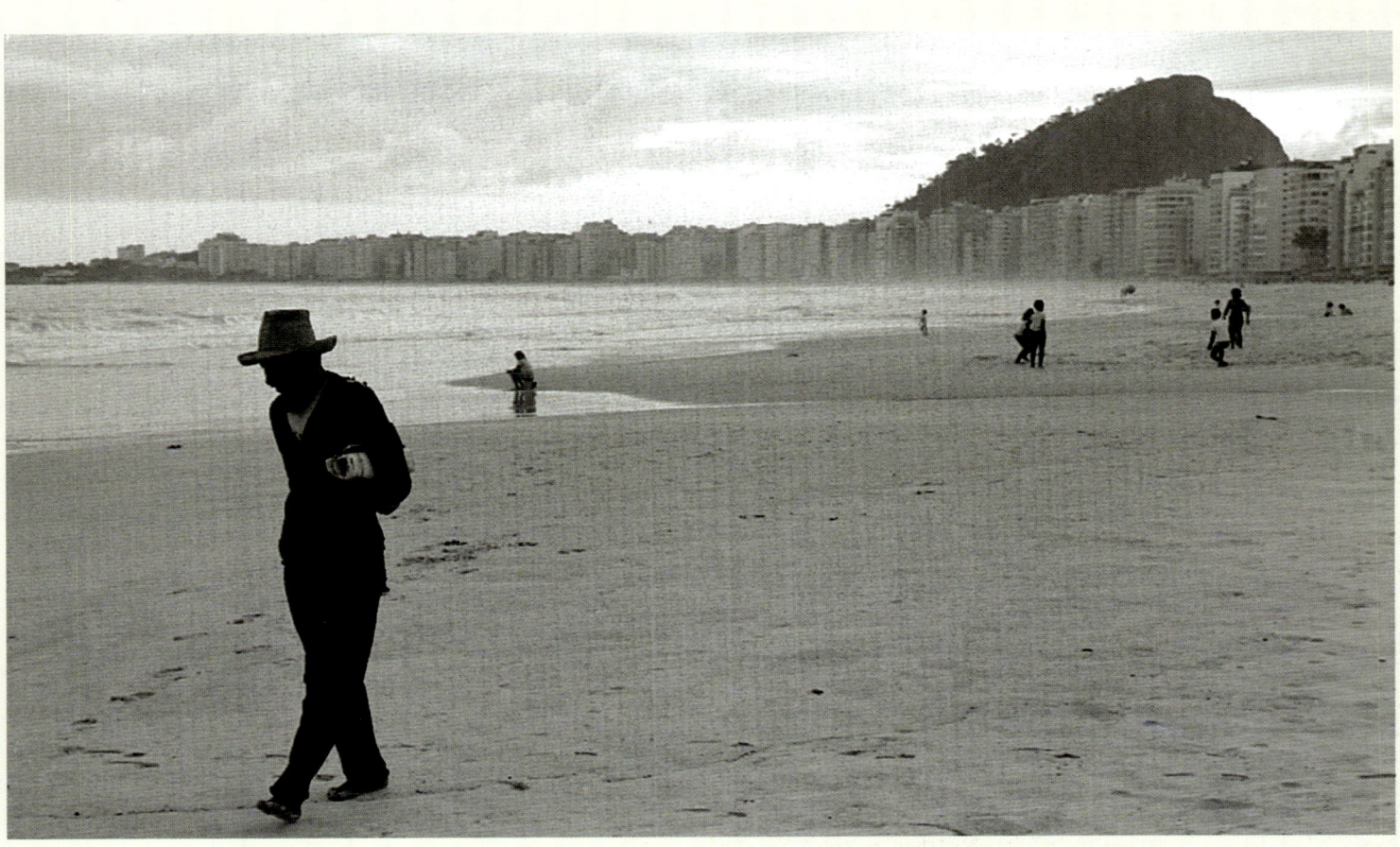

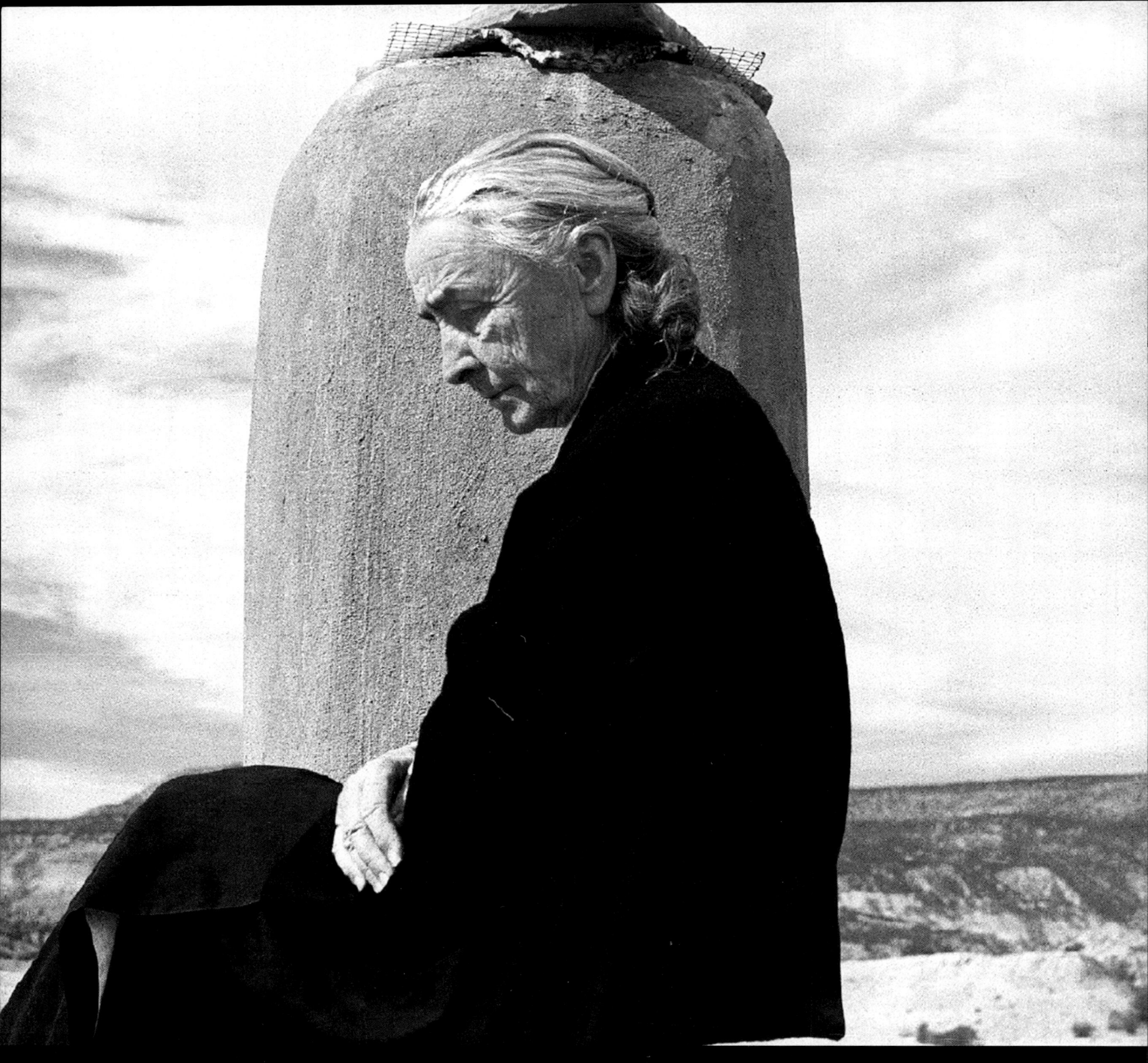

"I try to make my pictures seem reasonable and then, at the last minute, pull the rug from beneath the viewer's feet, very gently so there's a little thrill."

Looking back on his portraits of notable individuals including The Beatles, Marilyn Monroe, Georgia O'Keeffe, Presidents Ronald Reagan and Jimmy Carter, and Maya Angelou, John notes, "I usually daydream of pictures I will take before I go to take them. But I never find exactly what I've imagined. Still, these daydreams give me a point of view. I don't start to work until I have found something as interesting as what I dreamed. Alfred Eisenstaedt was right. He said, 'If you don't see a picture, don't take the camera out of your bag.'"

In 1987, *Life* magazine assigned John to photograph American painter Georgia O'Keeffe at her home near Santa Fe, New Mexico for "a little story." Fine photographers, including Yousuf Karsh, Philippe Halsman, and Arnold Newman had recently photographed her and John remembers one thing. "I'd seen all their wonderful pictures, and I vowed that I wasn't going to take a picture like any of them. Whatever it might be, I wanted something different." When John arrived to Georgia O'Keeffe's home in Abiquiú, New Mexico, her first question was, "How long will this take?"

"I said, 'It might take three or four days.'

She said, 'Why? They are planning just a little story.' This was true, but you never could tell at *Life*.

'It all depends on the pictures,' I told her, which was true. She said, 'We'll see,' and drove me over to her second house at Ghost Ranch for lunch. She talked proudly about the rattlesnakes she killed on her walks and pulled out these little matchboxes filled with rattles. I asked if I could take some pictures at the table. I was on my best behavior. She said, 'Of course.'

I thought it was important for her to understand that I was looking for something different from what Arnold and Philippe and Yousuf had been interested in. I also thought she would like the readers of *Life* to know she was a rattlesnake killer."

Because *Life* had asked John to do a "picture story," he knew that he needed to take a number of related pictures of O'Keeffe that somehow showed something different and surprising about simple acts like reading her mail, writing letters, taking walks, or grooming her dogs.

"I think it's terribly important to not sit around with a subject when you don't think there's going to be an interesting picture. Your meter [is] running all the time, and every time you go 'click' the subject thinks you took a wonderful picture. Why do you need more? So, you try to make every minute with a subject count."

Shortly after lunch, on the first day, John excused himself, saying that he wanted to drive around and get a sense of the land. O'Keeffe told him that she took a 30-minute walk in the morning and evening, so he arranged to return at dawn the next morning. Then he spent the day with her. He came back the next day mid-morning and stayed through her evening walk.

When John submitted his images of 78-year-old O'Keeffe to *Life* magazine, his editors were extremely pleased. They determined that the initial space in the magazine allotted for the layout of the "little story" wouldn't be enough to include all the images, so they held off on publishing the story until they had room to expand it. Eighteen months later, John's photographs of O'Keeffe were made into a ten-page layout, but *Life* then decided O'Keeffe might be a cover, and some quotes were needed from the artist. So John returned to Ghost Ranch to make a cover image (something he felt he didn't really know how to do) with *Life* editor Dorothy Seiberling.

"It was Dotty's turn to interview her and I suggested we go up on the roof. I got bored sitting there. I think it's a bad idea [to] take pictures when somebody is being interviewed because they invariably look intently at something outside of the picture and the viewer wonders what it is. Plus they are usually making awkward gestures and their mouths are twisted as they talk. But I got so bored that I decided to try to make the most lopsided picture in history and put her on the left side of the picture with nothing but blank sky on the right to balance. Curiously, it worked. She looks as if she's reflecting on something, but she isn't. She's coiled, listening to a question and getting ready to gesticulate." It became the cover image.

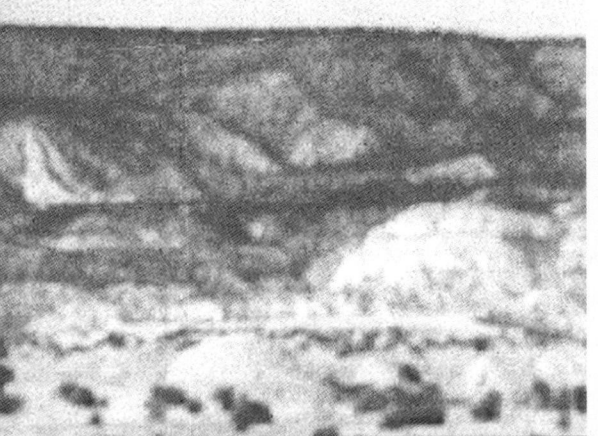

ABOVE: Georgia O'Keeffe on her roof. Ghost Ranch, Abiquiú, New Mexico, 1967.

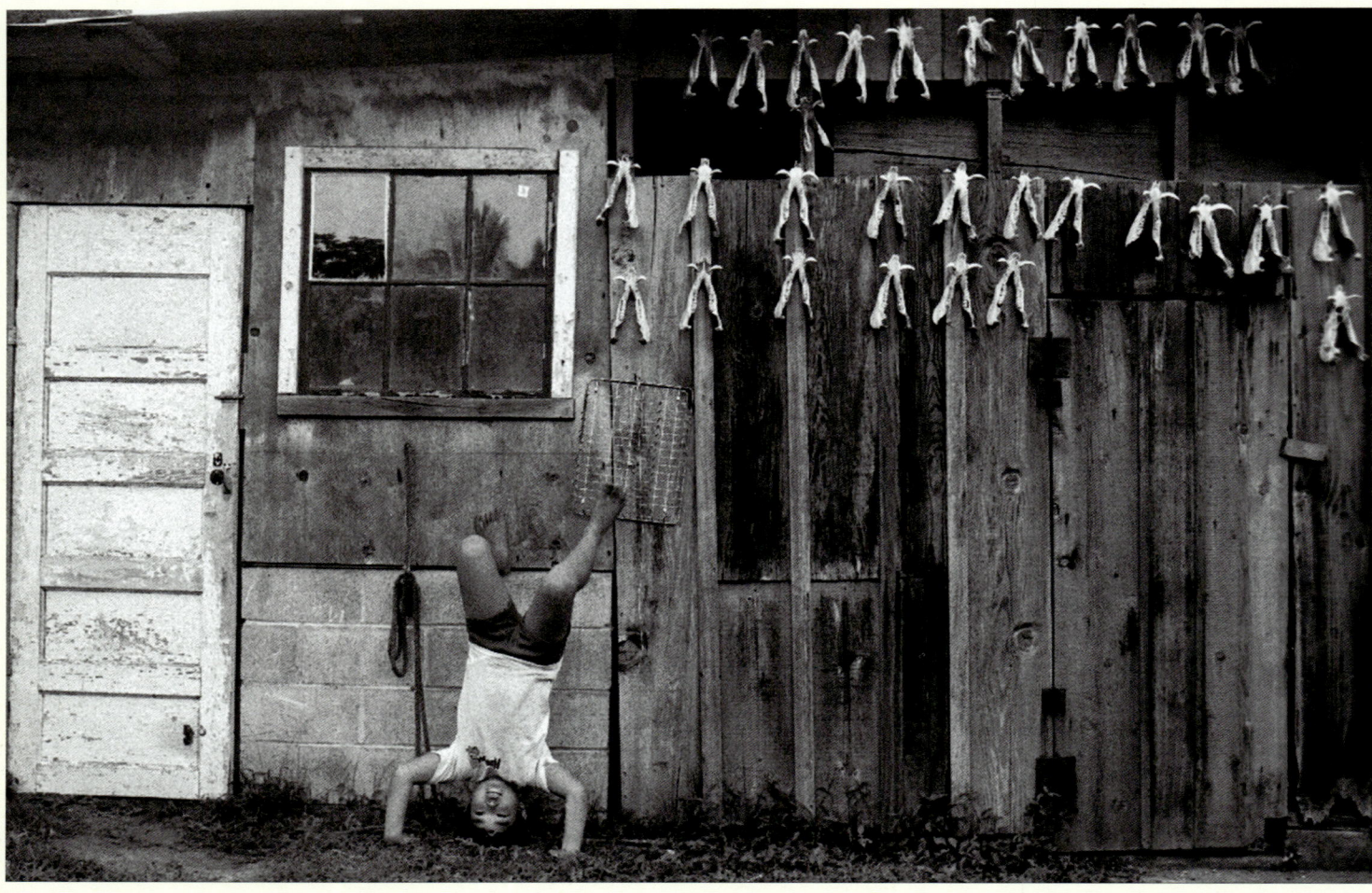

ABOVE: Calbert Imada, The Island of Hawaii, 1983.

VISION

John has always taken assignments (a word he dislikes) from a contrarian perspective. He enjoys revealing his subjects in unexpected ways, exemplified in many of his well-known portraits shot for *Life* magazine, including his portrait of The Beatles—the band members in mid-song as they treaded water in a freezing swimming pool during a cold snap in 1964.

"What I always found wonderful was that you imagined what was expected, and then you would never do that. Not exactly the opposite, but something different. The anathema to me was someone suggesting, 'This subject should be photographed this way.' I couldn't do that. I really couldn't. So, I either said, 'No, thanks.' Or I went and did something different. That was what made assignments interesting."

BEHIND THE IMAGE

John was in Hawaii shooting for *A Day in the Life of Hawaii,* a book by Rick Smolan and David Cohen. "I spent the morning in the Waipio Valley surrounded by nature, which is a green mess, and I was thirsting for a sign of human order. I had pressed David Fujimoto, my guide, to tell me what was unusual to see in the area. 'The Black Beach?' he suggested. Well, yeah. OK. 'The little old hotel in the Valley?' Hmmmm. 'Mrs. Duldulao's taro field?' Yeah. My enthusiasm was minimal. David was feeling a little frustrated when we came up for lunch. 'John, there is a guy with pig jaws all over his shed. Is that the kind of thing you're looking for?' I loved it. The man who killed the wild pigs whose jaws adorn the wall of the shed was not at home. Mrs. Imada said her husband remembered every hunt and where each jaw came from. Calbert, their son, said he could stand on his head, and showed me. I felt like a hunter, too."

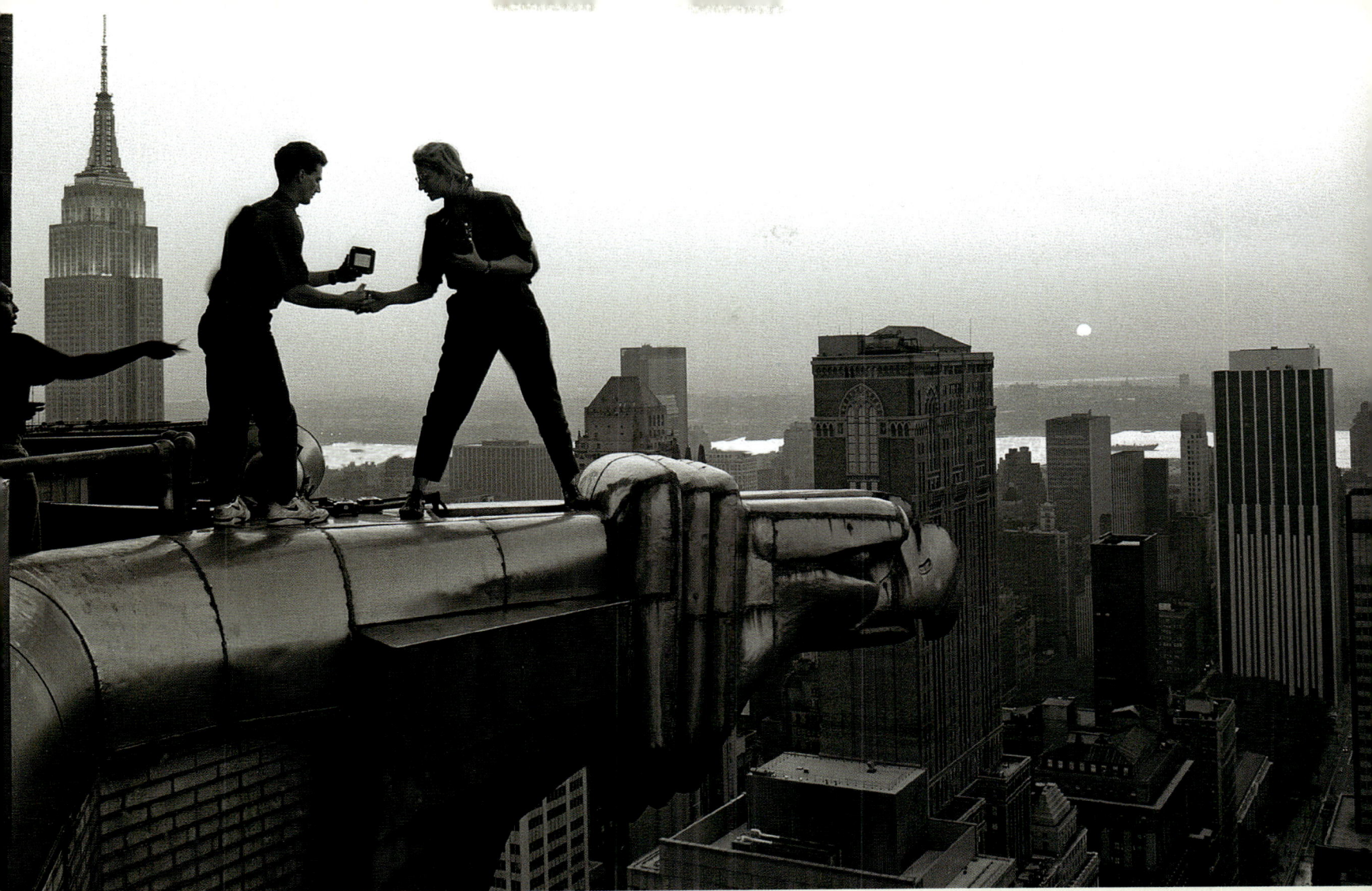

BEHIND THE IMAGE

In the early 1930s, Margaret Bourke-White's assistant photographed her crouching on one of eight gargoyles that extend from the 61st floor of New York City's Chrysler Building. Six decades later, with a book and an exhibition due that fall, Annie Leibovitz chose to pay tribute to Bourke-White by photographing in the same spot. She asked her friend, dancer David Parsons, to pose on a second gargoyle. Watching from the safety of a terrace, John was photographing Leibovitz for a fall preview section in *The New York Times*. He wondered if any photograph would justify the risks they were taking. Now he wonders not only about the risk but the reward, too. No one today knows what, if any, picture Bourke-White took from the perch. There's reason to believe she was just posing for some self-publicity. "Intrepid and eager for the world to know it," is how historian Alan Brinkley of Columbia University recently described her. And John says Leibovitz prefers a marvelous picture she took of Parsons when she caught his body in an odd position, balancing on one knee and his elbows, on the floor of her studio downtown earlier that afternoon.

Curiously, because John's subjects might be selected by others, he felt a great sense of freedom. He challenged himself to portray his subjects in the most interesting and unexpected way. John feels that had he approached a subject, say a woman with 16 children, for his own personal project, he would feel some obligation to do something "nice and expected," a portrait of a woman with her 16 children. "In my experience, because a publication was interested, I'm free to do what I want. I won't take the picture the publisher expects—and I'm not free to trash the woman. I'd excuse myself rather than do that. But I am free to have my own point of view because it's the publication's interest, not my picture, that's [of] meaning to the subject. Being a contrarian on assignment gave me a wonderful freedom."

"What makes a picture good? It's not just the composition, though that is important. It's not just the framing, which is important, too. It's not the texture or the timing or any of that. It's important that the picture is interesting. The subject may be as common as your little left finger, but then somehow you've got to make an interesting picture of a little left finger. Look for what is peculiar."

BEHIND THE IMAGE

"It is difficult to get the performer and the audience in a single picture. He faces one way, they face another. He is in the spotlight, they are in the dark. I had spent a week in Europe trying (among other things) to solve that problem, but it was not until we got to Atlantic City that I did. The audience at the Steel Pier stood right up to the edge of the stage, so they were as close to Armstrong as an audience could be. I put two or three lights up in the rear of the room to light patches of the audience and one over the stage to light the performers and those in front. Knowing Armstrong's routine, I sat beside the drummer and waited for Armstrong to sing 'Hello Dolly!' I knew he'd joke and spin around, which would solve the problem, but just as important, by then the audience would be happy, clapping, beaming proof of Armstrong's genius as an entertainer."

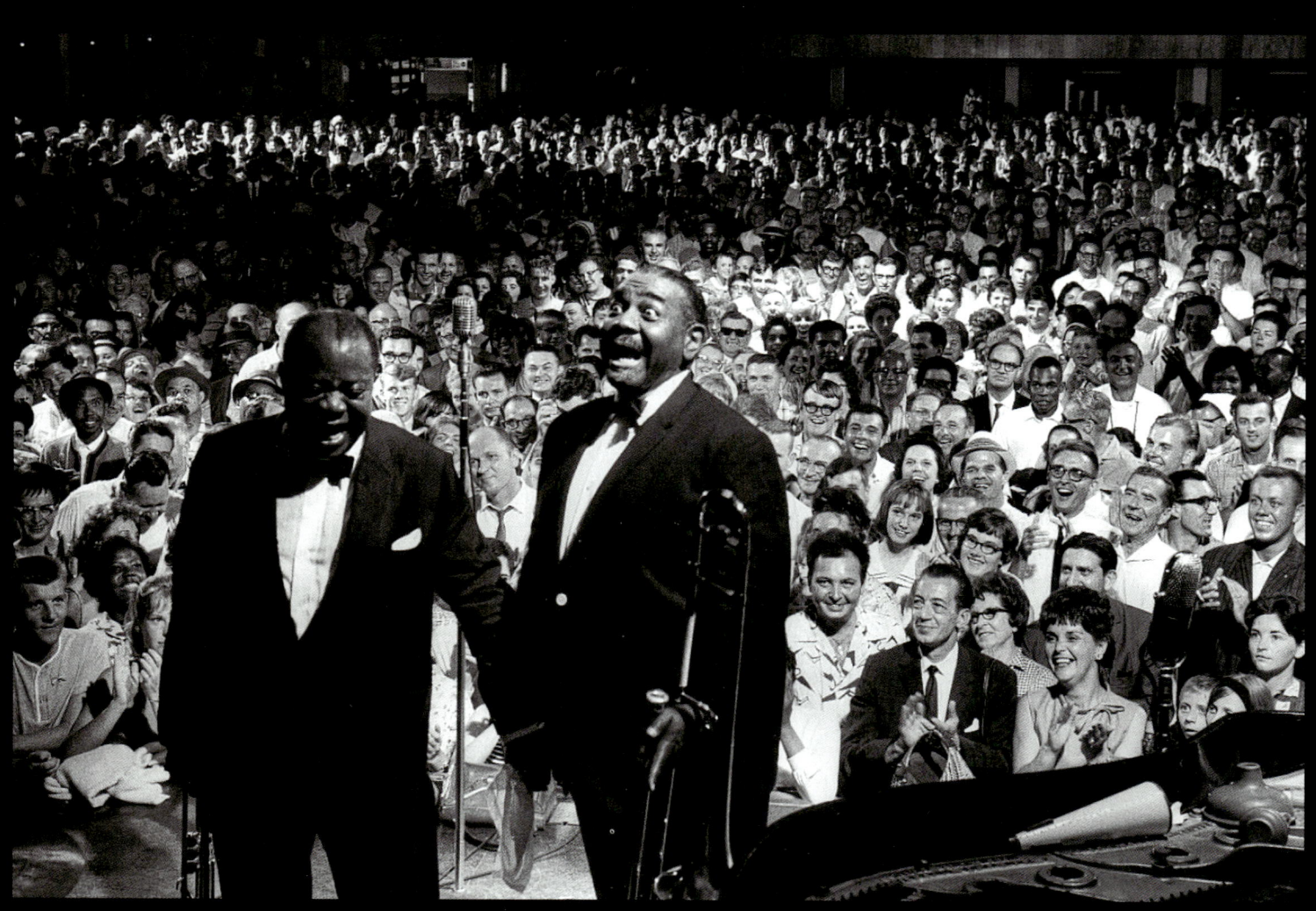

EQUIPMENT

For John, the mark of a good photographer has nothing to do with the size of the camera or the weight of the lens they use. Today, he captures his personal photographs with a small, 10-megapixel Canon G12. "It's not threatening to the subject. If you think of it in terms of English grammar, there is a kind of photography you can compare to the use of the third person narrative when you write. 'She went there, she nodded, she smiled, she bit her finger . . . whatever.' That's what I am interested in doing." Though John acknowledges the need for professional photographers to produce images of the highest quality, he feels that expensive SLRs with humongous lenses put more emphasis on the photographer making the photograph than on what the subject is doing. "When the subject turns to look at the camera, the picture turns (grammatically) into the first person. 'I went there. She smiled and reached toward my camera . . .' Taking the picture of the event becomes the event itself. Whereas, a less obvious photographer might lift a piece of the event unnoticed into a new picture world."

BEHIND THE IMAGE

"Medgar Evers, the NAACP field secretary, was shot dead in his driveway in Jackson in 1963. At his funeral in a high school auditorium, I stood on one side of the stage with other photographers during the ceremony. I'd like to say that I realized what this moment was when it happened, but I didn't. What is important about it is that in the midst of conflict over civil rights, the murder was reduced to a simple human document. It didn't make a difference what slogans were shouted or what political points of view or theories were held. You saw in stark human terms something wrong had happened."

LEFT: Louis Armstrong and trombonist Tyree Glenn, Atlantic City, New Jersey, 1965.

RIGHT: Medgar Evers' funeral, Jackson, Mississippi, June 18, 1963.

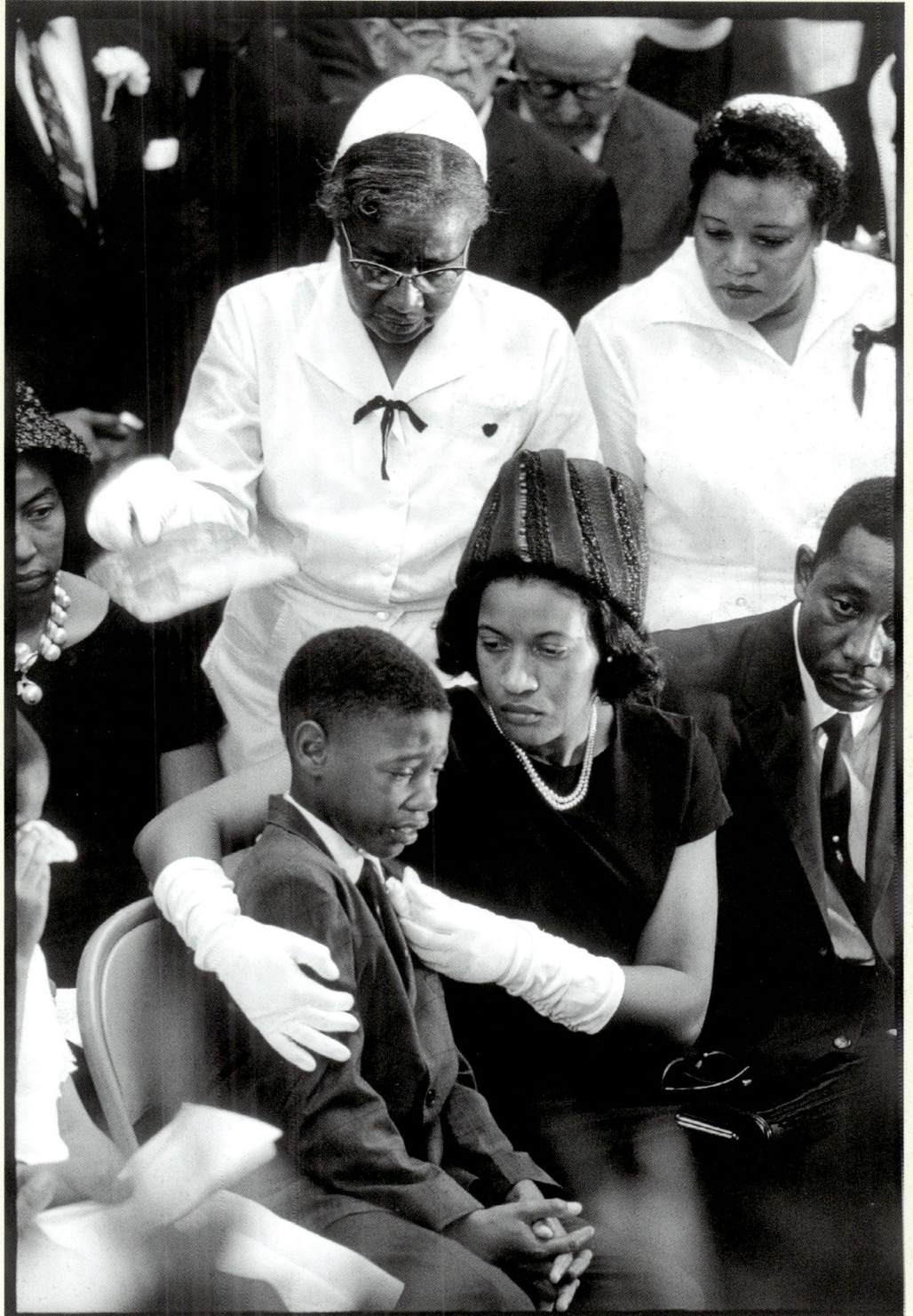

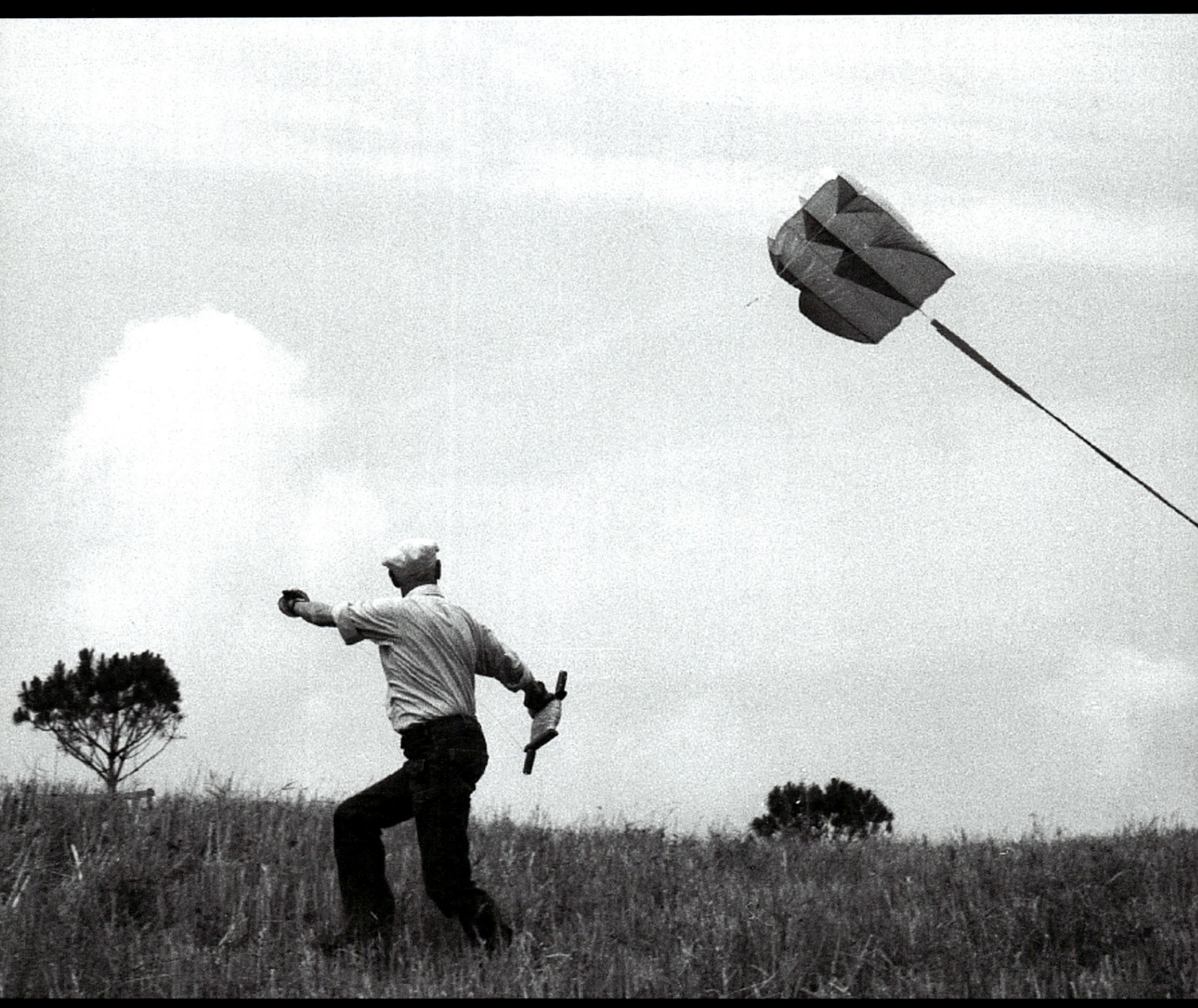

"Like doctors, photographers must be concerned with what's present. Wishing it were different doesn't help. You can't put a spin on anything. Either something is there and you photograph it, or it's not there and you don't photograph it."

ABOVE: Henri Cartier-Bresson flies his kite, Provence, France, 1987.

BEHIND THE IMAGE

⊙ "Cartier-Bresson hated to be photographed, but he agreed to be the subject of a picture story in *Life* magazine to help publicize an upcoming exhibition of his earliest photographs at the Museum of Modern Art in New York City. When I arrived in Paris, his first question was whether all the pictures could be taken from behind? While we quickly agreed that would be silly, and while he was both a wonderful man and a great photographer, at 79, Cartier-Bresson often seemed a simmering teakettle. Now and then something would set him off as if someone had turned the heat up on a stove. There'd be steam and the lid would be rattling; he'd be upset. Just as swiftly, he'd quiet down and be his attentive self again. So, the very first thing I did was take a picture of his face, because I felt it might be the only time that I could. I didn't know when the teakettle might boil. I was careful about pressing the point further.

At his summer house in Provence, he planned to go for a swim in the municipal pool, which I would normally think was a hokey picture opportunity, but I thought with Cartier-Bresson it might be interesting and certainly it would be hard for him not to show his face. Who knew what the possibilities were, what the pool was like and so forth. Anyhow, it turned out that it was closed for repairs, and on his way home, he stopped to draw for a few moments in a field. I photographed him from behind to show the landscape. The picture is pleasant but static. As he finished, I asked what else he might do? 'Nothing. No more is possible,' he said firmly.

His wife, Martine Franck (an excellent photographer), understood my disappointment. She rummaged through the hall closet to find a kite that Cartier-Bresson flew with their 15-year-old daughter and urged him to fly it for me. There was just enough wind to get it up. You can ask somebody to fly a kite. You don't tell them how to fly the kite, and how they run and what they do is their business. Suddenly, if they're doing it in front of you and your camera, it gives you some information to convey to a viewer, even when he makes sure you don't see his face."

A SECRET

Put good pictures in front of your camera. "When I became an editor as well as a photographer, I discovered to my surprise that good photographers are not good photographers because they have a special eye. Good photographers are good because they put good pictures in front of their cameras. Think for a moment about what cameras do, and this becomes obvious."

You will undoubtedly find yourselves in a situation when you might be troubled by the fact that you can't find a good picture. When this happens, hold back from shooting; put your camera back in your camera bag or pocket. "If you can't see a good picture, pressing a button will not make one appear. Think about the situation and see if you are ignoring something because you didn't think it is important—or see if you can raise a shade and flood a room with light, or get people to start singing or climb a hill to get a different view. And if you can't, just go home. All photographers take a boring picture sometimes. It doesn't count. No one wins them all."

CURATING

Following John's illustrious career as a documentary photographer for *Life* magazine, he spent 15 years in such roles as the picture editor for *Life Special Reports*, and was part of the group that tested and launched *People* magazine. He was instrumental in the creation of *Life* magazine as a monthly in 1978 and was its picture editor until 1987. John believes that a photographer should edit his or her own photographs down to as small a selection as possible before showing them to a publisher. "In general, everybody takes good pictures. It's become wonderfully easy to take good pictures, but there are very few telling pictures; there are very few pictures that make you stop and say 'Oh.' It's always been so. As Cartier-Bresson said, 'When you take a good picture it jumps out. But great pictures are very, very rare.'"

Elizabeth Fleming

www.elizabethfleming.com

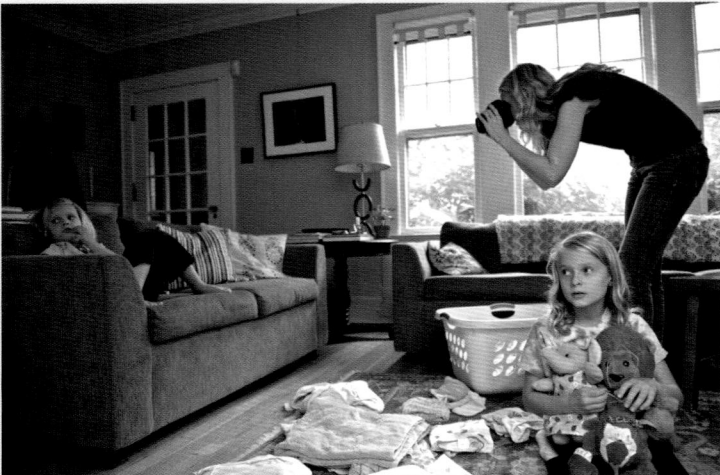

LEFT: Elizabeth waits for moments to unfold between loads of laundry.

Portrait of Elizabeth Fleming by Stephanie Calabrese Roberts

"Art wouldn't be interesting if it was completely appropriate."

PATH TO PHOTOGRAPHY

The oldest of three daughters, Elizabeth Fleming remembers her parents encouraging her to experiment with art and express herself creatively ever since she was a young child living in the suburbs of Philadelphia, Pennsylvania. They gave her a camera with black-and-white film when she turned 12, and Elizabeth remembers instinctively creating photographs that were dark and mysterious—shooting dim self-portraits, images of the moon, shots of her sister with fictitious injuries, and photographs of a pretend twin by way of double exposure experiments.

For as long as she can remember, Elizabeth has long held a fascination with mysteries, strange happenings, and ghost stories despite the fact that her explorations of this subject matter in books and movies often kept her from falling asleep at night. She remembers enjoying the dark humor and unexpected endings of Roald Dahl's stories, checking out each one of the books in the UFO/ghost story section of her school library, and obsessing over a Ouija board in her early teens. Extending this fascination

to the photographs, drawings, and paintings she created, Elizabeth remembers sharing her artwork with her father and enjoying listening to him use big words in his analysis of her dark and mysterious creations. Encouraged by the intellectual discussions prompted by her images and positive critiques from art teachers she respected in high school, and inspired by the edgy work of Balthus, Francis Bacon, and Egon Schiele, Elizabeth went on to pursue a Bachelor of Fine Arts degree from Washington University in St. Louis, Missouri, with an initial focus on painting.

During college, Elizabeth began incorporating old family-photograph cutouts within her paintings, and after taking several photography classes, shifted her focus away from painting and toward photography. "I'd have an idea in my head of what I wanted [the painting] to be, and it never looked like what I could envision. It just didn't quite fit. But when I took pictures they [still weren't necessarily] what I'd envisioned, but I liked [the results] even more than what I had in my head." During this time, Elizabeth remembers writing dark

poetry, and shooting nude self-portraiture and portraits of her roommates with a Hasselblad as well as domestic imperfections such as crumbs on the floor. While Elizabeth made attempts to experiment with her photographic style— to not isolate one object or person within her compositions or to lighten the mood of her images by minimizing the dark undercurrent revealed within her ordinary scenes—no matter how hard she tried to do something different, "It still kind of looked the same."

Following college, Elizabeth moved to Brooklyn, New York, "with grandiose visions of being discovered the day I moved into my apartment." Realizing quickly that she needed to find a job to pay the rent, she interviewed for a variety of freelance photography positions and within a month of arriving to New York, interviewed with and unexpectedly fell in love with commercial photographer James Worrell. While Elizabeth and James continued their relationship (and later married), she went on to freelance for a variety of fashion, editorial, and still life photographers and photo editors, yet struggled with the overly technical aspects

About the Series

"'Life is a Series of Small Moments' is an ongoing body of work about the intricacies contained within the emotional landscape of living with children, and of childhood itself. As the mother of two young girls I'm consistently reminded of how transient life is, and I find that watching my daughters grow and change so rapidly—and consequently being acutely aware of the passage of days—is a source of both wonder and sadness. Consequently, my photographs have become one way of processing my loaded relationship with time. As a result, I am attempting to create lasting documents of fleeting moments while also paying homage to memory, or more precisely, to how people connect with the impressions their memories leave behind. In isolating various objects and/or people within my images, I hope to draw attention to things the eye often skims over, while visually representing the ache that I suspect many of us feel when we look back on our own and our family's pasts.

I also believe there is the potential for a sense of intimacy in the gap between mystery and revelation. Through resting in this middle place, I am both showing and withholding as I aim to create a certain tension, one that allows for identification through the process of 'peering in,' as it were. This alternation between discovery and hiding is, for me, another way of connecting to the emotional and often volatile makeup of childhood. I find myself compelled to examine the ordinary in relation to the familiar as a means of bearing witness to the complex and often allegorical nature of domestic life."

ELIZABETH FLEMING

BEHIND THE IMAGE

"[My daughter] Edie's in the bathtub because she had painted her face with watercolors. She'd been completely covered in black and red and blue so I put her in the bath to wash off, and only that one spot on her eyebrow was left. She'd been rinsing her face under the faucet, and then she turned around and lay back for just a second. It was a lucky shot."

BELOW: *Painted*, 2007.

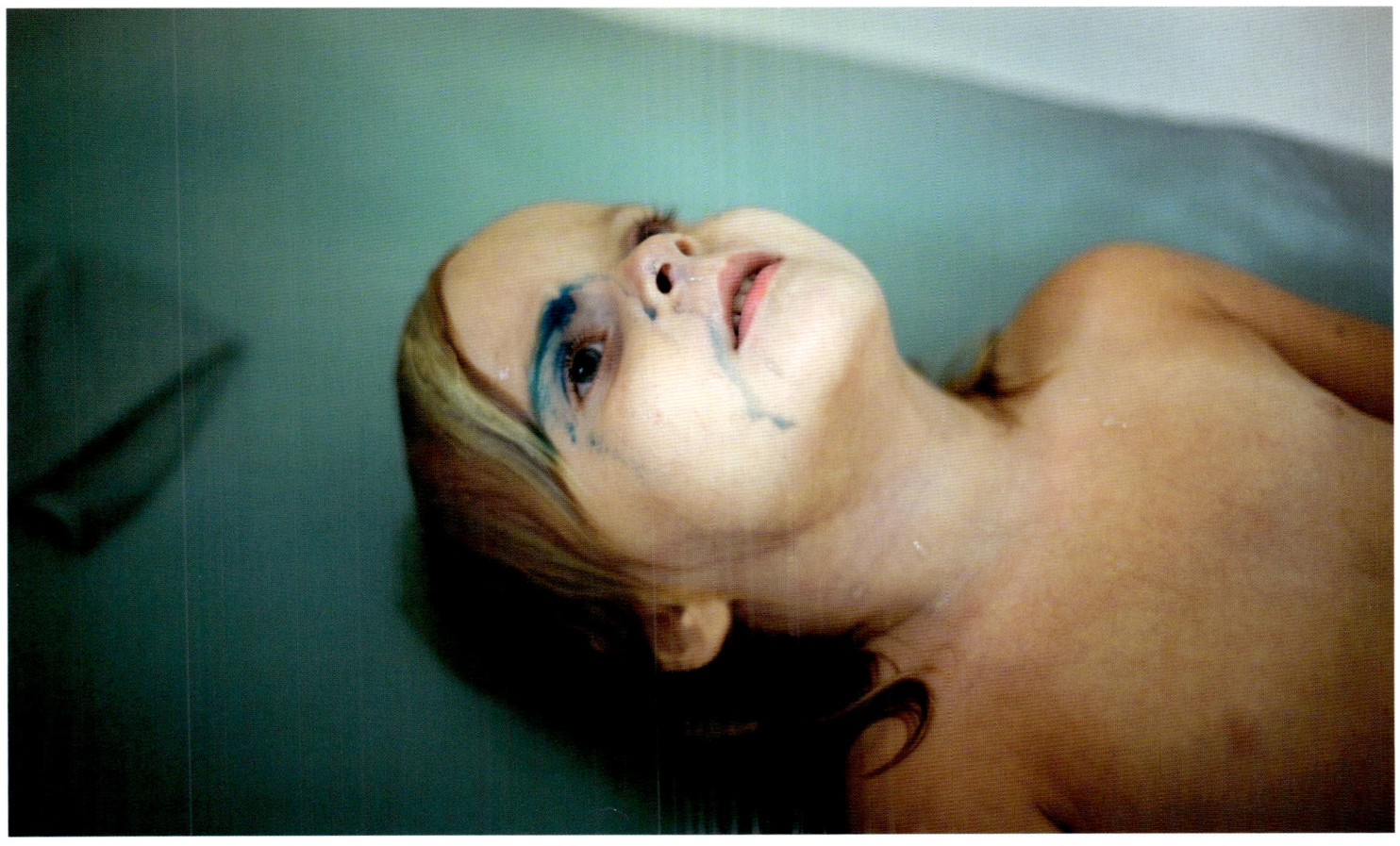

of commercial photography and the lack of creativity in her roles. Pressured to find a more fulfilling job in the field of photography, she took a position as an assistant photo editor at *HomeStyle Magazine* in Manhattan. While Elizabeth found it exciting to meet and book photographers for assignments and review their work, managing logistics and juggling details left her feeling uninspired and with little time to pursue her own photography. In 1999, after a summer tour through Europe, Elizabeth enrolled in graduate school at the School of Visual Arts in Manhattan to continue her exploration of photography, film, and related media. During graduate school, Elizabeth was a curatorial intern for the Whitney Museum and assumed a full-time position as the Biennial Assistant for another year before leaving to focus on the creation of a family. Eight months after the birth of her first child, Elizabeth and James traded a one-bedroom apartment in Brooklyn for a picturesque home in the suburbs of New Jersey.

BEHIND THE IMAGE

"I can't remember why I had the box. Something came in it, and we took it upstairs, and June was playing around with it. I'm not sure how it ended up outside the bathroom. I like that you can almost see her toes through the tights."

BEHIND THE IMAGE

"I shot this picture very early in the spring when it was just barely warm enough to be in the yard. Edie had been digging in the piles of dirt (previously our vegetable beds) with a little plastic shovel and burying rocks and sticks in the mud. Her hands were freezing and I asked her to hold them up so I could see how dirty they were. Her palms are bright pink because she was so cold."

BELOW: *Earth*, 2008. **RIGHT:** *Hiding*, 2009.

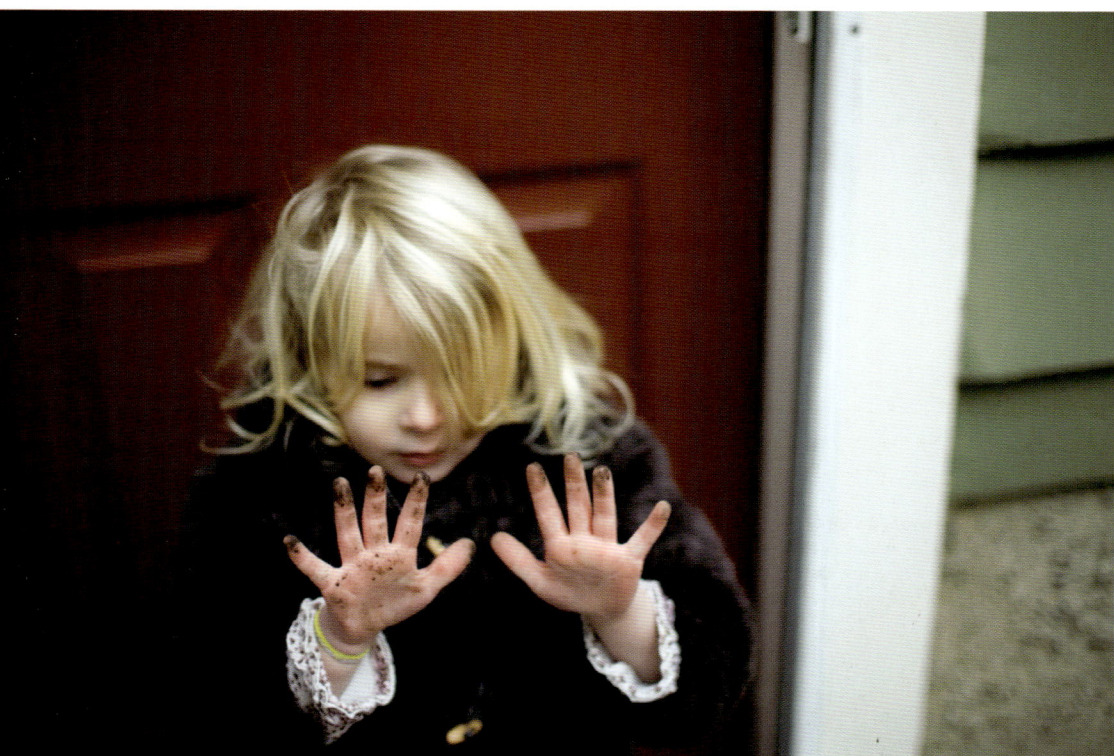

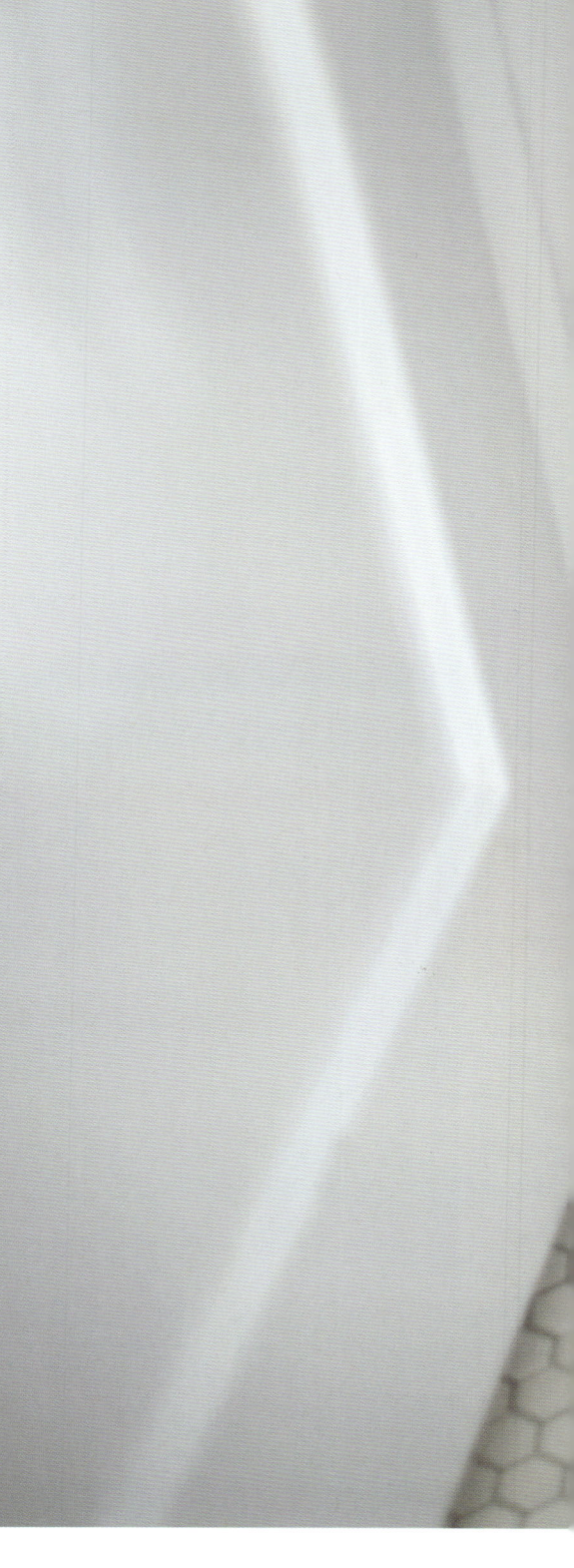

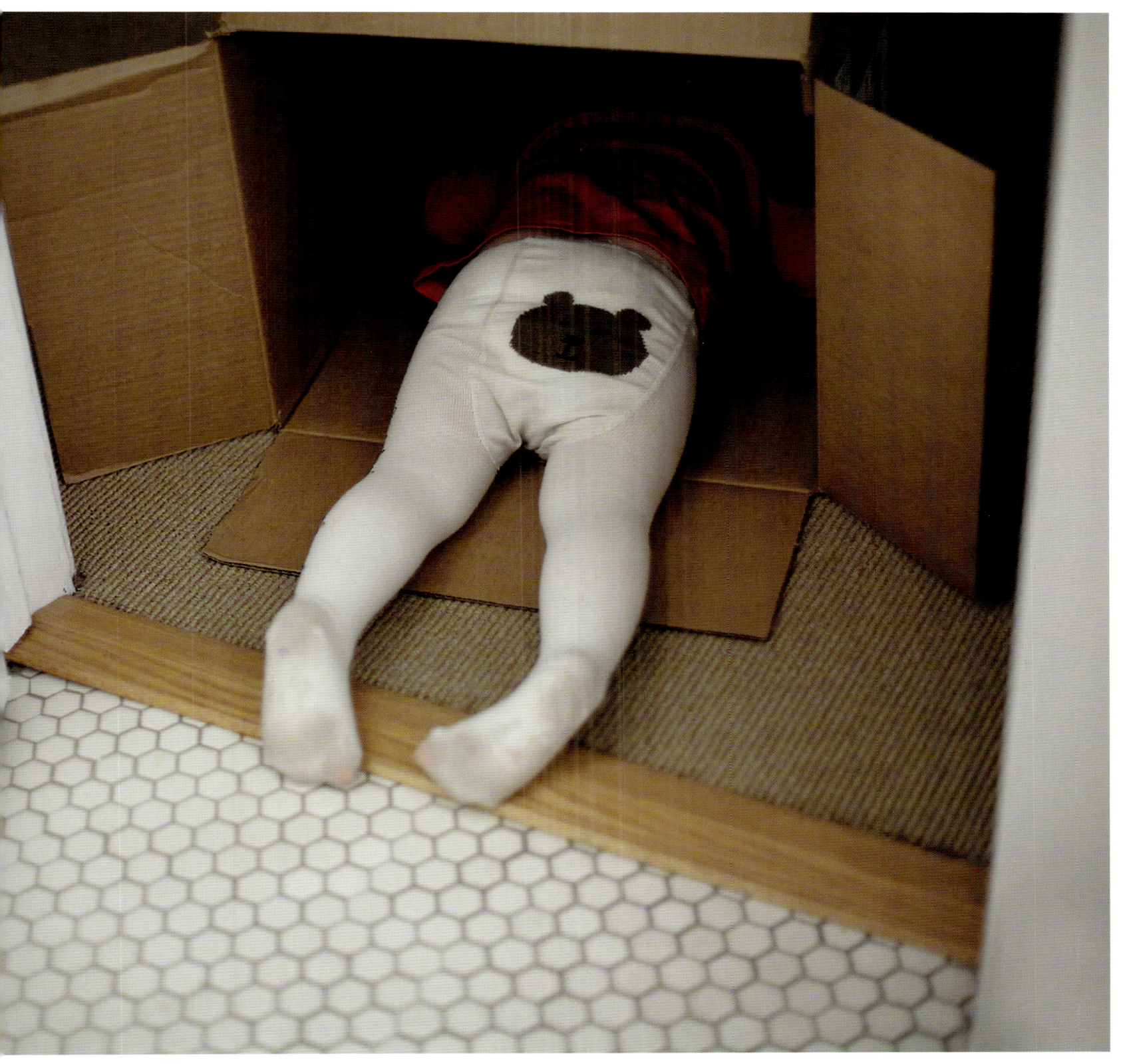

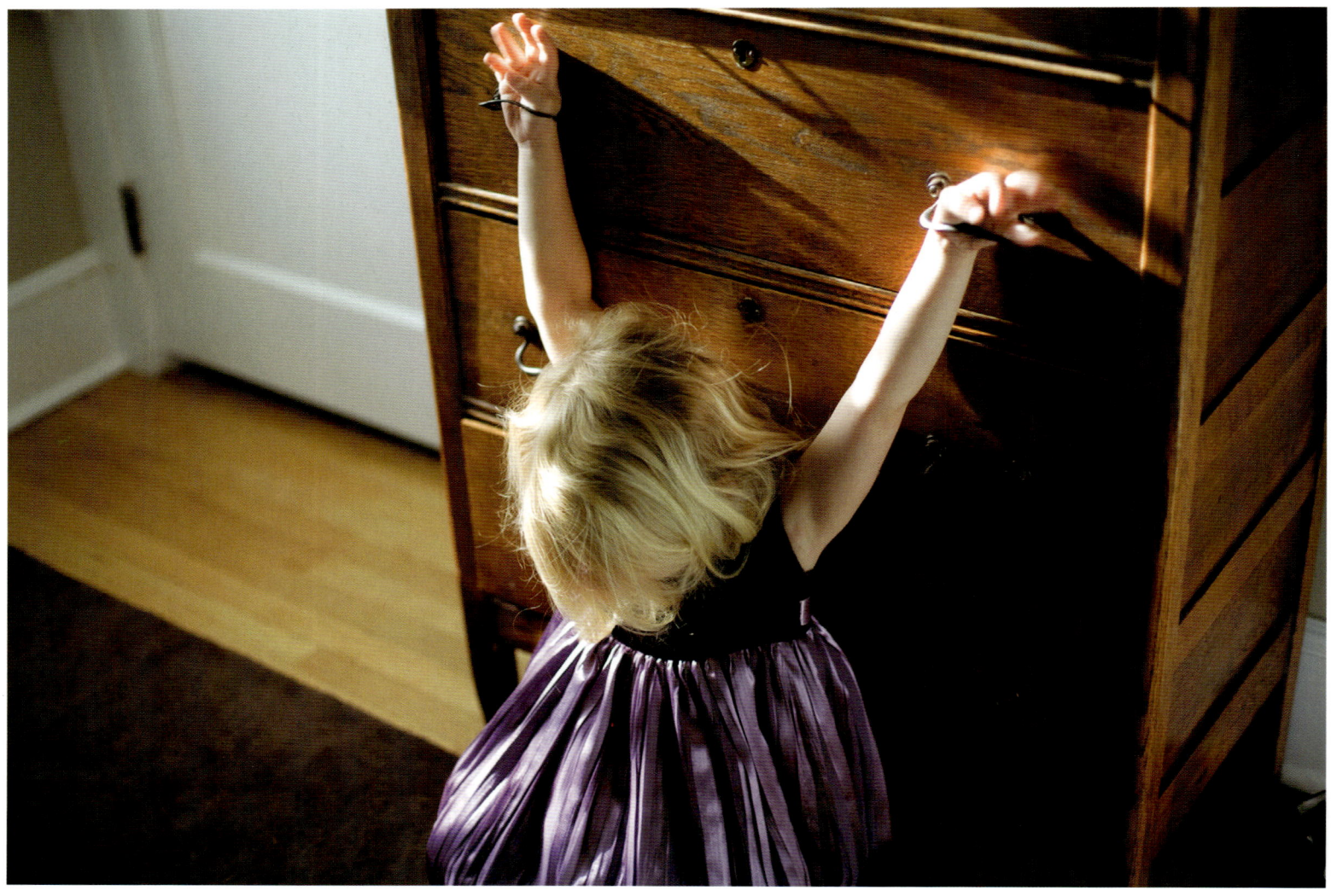

ABOVE: *Hanging*, 2009.

INSPIRATION

The birth of Elizabeth's first child, Edie, and a new home with blank walls to fill, brought a surge of creativity and intriguing new subject matter to study through the lens of her first digital SLR. "I started taking domestically-inspired pictures that were similar [in style] to what I had been doing in college and grad school—close-up images with a shallow depth of field that portrayed her drooling, nursing, and having tantrums. I used only natural light and tried to transform ordinary details into something more poetic. Then I did a whole hazards [series] where I took pictures of outlets and anything that might cause her to choke or impale herself." Over time, after the birth of her second daughter, June, Elizabeth began to shoot more frequently in an attempt to pause and capture fleeting and curious moments of childhood and her domestic life. She became more comfortable exposing a wider-angle view—revealing more of the setting and the complexity of her feelings in the moment. These small moments, inspired by a mother's love and genuine fascination with her subjects, infused with the less obvious, darker side of Elizabeth's nature, evolved into an ongoing series of award-winning fine art photographs that have been exhibited in art galleries and photography centers across the country.

BEHIND THE IMAGE

"Edie was playing around the dresser in [her sister] June's room and she put her hands through the handles and started hanging, so I ran downstairs and got my camera. She wore that dress to school, I think, every other day when she was four. She loved that thing. She wore it until it came apart."

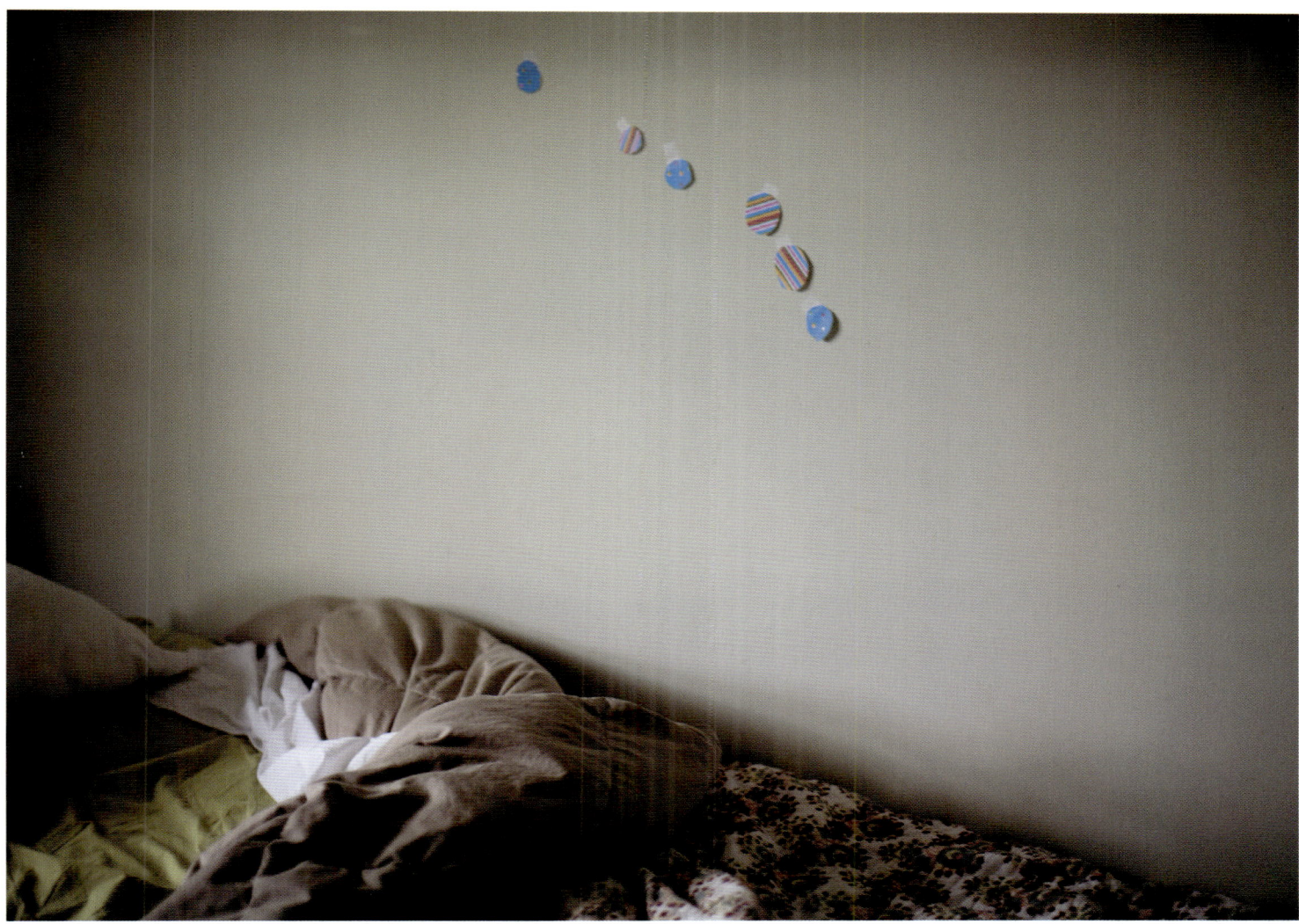

ABOVE: *Planets*, 2008.

APPROACH

"It's documentary, but it's more like my way of finding a little bit of sanity in insanity. It's a different way of looking at my life. It's not necessarily a representation of *this is how it is*. Things are so wild with kids. Being able to really look at the girls and capture them in this way [is different than what I see when] I'm just interacting with them. If I step back with the camera, they get that sort of faraway look, and I'm really glad that I have that to hold on to."

A glance through Elizabeth's home reveals a creative environment that would inspire almost anyone—hand-cut letters and colorful drawings taped to the walls, kid-inspired installations of found objects and art books within reach, a dining room dedicated to crafts, and a makeshift scarecrow made of cardboard boxes and pillows propped up on a chair in the living room. Elizabeth keeps her camera in the same spot (on a shelf in the study), and on the same aperture setting for quick access to spontaneous moments as they happen. She may shoot hundreds of photographs over the course of several months and select just one to add to her "Life is a Series of Small Moments" ongoing series. In a single setting, Elizabeth might shoot up to 30 images of her subject(s), experimenting with subtle changes to the point of focus within a shallow depth of field.

BEHIND THE IMAGE

"My in-laws were coming to visit. Edie had just gotten this craft paper—these little squares—and she said she wanted to decorate the room for [her grandparents]. She started cutting out the shapes and she wanted circles so I helped her. That's why they're less messy and more round. But she taped them by herself up on the wall just where she wanted them."

"My questions when I struggled were less about 'Am I exploiting them?' and more about 'Am I neglecting them in order to make my art?' I question everything, and think about everything, and obsess about everything. And that's one of the few things where I feel like I am comfortable with it because I guess I wouldn't be able to make the art come out right otherwise. I think some people can fake it but I can't."

VISION

You can sense a bit of Elizabeth's rebellious nature and her fascination with mystery and intrigue beneath the smooth surface of reality in her images. Elizabeth is drawn to explore and make images of what went wrong, what hurts, and what was rejected, scared, or soiled, yet she reveals these discoveries as one-frame scenes in fairytales. While there is a certain dark quality present in these moments, she portrays them in a dreamy, feminine, and almost sensuous way.

"I think there was a part of the being nice, being good, and being polite kind of thing [that felt unnatural]. It's not that I came from a family that was all *Sound of Music* or anything, but there was an emphasis on being socially adept. And I was more of an introvert, so I definitely rebelled against that a bit. I'm social enough and I like being around people and my friends, but I didn't do as well being thrown into group situations." Photography has given Elizabeth a creative outlet to process her struggle with depression—a way to expose the reality of what's often hidden beneath a socially acceptable, "appropriate" facade.

EQUIPMENT

Elizabeth shoots with a Canon digital SLR and a 50mm lens, with her aperture most often set to $f/1.4$ to offer a shallow area of focus on her subject within a blurred, dreamlike setting. She shoots exclusively with natural light and often underexposes her images with a slow shutter speed setting. Elizabeth processes her images on a Mac Pro in the office and "napping room" on the third floor of her home using Adobe Lightroom to manage and organize her images, and Adobe Photoshop for fine-tuned tweaks to color, contrast, and exposure.

SHARING

Elizabeth began her blog, *Tethered*, in 2008 as a creative outlet for her writing, to share experiences with her photography, to document and share inspiring discoveries, and to feel part of an extended creative community, but she remembers feeling conflicted about spending more time "in [her] own world" as a new mother. In spite of feeling that initial guilt, she found that she "was really into the writing. It was nice to be able to write about other people's work if I saw something that I liked, almost even as a record for myself instead of just forgetting about it or jotting it down in my sketchbook and not looking at it again." Elizabeth appreciates the blog now as a personal documentary of her thoughts and discoveries.

A SECRET

Stir your imagination and vision within the boundary of nonfiction.

What makes Elizabeth's approach unique in the genre of documentary photography is the conceptual nature of her personal work and the portrayal of her children in a non-sentimental way. The setting is real—her home—yet the view and peculiar moments she exposes (scenes that might otherwise have been swept under the rug) appear almost fictional, leaving the viewer a little puzzled, unsettled, or simply curious. Consider ways in which you too might stir the viewer's imagination and intrigue with your work, or simply elicit a surprising emotional reaction to scenes discovered within the boundary of nonfiction.

BEHIND THE IMAGE

"They had gotten wet from Edie playing outside in the sprinkler so I hung them on the doorknob to dry them out before I threw them in the hamper."

RIGHT: *Keyhole,* 2007.

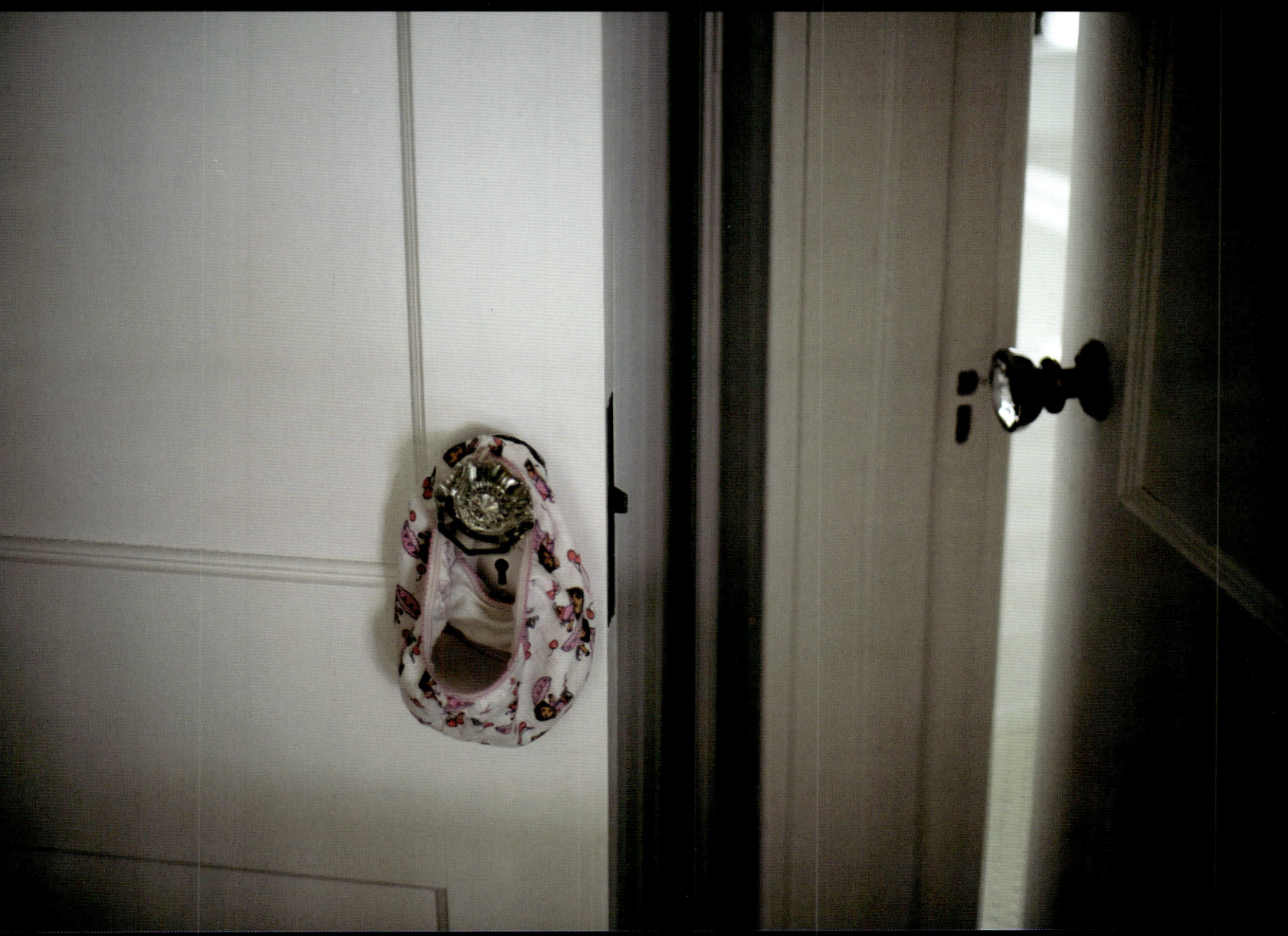

Rick Smolan

www.againstallodds.com

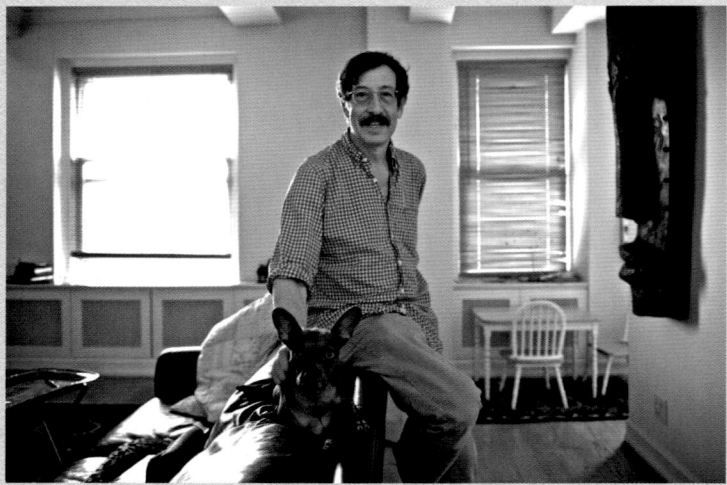

LEFT: Rick in his Manhattan home protected by his dog Bella.

Portrait of Rick Smolan by Stephanie Calabrese Roberts

"My first reaction to getting an assignment was always incredible elation, and then suddenly, abject terror thinking that if I blow this assignment, my career will be over. I bet everything on every assignment, and always felt like each one might be my last."

PATH TO PHOTOGRAPHY

At age 14, Rick Smolan received a camera from his father and took it with him on a summer trip to South America with his history teacher and a fellow student. Rick was painfully shy as a child and teenager, but discovered that having a camera in his hand, especially in a foreign country, gave him a way to relate with people without speaking their language. "I was this scrawny little kid. I couldn't play sports. I couldn't talk to girls. So, the camera became a way for me to be there without really being there. I could walk up to the sports guys and cheerleaders and take pictures of them. I could insert myself into any one of the different groups and [eventually] everybody accepted me because I was there glorifying what they were doing."

Feeling the desire to establish his independence and seek adventure beyond the confines of his neighborhood in the suburbs of New Jersey, Rick (the eldest of three) enrolled in a high school exchange program at age 16 and spent a year living with a family in Barcelona, Spain. There he persuaded the owner of a small photography store down the street from his school to teach him how to develop film and make prints in exchange for being able to use the darkroom for his own work, "So while the other kids my age were out drinking for the first time and getting stoned, I was in the darkroom breathing chemicals and I just loved it. Being in the darkroom, watching the images appear in the trays, was just magic."

Rick continued down the path of photography through high school and shot pictures for the school yearbook, but remembers having tense arguments with his father when he began to express an interest to focus on photography in college. Convinced that he didn't want his son to end up in a studio shooting portraits or weddings, Rick's father refused to let him apply to any college that offered a photography program. At the time, Rick had no idea that his father had been a photographer on an aircraft carrier during World War II (a position that, at the time, was looked down upon and considered an "unskilled" role).

Rick went on to Dickinson College, a liberal arts college in Carlisle, Pennsylvania, and secretly crafted a photography major with the help of a supportive art professor, giving him opportunities to shoot fellow students throughout his studies. Rick shot for the college yearbook and in 1971, with prompting from his art professor, submitted a box of 100 photographs to Images, a stock photo company in Nashville, Tennessee. Shortly thereafter, Rick received $1,000 in exchange. Thrilled by the reality of making "incredible money" for his images and inspired by the thoughtful critiques and assignments he received from the agency's owner (and photojournalist), Jack Corn, Rick continued to sell his images to publications via the stock agency throughout college. As Rick neared graduation, Corn suggested Rick share his work with John Durniak, the photo editor for *Time* magazine in New York. Armed with his yearbook in hand, Rick showed up for the meeting.

"John Durniak was known for taking hungry young photographers and throwing them into [assignments] for which they had no qualifications—to see what they would do. I didn't know this. I just knew that my first assignment was to photograph [British playwright] Tom Stoppard. Durniak wanted me to do a [spontaneous] portrait of Stoppard, so they introduced me to him on the 30th floor of the Time-Life Building just before he was about to leave. He had just written a play called *Jumpers* so when we walked out of the elevator together, I got him to jump off the little potted plants in front of the building." Durniak gave Rick a second assignment and then, in 1975, a third—a color cover story that would feature American opera conductor Sarah Caldwell.

"I knew nothing about opera. I had never shot in color. And I didn't know how to light a portrait." Rick arrived to Caldwell's dimly lit home in Boston in the pouring rain. Unable to shoot in natural light and unaware how to properly use his flash, Rick scrambled to remove all the lampshades off of her lights, but with only 15-watt lightbulbs in the lamps, the situation didn't improve. "She was getting more and more irritated with me, and I just realized

my career as a photographer was basically over. Instead of being upbeat and vivacious and trying to get her to smile, I was sinking into this horrible depression."

And then there was a knock on the door.

A CBS film crew arrived at Caldwell's door to shoot a story for *60 Minutes*. The crew proceeded to light the entire house and enabled Rick to get his shots. Saved by the intrusion (and the light), Rick shot his photographs of Caldwell over the shoulders of the video crew during breaks between their filming. "When they left, I remember she looked over at me in the corner and asked, 'Have you ever shot a cover story before?'"

Admitting that he hadn't, Rick quickly rallied to recover what he believed could have been the end of his career as a photojournalist. Recalling a heated phone conversation he had overheard Caldwell having with a car service about a driver cancellation, Rick proposed that he become her chauffeur for the next week and offered to drive her to New Hampshire in his rental car. "I said, 'Look, you're right, I haven't shot a cover story before. I'm a pretty good photographer, but I don't feel I've captured your personality and how incredible you are at what you do.' (I knew nothing about what she did.) And I said, 'I'd love to just be a fly on the wall. I could be your driver, and I would carry your bags. I would do whatever you want, and I would be quiet, and I'd stay out of your way.' I could tell the idea of having a personal driver amused her."

So Rick drove Sarah Caldwell to New Hampshire and spent a week documenting her at as she worked. At the end of the week, she invited Rick to join her on a trip to Mexico where she was developing a new opera. "I called and told *Time* that I was going to Mexico with Sarah, and I remember the woman on the phone just being completely stunned because they had expected me to be eaten alive by Sarah and instead I had been adopted." On his tenth day in Mexico (it was his birthday), Rick rushed out that morning to the newsstand to find his portrait of Sarah on the cover of *Time* magazine.

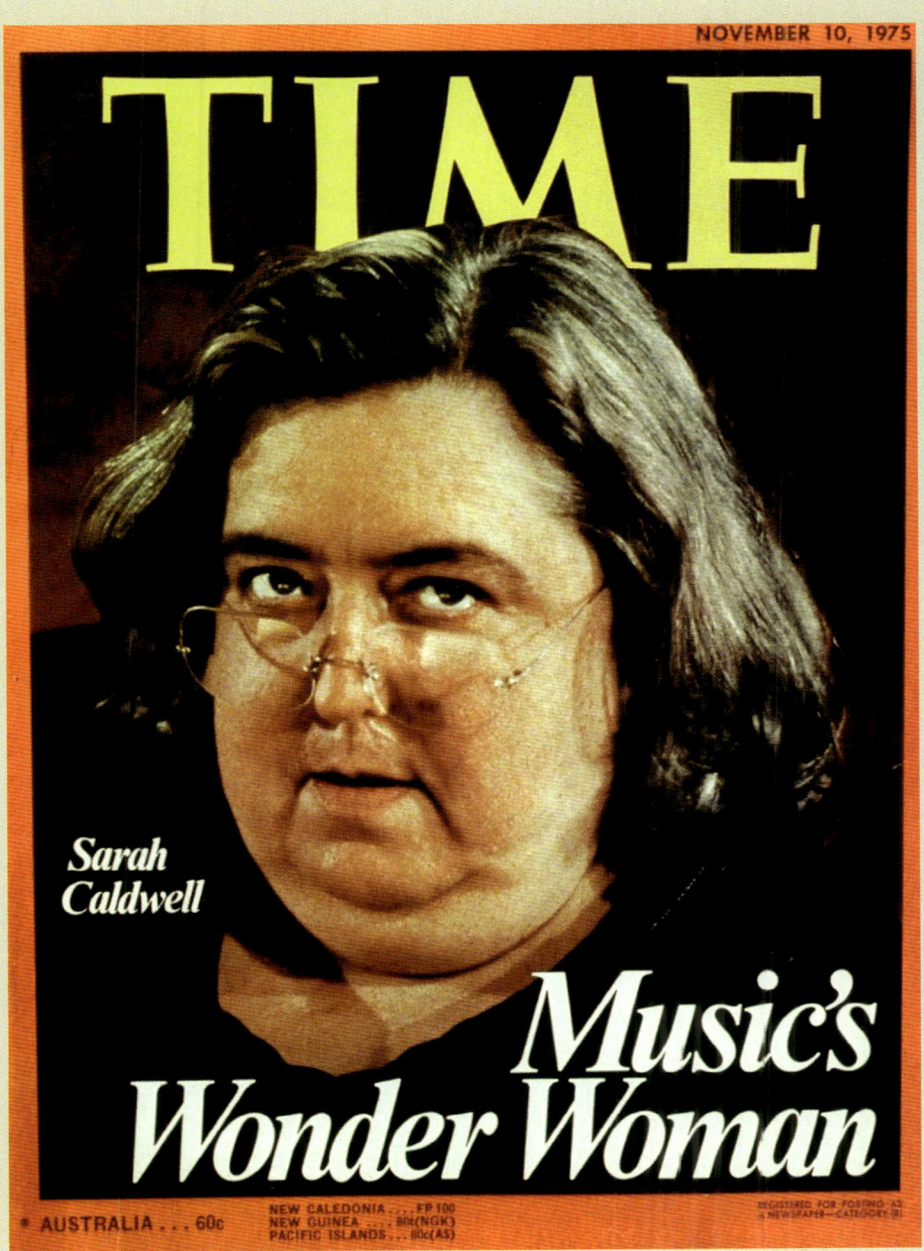

NOVEMBER 10, 1975

TIME

Sarah
Caldwell

Music's
Wonder Woman

● AUSTRALIA . . . 60c

NEW CALEDONIA . . . FP 100
NEW GUINEA . . . 80t(NGK)
PACIFIC ISLANDS . . . 80c(AS)

LEFT: *Time* cover featuring Rick Smolan's photograph of Sarah Caldwell.

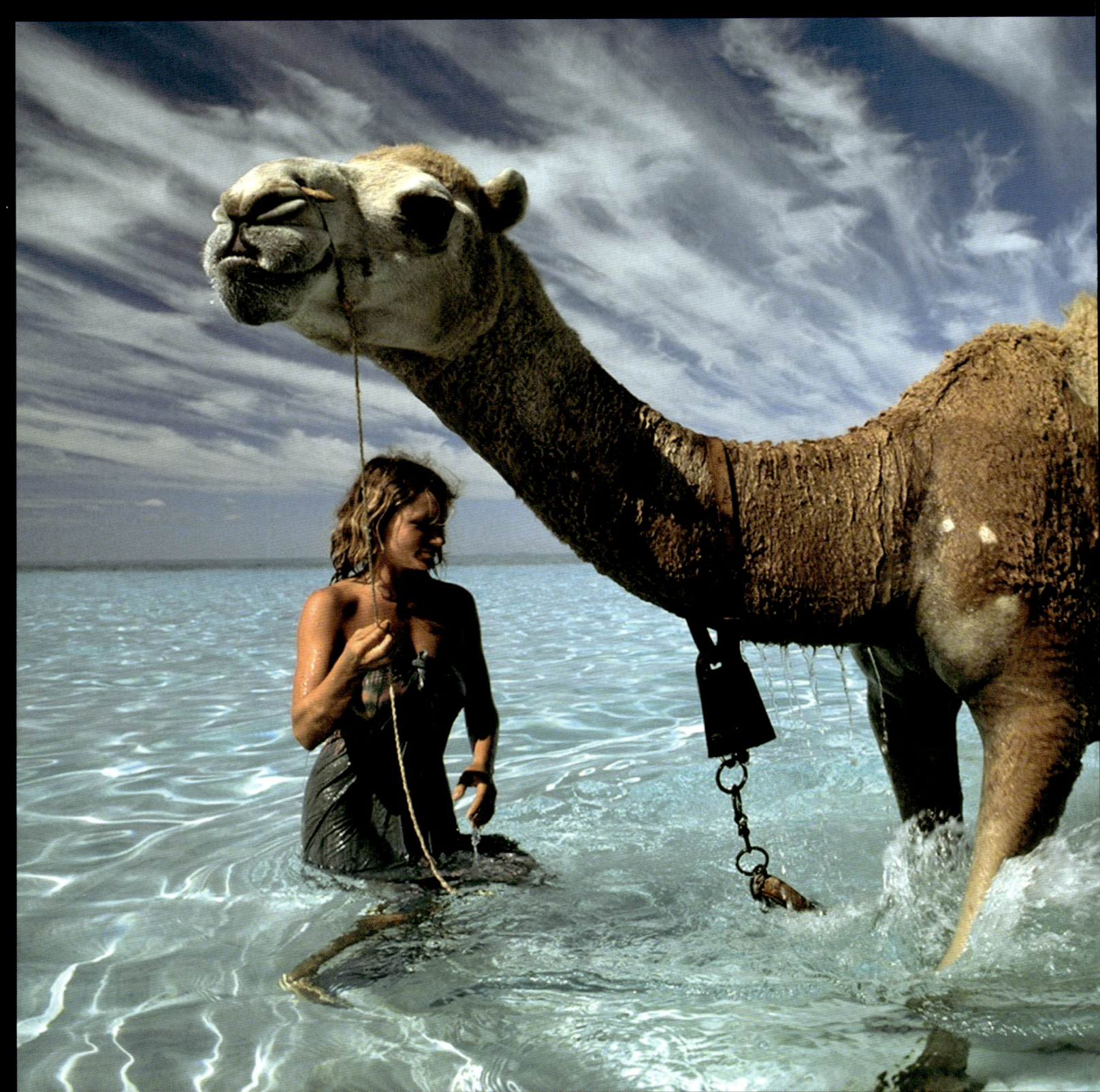

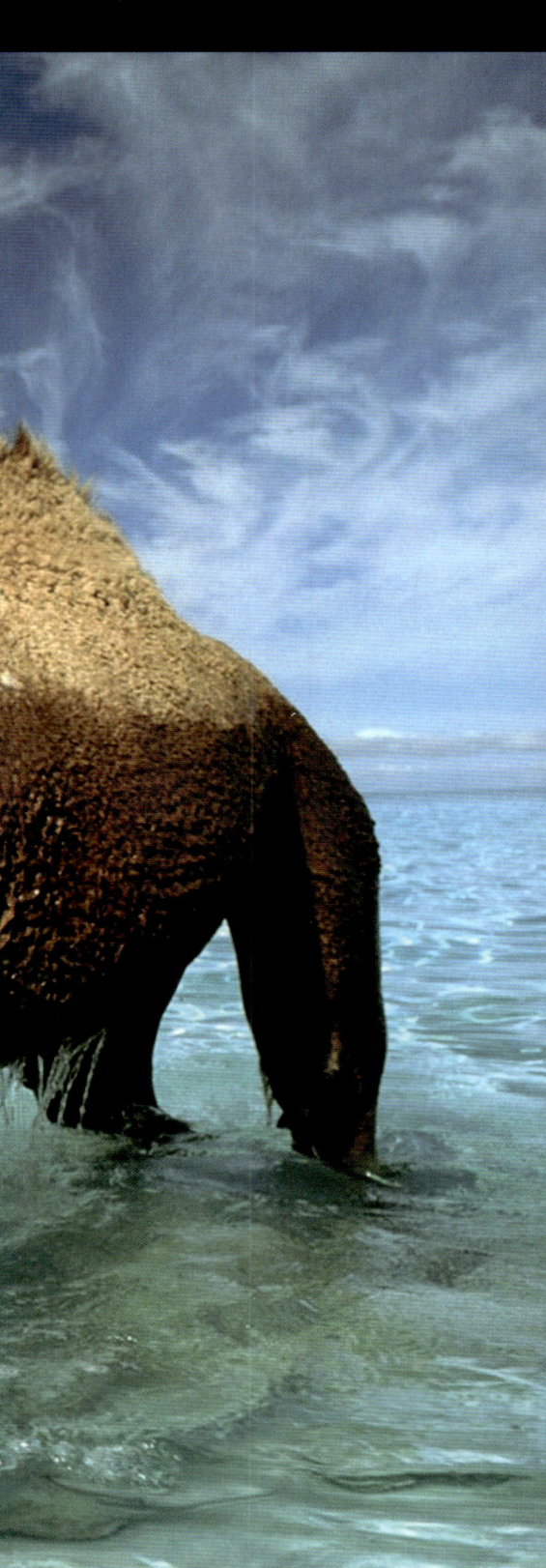

INSPIRATION

After shooting assignments around the world for publications including *Time* and *National Geographic*, Rick experienced a personal challenge, which unexpectedly led to a pivotal disappointment. The result for Rick was a shift away from shooting professional assignments and an embracing of the idea of collaborative photography-based storytelling experiences.

After Rick documented Robyn Davidson's journey across Australia in 1977, she posed a challenge to him. "She said something like, 'All of you photographers are just basically prostitutes. Someone calls you up and pays you to care about something for a week, so you care 'deeply' about it for a week, and then go on to the next thing. I think my trip is the first time you've actually ever cared about anything and stuck with it and let it became a part of you. Now you have to make a choice. Are you going to go back and just be a hired gun again or are you going to go use your skills to actually affect things instead of just documenting them?'"

Thinking past the "adrenaline rush" of each assignment, Rick did begin to feel a sense of frustration with the heavy-handed editorial control of his mainstream publishers. Yes, he was a storyteller, but someone else was using his photographs to tell their story. He felt that many stories featuring his photos often missed critical elements of the truth, and very often the most telling photographs were omitted from the story because they were deemed too political or divisive. "You started to feel after a while that the editorial was just filler or entertainment to sell the ads. I think part of me just wanted to go off and try it to see if I could actually move the needle—to see if I could actually change something, help the people in my photos, or right an injustice."

BEHIND THE IMAGE

Rick was verbally accosted by writer and camel trainer Robyn Davidson for taking an impromptu picture of her washing the windows of his hotel in Alice Springs, Australia. Rick later learned about her plan to travel across the Australian outback alone, by camel—a 1700-mile journey. Interested in her story and confident in her strong will to make it happen, Rick persuaded the National Geographic Society to fund her trip. Hesitant to publicize her personal journey, Robyn reluctantly agreed to let Rick photograph her journey from Alice Springs to the Indian Ocean. Rick made this image of Robyn and Bub toward the end of the journey using a 15mm fisheye lens. "Bub was the camel who seemed to be the most delighted by water even though he couldn't drink it. He [was] splashing around like a toddler."

LEFT: Robyn Davidson and her camel Bub reach the Indian Ocean.

RIGHT: *National Geographic* cover featuring Rick Smolan's photograph of Robyn Davidson.

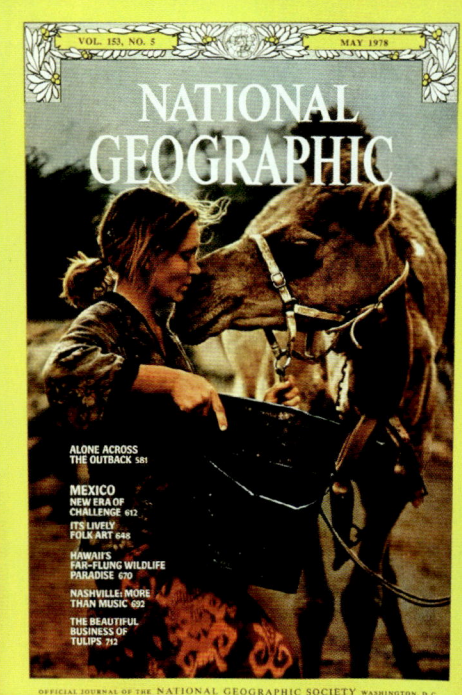

INSPIRATION

In 1978 *Time* magazine assigned Rick a three-day project to shoot a story about Amerasian children—children who had been fathered and abandoned by U.S. military men in Southeast Asia. "It was unbelievably upsetting. There were 40,000 children, many of whom looked very Western. The more Western you looked, the more abused you were. Children were beaten up, ridiculed, and ostracized." Rick instantly related to the children's social struggle and felt that exposing the story would be a way to increase awareness for their plight. Unhappy with the publisher's soft version of the troubling story Rick attempted to reveal within the confines of the assignment, he decided to continue the documentary on his own for six months—to "invest in doing a story I could hopefully affect [the outcome of]."

As Rick expanded the story, what he discovered was a complex situation. He followed and documented U.S. military men frequenting bars in search of prostitutes, despite the fact that the military denied it was happening. He discovered that young Asian women deliberately went bars to seek out the military men in hopes of getting pregnant—seeing it as a way to escape their current situation and begin a new life in America.

"You would think this is a story about these bad GIs impregnating these poor girls. But as I spent time with them, I could see that either nobody was the bad guy, or everybody was the bad guy. Part of it was the girls seducing the guys. Part of it was the guys getting the girls pregnant."

Grounded in the complexity of the big picture, Rick then approached Pearl S. Buck International, a humanitarian non-profit organization, to connect with and share stories about the Amerasian children. For his first subject, he chose Eunsook Lee, an 11-year-old, very Western-looking girl being raised by her grandmother. Rick spent a week with the girl and her grandmother, photographing Eunsook, and was stunned that unlike any of the other Amerasian children he had spent time with, Eunsook was confident and very much a leader among her classmates. At the end of the week, when Rick sat down with his translator to thank the grandmother and make a request to return in a few months to continue shooting, "The grandmother started crying and I thought I had done something wrong." Through the translator, the grandmother shared that she was dying and wanted to know if Rick could take Eunsook to America and find a home for her.

"I was 28 at the time, not married, living in hotels . . . so I said, 'Look, as much as I adore Eunsook, I'm not really the right person to take care of her.'" Inspired to help find a home for Eunsook, Rick wrote a heartfelt letter to his best friend Gene Driskell and his wife Gayle, asking if they would be interested in adopting Eunsook. "To my astonishment, Gene wrote back immediately and said 'Okay.'"

While Eunsook's story and her eventual adoption continued to unfold, Rick pitched his extended Amerasian story to a variety of American magazines, though none of them would agree to publish it because of the sensitive subject matter. *GEO* magazine, an international publication known for publishing gutsy work, stepped up just before Rick had lost hope. Shortly before the story went to press, Rick reviewed all of the layouts and made one final call to the picture editor to check the captions for his photographs. "As I was about to hang up, I said, 'You didn't ask me about the opening spread of the GIs in the bar picking up the girls. And what about the picture of the little girl holding the photograph of her father?'"

After a long pause, the pictured editor shared that ad sales hadn't been going as well as the publishers had hoped. The reason? The magazine had become too gutsy. Rick was distraught. He had promised his subjects that he was committed to sharing the whole truth and that he would not let the story get "watered down" as it had been by his previous publisher and other photojournalists. Rick promptly requested that *GEO* release the story back to him if they chose to "take the guts out of the story." They refused. Rick demanded that they remove his name from the story. They dropped it as a cover story, and "no one paid any attention to it. That was the last assignment I ever did. That's when I thought, 'I can't do this anymore and I sank into a terrible depression. After a few months of moping around I decided to go back to stay with some photographer friends in Australia. One day a little lightbulb went off and I thought to myself, wouldn't it be interesting if we could gather all of our heroes, our peers, and some younger photographers and just do a project ourselves?'"

This seed of an idea, an act of rebellion fueled by a passion for true stories, led to Rick's first groundbreaking collaborative photography project. On March 6, 1981, Rick sent 100 diverse photojournalists ranging in age from 25 to 65, who specialized in everything from fashion photography to war photography, to document visual stories throughout Australia during the course of a single 24-hour period. The effort generated 96,000 photographs and stories that lead to the creation of *A Day in the Life of Australia*. The book defied book publishing standards because it was self-published (35 publishers had turned Rick down) and relied upon corporate sponsors (including a five-year-old company called Apple Computer, Inc.) to fund the project. This corporate-sponsor funding strategy became an overwhelmingly successful model, enabling Rick, his wife and business partner Jennifer Erwitt, and their team to create numerous award-winning media products including books, television specials, interactive CDs, websites, and traveling exhibits.

APPROACH

Rick finds that his best assignments come as a result of being open and flexible to follow a story wherever it might lead. He's often extended his time with his subjects, submerging himself within the background of an experience to document the natural evolution of a story, as he did with Robyn Davidson in Australia for the "From Alice to Ocean" project. "*National Geographic* didn't expect me to spend three months with Robyn. They thought I was going to spend a couple of days three or four times during the year. But for lots of reasons I wanted to go on that journey. It's like peeling back layers of the onion. At first, people have their photographic face on. If you're just there to take their picture, some people are very good at keeping that photographic face on. But if you're there day after day after day, people eventually revert back to who they really are."

Honoring his intuition and placing trust in the unknown path of a story unfolding in his midst, Rick instructs hundreds of his professional freelance photographers assigned to his collaborative photography projects to seek and follow stories using this same approach. "Part of the goal of these projects is the element of surprise. If we only get pictures that illustrate our preconceived ideas, we haven't done a very good job. So when we make up assignments for the photographers, we do something really unusual. We tell them 'Once you get out there, if you want to scrap the entire assignment, you need to tell the people who are expecting you that you have changed your plans, but you are free to improvise.'"

BELOW: Eunsook and her grandmother, Pajoo, South Korea, 1978.

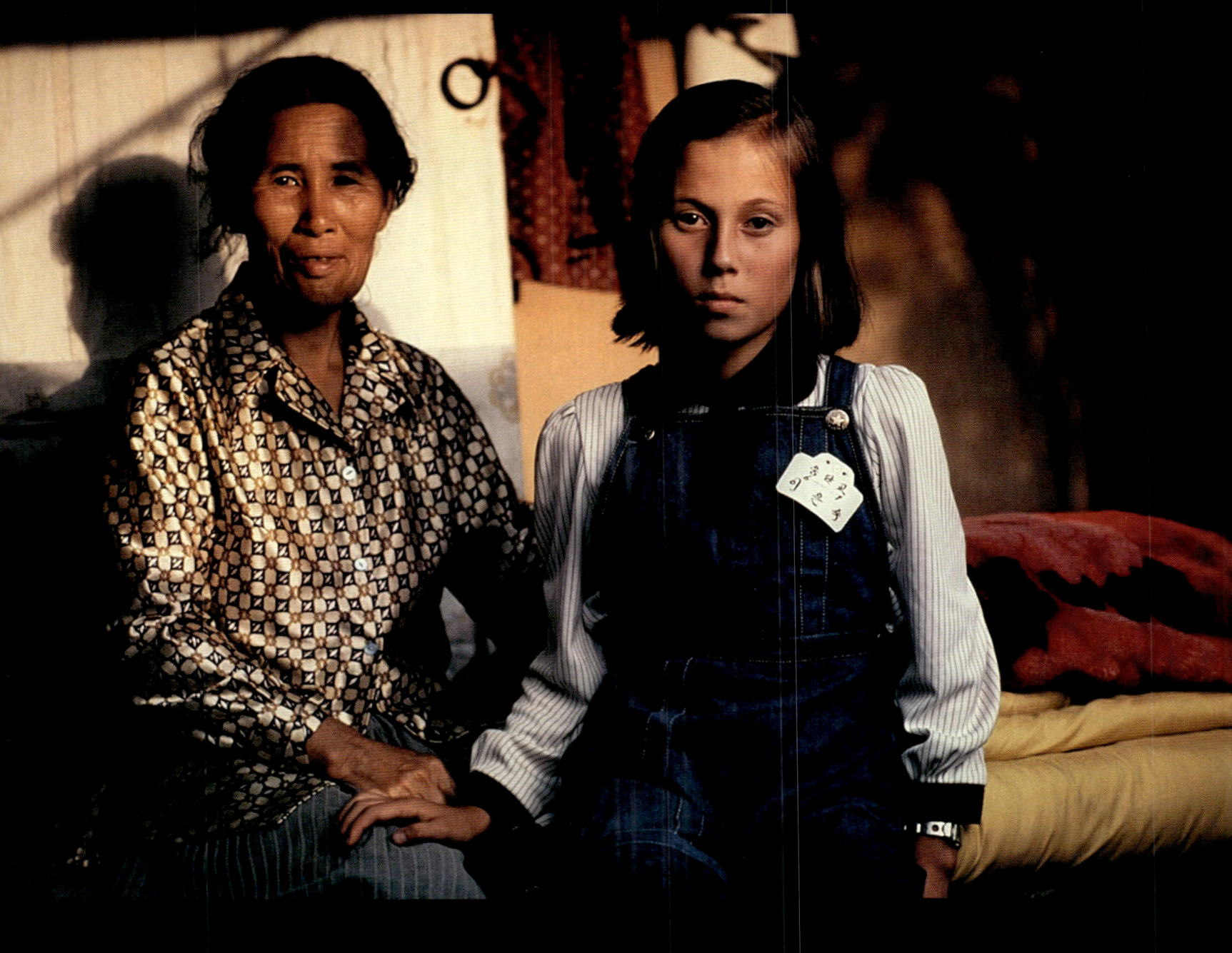

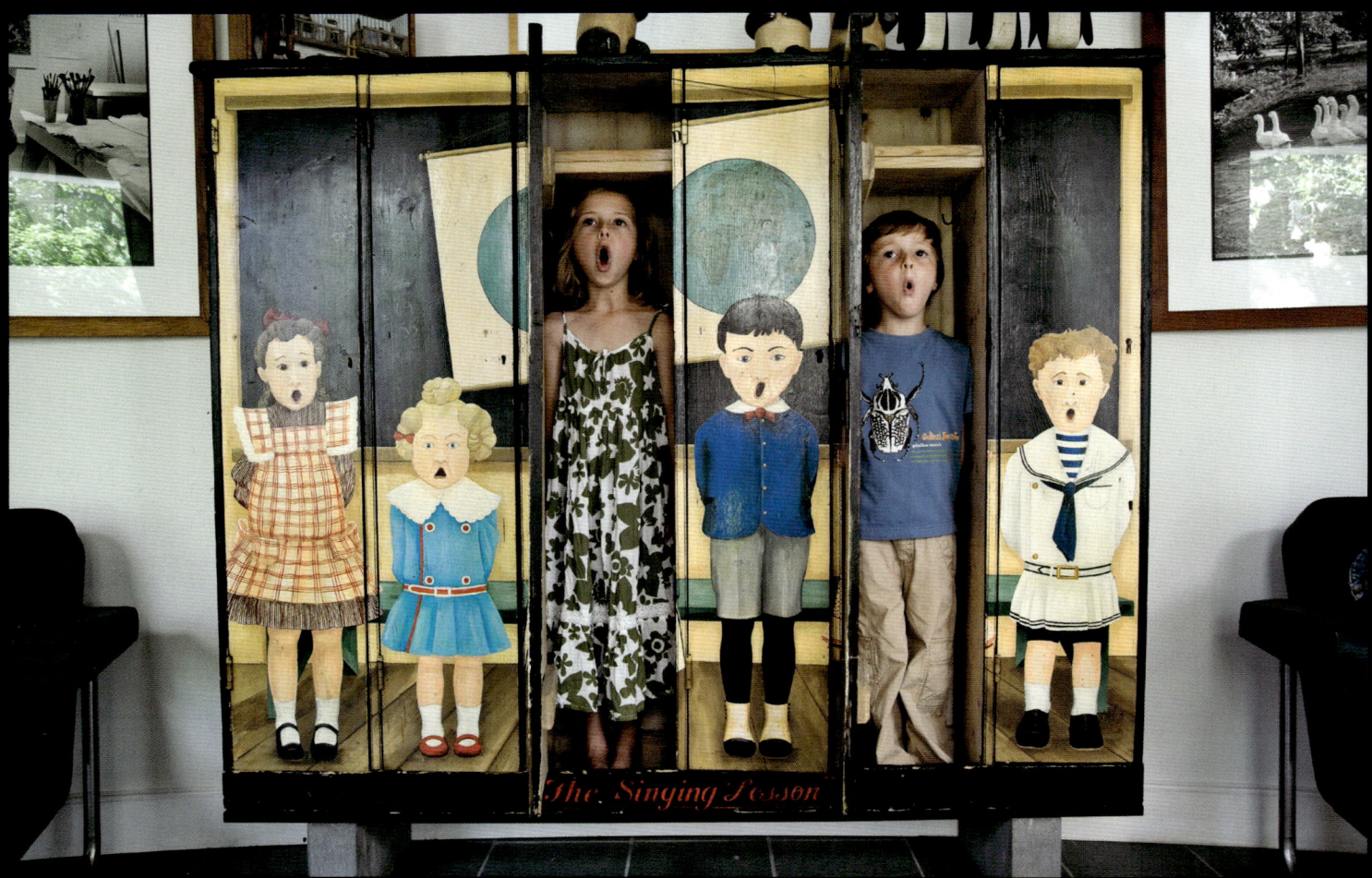

ABOVE: Phoebe and Jesse visiting at grandfather Elliott Erwitt's home.

VISION

Today, Rick makes photographs almost exclusively for himself, his family, and his friends. Focusing his camera primarily toward the documentation of day-to-day moments of his children, some might call his images "sentimental," but he doesn't mind. Occasionally, you might find one of his personal photographs featured in one of his books, but Rick most often expresses his vision and passion for story through the eyes of an expansive, interdisciplinary team of creative specialists he brings together for his collaborative projects. Like a relay race with 200 runners, Rick engages a team of people with diverse skills who each do their part and pass their results on to the next team. Rick thinks of himself less as a lone photographer, and more as a "photographic

orchestra conductor"—inspiring photographers, writers, designers, project managers, volunteers, and corporate sponsors to document our world in unexpected and emotionally engaging ways.

EQUIPMENT

Rick primarily shoots documentary images of his family and friends with a Nikon D700 and a 24–70mm or 70–200mm lens, and most often in natural light. He avoids using a flash because he feels that artificial light has a tendency to "blow out the mood. I'd rather have it slightly unsharp and moody than sharp with no mood." Rick organizes and processes select photographs in iPhoto on a big-screen iMac in his home office—a modest beige room jam-packed with colorful books, magazines, artifacts, and stacks of paper overlooking New York's Central Park.

BEHIND THE IMAGE

Ever since Rick's children were toddlers, for many years, the first thing that Phoebe and Jesse did when they arrived at their grandfather Elliott Erwitt's East Hampton house on Long Island was to climb into his painted school lockers to see how much they'd grown since their last visit.

Rick readily experiments with new digital cameras and enjoys the feel of shooting with a rangefinder camera. For quick captures, he also shoots and processes images with a variety of photography apps on his iPhone.

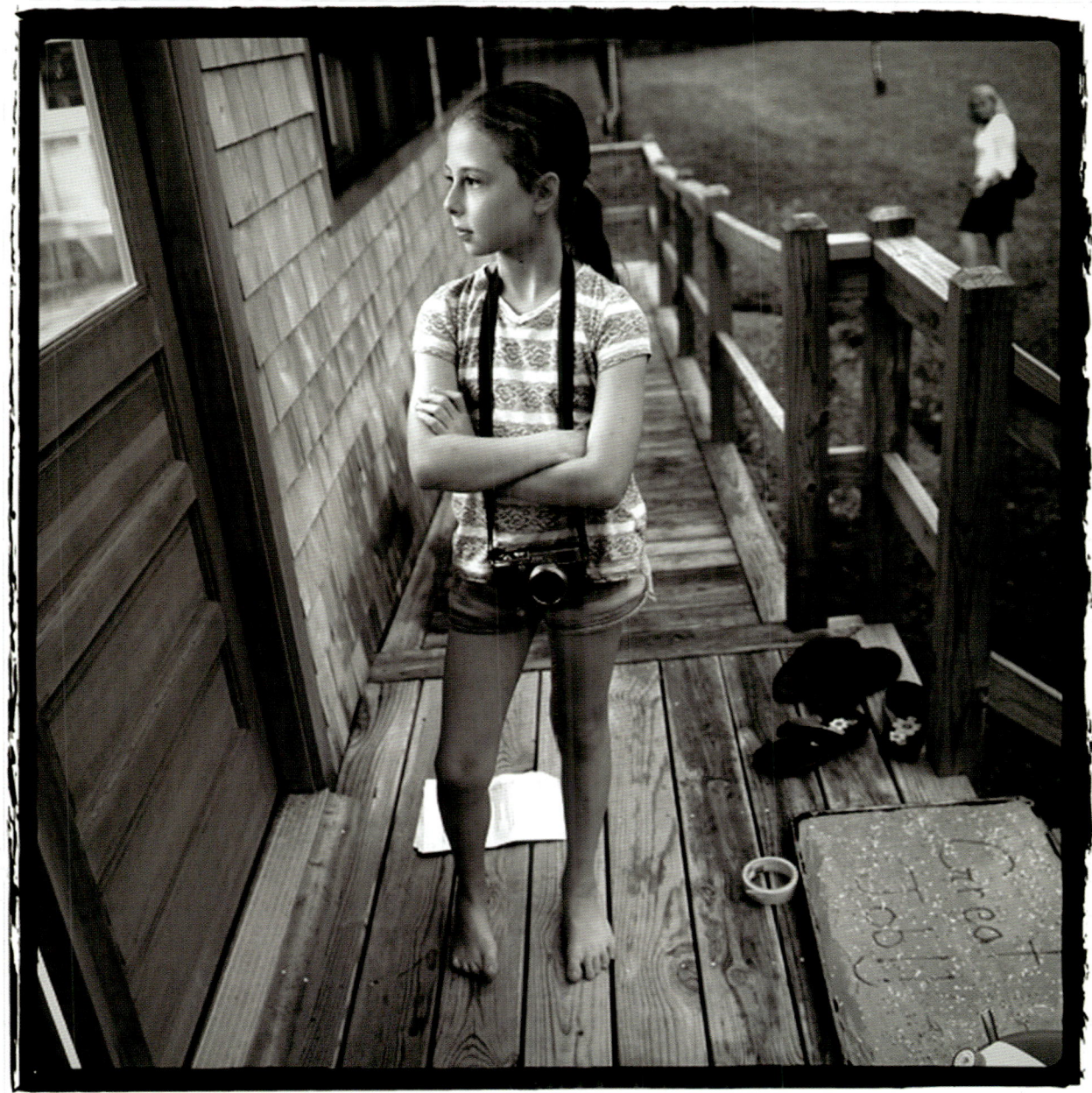

ABOVE: Phoebe with her dad's digital rangefinder.

BEHIND THE IMAGE

Rick enjoys documenting his children and watching them express themselves creatively. He's impressed by his 11-year-old daughter Phoebe's confidence and photographic ability. "I'm not shooting every second anymore. A lot of times I'm just hanging out with the kids. As opposed to my old method of being invisible in the background, with them I'm present as their dad. But once I see them doing something intently, I back up and start documenting what they're doing." Rick shot this image with his iPhone.

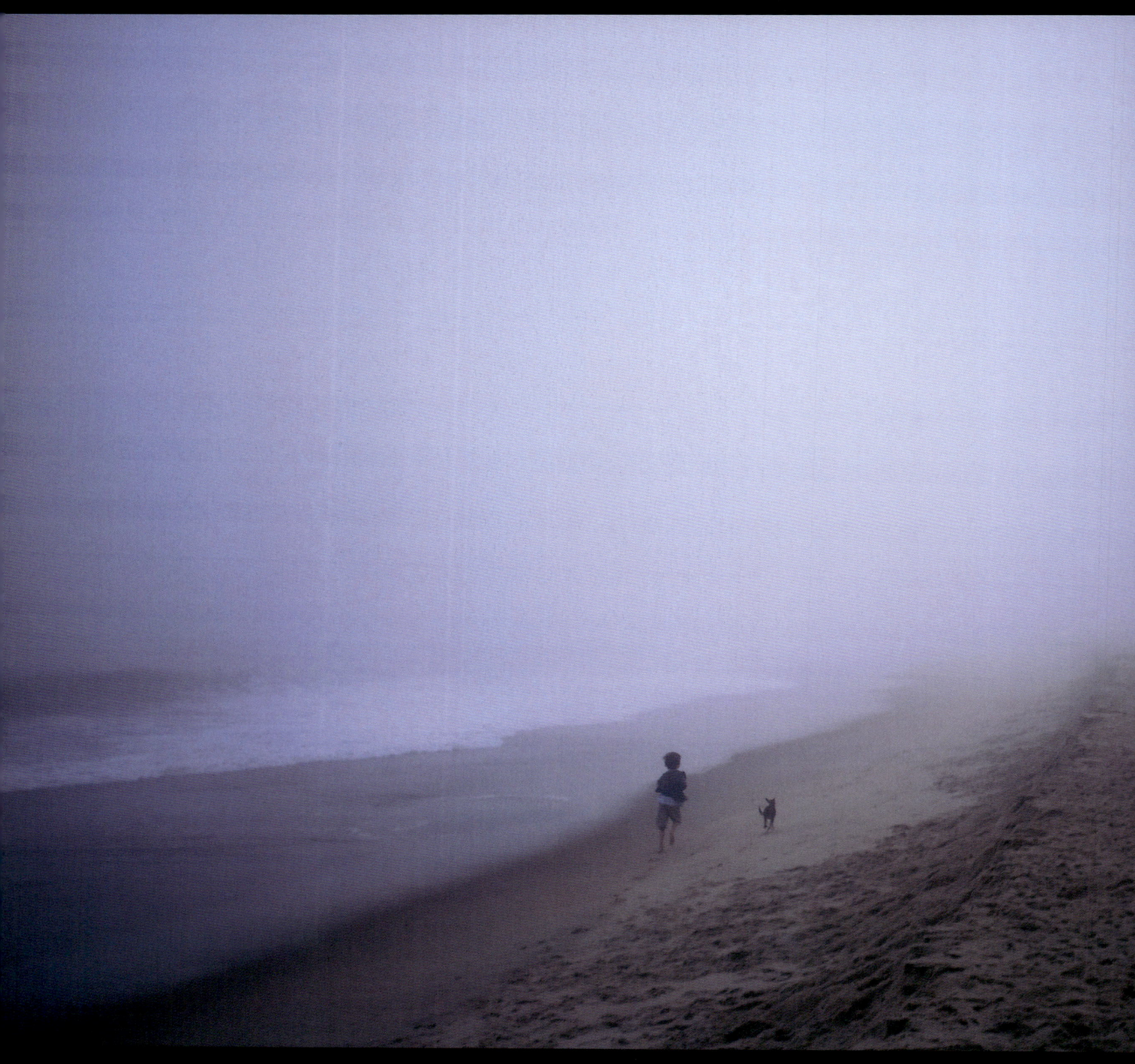

BEHIND THE IMAGE

🔴 "This image, shot [in the] summer [of 2011], is one of my favorite pictures ever. We were spending a month at [my father-in-law] Elliott Erwitt's Long Island summer house in East Hampton, New York. Sometimes in the late afternoon, this deep fog rolls in along the beach. You feel like you're in a dream. It's quite magical. My son Jesse took off running down the beach with Bella, our rescue dog. I just love the mood of it. I was testing out the new Fuji X100 digital rangefinder camera, so this was shot with a fixed 35mm lens.'

BEHIND THE IMAGE

🔴 Rick took his children to the World Maker Faire, in Queens, New York, in 2011. "As you go back and forth on this swing, it looks like you're about to hit the waterfall. Just as you get to a certain point in the middle, the sensors know you are there and the waterfall turns off. When you come through, and the waterfall turns back on, so of course the kids [including my nine-year-old son, Jesse] love it because if you do it right, you can still get yourself wet."

LEFT: Jesse with his dog Bella, East Hampton, New York.

BELOW: Jesse at the World Maker Faire, Queens, New York.

A SECRET

Give yourself the freedom to differentiate your professional images from your personal images.
The style of your professional photographs and your personal photographs may or may not be markedly different from each other. If your styles do diverge, consider creating two websites, or two galleries within a single website, to differentiate, present, and share your professional work apart from your personal work. If your professional and personal styles are more similar, give yourself the freedom and space to explore a new path in your personal work. You might be holding yourself back for fear of detouring from a signature style in your professional work. Try shooting in a way that differs greatly from your current work, and see how you feel about it.

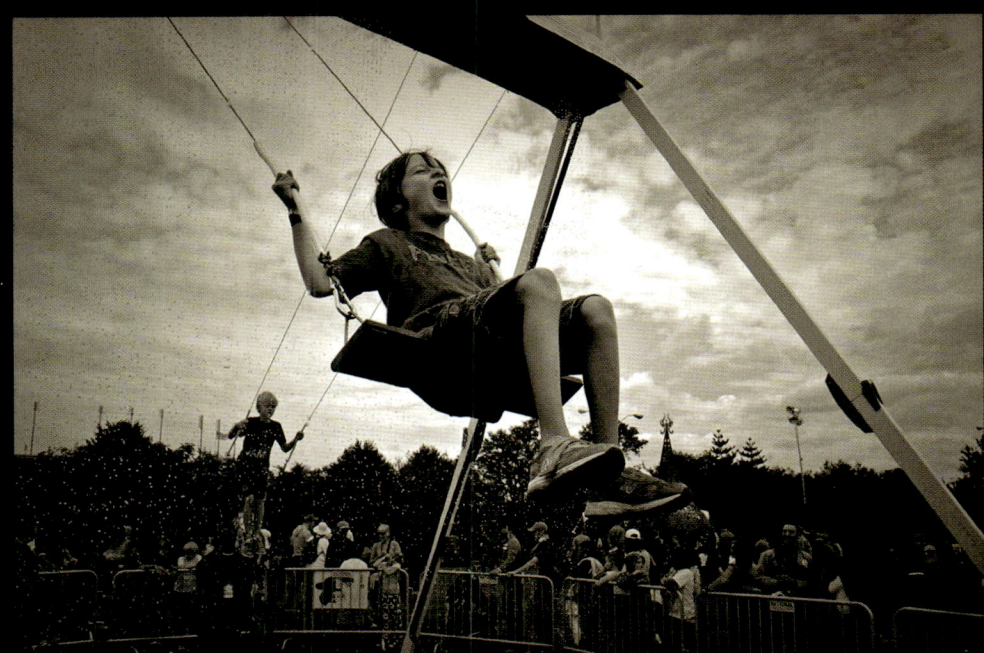

Elliott Erwitt

www.elliotterwitt.com

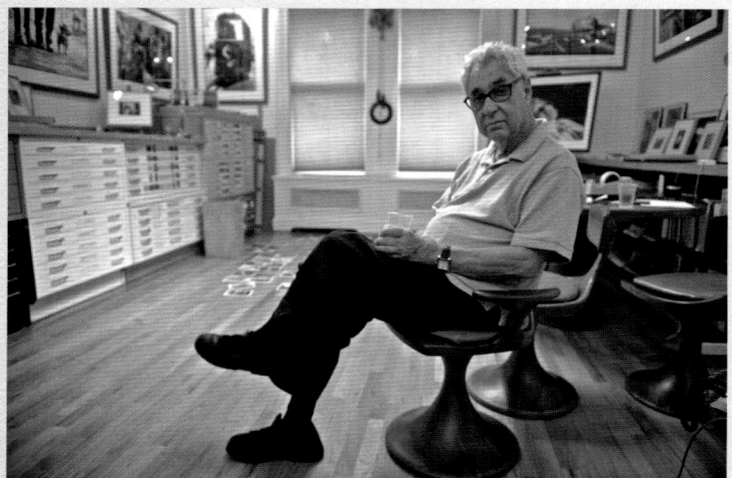

Portrait of Elliott Erwitt by Stephanie Calabrese Roberts

"People describe things to me, and I can't make a judgment about my own humor or lack of it. I suppose I like things that are amusing rather than things that are tragic, but then who doesn't? I'm not drawn to dramatic photographs, as many of my colleagues are. But I can't make judgments about myself. I'll leave that to you."

LEFT: Elliott Erwitt seated in his studio.

PATH TO PHOTOGRAPHY

Elliott Erwitt started taking pictures in 1942, at age 14, after he bought an old glass-plate camera for five dollars in Los Angeles, California. Having spent most of his childhood in Milan, Italy, he and his Russian parents lived in France for several years before immigrating to the United States when Elliott was 11. Apart from learning two new languages and being "like most kids, nothing special" and "a bit shy by nature," Elliott recalls assimilating well in France, New York, and eventually Los Angeles, all within a three-year time period. "I can get along with most anybody, if they're not aggressive."

While attending Hollywood High School, following the split of his parents, Elliott initially turned to photography for the sole purpose of making money. "I've been on my own since I was 16. I had to figure out ways to earn my keep, and working in a [commercial] darkroom was one of them. I was processing "signed" pictures of movie stars for fan clubs. It was mass production. I was not doing anything very tricky." Though uninspired by his darkroom job, Elliott continued to make his own photographs of his neighbors' kids, his friends, and school

events including the senior prom. He went on to study photography and filmmaking at the Los Angeles City College and the New School for Social Research.

At age 22, in 1950, Elliott moved to New York City to make photographs and pursue a career as a freelance photographer. During this time, he made images with a Rolleiflex camera and connected with influential mentors and photographers, including Edward Steichen (who led the Department of Photography at New York's Museum of Modern Art) and Roy Stryker (who led the documentary photography movement of the Farm Security Administration during the Great Depression). Both gentlemen took an interest in Elliott's photography and helped him find work until he was drafted to the U.S. Army in 1951. "I don't think that I could ever hold a steady job. In fact, the only steady job that I ever held was the one in the United States Army for two years, but that was not of my own volition. But it worked out all right. I had a good time in the Army."

Elliott felt fortunate to have been stationed in Europe while in the Army (specifically France and Germany), and appreciated the fact that he

didn't have to worry about paying rent. He worked as a photographer's assistant and darkroom technician and remembers making photographs for documentary purposes of things like automobile accidents and traveling generals—"nothing very interesting. But it gave me the opportunity to take my own pictures, which was nice." Elliott had begun to define an invisible line that separated his professional photography from his personal photography.

Following his military service, Elliott moved back to New York City in 1953 to resume his burgeoning career as a freelance editorial and commercial photographer. He joined Magnum Photos, a prestigious cooperative photography agency, by way of an invitation from its founder, Robert Capa, whom he had met in New York and visited on his days off while he was stationed in France. Elliott went on to produce editorial work for a variety of well-known magazines including *Collier's* and *Life*, and commercial assignments for numerous clients, including a well-known tourism campaign for Puerto Rico orchestrated by advertising giant Ogilvy & Mather (a campaign he shot again in 2009 to commemorate its 50th anniversary).

"Photography is nothing more than noticing things and putting them in context. That's it. Pretty simple stuff."

Elliott feels fortunate to have been sent on assignments that have led him to interesting pictures. "I did a book [for Time, Inc.] on Eastern Europe [Poland, Hungary, and Czechoslovakia] during their bad times. That was interesting to do. I traveled a lot in the Soviet Union when it was difficult to work there. I've gone on state trips with presidents of countries. I was accredited to the White House during the Kennedy years. I've also taken pictures of ice cubes for Four Roses ads and architectural projects ending in books and exhibitions, including one at the Metropolitan Museum of Art. I'm a photographer, you know, I'm a taxi driver. I'll do whatever."

A father of six, Elliott has worked diligently throughout his life, relying on his photographic eye in the professional sense to earn a living to support his family, while remaining committed to his love of photography in the "amateur" sense. Not surprisingly, Elliott is best known for his "amateur" photographs—the photographs he made on the back end of his professional assignments simply because he was moved to make them. In 2011, Elliott received the Infinity Award for Lifetime Achievement from the International Center of Photography. Now in his eighties, he continues to shoot as a professional and amateur photographer, produce books of his personal photographs (45 to date), and is confident that his best pictures are still to come.

BEHIND THE IMAGE

"It's a family snapshot. It's the only frame like that on the entire film. You come upon a scene of your children that seems nice; you take a snap, and go away. [If] you see that maybe there is something that's quite good [on the contact sheet], you print it. It's that simple."

BELOW: New York City, 1953.

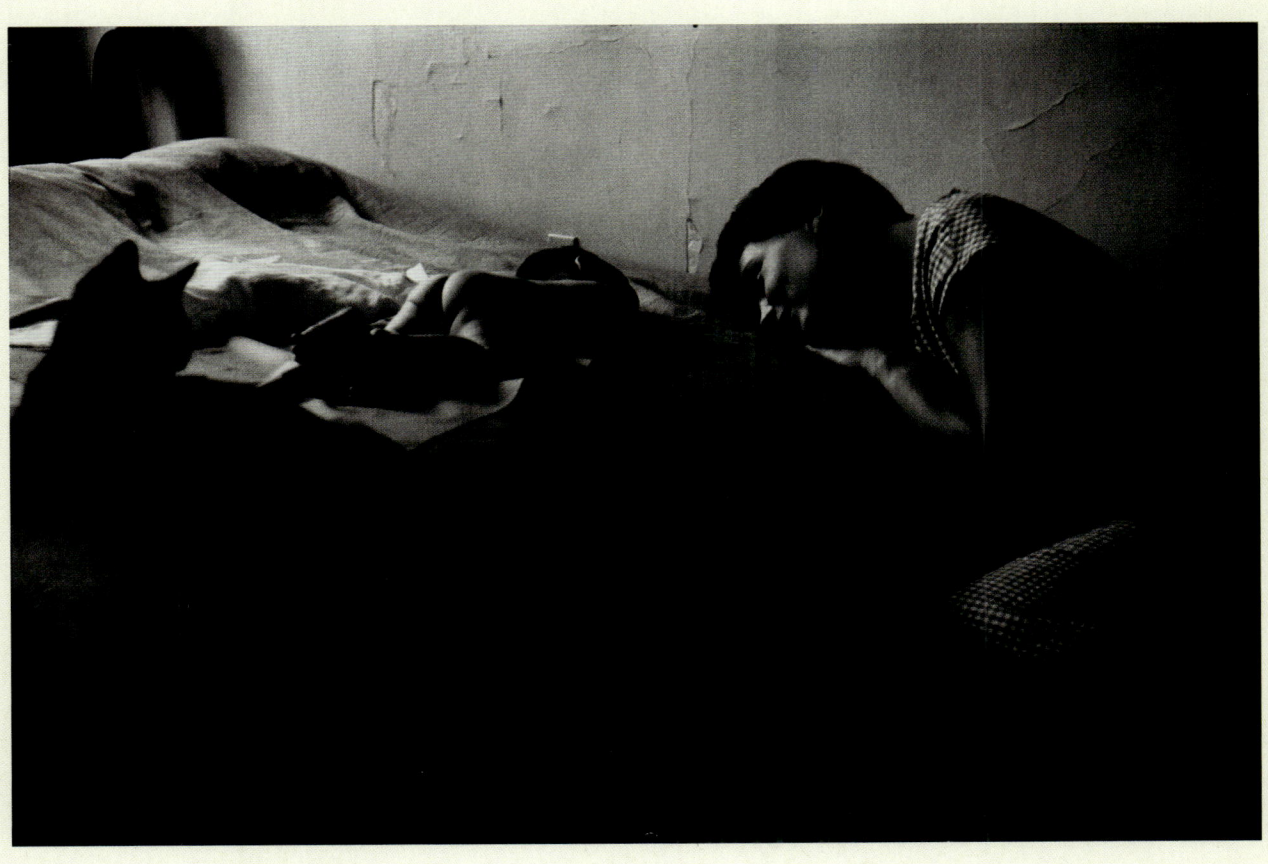

INSPIRATION

Elliott found photographic inspiration from Henri Cartier-Bresson and felt most significantly moved by an image Cartier-Bresson made in 1932 in Paris titled "The Quai St Bernard, near the Gare d'Austerlitz train station," citing its emotional and evocative appeal.

Elliott has long maintained an appreciation for fine artists and filmmakers who pushed the creative boundaries of their time, portraying familiar subjects in unfamiliar and unexpected ways as a form of personal expression. He has felt most visually influenced by neorealist films including *Umberto D of Vitorio de Sica* and *Day of Wrath of Carl Dryer*, characterized for their authenticity and documentary style of cinematography that appeared soon after World War II. Elliott has admired and been inspired by German and Italian expressionism—artists who aspired to express meaning and emotion, rather than physical reality—specifically French expressionist painter Chaïm Soutine and painter Amadeo Modigliani.

While Elliott constructs his art—his "amateur" photography—within the landscape of what's present, he does so with an acute instinct for revealing significant moments within insignificant settings. His images evoke emotion, exposing his sensitivity and compassion for the comedy and complexity of the human condition. Standing before his subjects, he makes no judgment, takes no stance, yet gently nudges us to notice curious, humorous, and ironic moments often overlooked as we hurry through life. His

BEHIND THE IMAGE

◐ "I guess you can tell that men are more interested in naked women even though they were painted by Goya more than 150 years ago." On seeing the paintings, Elliott stood back and waited until the subjects entered his frame in just the right way. "You've got to be patient. You can spot a picture sometimes that isn't quite ready, and wait around. Most of the time it doesn't work to wait around, but sometimes it does."

personal images require no captions beyond a location and date because they speak quite simply and succinctly for themselves.

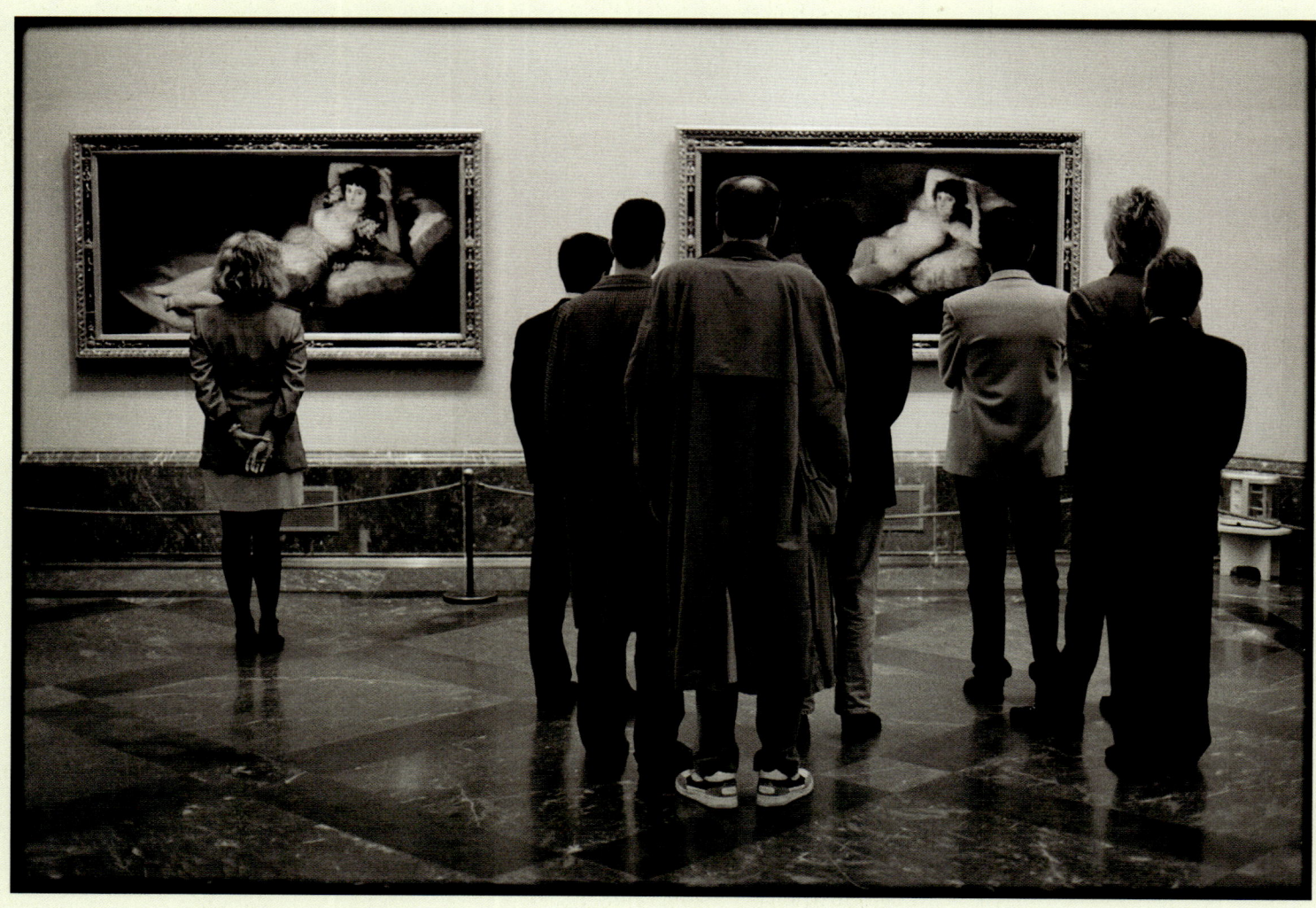

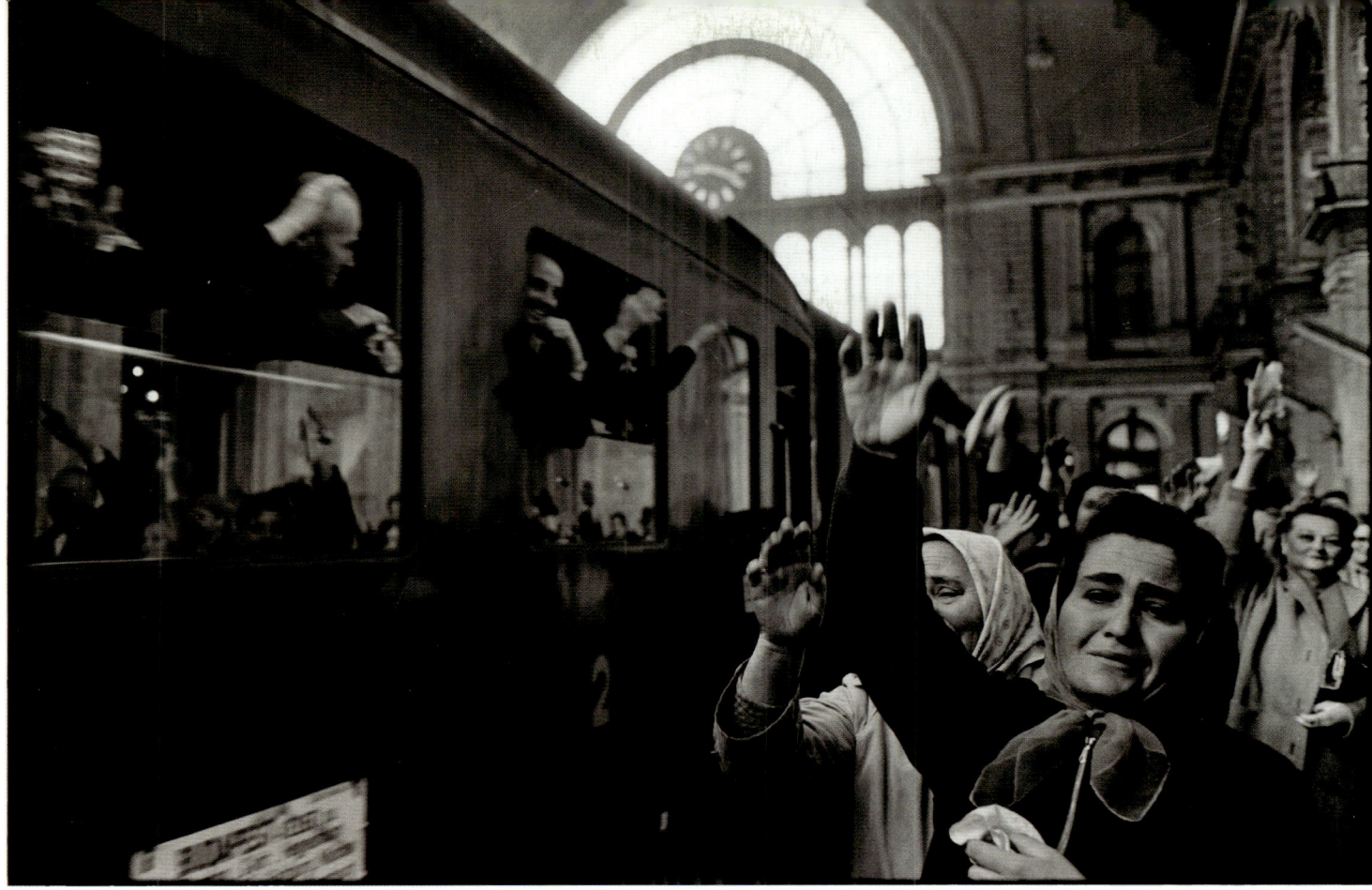

APPROACH

Elliott takes great pride in continuing to work as a commercial photographer even into his eighties, shooting assignments for a variety of clients, with subjects ranging from dog shoes to entire countries. He has reached a point in his career where his clients trust his instincts and give him (mostly) free rein to define his vision and approach to his assignment in the way he sees fit. "Let me elaborate on that. I'm not going to take pictures of my toes." The open nature, broad challenge, and brevity of the brief for an assignment has always motivated him.

"My first big campaign for Puerto Rico, my brief from David Ogilvy, was 'go and take some nice pictures.' The brief here [from my recent single malt whisky client who sent me to] Scotland was also 'go and take some nice pictures that represent Scotland and that make people think well of Scotland.'" In approaching a broad country assignment such as this, Elliott finds

LEFT: Prado Museum,
Madrid, Spain, 1995.

someone who knows the place, sits down with them and finds out what's going on and where. "The rest is just going to these places and looking." For the Scotland assignment, he visited the country twice, for three weeks each time.

Elliott never tires of noticing possible photographs, whether he has a camera in hand or not, and he feels comfortable making photographs in any setting (including nude beaches), though he avoids violence and holds back only from making images that he feels might be humiliating for his subject. "Apart from that, I think anything is fair game." He often makes new discoveries and finds inspiration in his extensive personal image archive, which spans the length of his career. In fact, the idea for his book, *Sequentially Yours* came to him after looking through stacks of his contact sheets. "There's always a before picture, [a] during picture, and [an] after picture—or there often is—and sometimes that arc is quite interesting. It seemed like a good idea, so I looked through my work and found enough material to do a rather substantial book."

ABOVE: Budapest,
Hungary, 1964.

BEHIND THE IMAGE

"[I took this picture] during the time I was working on a book in Eastern Europe for Time, Inc. I went to the train station because it's a highly charged place. People come and go, and when that happens people will get emotional. That's like shooting fish in a barrel. If you go to places like that, you're apt to get something."

"What makes photographers interesting is good pictures, which are produced if people have a visual sense and a sense of heart, you might say."

"I can tell you that nothing goes through your mind when you're taking pictures. That's an intellectual kind of exercise. If you're doing a setup [or orchestrating a specific subject in a specific setting], then of course things go through your mind. But if you're walking around looking for stuff, nothing goes through your mind. Things go through your eyes, not through your mind. Maybe when you edit, they go through your mind."

VISION

"It's easier to take pictures of dramatic events and things, of course, but you can take pictures anywhere. I wish more people did. It's more difficult now because there are fewer places for good photography to be shown, to be used, and so I think the tendency for many photographers, with the exception of my colleagues at Magnum, is to work when they're assigned and not so much on their own. That's unfortunate." While Elliott has spent his entire career earning his living from editorial and commercial photography, he's consistently expressed his vision through his personal photographs. These are the images he enjoys making most. His subject matter, settings, and situations vary greatly (though he does exhibit an affinity for children and dogs), yet the purity of his instincts for documenting intriguing, amusing, and often laugh-out-loud absurd everyday moments has remained the same.

While Elliott takes pleasure in the fact that his images amuse his viewers, he hopes that they don't "just make them laugh. I hope [they] inform people about visual information. I hope that not all my pictures are 'ha-ha' pictures.

I think there are some quite serious ones. But certainly I'm pleased that I'm being recognized these days. That's nice. It's better than the opposite."

EQUIPMENT

More often than not, and always when he travels, Elliott has a camera with him. He uses whatever camera is appropriate for the job, but for his personal images he prefers his film-based Leica rangefinder. "I will do digital with an assistant (because I don't understand those cameras) if I have to, because of an assignment. That's quite rare. I shoot almost totally on film. Everything is processed in my darkroom here in the studio, everything is printed here. I haven't entered the digital age, except for email. That's about it."

DIFFERENTIATING PROFESSIONAL AND PERSONAL IMAGES

Elliott has always carried two cameras with him on an assignment. He uses one camera for his professional images and another camera for his personal images. For the most part he can differentiate his images in this way, but

"sometimes they cross. Everything is personal, really, unless it's taking pictures of ice cubes for Four Roses Whiskey or something like that. Then it's not personal. When you're working for a client, it's not really personal because you're being paid to do something that the client will accept, so you have to put yourself in their shoes, which is perfectly fine. So in that sense, that is not personal, that is a professional assignment. When you don't have a client, that's personal. Sometimes when you have a client it could also be personal, especially when they [trust your vision]."

BEHIND THE IMAGE

"I was just walking on the street while on vacation in Kyoto. I carry my camera when I travel, so if I see something I snap it. As they say now, 'If you see something, do something.'"

RIGHT: Kyoto, Japan, 1977.

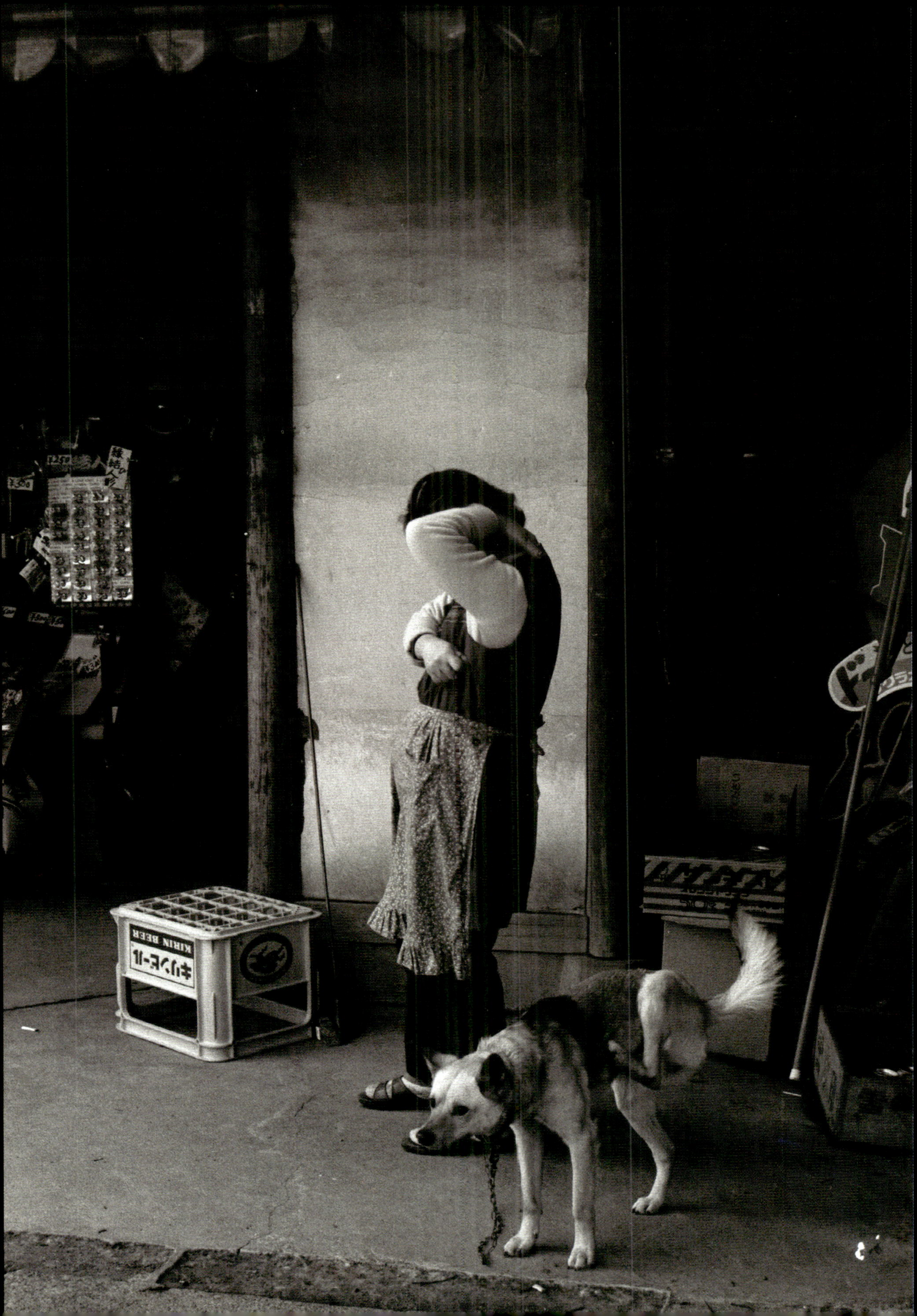
KIRIN BEER
キリンビール

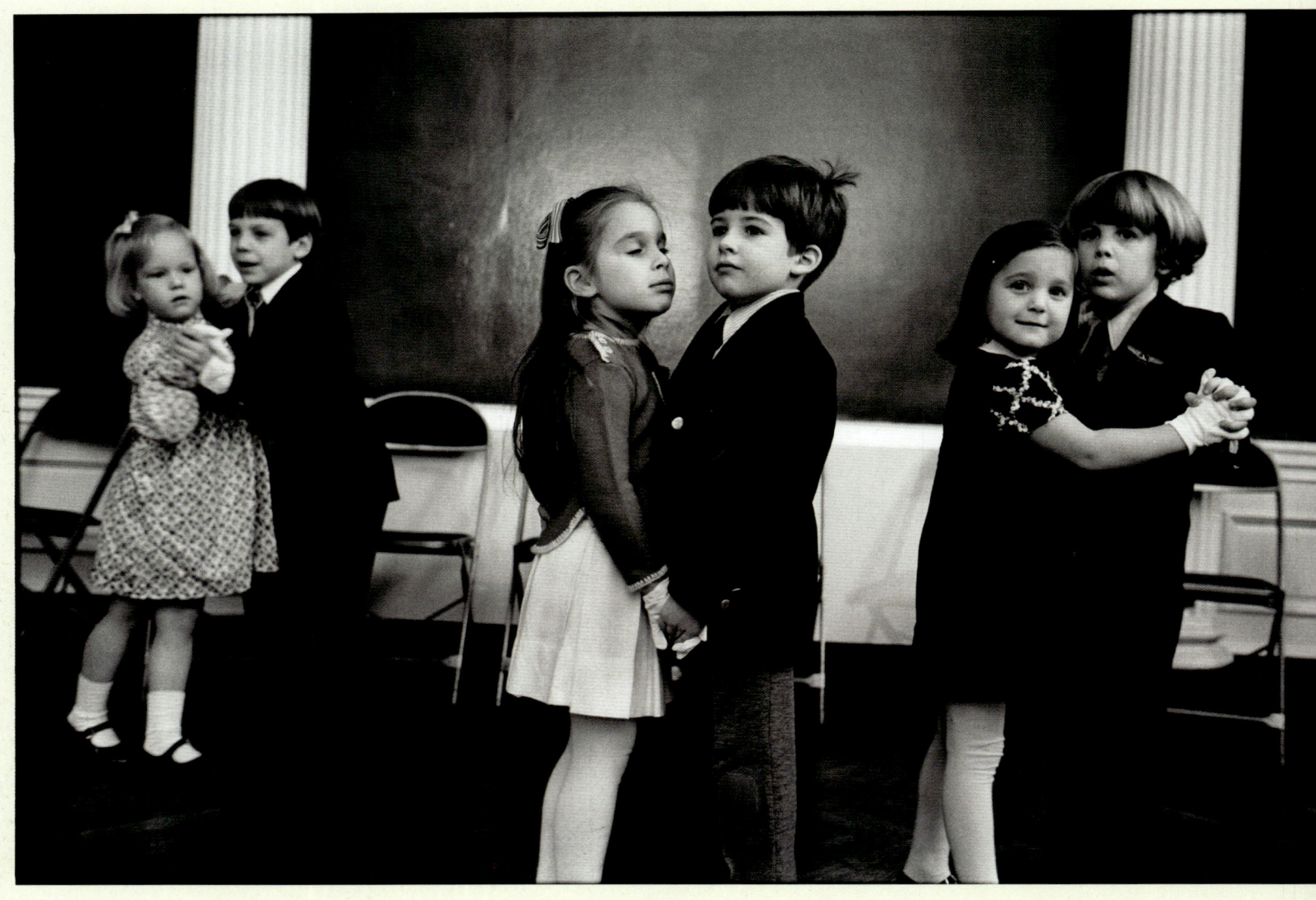

BEHIND THE IMAGE

"[I took this picture on] an assignment for some little magazine, to take pictures of Upper East Side children's dancing class. They were dancing to Lester Lanin [a musician who led ensembles that performed in the homes of wealthy socialites in Philadelphia and New York]. Future lions of industry."

"I can say that photography has given me a kind of interesting life, and I'm grateful to photography for that. I've enjoyed both aspects of my photographic life, the commercial and the private, and I'm glad that I never had to work for anybody for longer than a couple of weeks."

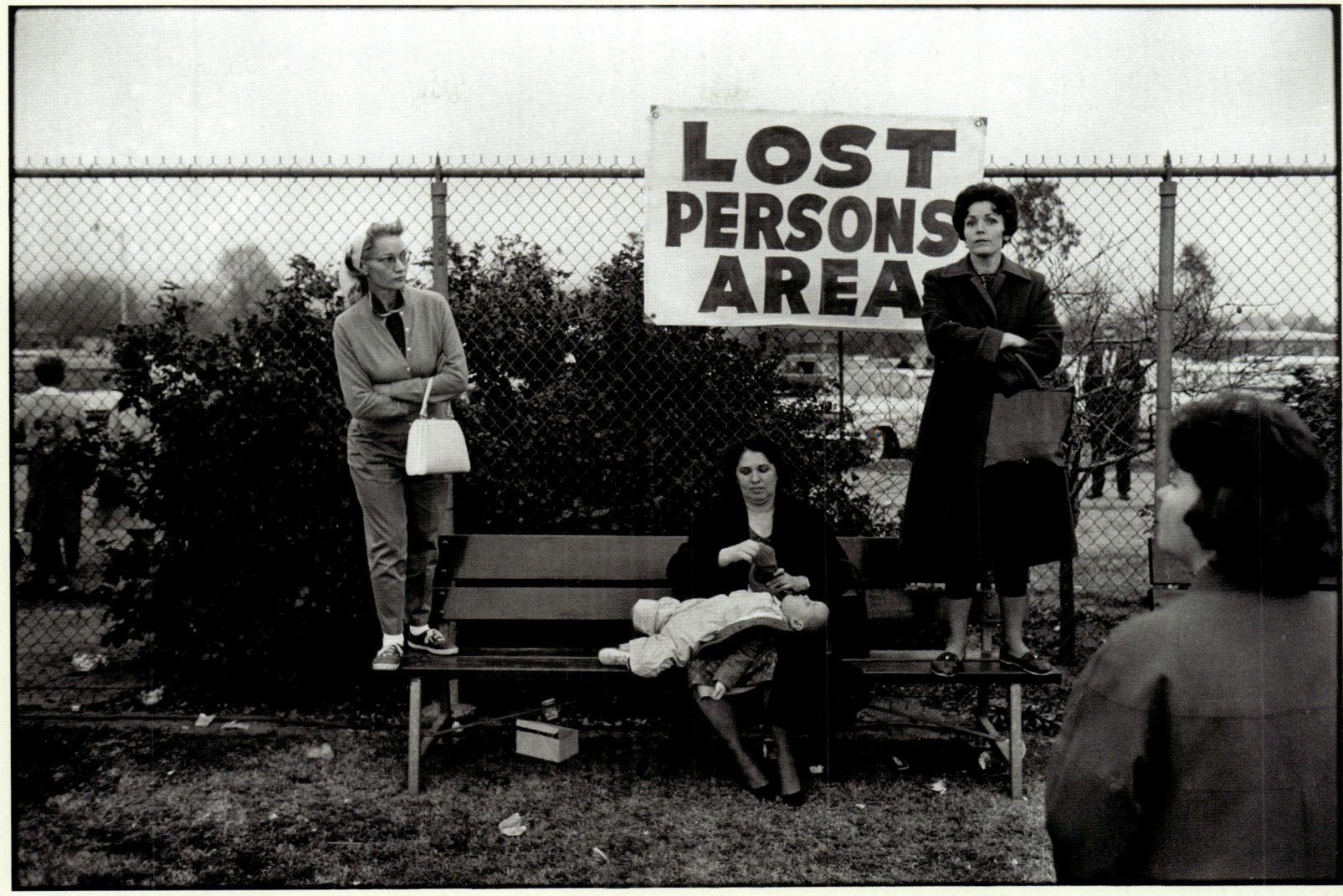

ABOVE LEFT: New York City, 1977.

ABOVE: Pasadena, California, 1963.

A SECRET
Shoot what you love and let it evolve into a project.

Put yourself in front of subjects you like as often as you can. If you like taking pictures of your children, take pictures of your children. If you like taking pictures of strangers on the street, take pictures of strangers on the street. If you're not sure what you like to shoot, take time to review your image archive and look for connections or repeating subject matter and let your project choose you.

"I found that I had a lot of pictures of dogs, because I like dogs and I take pictures of them. So I looked them over, guarded them, and thought maybe I should take some more. So far, I've done eight dog books."

BEHIND THE IMAGE
Attracted by this sign at the Rose Bowl Parade, Elliott waited for his subjects to naturally fall into place.

2

STRETCH YOUR CREATIVITY
& UNCOVER YOUR VISION

Your vision subconsciously influences what you see and what you choose to expose in your photographs, yet it might be difficult to define and articulate what makes your subject matter selections and the way in which you portray life's moments unique to you. In spite of the fact that documentary photography is focused on capturing an external view of our subjects, stories, and settings, I suggest to you that it's largely an introspective act. For me, photography is less about technology and technique and more about the magical concoction that combines the thoughts in my head with the feelings in my heart, inspiring me to focus and click.

Your vision defines your unique view of reality—your life perspective—and will be expressed subconsciously in the images you make. Whether you realize it or not, your vision has been building since you were born. It's the sum of your past experiences and what you are seeing, feeling, and thinking in the present moment. It might evolve very gradually over time, or it might shift more dramatically depending on particular life experiences. If you placed a group of photographers in the same setting and assigned them to shoot a single subject, undoubtedly the experience would yield a diverse collection of images. No two photographers see in the same way, as evidenced by the documentary photographers you read about in the previous chapter.

The process of uncovering your vision is a lot like learning to color outside the lines of a coloring book when you were a child—to put aside a set of predetermined subjects and defined boundaries, and to get comfortable drawing your own lines and shapes on a blank piece of paper. Grant yourself the freedom to stop making the photographs you think you're supposed to be making to please an audience, and begin making photographs or curating your work in a way that pleases you. The best way to uncover your vision is to follow your instincts, shoot frequently, experiment often, study your images, and look for trends. Your vision may not be apparent in the glance at a single frame, but you can uncover clues that point toward your unique vision by stretching your creativity with your photography—your subject selection, your approach, your perspective, your processing style—over an extended period of time. Experiment with the shooting and processing ideas in this chapter to stretch your creativity and help you uncover your vision.

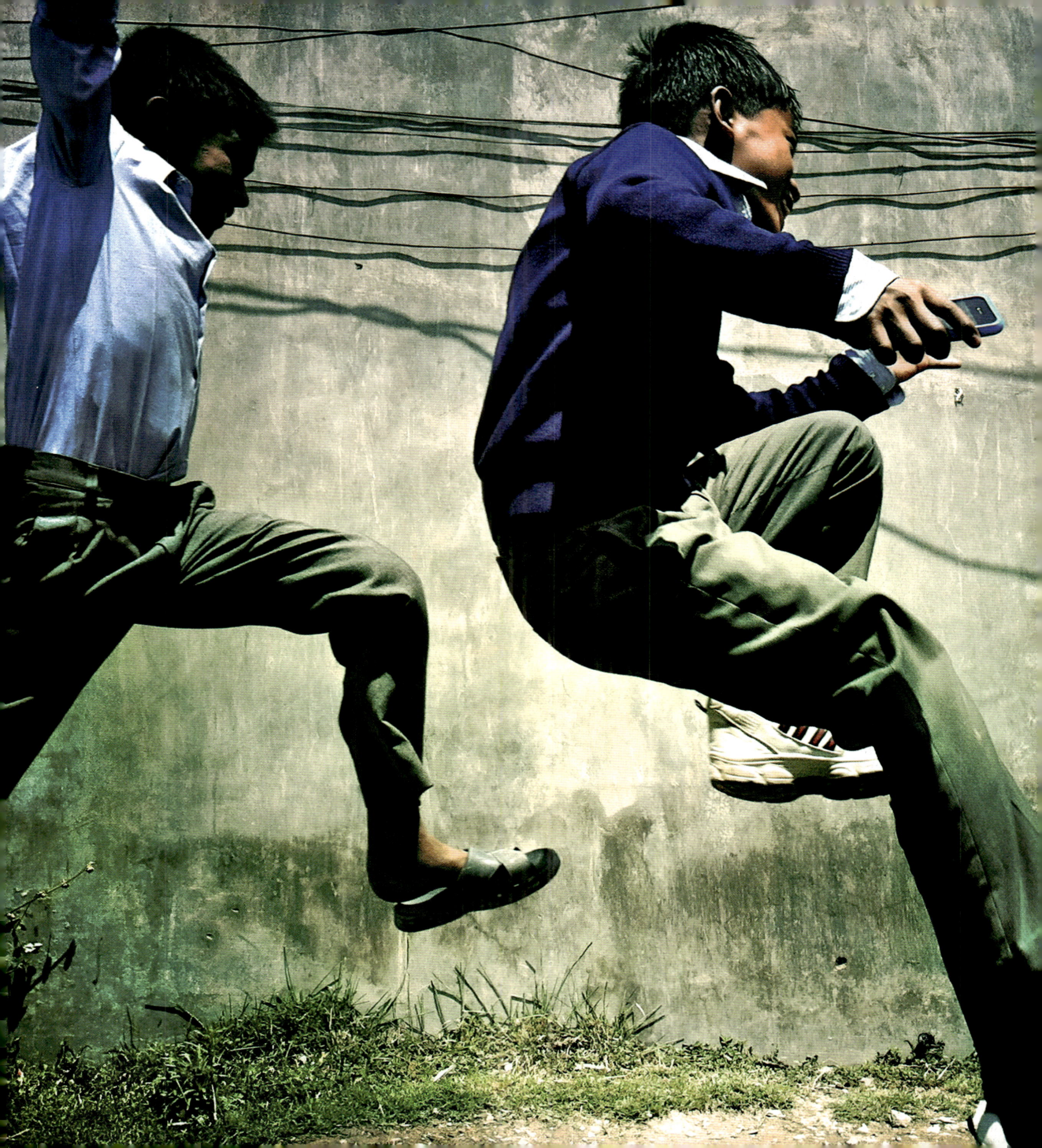

Avoid the Expected Shot

One of my favorite things to do at a significant event or setting is to turn my focus away from the predictability of the main attraction, and explore what's happening on the periphery— to seek out what's not so obvious. Magic can often be discovered in moments of distraction or behind the scenes. If you're a professional photographer working on an assignment, naturally your client will have expectations that must be met. Get the shots the client requests and expects, but then give yourself the freedom to step back and let your eyes wander. If you're shooting for yourself, think about ways to seek and capture something unexpected. For example, if you're planning to shoot your daughter's drama performance, consider that moments behind the scenes might be more humorous than what happens on the stage. If you're taking photographs of a friend's wedding day, naturally you'll photograph the obvious moments of the couple exchanging vows, sharing their first dance, and cutting the cake, but make sure you arrive early to follow the bridesmaids as they prepare for the ceremony and the bride as she steps into her gown.

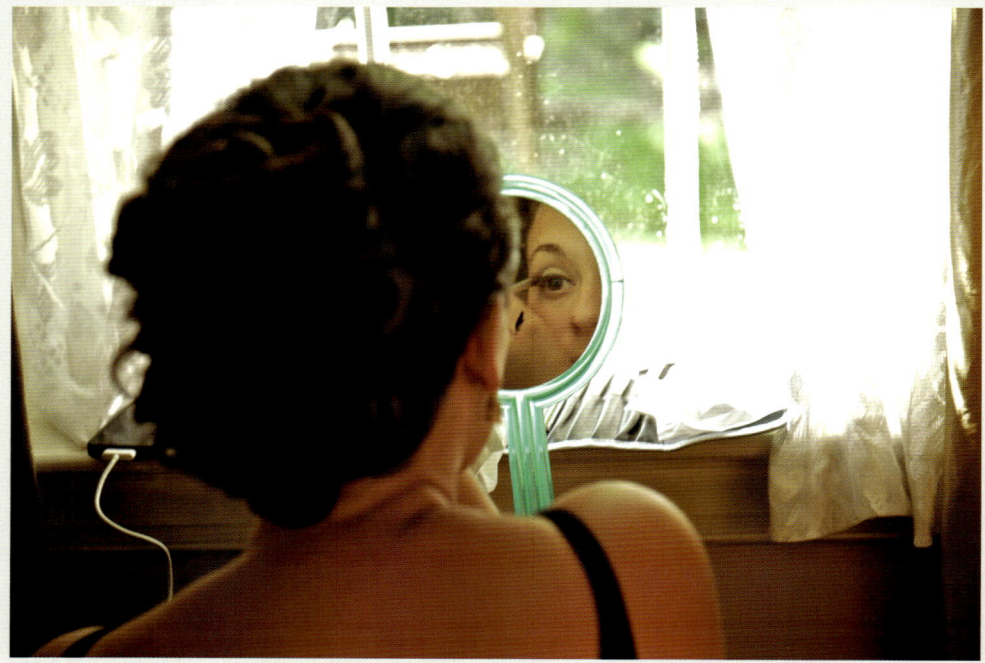

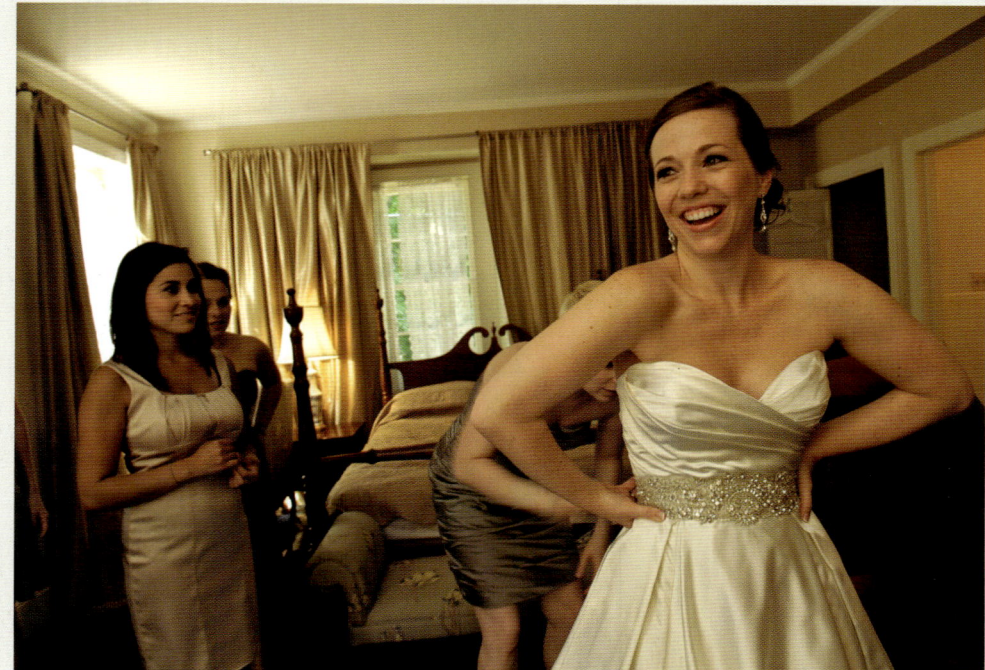

TOP RIGHT: A bridesmaid defines her eyes in natural light.

RIGHT: Bride Jessica, assisted by her bridesmaids, steps into her gown before the wedding ceremony.

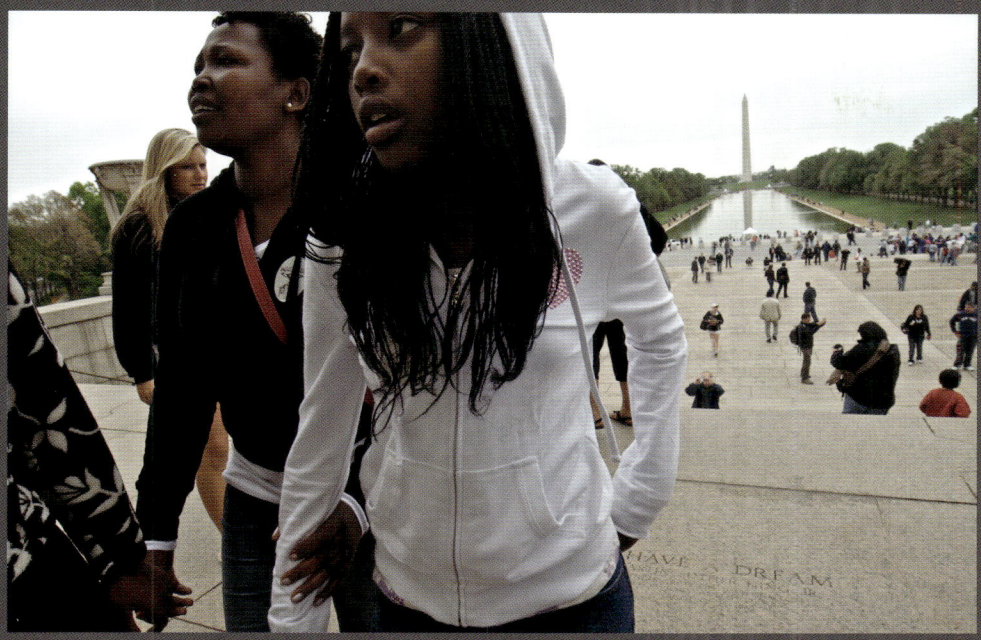

"When you see everyone shooting in the same direction, it's usually a sign that there's something to be seen somewhere else."

LEFT: Grace, Odette, and Mutoni continue to climb the steps of the Lincoln Memorial in Washington, D.C. after pausing to stand in the space where Martin Luther King Jr. gave his "I Have a Dream" speech.

BELOW, LEFT AND RIGHT: Visitors of the Lincoln Memorial in Washington, D.C. compose their images of the 19-foot tall statue of Abraham Lincoln.

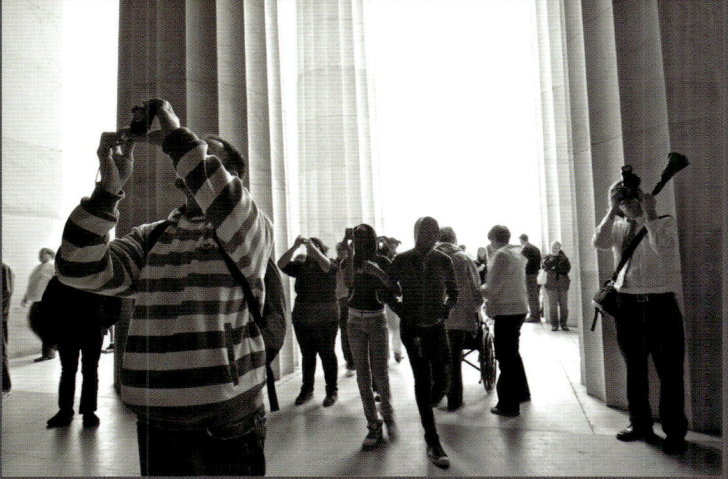

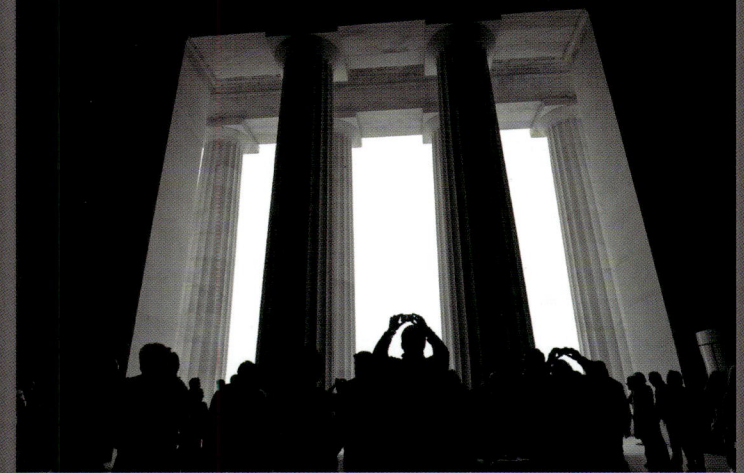

SHOOT BACKWARDS

At the time these photos were taken, I had spent nearly a week documenting the story of my Rwandan friend Odette and her reunion with her two daughters, Grace and Mutoni, after four long years of separation. Shortly after the girls arrived from Uganda to their new apartment home outside of Washington, D.C., Odette was eager to immerse them in American culture, so we wandered through a few museums, rode a carousel, and stood before a handful of our nation's most photographed monuments.

I must admit, making images of familiar landmarks and tourist attractions such as the Lincoln Memorial holds minimal interest for me, but I am attracted to people and intrigued by the ways in which they consume new experiences. The image potential of Odette and her daughters' reaction to the sight appealed to me enough to haul my SLR with a thick 14–24mm lens up the expanse of stone steps to see President Abraham Lincoln seated in contemplation on a wet day in May. Not surprisingly, I found the most interesting images when I (respectfully) turned my back on "the shot" of President Lincoln, and focused my lens on the amateur photographers in the opposite direction.

Avoid the Expected Shot

SUBDUE THE MAIN ATTRACTION

Each December, piano instructor Suzanne Polk Roberts orchestrates a holiday piano recital for her young students. Here, they perform before an audience of friends and family on the grand piano at Villa Serena in Conyers, Georgia. While the audience was fixated on the sights and sounds of the proud performers, I took a few steps back with a wide-angle lens to follow the young fans on the periphery.

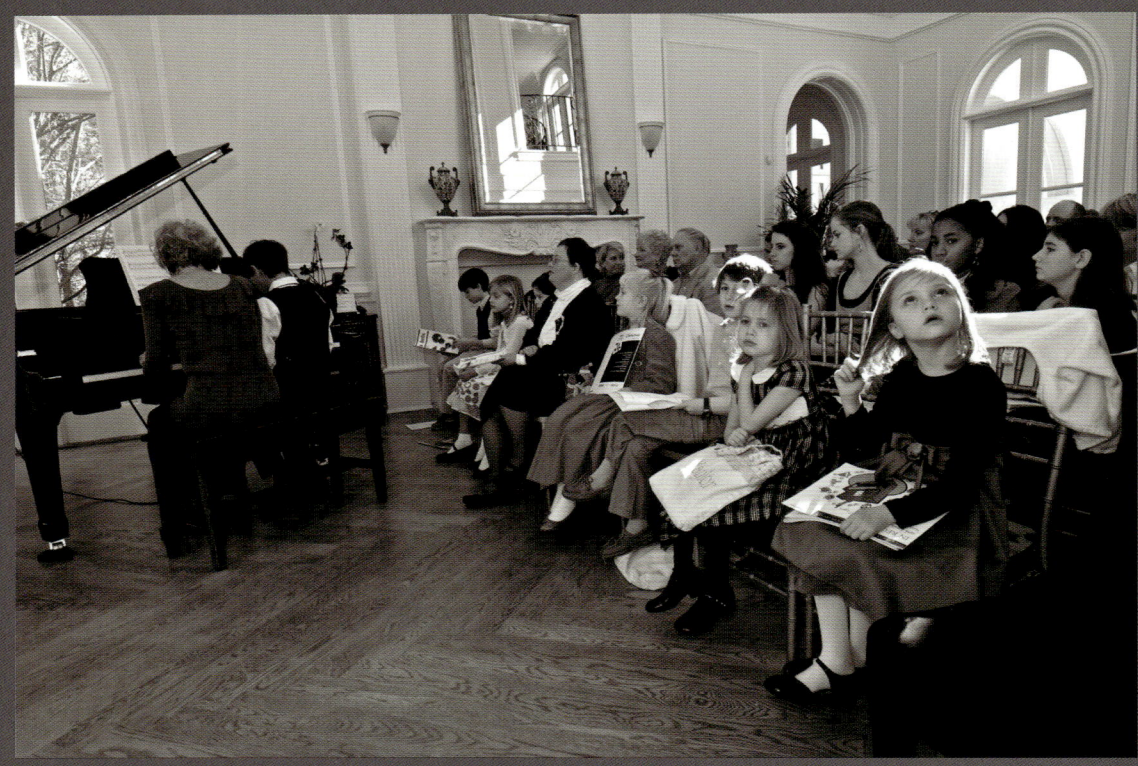

TRY THIS

To avoid the predictable shot of a landmark destination:

- Focus on an insignificant detail or a repeating shape.
- Create an abstraction out of geometric shapes, lines, fields of color, and shadows.
- Notice the placement of unexpected manmade objects or creatures.
- Follow people moving in and around the subject.
- Get down on the ground and look up or climb to a high place and look down.
- Reveal something interesting in a reflection.
- Turn around and shoot backwards.

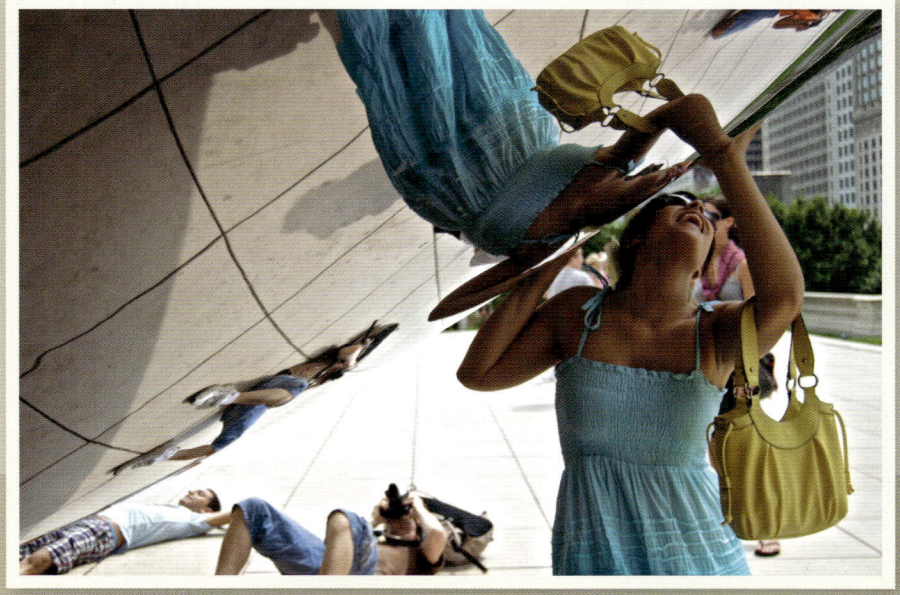

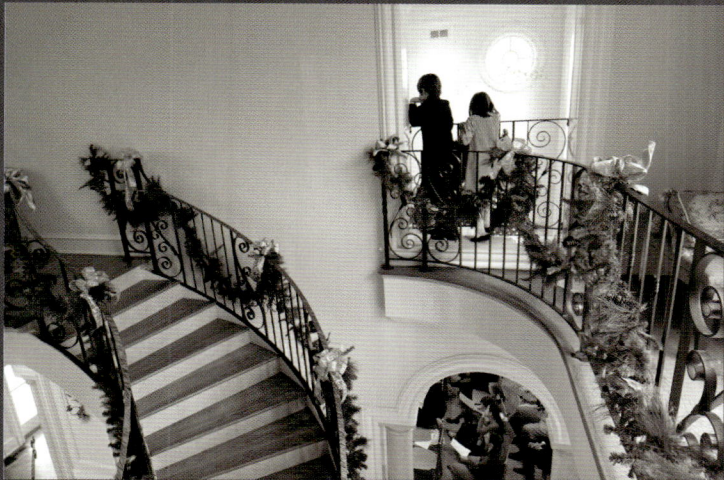

LEFT: Siblings Bo and Mary Elise quietly take in an aerial view of the audience and performers below.

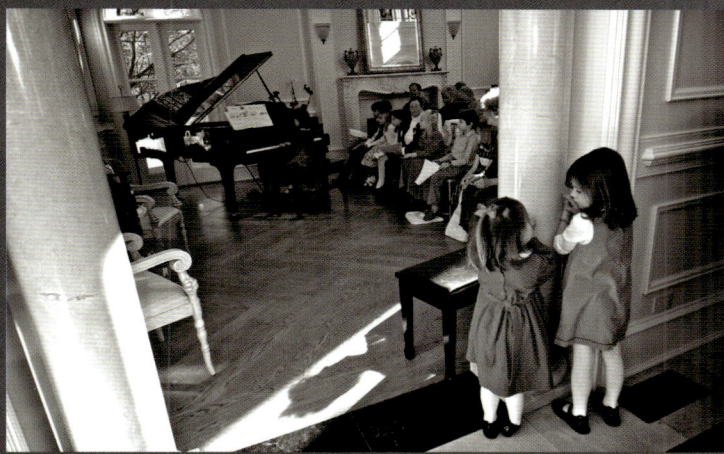

BELOW LEFT: Sisters Reese and Grayson exchange whispers during the performance.

BELOW: A twelve-year-old boy from Bogotá, Colombia discovers an aerial view and daydreams while he waits for his new American-born siblings to perform.

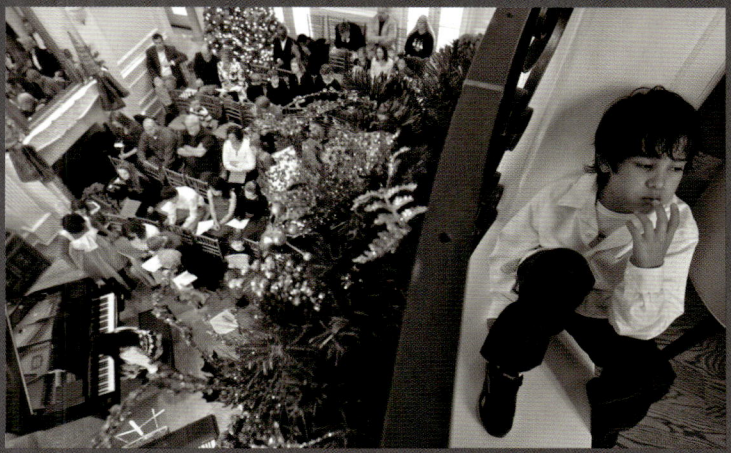

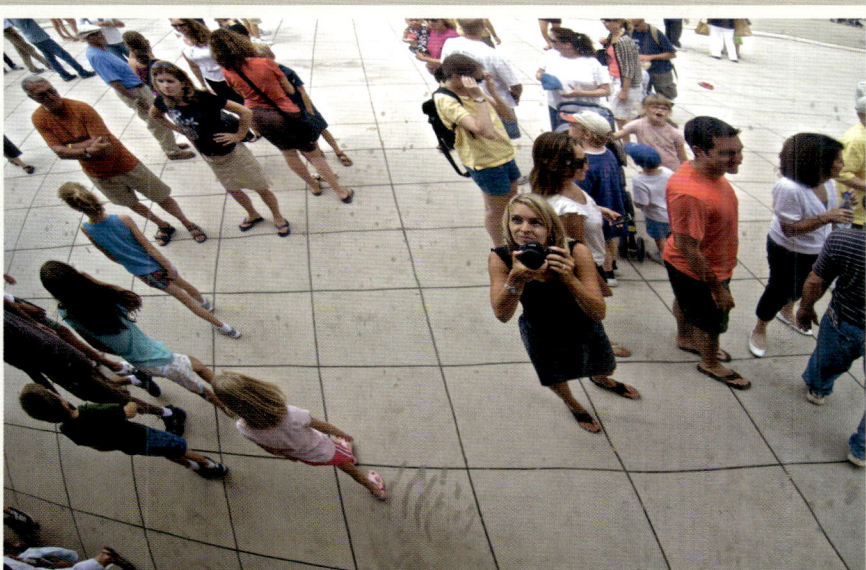

OPPOSITE AND LEFT: Chicago's Cloud Gate, a bean-shaped public sculpture comprised of highly polished stainless steel pieces, is a popular tourist attraction. Rather than shooting the familiar wide-angle view of the landmark in the context of its surrounding cityscape, I zoomed in on the fascinated expressions found reflected in its surface to offer unique views.

Let the Background Drive the Foreground

If I'm flexible on time, one of my favorite things to do when I'm shooting in an urban setting is to seek out an interesting background for action. I might be attracted to a textured building façade or a unique sign because of its color, graphic shapes, or message. Sometimes I'm attracted to a simple and clean expanse of open space like a painted concrete wall or a soothing horizon.

Making a deliberate choice about your background and the positioning of your feet relative to a variable subject in the foreground is a smart approach, as it gives you time to assess the light and adjust your camera settings before your image falls into place. It also simplifies the composition process, because you've already composed a substantial portion of the shot.

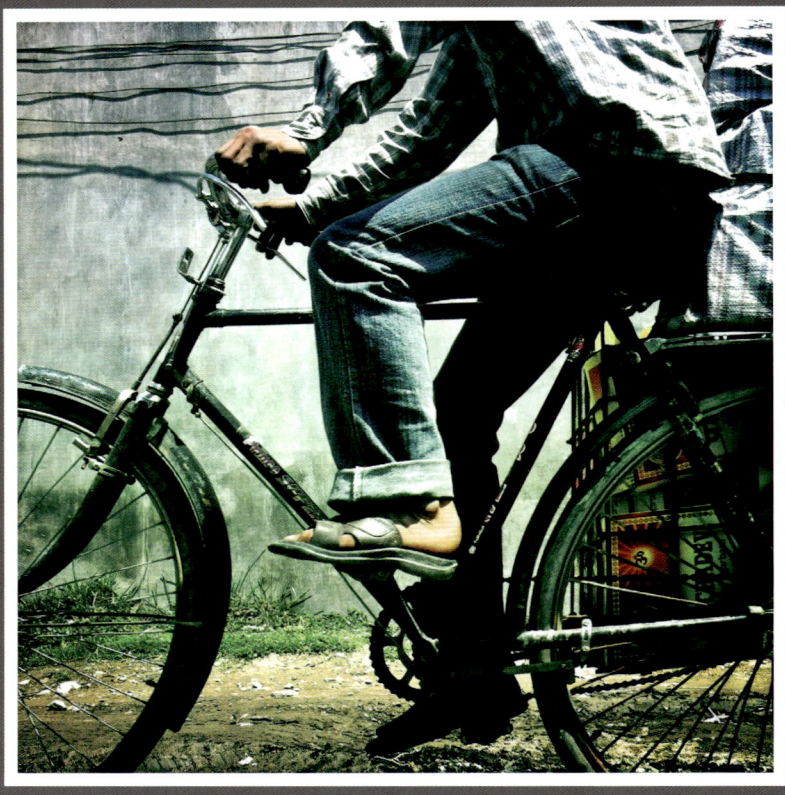

ABOVE: Boy on a bicycle in Kathmandu, Nepal.

RIGHT, FAR RIGHT: Koseli School students in Kathmandu, Nepal create motion while their fellow students stand ready with their cameras to let the background drive the foreground during their Lens on Life photography workshop.

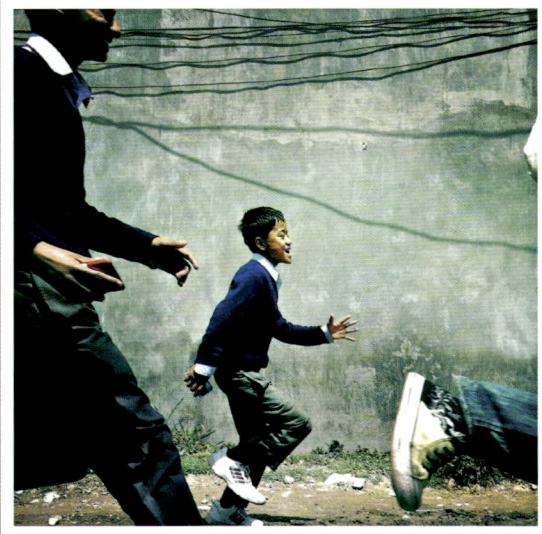

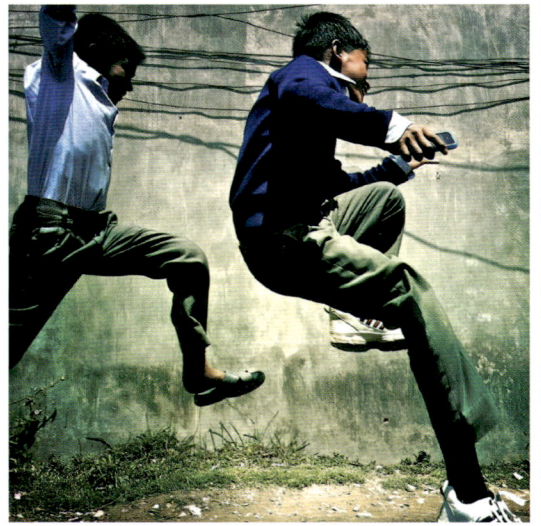

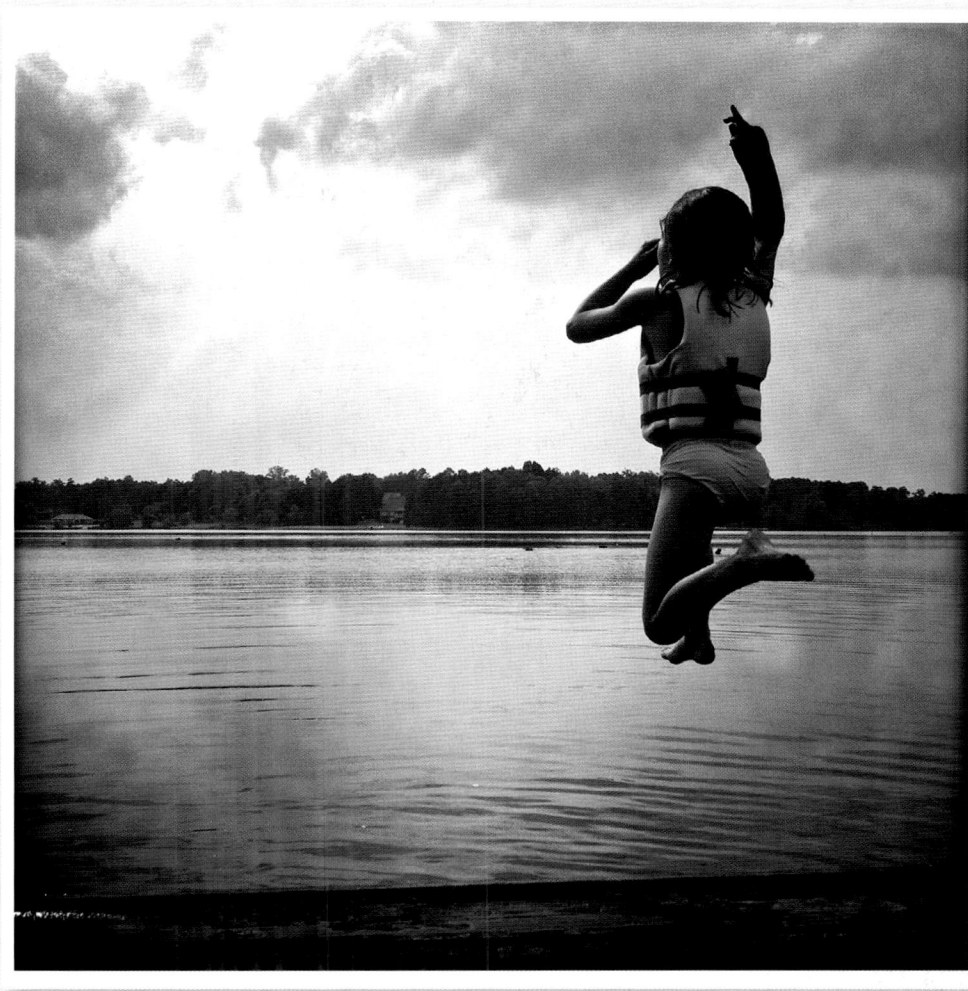

When I find an intriguing background with good potential for action in the foreground, I plant my feet and align my body to compose the scene within the boundaries of my chosen background. If I'm shooting with my SLR, I'll adjust my ISO, aperture, and shutter speed settings to accommodate the available light and sense of motion I want to portray in the foreground, then make a few test shots as my subjects move past or toward my background. When my settings are where I want them to be, I simply stand still and wait patiently for something interesting to occur in the foreground. I watch people move in a way that's natural for them, and when the shapes, organic lines, and colors connect with the background in a way that clicks, I shoot.

ABOVE, RIGHT, FAR RIGHT: My children, Lake Nunnally, Georgia.

LENS ON LIFE, INC. NON-PROFIT ORGANIZATION
Stephanie founded Lens on Life, Inc. in January 2011 to inspire creativity and provide photography education to children and young adults living in material poverty around the world.

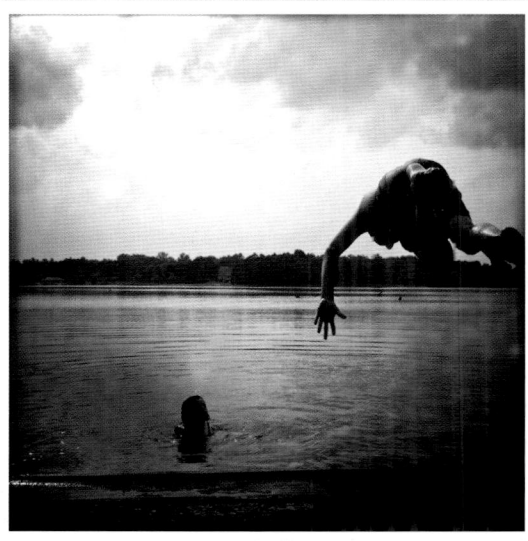

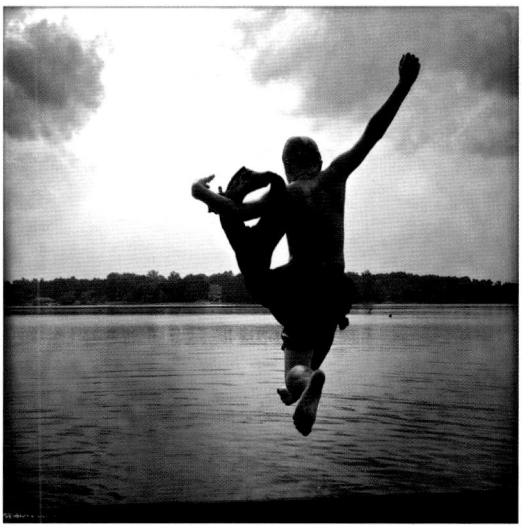

Capture Spontaneous Gestures & Reactions

Documenting spontaneous human gestures and unpredictable reactions to curious, humorous, or even awkward moments moves me—like record-scratches that pierce the predictable rhythm of life. They create tension and make me feel a little anxious, but in a good way. Don't shy away from shooting these spontaneous moments because your subject isn't smiling, or because elements have aligned in ways that create visual tension. Be a witness to that tension and expose the truth, because we shouldn't let the rhythm of life get too predictable. Awkward moments humanize us, and reflect the reality of life. Consider it endearing evidence of our imperfection.

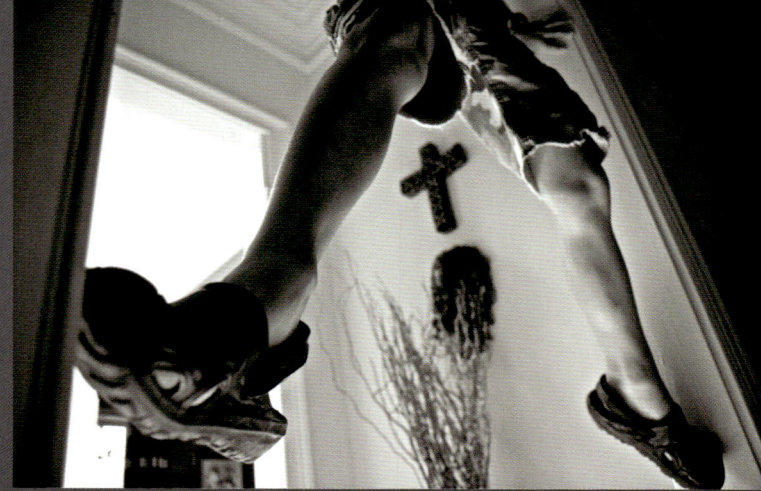

ABOVE: My son scales the doorway. Before you stop your subject from doing something "wrong" or unexpected, consider the visual impact of spontaneous actions.

RIGHT: Webster/ Tate wedding reception attendees, Apalachicola, Florida.

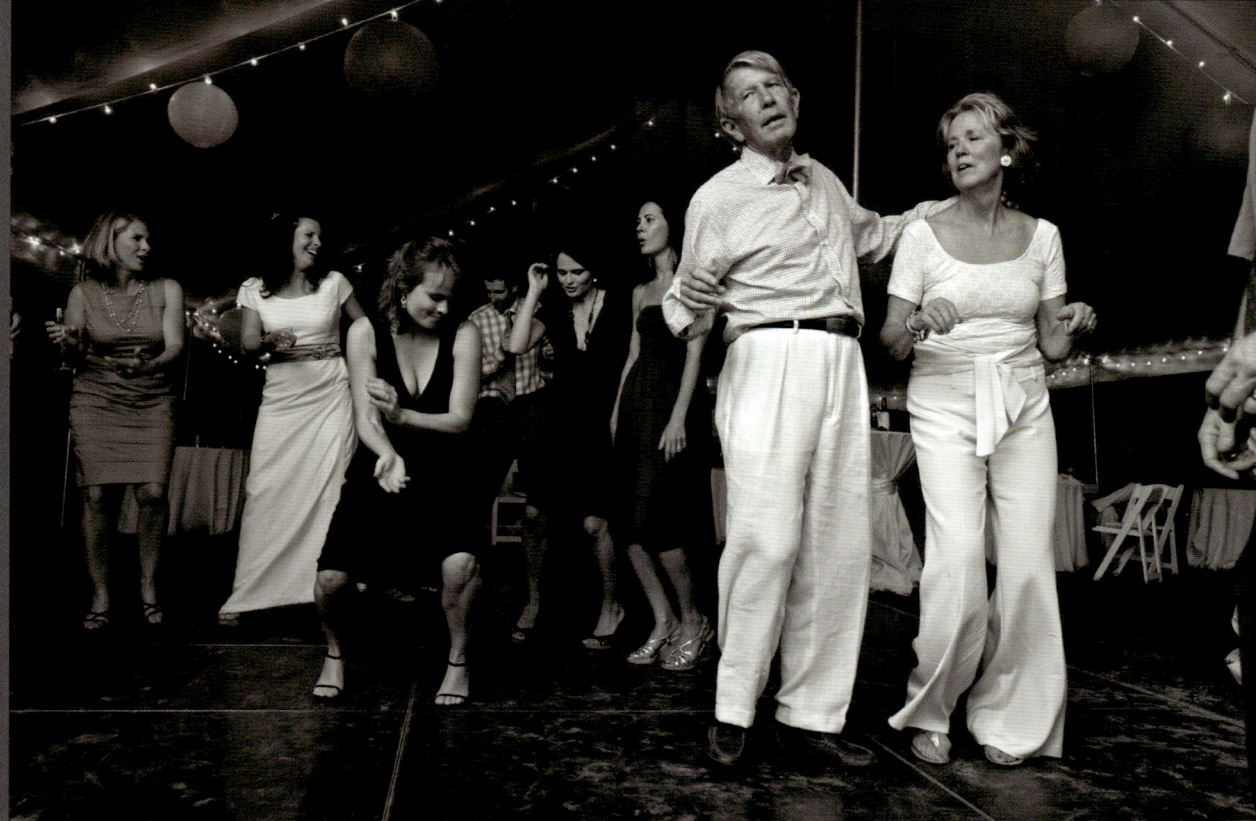

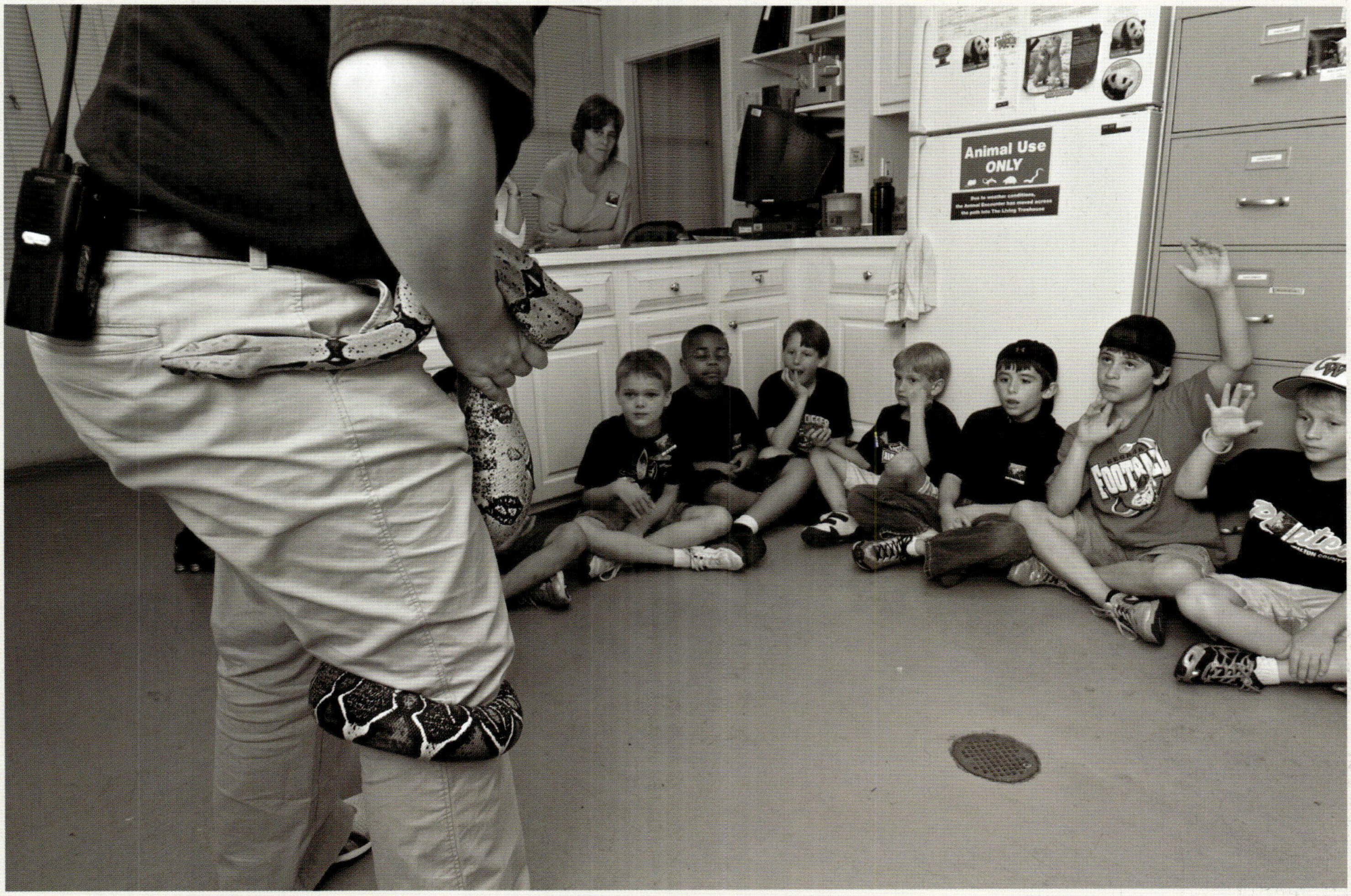

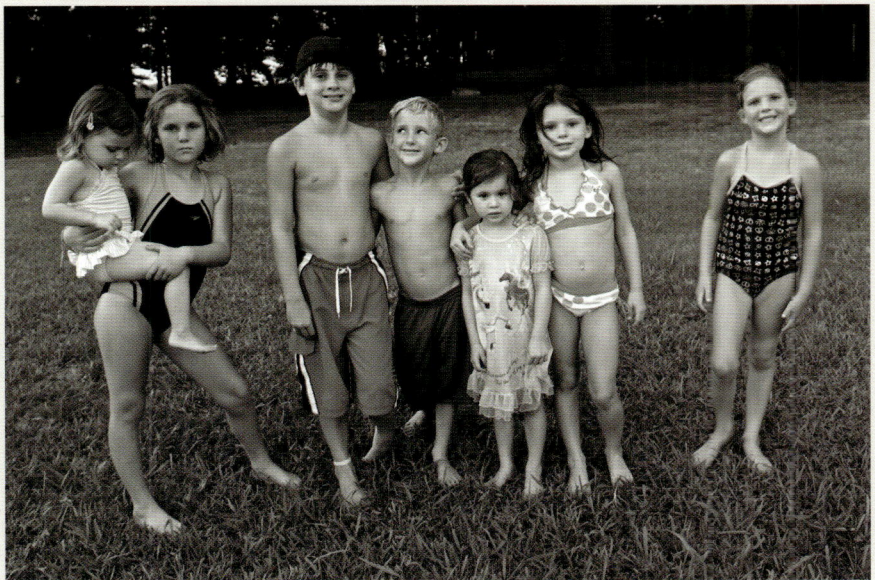

LEFT: Cousins pose on Nunnally Farm.

ABOVE: Boa constrictor hugs a zoologist, Zoo Atlanta.

"I really believe there are things nobody would see if I didn't photograph them."

DIANE ARBUS, PHOTOGRAPHER

When you're getting started with documentary photography, you might feel a little uncomfortable sharing an honest and imperfect view of your subject, especially if you share a close relationship. I'm not suggesting you shoot with malice or the intent to embarrass or expose your subject in a hurtful way. However, I do believe that if your heart is grounded in respect and wonderment for your subject, it's okay to be honest in the portrayal of the moment, even if the moment is a little bit awkward or quirky. As documentary photographers, our aim is to shine a light on what's true, and the truth is we often connect most deeply with one another in the context of awkward moments.

If you are in tune with the people around you, you can often sense the approach of awkward moments. For me, following and catching them is like tracing the fleeting lift and lilt of a bubble and attempting to anticipate the pop. For this reason, I shoot most often with the camera on my iPhone because it's always with me, and because I can quickly and casually lift the device and make an image without holding it to my eye, lest I disrupt the magic of the moment. Consider processing an awkward moment in black and white so you can focus visual emphasis on the intriguing expression or gesture of your subject and soften uneasiness by removing the complexity of color.

ABOVE: Who's watching whom? Lake Burton, Georgia.

RIGHT: Three by the tree, Nunnally Farm.

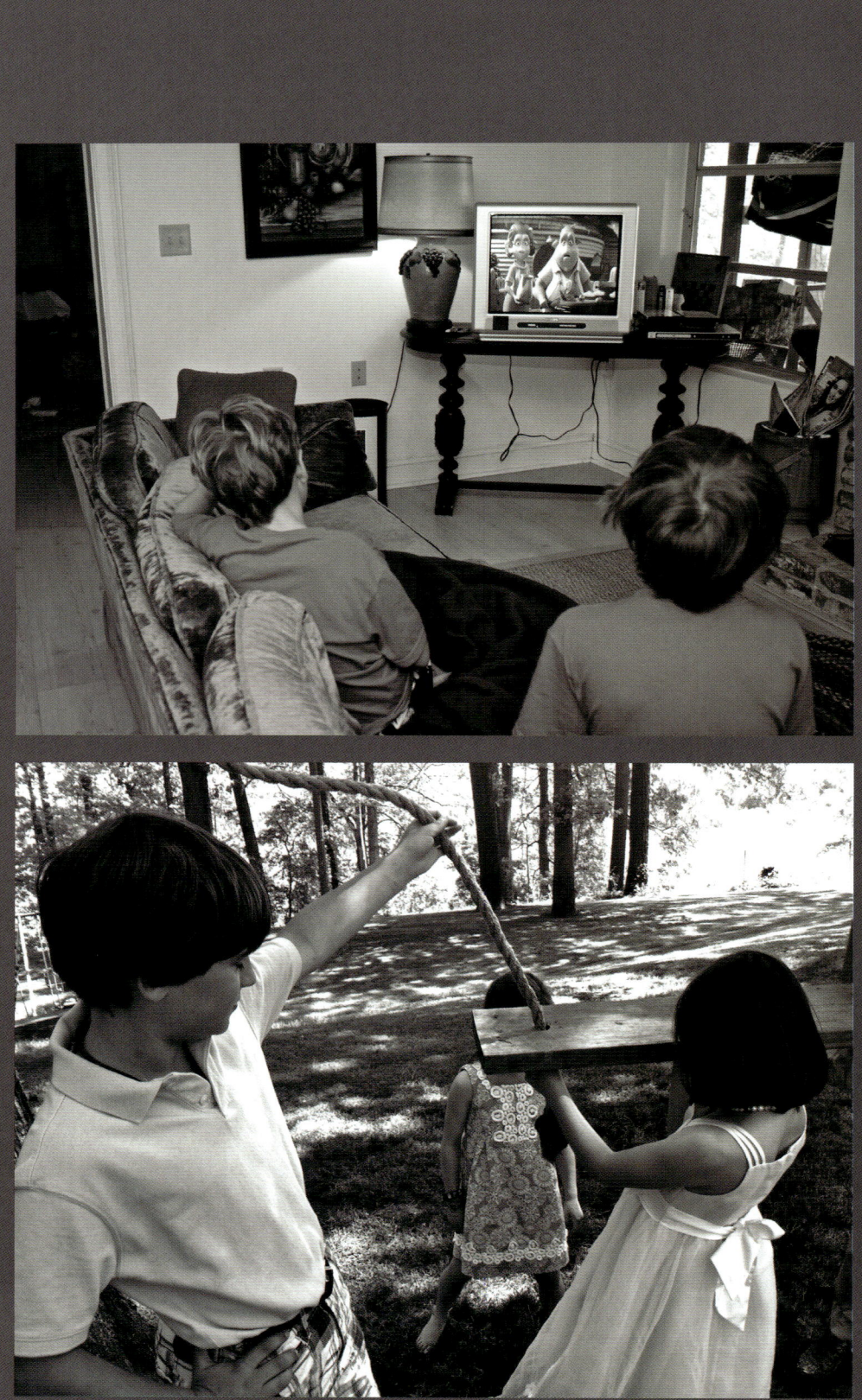

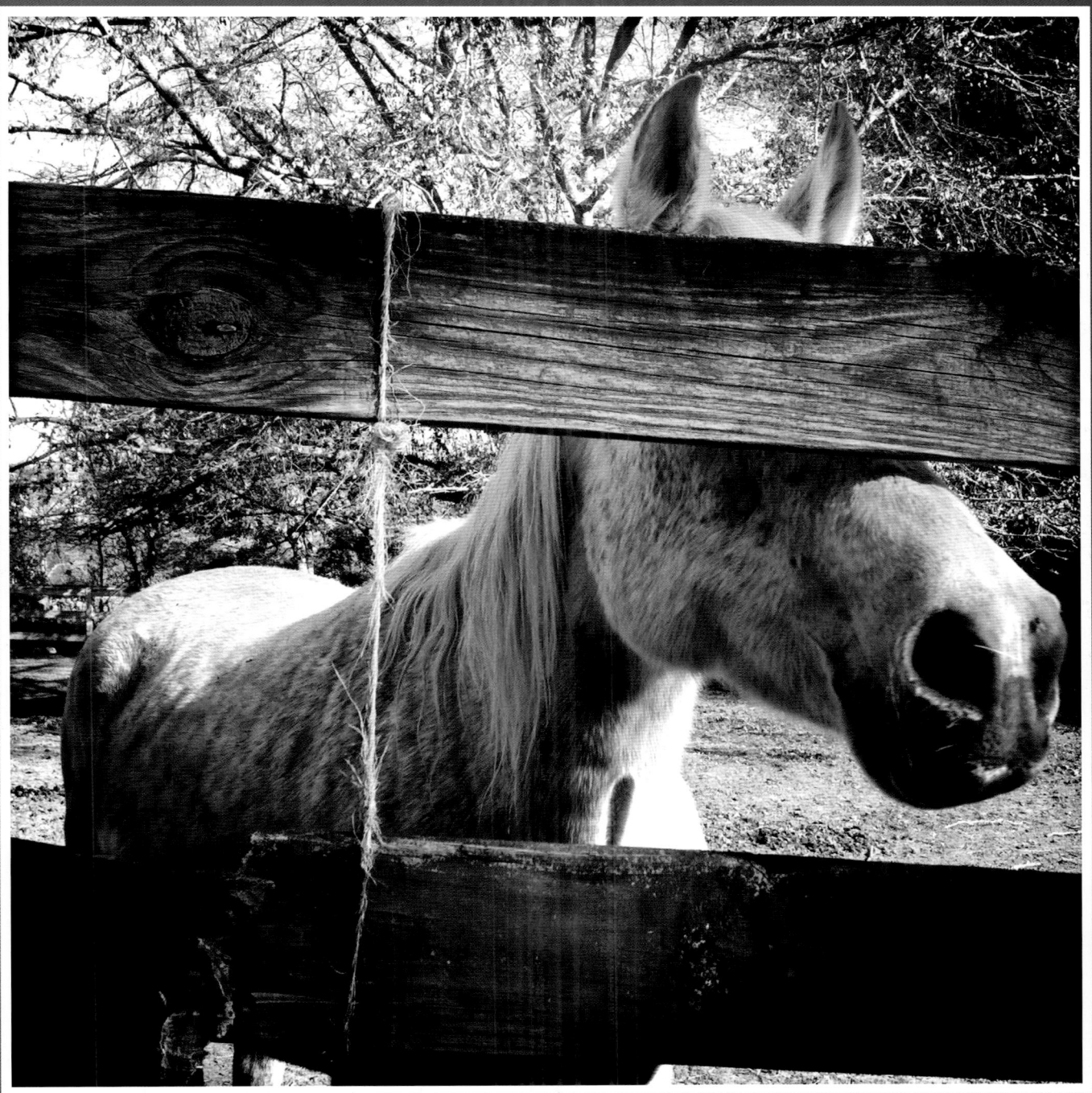

ABOVE: Mel's horse,
Canton, Georgia.

Create Drama with a Slice of Light

Dim environments can be challenging, as they offer little contrast and can result in images that are flat unless you have an artificial light source such as a speedlight, or external mount flash. However, using a flash could have a negative impact on the mood of the setting. In the absence of light, consider ways in which you might position yourself in your setting to receive a dose of spontaneous natural light to create a high-contrast, dramatic moment. While you anticipate spontaneous light, adjust your camera settings so that your camera can let in as much light as you think you need to expose the details of the environment. A wider aperture setting would let in more light, but reduce the clarity of elements in the background of your primary focus area. A more narrow aperture setting would give you more detail, but require a slower shutter speed to let in the light you need to expose the setting. If you have a tripod or a place to stabilize the camera, you can accommodate a slower shutter speed while retaining image clarity. If you don't have a method of stabilizing the camera, widen your aperture so you can accommodate a faster shutter speed.

BELOW: The electricity often goes out around the same time each evening in homes throughout Konombe, Rwanda. When the lights go out, houseboys and housegirls might appear with candles, matches, and teacup saucers or small dishes. Lighting the candle, they drip wax on the teacup or small dish and steady the candle in the center. I positioned my camera on the table to allow for a 10-second exposure.

SETTING

ISO 1600

FOCAL LENGTH: 14mm

APERTURE: ƒ/22

SHUTTER SPEED: 10.0s

FLASH: not fired

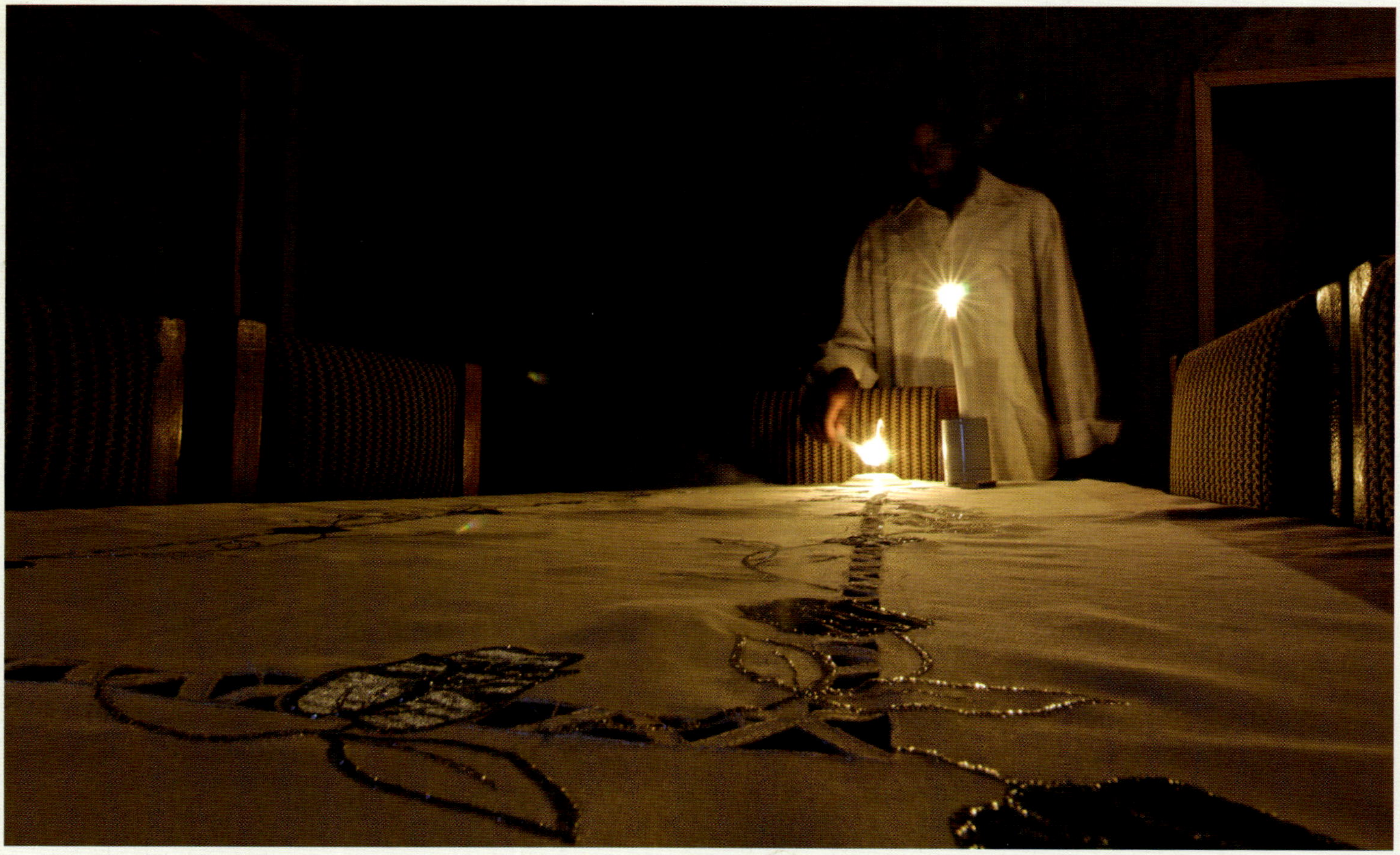

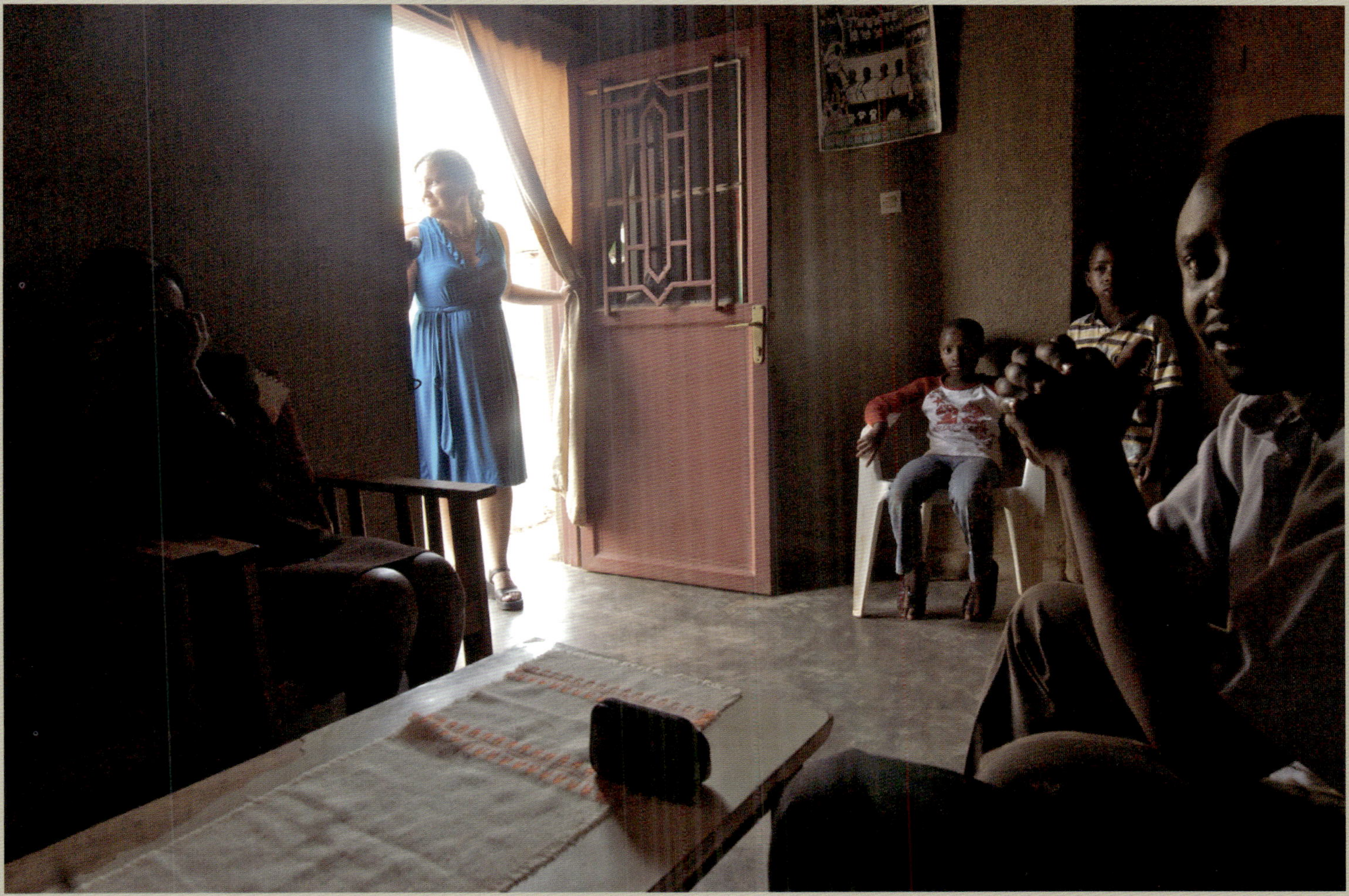

For the images on both of these pages, I chose to use a narrow aperture setting, so I increased my ISO substantially from my standard 200 setting to 1600 and 2000, respectively, to accommodate for the low-light environment. The higher your ISO setting, the more grainlike noise you'll find in your digital photographs. In both cases, I felt that a grainy texture could intensify the dramatic mood of the setting caused by the high-contrast area of focus in the moment.

ABOVE: Jen Lemen turns toward Betty while heading to the kitchen, a small room just beyond the front door of Betty and Frank's home in Konombe, Rwanda. For everyone else, my camera remains the center of attention in the room.

SETTING

ISO 2000
FOCAL LENGTH: 14mm
APERTURE: f/9
SHUTTER SPEED: 1/20
FLASH: not fired

Explore Your Environment to Document What's Inside You

When we think about documentary photography, our thoughts might move initially toward photojournalism or newsworthy moments—images that portray a view or a perspective of our external world. What we see. But I suggest that the documentary genre can and should be stretched to meet the needs of the photographer, and needn't be limited to the notion of a visible exterior. Let's think about it more introspectively and challenge your mind to see beyond the physicality of your subject.

Consider using the limitations of what's present in your environment to document the evolution of what's going on inside of you.

Keeping a camera with you at all times gives you an opportunity to quickly make images to express who you are, what you're thinking, or how you're feeling in a more conceptual way. Think of this form of documentary photography as visual journaling, using physical elements of your environment as you would use words to express thoughts or feelings.

Beyond the selection of subject matter, think about ways you can use composition, perspective, light, color, and texture to express yourself. If you're feeling lighthearted, inspired, or hopeful, you might subconsciously be driven to visuals that exude light and contain expansive fields of soft color or white space. You might be drawn to organic objects with curved or delicate edges. If you're feeling constrained or heavy with conflict or loss, your images might reveal dark shadows, complex shapes, broken lines, jagged edges, or gritty, textured surfaces. You may not consciously understand how your current state of heart and mind might influence the images you make, but shooting daily and studying these images over time can reveal clarity in your emotional landscape.

TRY THIS

At least once each week, carve out and schedule a one-hour break in your day to explore an unfamiliar environment.

Use this time to go for a quick drive, walk beyond your neighborhood, pedal your bike off the usual route, or ride the train and get off at an unfamiliar destination. Let yourself wander and find inanimate objects (organic or manmade) that seem to express your feelings of the moment.

I was teaching an iPhoneography class to a group of adult students in Atlanta one Saturday. During our lunch break, I hopped in my car and drove around, scanning the landscape for something interesting. Maybe it was the contrast of the bright orange doors tucked behind a foreboding chain link fence that first attracted my eye. I parked the car to explore the scene and my attraction to it. Initially I made several images of the repetitive orange doors through a hole in the fence, but those images felt like an inaccurate representation of how I was feeling.

The view was too clear and unobstructed. In that moment of my life, I was feeling as though many of my honest thoughts were hidden behind a bright façade and that actions I desired to make were not possible due to challenging obstructions and limitations. I found these feelings reflected to me physically in the form of the covered car behind the fence and the black area of spray paint covering the identity of a parking space. As I moved closer toward the car, I found a tear in the cover, exposing the identity of the car, despite the layers of obstruction. I didn't seek it out, yet following the attraction of my eye led me to a moment that accurately reflected how I was feeling.

RIGHT:
Covered Up.

FAR RIGHT:
Protection Mechanism.

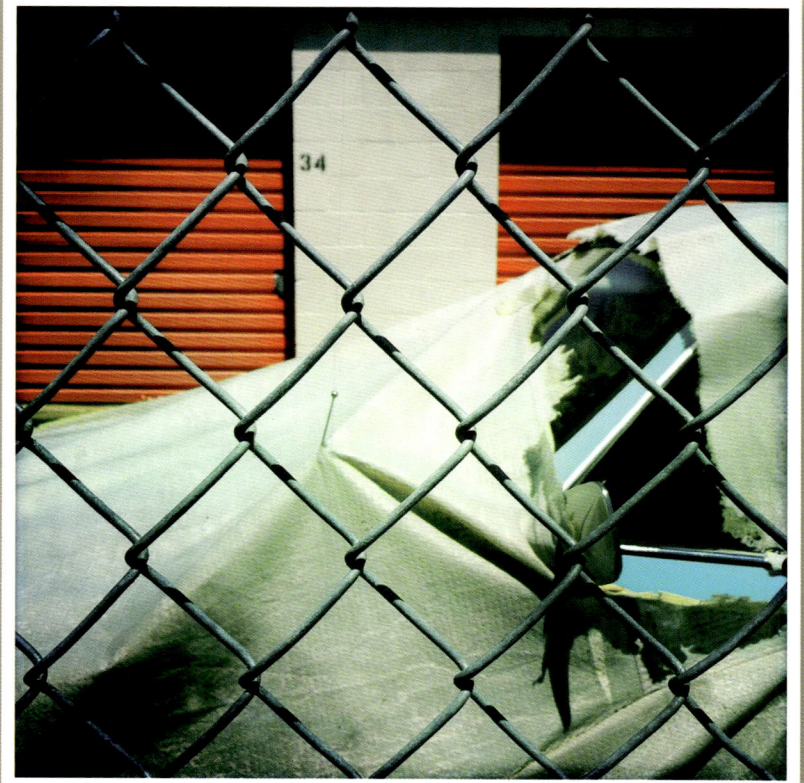

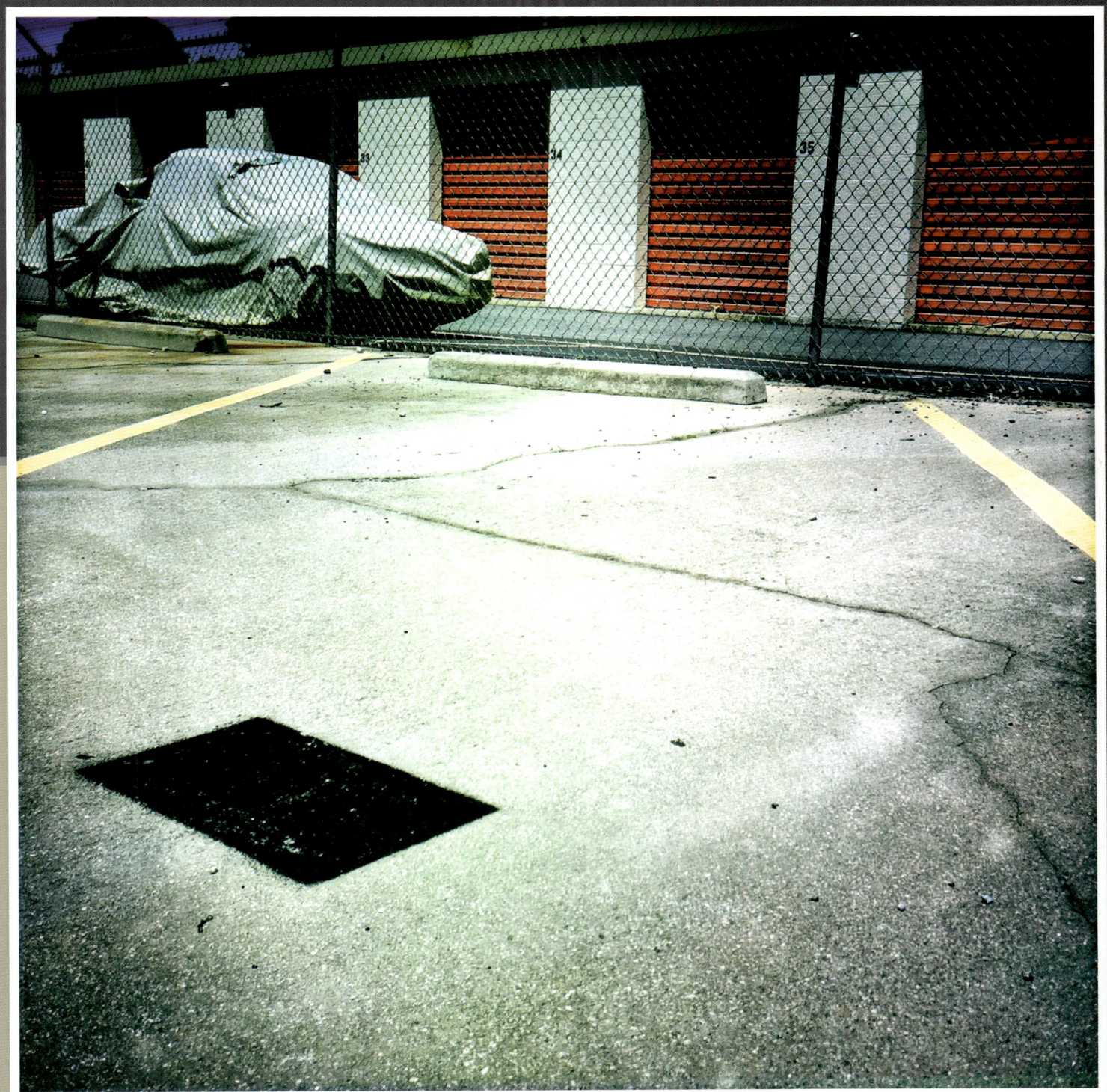

I made these images on Wednesday, August 17, 2011 within a one-hour period of time to document and help me process how I was feeling in the wake of a strained relationship. Using the Instagram app on my iPhone camera, I took pictures of domestic artifacts in and around my home. I didn't place or move any of these objects, but rather positioned myself in relation to each object to visually articulate how I was feeling. I used the Tilt-Shift feature within the Instagram app to place clarity on my area of focus and blur the background, giving the illusion that these images emerged from the depth of my mind. I then applied a simple filter to each of the images in the sequence to distort reality and visually connect them. I titled each image and shared the sequence online with my Instagram followers as a way of extroverting my thought process. Documenting and acknowledging my honest feelings gave me a sense of peace.

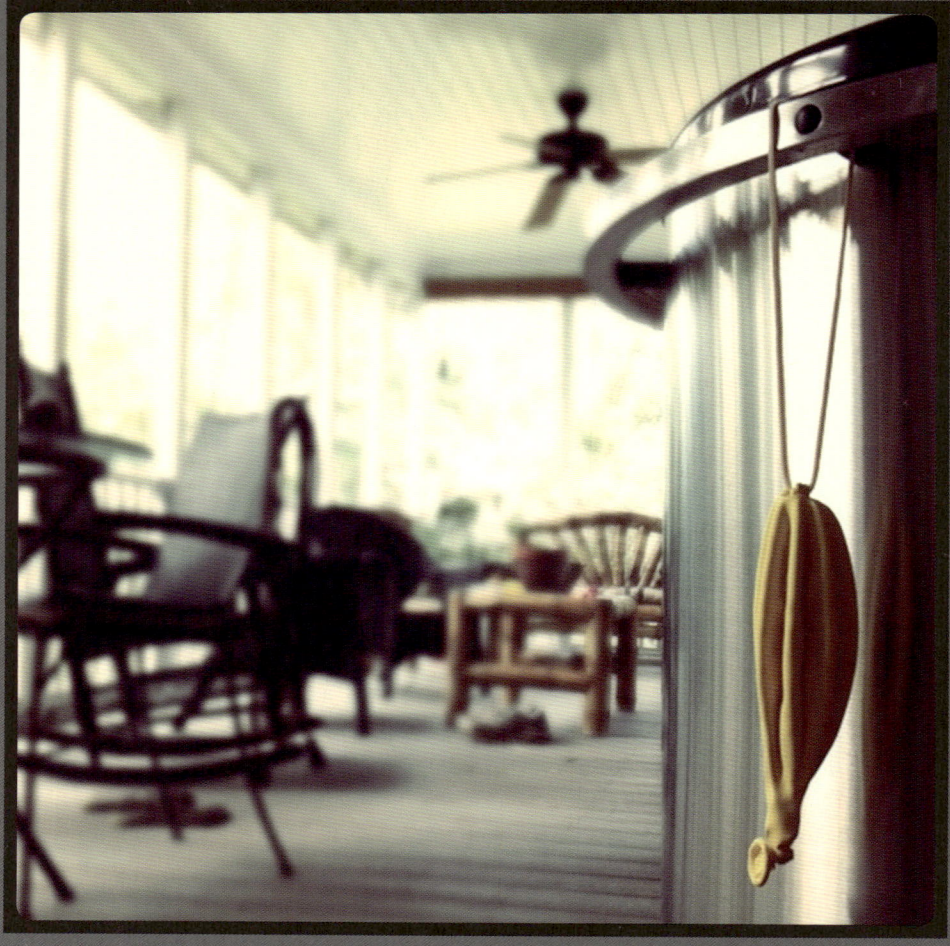

Deflated.

TRY THIS

- Let your eyes wander in your own home, and guide you toward elements of the setting that connect with you in that moment.
- Shoot these points of connection.
- Title each image with a word or phrase that articulates how you feel about it. If you share these images publicly, a title can help provide context or intrigue your viewers so they can see the physical object in a more conceptual way.
- Review the series of images and see if you can find a thread that connects them.
- Process the series of images in a consistent way and present them together.

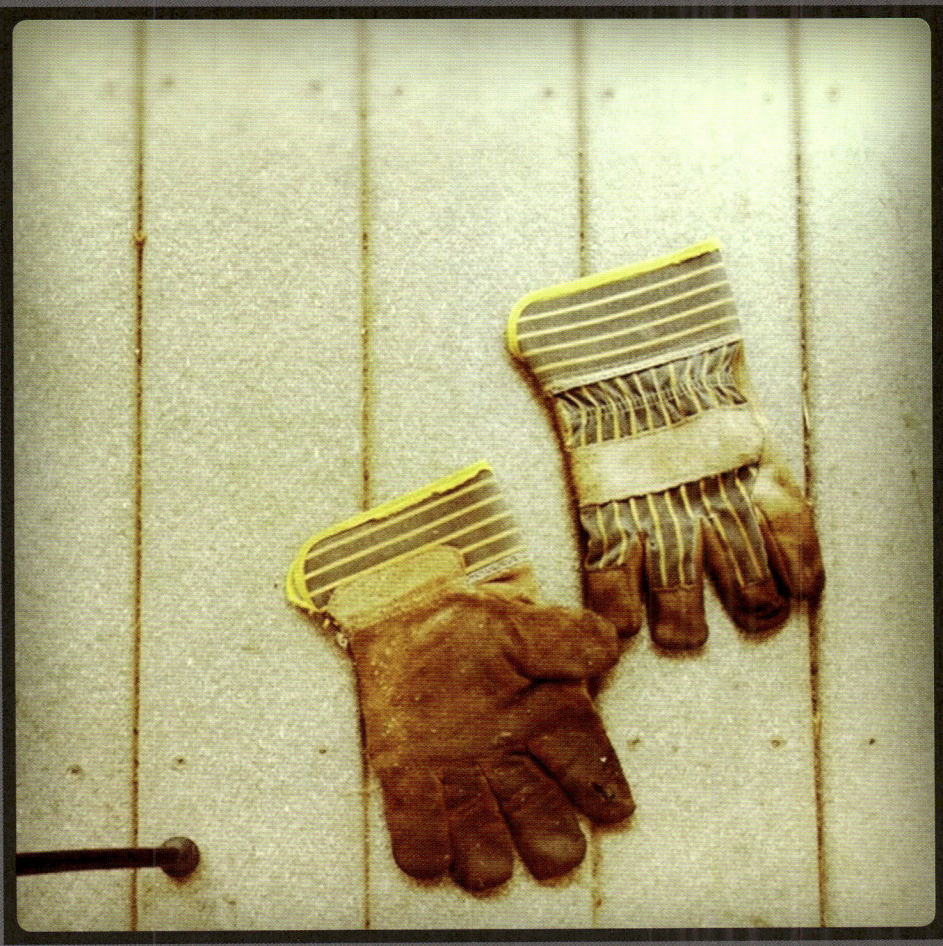

Discarded.

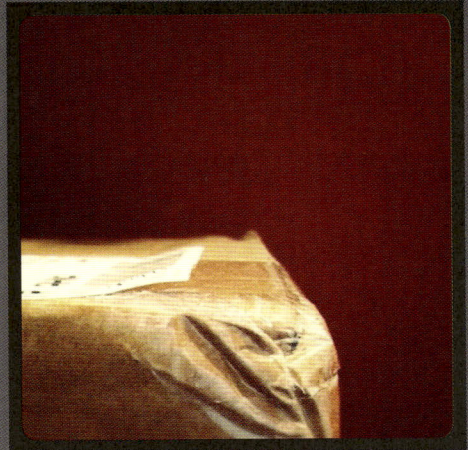

Dented.

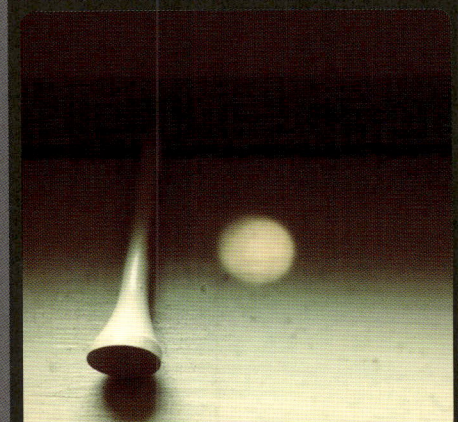

Disconnected.

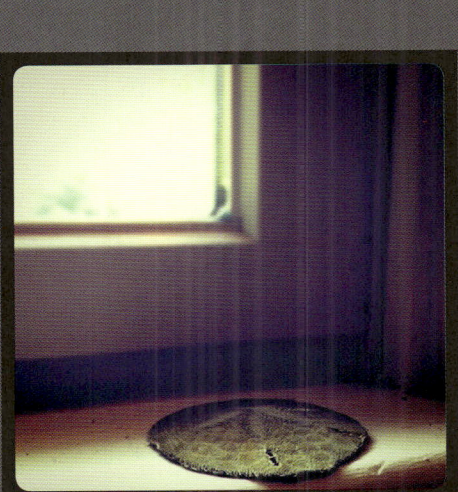

Displaced.

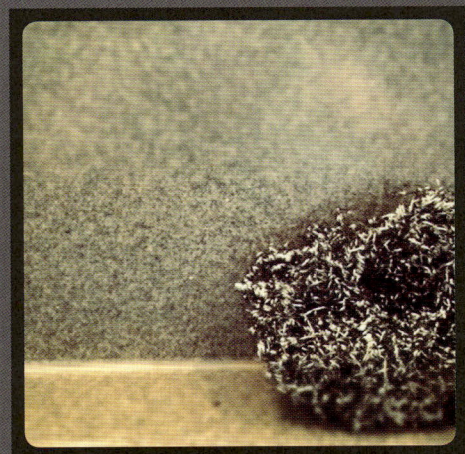

Distorted.

Dig for Clues in the Visuals of Your Past

On the journey to uncovering your vision, you can often find clues in the faded visuals of your past—the images you didn't capture with a camera, but have remained with you in your mind's eye. Since childhood, you've been subconsciously picking up visuals that resonated with you (significant and insignificant, positive and negative) like special stones, collecting them along the path of your life. While you shared many of your childhood experiences with family members and friends, each visual you chose to capture and store in your mind was crafted from your unique perspective. You chose the subject matter in its setting, and identified your areas of focus for each memory. This collection of childhood memories represents a significant chapter in your personal documentary and provides the scaffolding for your vision as a photographer.

As we continue to collect memories on our path through life as adults, our life experiences become increasingly more complex. Our minds expand and hold heavy challenges, excessive tasks and routine chores, complicated schedules, missed calls, demanding careers, mixed emotions, full inboxes, and shelved desires. We carry the weight of these things on our backs each day, eclipsing our vision and creativity. For me and many photographers I know, photography is an attempt to unload that weight, even for just a few seconds—to pause and lose ourselves in the present moment long enough to capture its magic in the form of a photograph. It's an escape that can take you back to the curiosity and sense of wonder you felt as a child.

If you feel that you might be shooting without a firm grasp on your vision, put your camera down and give yourself some time and space to excavate, document, and linger on the clues found in the visuals of your childhood—the images in your mind's eye. Documenting these visuals can help you identify what attracts your eye and what drives you to press the shutter. Many of your best images will come from people, experiences, and places that feel familiar to you in some way because they connect you with your past.

TRY THIS

- Put your camera down for one week, and let yourself get lost in your childhood memories. Give your mind some time and white space to let visuals emerge. They may start out as faint lines, but wait patiently until shades of gray consume empty spaces, and details such as color and texture lend clarity.

- Linger on each of these images in your mind and document them in the form of words and phrases. They don't need to be complete sentences. Use words to recreate the moment from your perspective. Let one moment lead you to the next.

- Collect the visual phrases and see if you can find connections among them. Your images are a reflection of you. Embrace what's true. They will undoubtedly shed light on subjects, settings, and details that attract your eye today.

- Ask yourself these questions:
  - What moments come to mind?
  - Do the settings vary or are you drawn to a particular time period and place?
  - Who are the individuals in these scenes and how can you describe them?
  - What visual details emerge in each of these moments?
  - Can you recall an expression or a gesture?
  - How do you feel immersed in each moment?

If you need help getting started with this exercise, flip through your old family albums or spark a conversation with a family member or friend to help you visualize moments and fill in the blanks.

- See how these visual phrases have influenced your photographic subject matter to date to lend clarity around your unique vision. And see if the visual phrases influence your images and documentary projects to come.

VISUALS FROM THE PAST AS SEEN IN YOUR MIND'S EYE

This sequence of visuals appeared for me when I let myself get lost in childhood visits to my grandparents' homes. I followed the thread and tapped out these short phrases within the confines of a 140-character limit and shared them on Twitter. Reading them later, I felt inspired by the texture in the details.

Seeking new, she discarded what was well-worn and true. Faded curtains and front porch swings. Rusted chains. The hum of cool air by the window.

Pap and his brothers taught me how to play poker around his kitchen table. Chairs creaked. Pennies slid. I sipped root beer from the can.

Beneath a faded apron she commanded the kitchen. Wedding soup and thick meatballs. She spoke only in Italian and hugged me so tight it hurt.

She hid curlers beneath a blue bandana. Sipping coffee from a white teacup, she stamped the rim with painted lips and tapped the tip of her Lark.

She studied the cracks and curls of linoleum. Peeled paint and too many dandelions. Blowing seeds in the garden out back.

He added green peppers and hot dogs to the scrambled eggs. Black coffee. Snuff in pocket. King of croquet. I wondered why he never wore shorts.

Delicate models of cars and sailboats sat high on the shelf. "Don't touch." He made kites and flew them in high winds.

Twin beds . . . his and hers. She shuffled cards and carried a faux mink stole. He picked up the pinecones and pruned the azaleas.

Turn the Focus on Yourself:
Jen Lemen

CONNECT AND FOLLOW

Jen Lemen
WEBSITE: www.hopefulworld.org
BLOG: www.jenlemen.com
TWITTER: @jenlemen
INSTAGRAM: @jenlemen

Getting comfortable with self-portraiture can be a challenge. As documentary photographers we focus our lens outwardly, and feel most at ease when we attempt to play the role of invisible witness. What you may not realize is that much of photography is about understanding who you are—getting comfortable with your own vulnerability so you can build a capacity to reveal your subjects with empathy and sensitivity. Learning to expose an authentic view of yourself can help you develop an appreciation for your own imperfections, and gain confidence in the value of your presence and unique perspective.

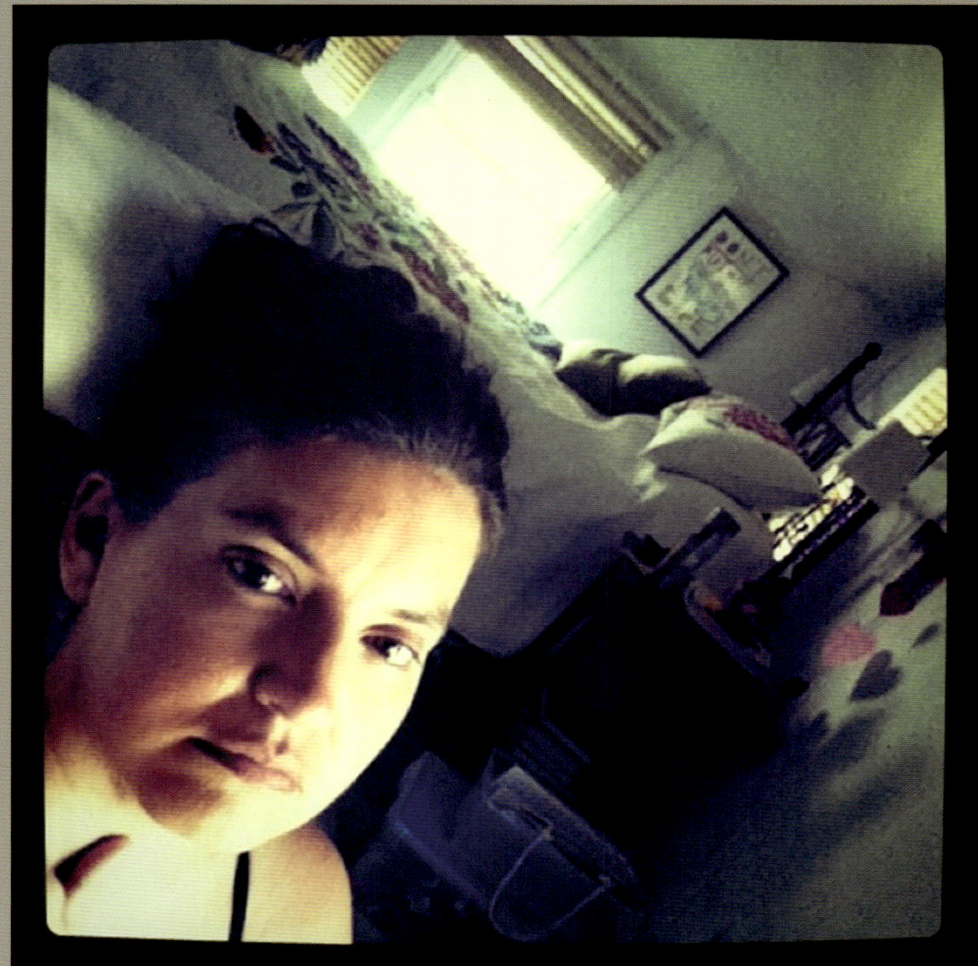

"I was feeling really down in this moment, but after looking at the image within the context of my room, I was comforted by my bed, the shadow of the heart, and the words on the framed print: 'Don't put off your happy life.'"

"Part of the reason to do self-portraiture is to learn how to externalize that judging voice so you're not so hard on yourself. So you can look at yourself and say 'Yes, my hair is not perfect in that picture or I don't look exactly as I thought I would look, but that's me and this is my life, and everything is changing. Tomorrow I'm going to look a different way. Some day I'm going to die and my body won't be here at all.' I think self-portraiture helps you grow your self-acceptance so you can desensitize yourself to that judgment."

Jen Lemen, founder of Hopeful World Publishing, is an artist, writer, photographer, world traveler, mother of two children, and friend to many. Jen has been documenting and expressing herself creatively through written and spoken word and creative visuals to a global audience through her popular blog since 2002. In the spring of 2010, she began to experiment with self-portraits as a way of processing her impending divorce, and the aftermath of helping two young girls in Uganda reunite with their mother in the United States after a four-year separation. Under the strain of these experiences, Jen felt weak, vulnerable, and very much alone for the first time in her home. "I couldn't just turn to someone and say, 'How do you think I'm doing right now?'—to mirror my feelings back for me." She decided to start making self-portraits as a way of seeing and documenting an accurate reflection of how she was feeling during this intense time of transition in her life.

Initially, Jen began shooting her self-portraits exclusively for herself to avoid judgment from an online audience. She didn't want the pressure of trying to look good. "When I first started looking at these self-portraits, I was shocked at how vulnerable and tender I looked. I was in a broken and fragile state and it was really clear to me in the images." Jen was also surprised to find that in spite of the visible signs of weakness, she discovered beauty in herself—a quality she had overlooked.

Jen continued to experiment with self-portraits and eventually began sharing the images on her blog as a visual way of expressing how she was feeling "in the moment" to her readers—revealing herself in a more vulnerable light. "In the past I felt that people over-estimated my strength and underestimated my vulnerability, and I just wanted to create a more honest portrayal of myself." Jen received a warm and encouraging response to the authenticity revealed in these self-portraits on her blog, giving her confidence to continue experimenting with self-portraiture as a method of personal expression on an almost daily basis.

Jen often creates her self-portraits in the "between spaces," when nothing is really happening or when she's bored and feeling inspired to document and share a mood or a feeling that couldn't otherwise be expressed in words. "When I turn the camera outside, I tend to shoot much of the same things—flowers, found objects, little details—and sometimes it just bores me. Using myself as a subject is more pliable. I can change myself… and play around with how I look. It's funny how deadpan a lot of my pictures are because I'm such an expressive person when I talk, but I like not performing for the camera. I just want to be myself without trying, and be seen for who I really am."

Having a long-standing and far-reaching online persona centered around hopeful and inspiring stories of courage, connection, and personal transformation, Jen feels as though there's been a disconnect between her public perception and a holistic picture of who she really is. "The self-portraits add a dimension to me that other people might not consider. I don't think most people would describe me as being 'really feisty and sexy' right off. They might say I'm spiritual or inspiring because of my work and my stories, but there's this other more visceral and human side of who I am. The self-portraits help shake up that perception."

Turn the Focus on Yourself:
Jen Lemen

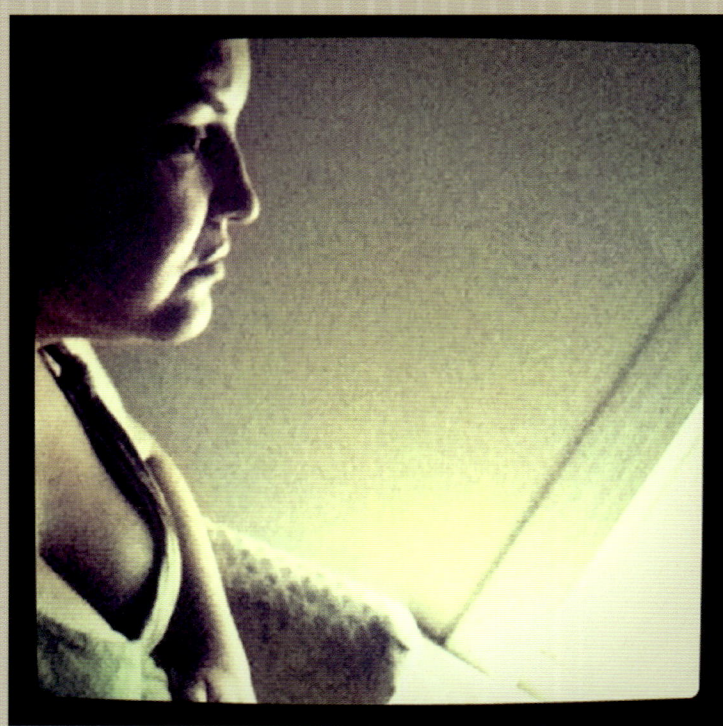

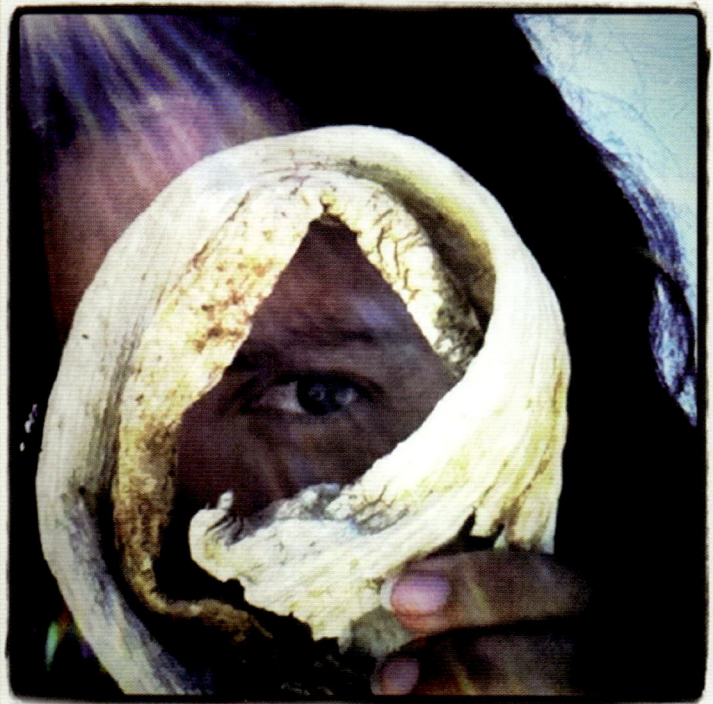

Jen felt isolated in this image. "My face looks really hard, but my body looks so soft. It seems to accurately portray the disconnect I was feeling between my head and my heart on that moment."

While on a retreat with friends at the beach, Jen had been considering what part of her identity she wanted to illuminate. "This image reflects my desire to play a more spiritual role—to be seen as a mystic or an oracle."

"When I first started looking at these self-portraits, I was shocked at how vulnerable and tender I looked. I was in a broken and fragile state and it was really clear to me in the images."

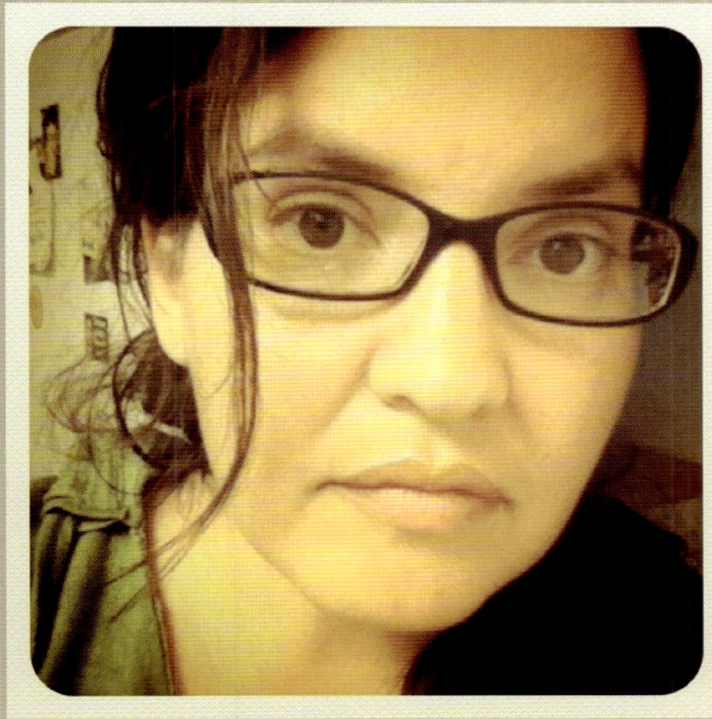

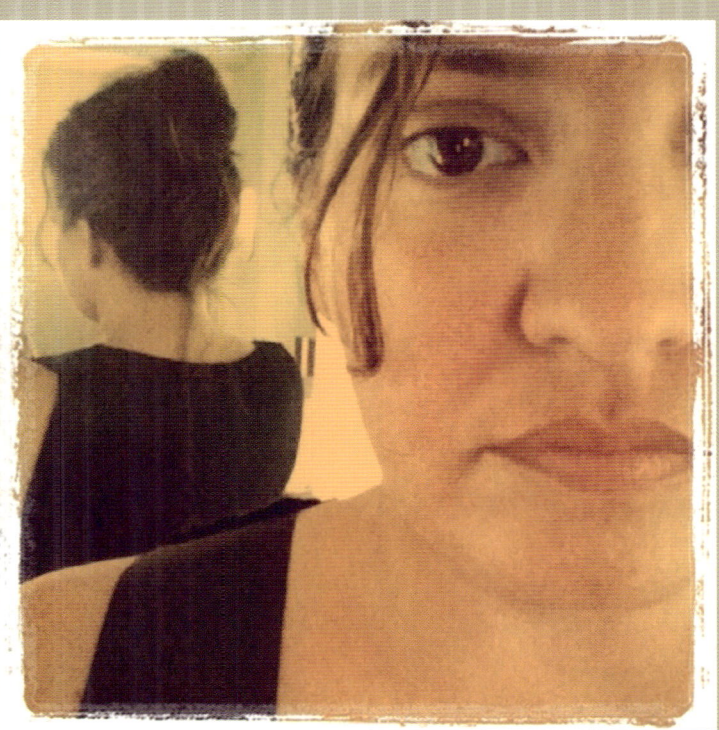

Jen spent several days living and sleeping in this Ethiopian dress and hoodie. "I was feeling really tired, so I took the image to check in and see if I looked as tired as I felt. And I did."

"I was feeling divided and very aware that there are two sides to every story, even two views within yourself—the side you hide and keep to yourself and the side you show to the world. I don't even think this picture looks like me."

Turn the Focus on Yourself:
Jen Lemen

"I'm trying to connect with what's underneath me, but I felt
as though even my attempt to portray this in an image failed."

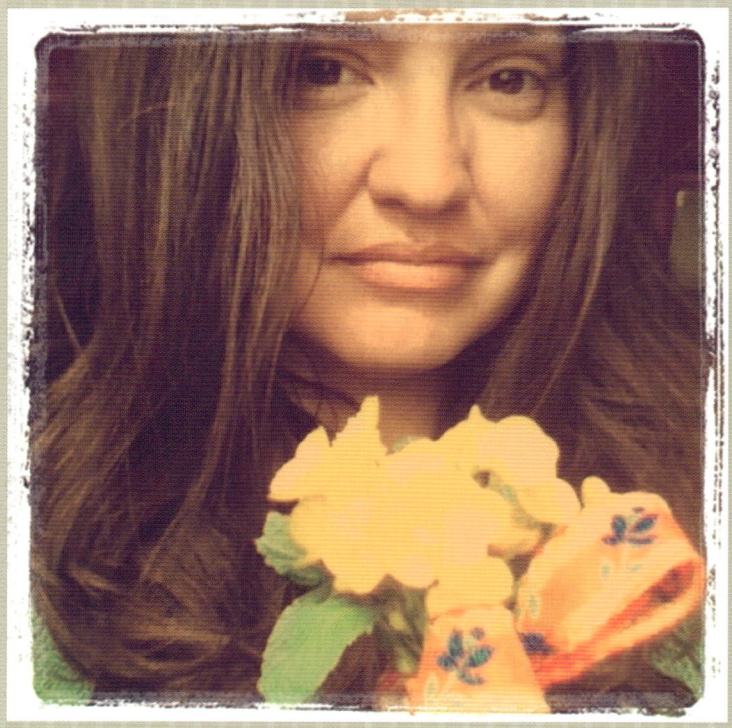

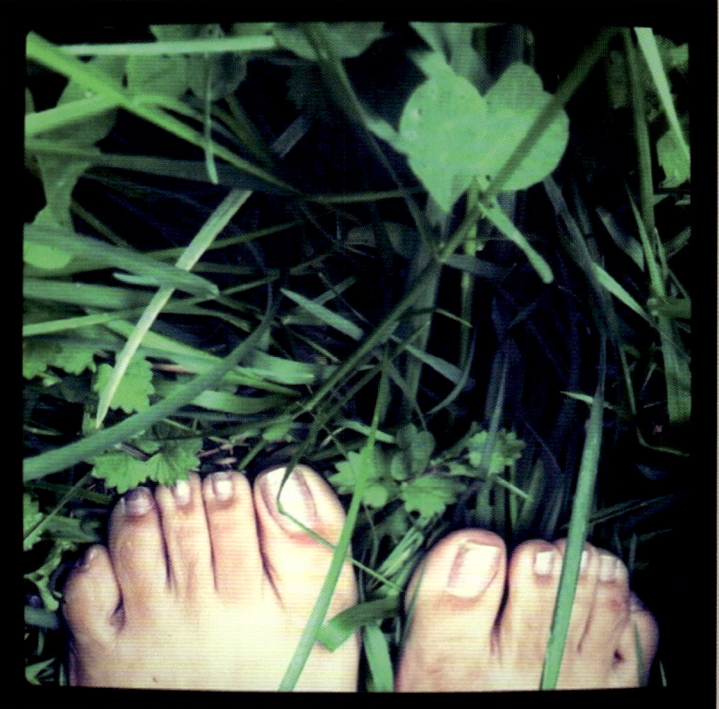

"I look really put together, but my hair was actually really dirty and I had been crying all morning." A friend had encouraged Jen to do something that would lift her spirit, so she went outside, made a buttercup bouquet, and SMS'd this image to her friend to convey how much his kind words had touched her.

Jen often shoots the placement of her feet as a method of physically grounding her spirit. "In the online world, everything gets so disembodied. You can't really tell where you are, so I went into my backyard to ground myself in the grass, but what's funny is that you don't get a sense of gravity in the image. I'm trying to connect with what's underneath me, but I felt as though even my attempt to portray this in an image failed. The only thing I could connect to was the worn look of my feet."

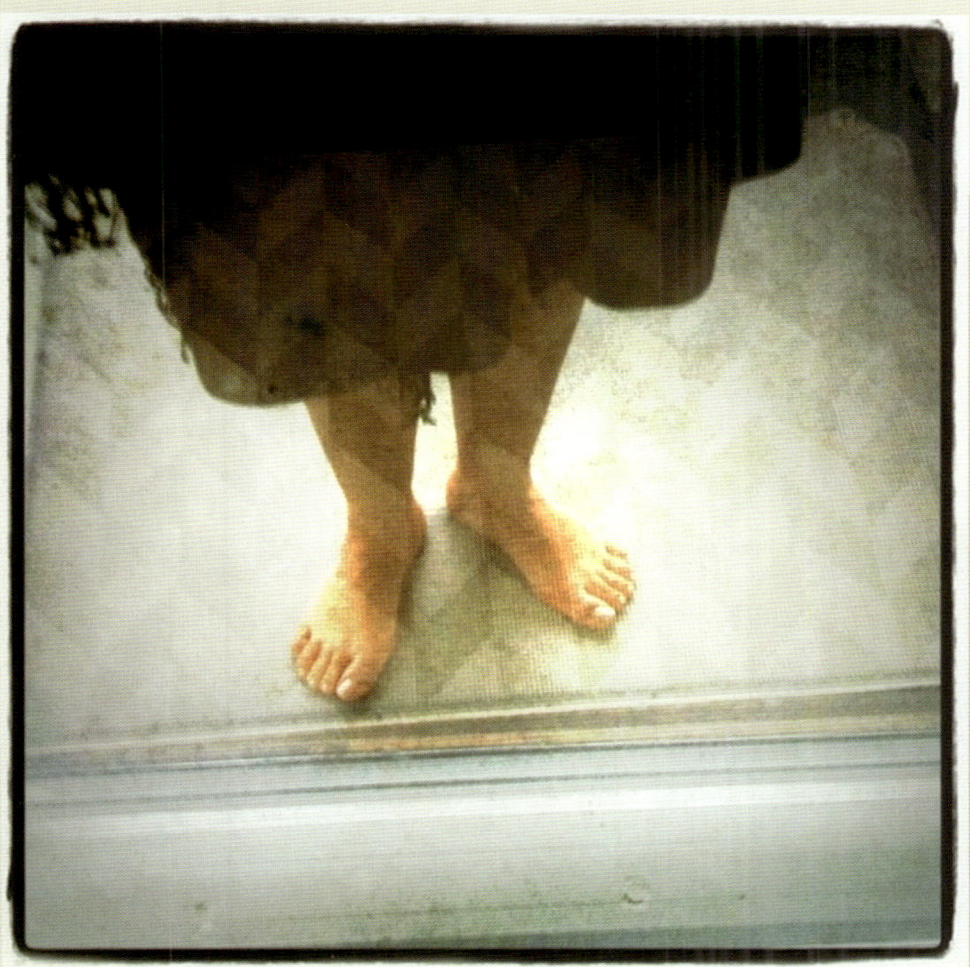

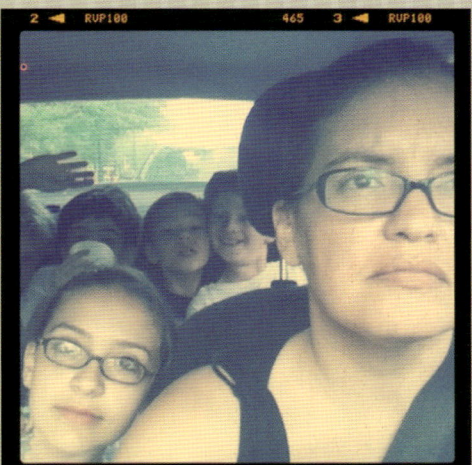

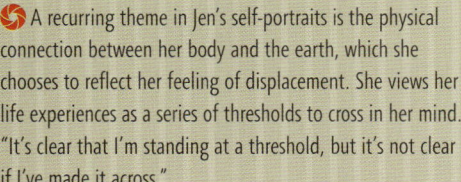 A recurring theme in Jen's self-portraits is the physical connection between her body and the earth, which she chooses to reflect her feeling of displacement. She views her life experiences as a series of thresholds to cross in her mind. "It's clear that I'm standing at a threshold, but it's not clear if I've made it across."

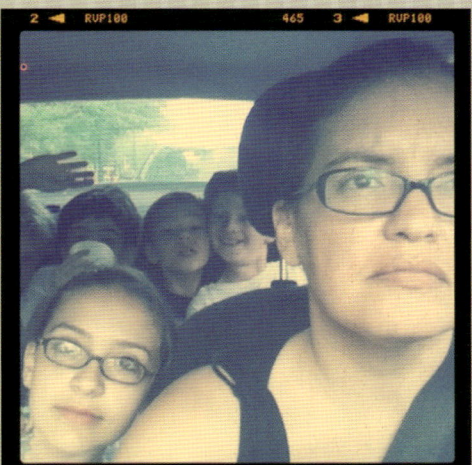 This is a typical motherhood moment for Jen—piling her kids and neighborhood friends in the car and heading out on a mission for ice cream. "I'm tuning out the activity in the backseat to drive the car, yet I'm still very much present and unfazed by the chaos of the moment. This is how I am."

"It's clear that I'm standing at a threshold, but it's not clear if I've made it across."

Turn the Focus on Yourself:
Jen Lemen

". . . I felt as though I was revealing a secret by sharing how alone and frail I felt in that moment."

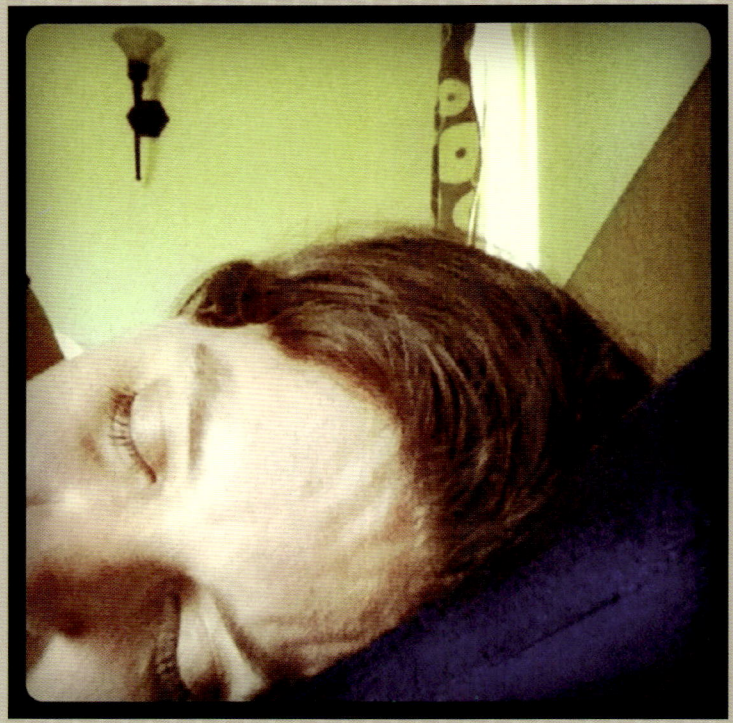

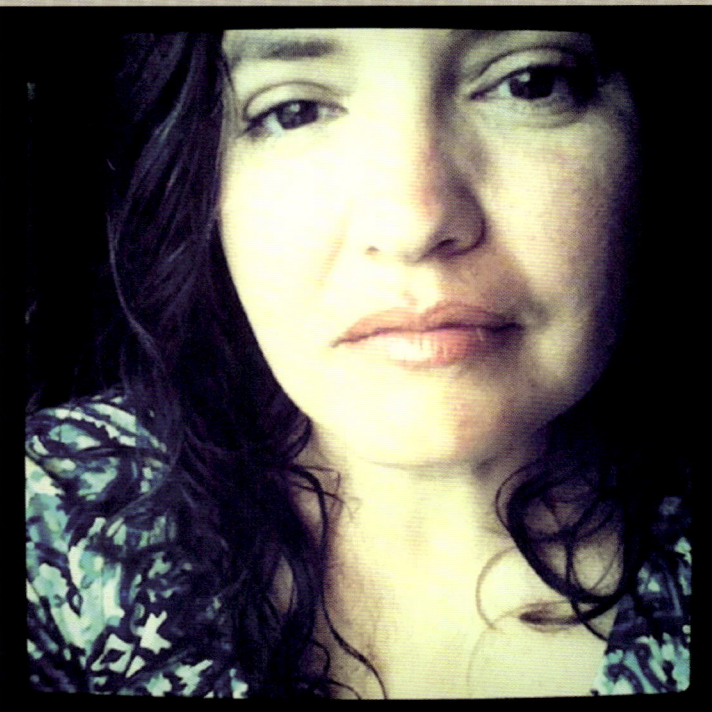

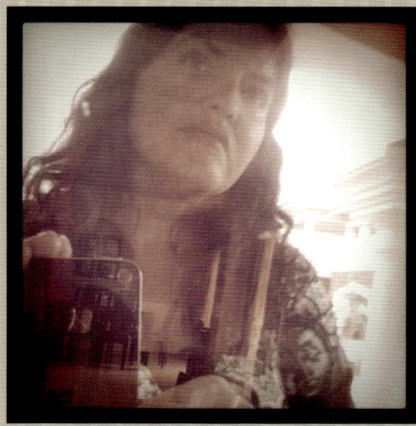

While working in Kathmandu, Nepal, Jen became extremely ill with a parasite for several days. "I felt vulnerable sharing this image online, even though it showed so little of my face. I felt as though I was revealing a secret by sharing how alone and frail I felt in that moment."

"Later that same day, I was beginning to feel better, so I took a shower and put on some makeup and pretty clothes. I felt really lucky in these moments, seeing my transformation in these images. I had made it through a really difficult spot."

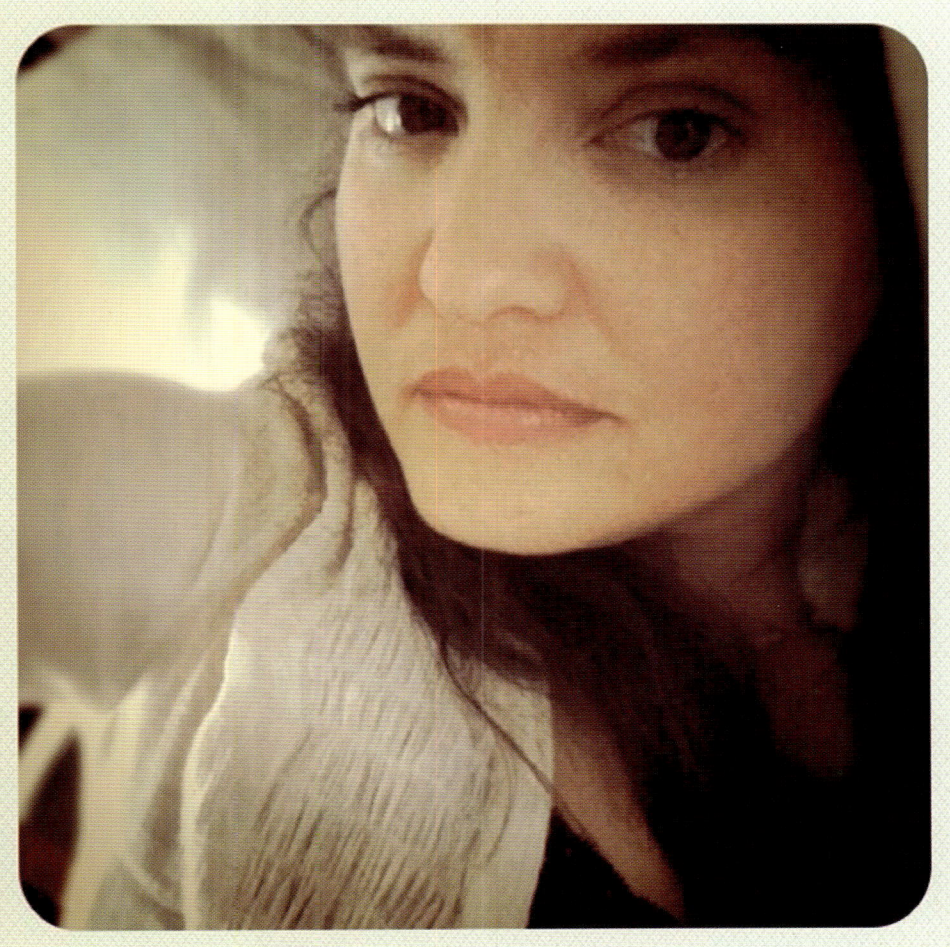

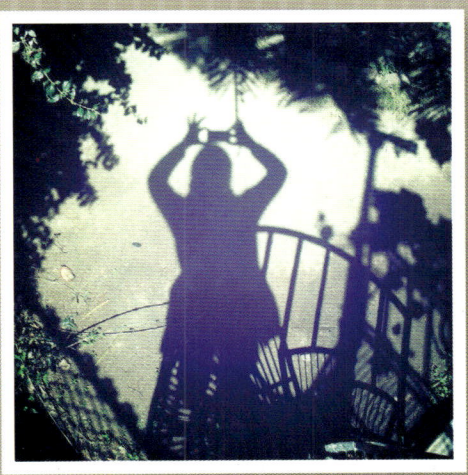

🔴 Jen shot this image from the rooftop of a building at Koseli School in Kathmandu, Nepal as an attempt to anchor her presence without being physically connected to the ground. "I like the illusion of how this image makes me look like I'm falling. It's unclear where I'm standing. I look displaced."

🔴 Jen had been awake all night preparing a speech in her hotel room and quickly snapped this portrait in the morning to see how she might look to the 100-person audience awaiting her presence. "I was feeling tired, edgy, and unsure about myself, but seeing this image showed me that I looked really soft and lovely, in spite of how I was feeling on the inside. It helped me feel more confident in myself."

"I like the illusion of how this image makes me look like I'm falling."

Turn the Focus on Yourself:
Jen Lemen

"Sometimes your self-portrait
is like a message in a bottle."

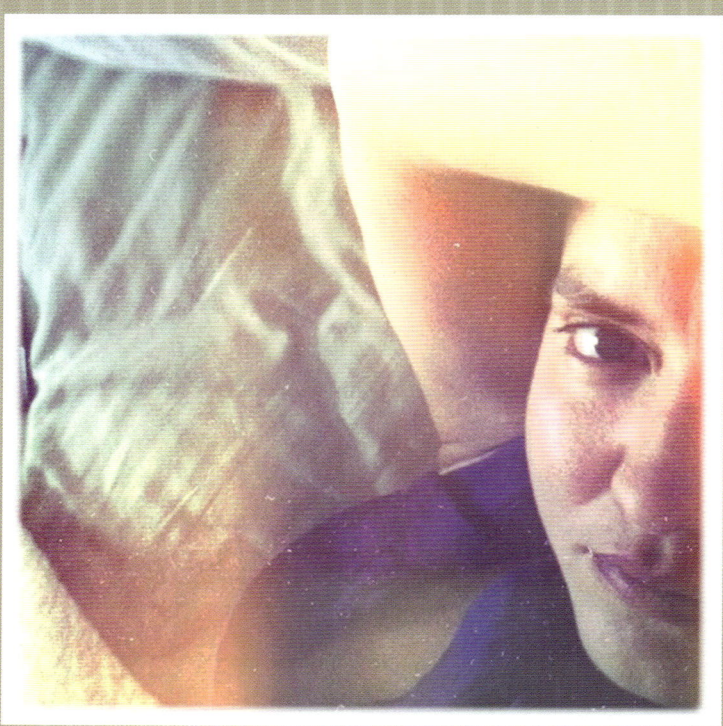

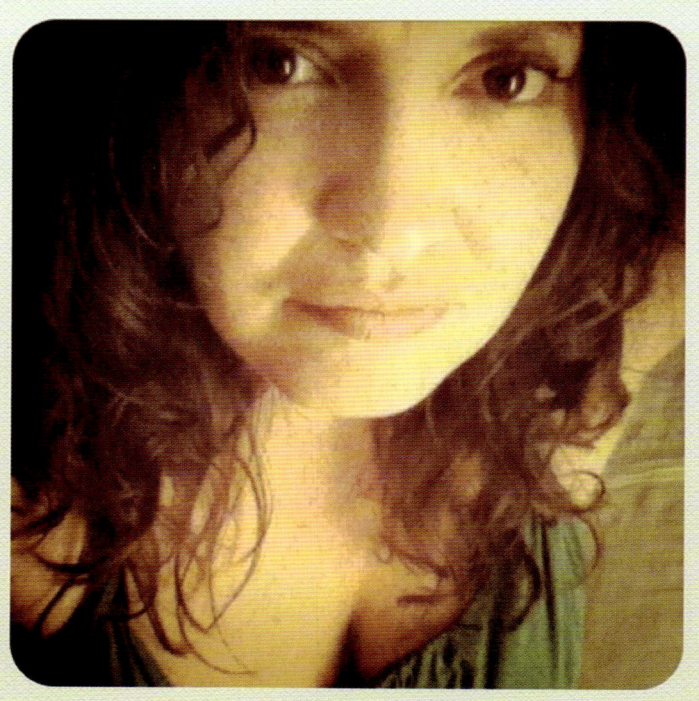

Following Jen's separation from her husband, she felt isolated and very conscious of the fact that there was no one to see her in the morning. "I rolled over and took a series of images of myself in bed one morning to see if I could still look sexy without being overly suggestive." She was pleasantly surprised.

"I had gone out to dinner with someone, but I really wished my date had been with someone else. So I shot this image and shared it on Twitter. Sometimes your self-portrait is like a message in a bottle. The message for this one was 'It could have been you.'"

"I like that the image feels soft and feminine without being overly sensual."

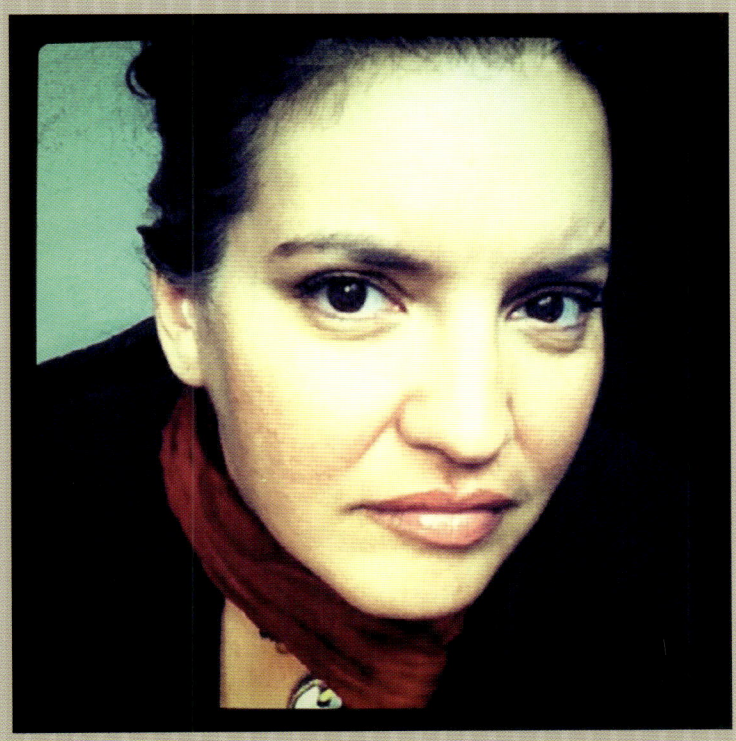

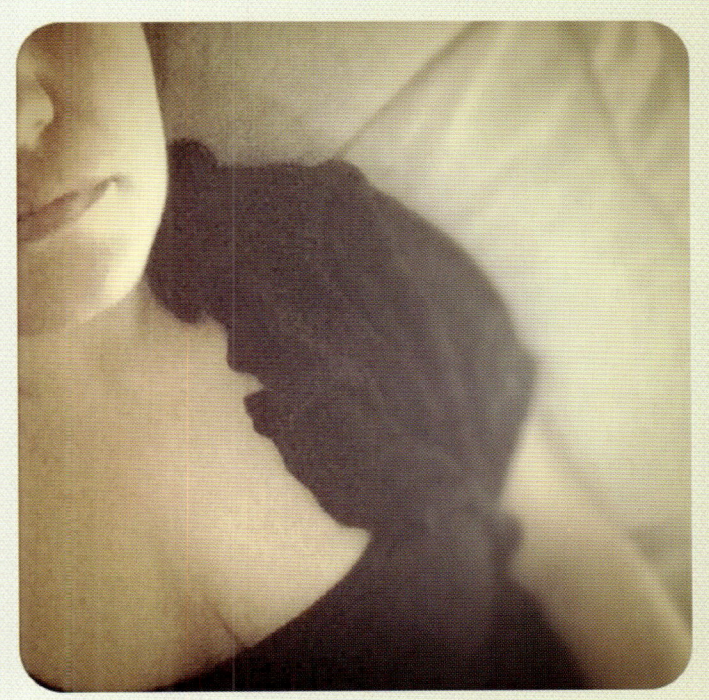

Jen made this image the morning after she revealed a secret to a new friend. "In this moment, I didn't know if our exchange was going to change our friendship or not, so I was just hanging in the wait, wondering what might happen." Jen wrapped this red scarf tightly around her neck as a tangible protection mechanism—to help keep her from feeling overexposed.

"I made this image to document a conscious portrait of my body as a way of learning to accept and appreciate my body for the way it is." Jen chose to exclude her face from the image, as it made her feel less vulnerable. "I like that the image feels soft and feminine without being overly sensual."

Turn the Focus on Yourself:
Jen Lemen

"Sunflowers are really simple with complex texture when you look at them closely . . . It's a form of self-portraiture for me."

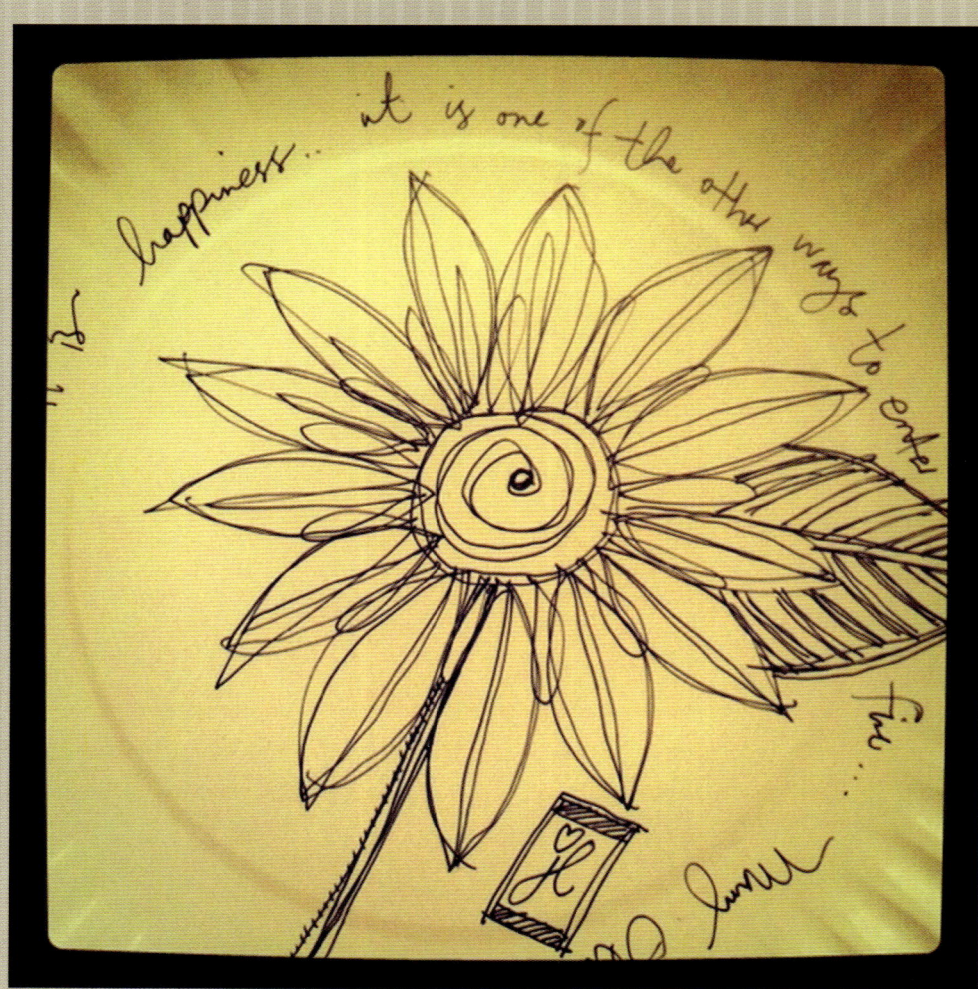

Jen's been drawing sunflowers for as long as she can remember, in books and on paper, napkins, and paper plates. "I've sketched thousands of them. Sunflowers are really simple with complex texture when you look at them closely. I love the versatility of them. They can be tall and strong. You can cut them down and put them on the table. You can eat them. You can feed the seeds to the birds. It's a form of self-portraiture for me."

"When you look at it closely, there's so much to see. As a symbol, it feels like an extension of me."

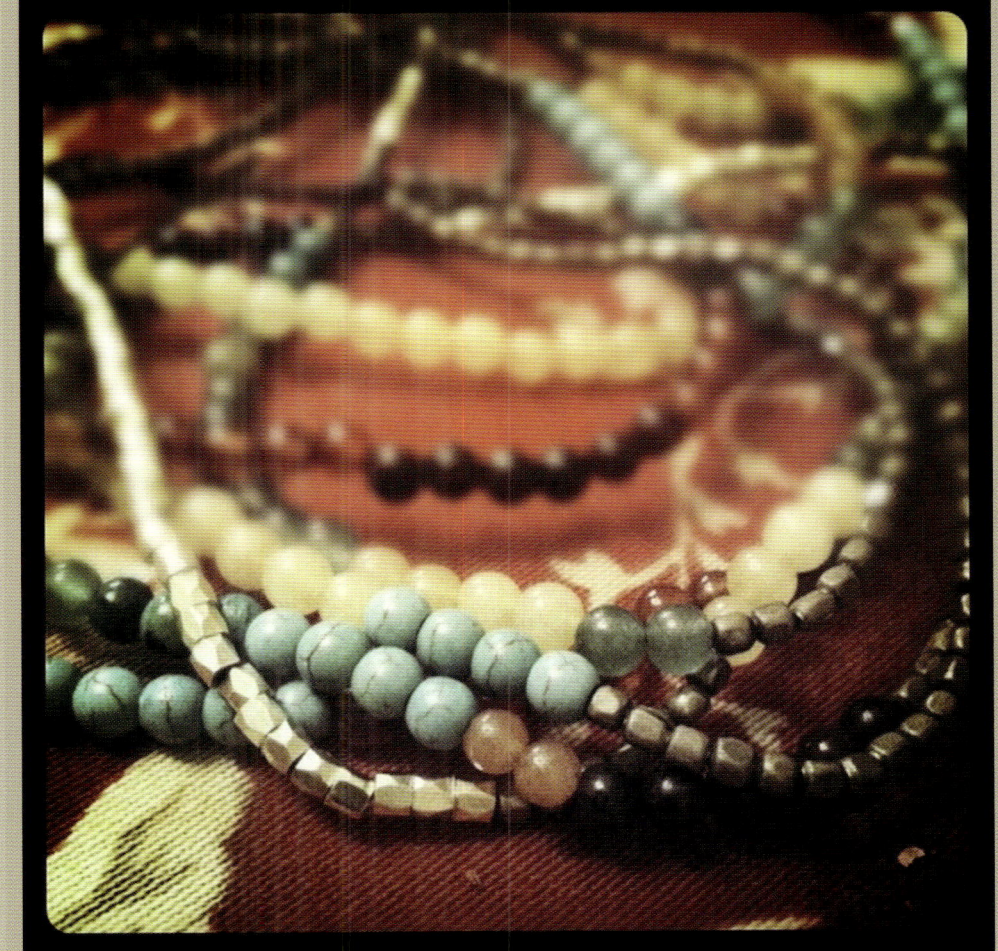

Jen is known for her eclectic accessory collection acquired piece by piece from faraway lands—bangles from Rwanda and Nepal, and handmade necklaces and scarves from Tanzania, Zanzibar, and Uganda. "I found this necklace in Oregon. The design doesn't even really make sense, but it's such an intricate mix of beads and stones and colors. When you look at it closely, there's so much to see. As a symbol, it feels like an extension of me."

Hunt for Clues to Help Reveal Your Story

Choosing to notice and incorporate details such as interesting physical elements of the environment within your documentary images can reveal subtle clues about your subject, offer context for the action, and immerse the viewer more fully within the story of your moment. Using a wide-angle lens (14–30mm range) to expose more of the setting, you can follow your subject while keeping a keen eye on changes that may occur in the background. Is there a spontaneous gesture, intriguing sign, or curious reflection in the window behind your subject that lends visual intrigue, humor, or irony to the moment? Does a cluttered room or an unopened bottle of orange Fanta on the table convey something about your subject?

To demonstrate the value of details, let's conduct an experiment. Study the images in this section, look for clues, and craft a story for the image. As you look at each image, ask yourself these questions:

- What's happening in the image?
- Who are the characters and what do you assume about them?
- Where is the setting and why is it significant or insignificant?
- How does the image make you feel?
- What visual clues did you use to help craft your story?

When you're finished, turn to the end of this section to reveal the truth behind each image, and ask yourself these questions:

- Did the details within the images provide accurate clues or distort your impressions?
- Which details proved to be most valuable in crafting your assumptions about the image?
- What details did you miss?

What's happening in the image?

Who are the characters and what do you assume about them?

Where is the setting and why is it significant or insignificant?

How does the image make you feel?

What visual clues did you use to help craft your story?

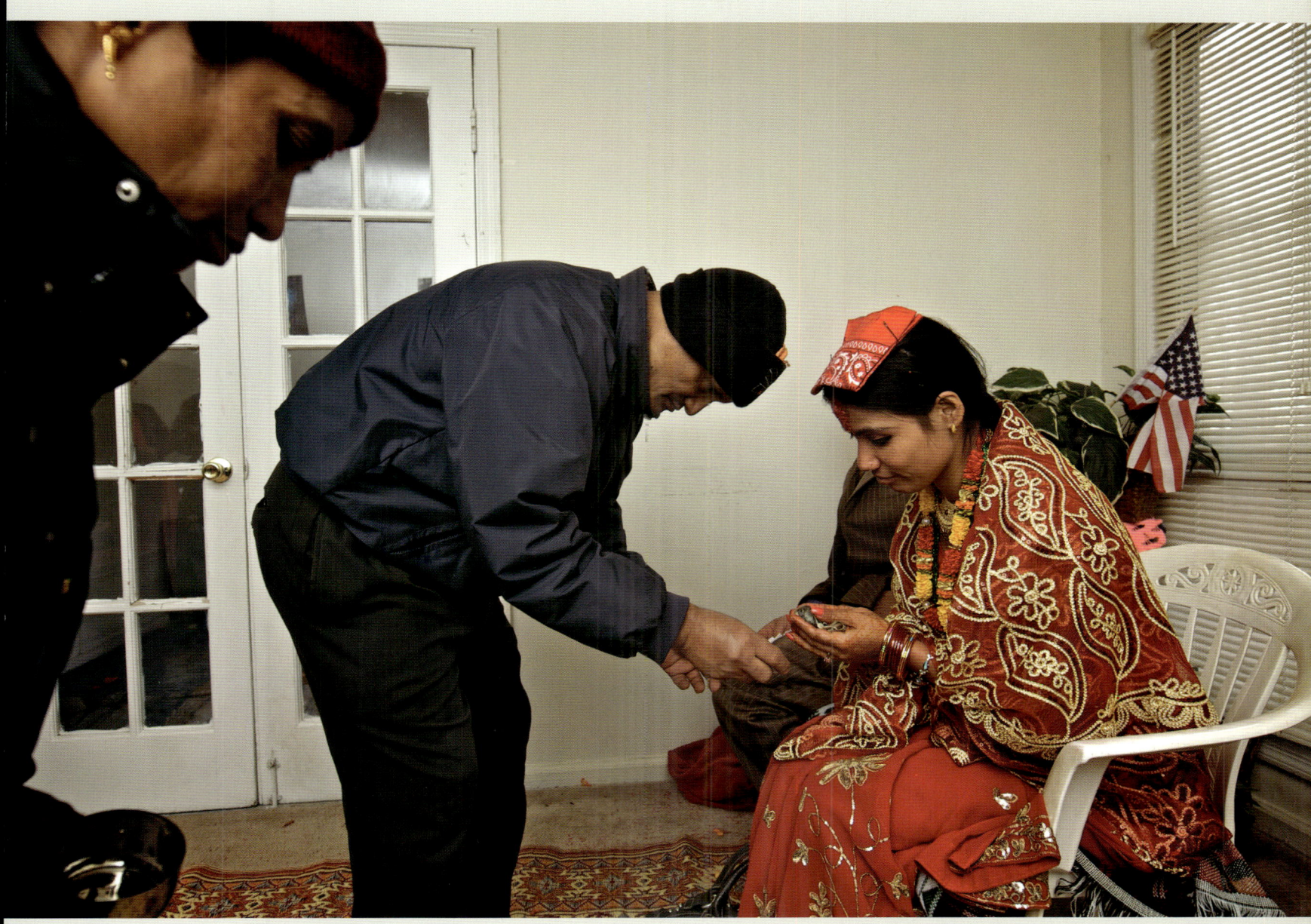

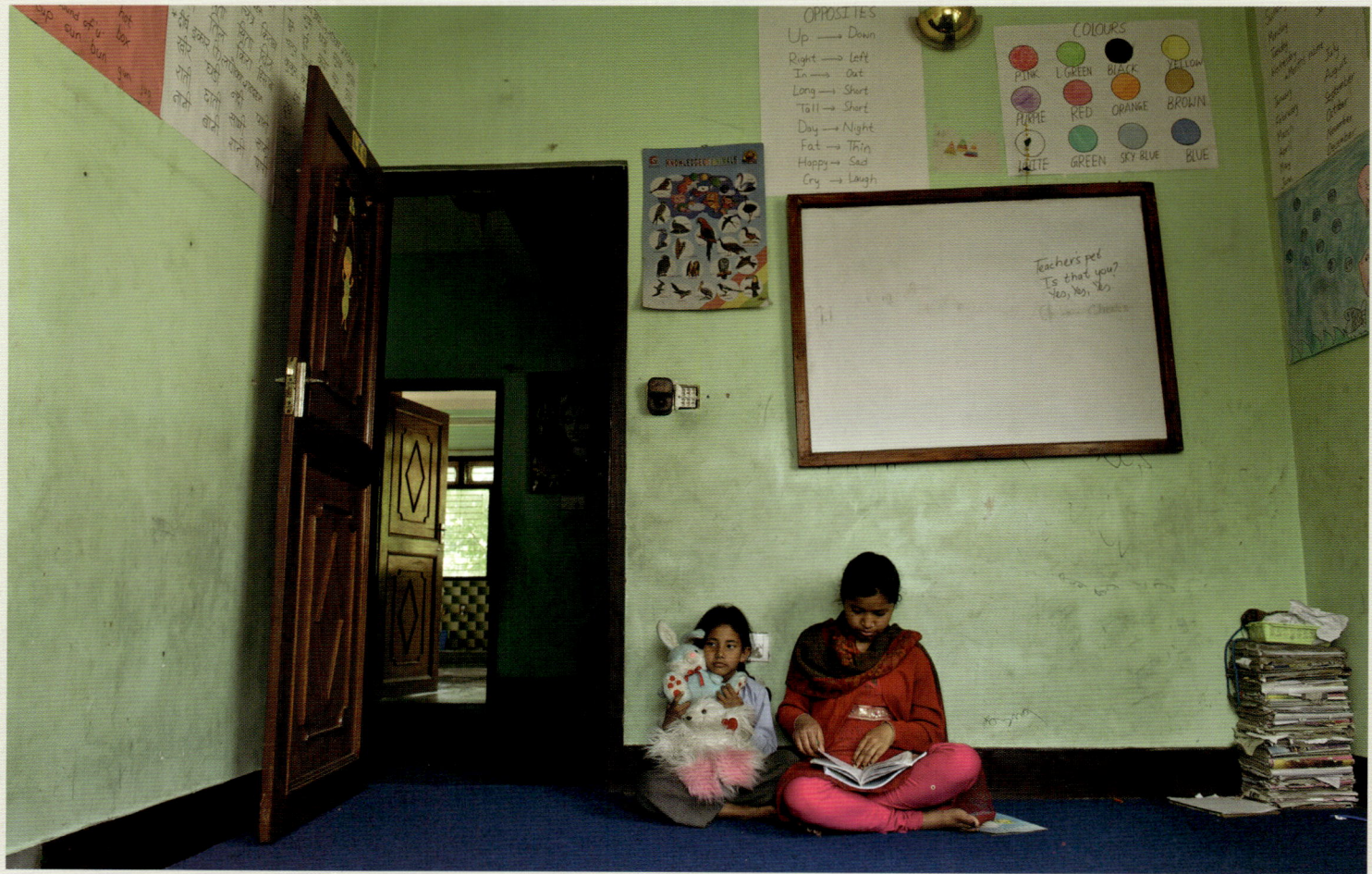

◐ What's happening in the image?

◐ Who are the characters and what do you assume about them?

◐ Where is the setting and why is it significant or insignificant?

◐ How does the image make you feel?

◐ What visual clues did you use to help craft your story?

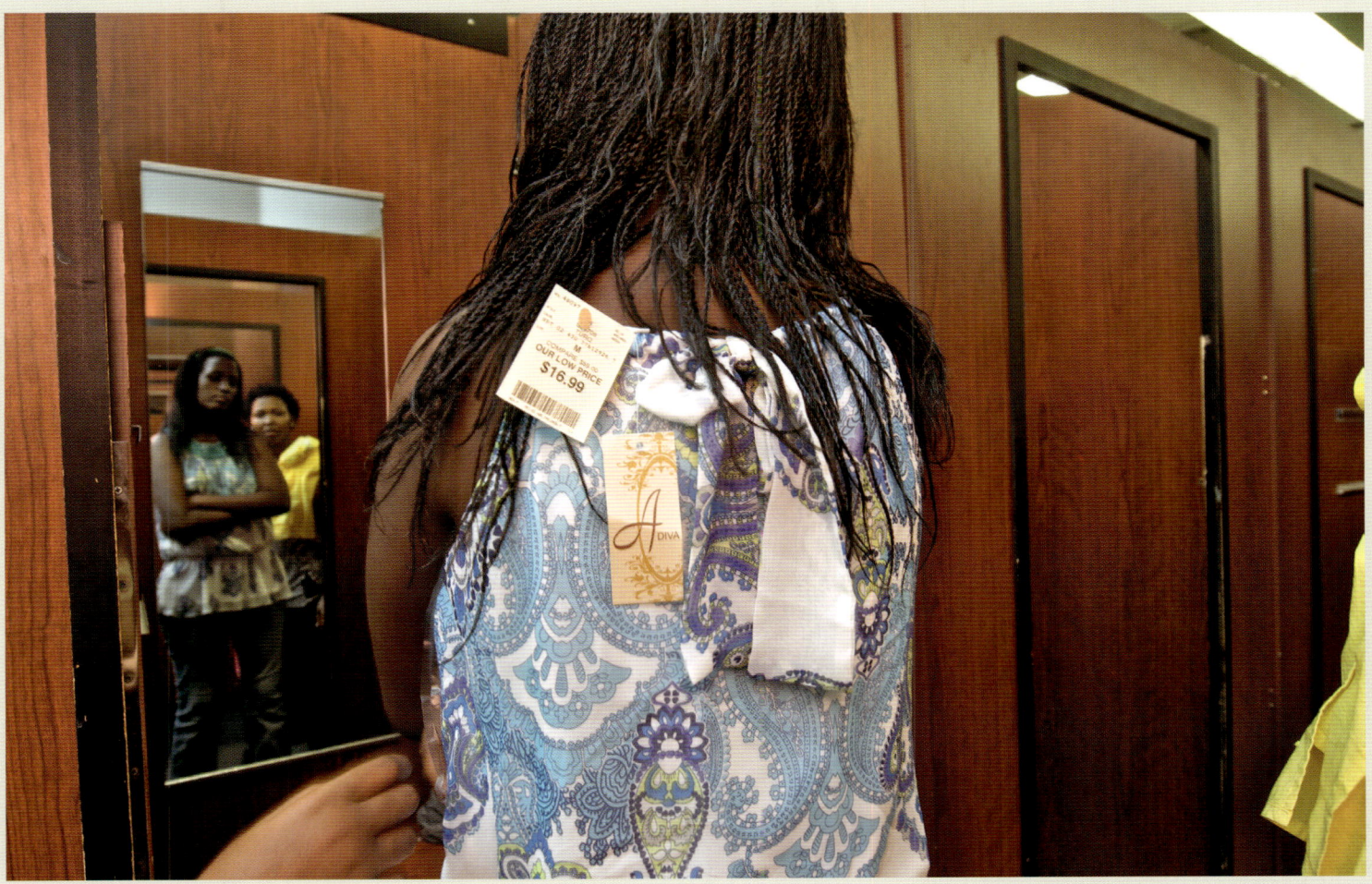

What's happening in the image?

....

....

....

....

Who are the characters and what do you assume about them?

....

....

....

....

Where is the setting and why is it significant or insignificant?

....

....

How does the image make you feel?

....

....

....

What visual clues did you use to help craft your story?

....

....

....

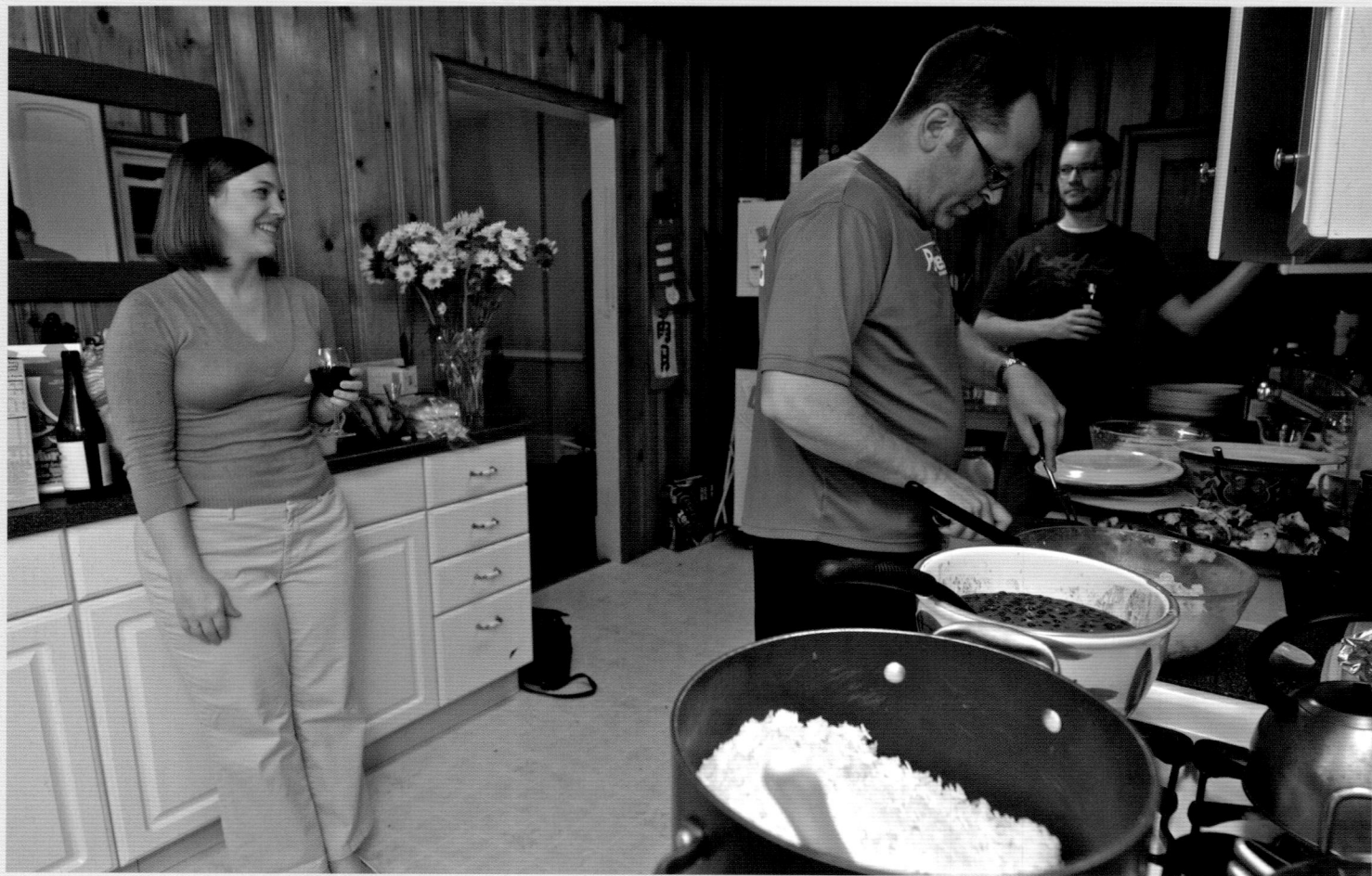

◉ What's happening in the image?

....

....

....

....

◉ Who are the characters and what do you assume about them?

....

....

....

....

◉ Where is the setting and why is it significant or insignificant?

....

....

◉ How does the image make you feel?

....

....

◉ What visual clues did you use to help craft your story?

....

....

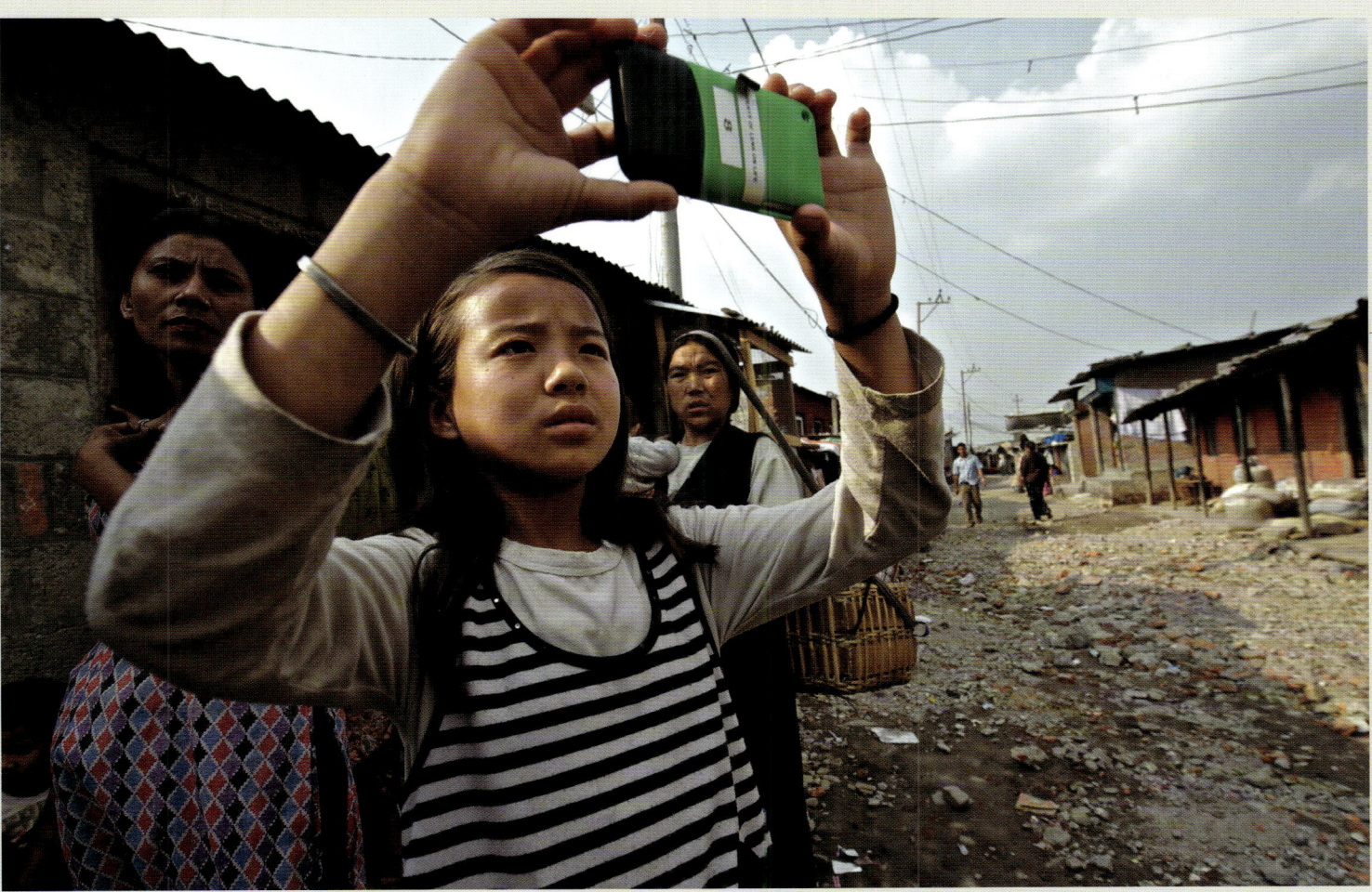

What's happening in the image?

Where is the setting and why is it significant or insignificant?

How does the image make you feel?

Who are the characters and what do you assume about them?

What visual clues did you use to help craft your story?

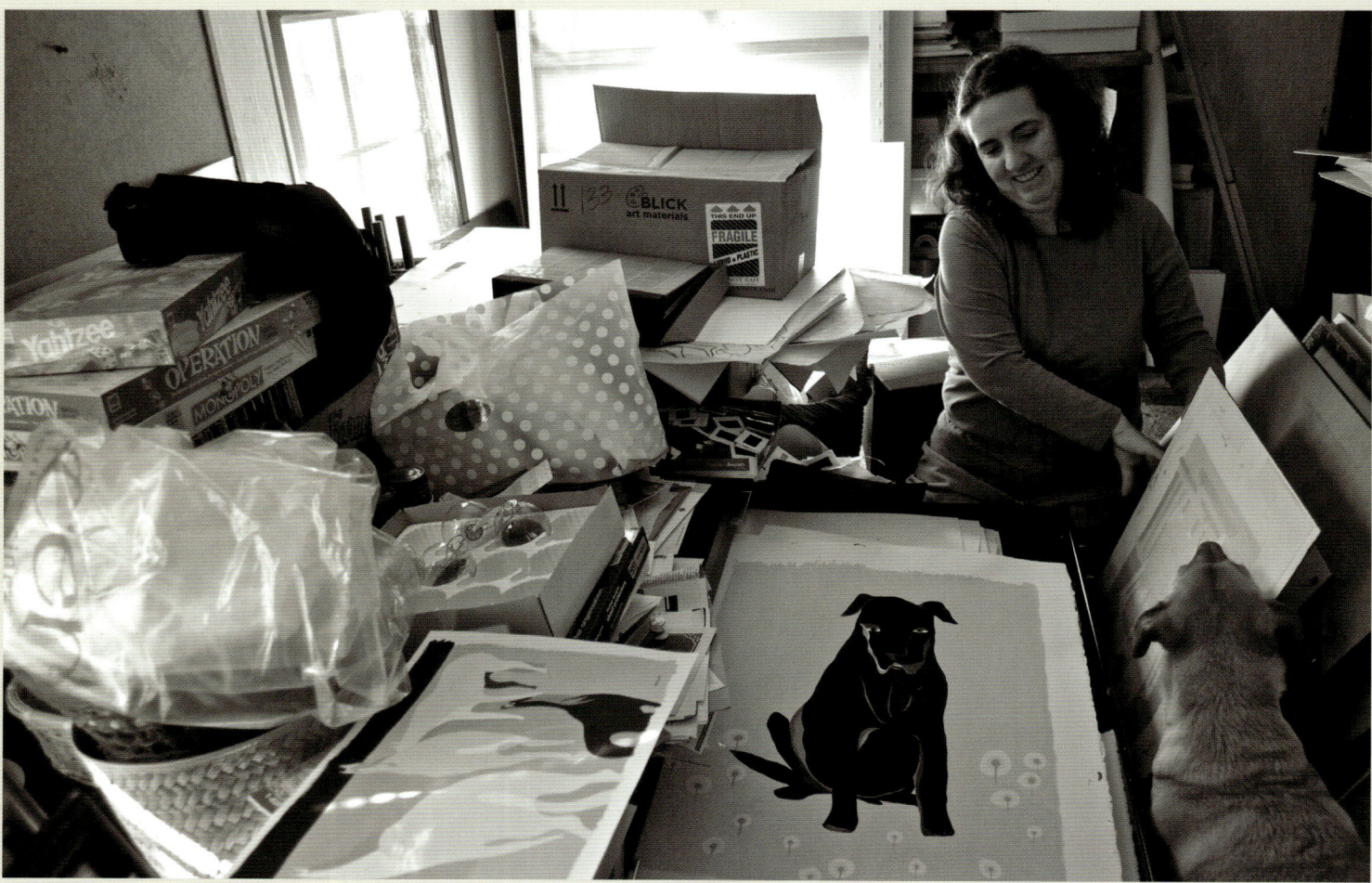

What's happening in the image?

....

....

....

....

Who are the characters and what do you assume about them?

....

....

....

Where is the setting and why is it significant or insignificant?

....

....

How does the image make you feel?

....

....

What visual clues did you use to help craft your story?

....

....

....

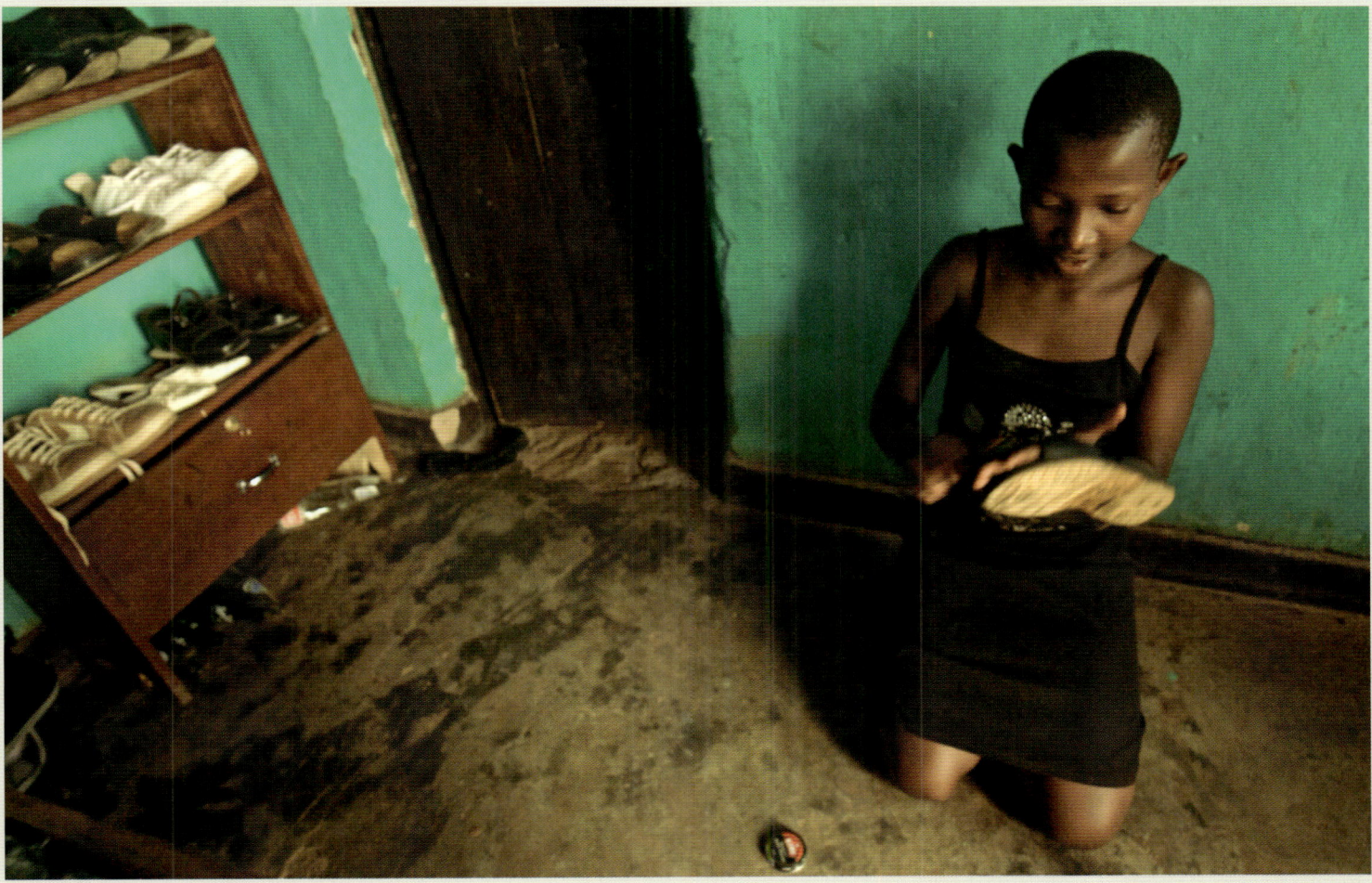

What's happening in the image?

Who are the characters and what do you assume about them?

Where is the setting and why is it significant or insignificant?

How does the image make you feel?

What visual clues did you use to help craft your story?

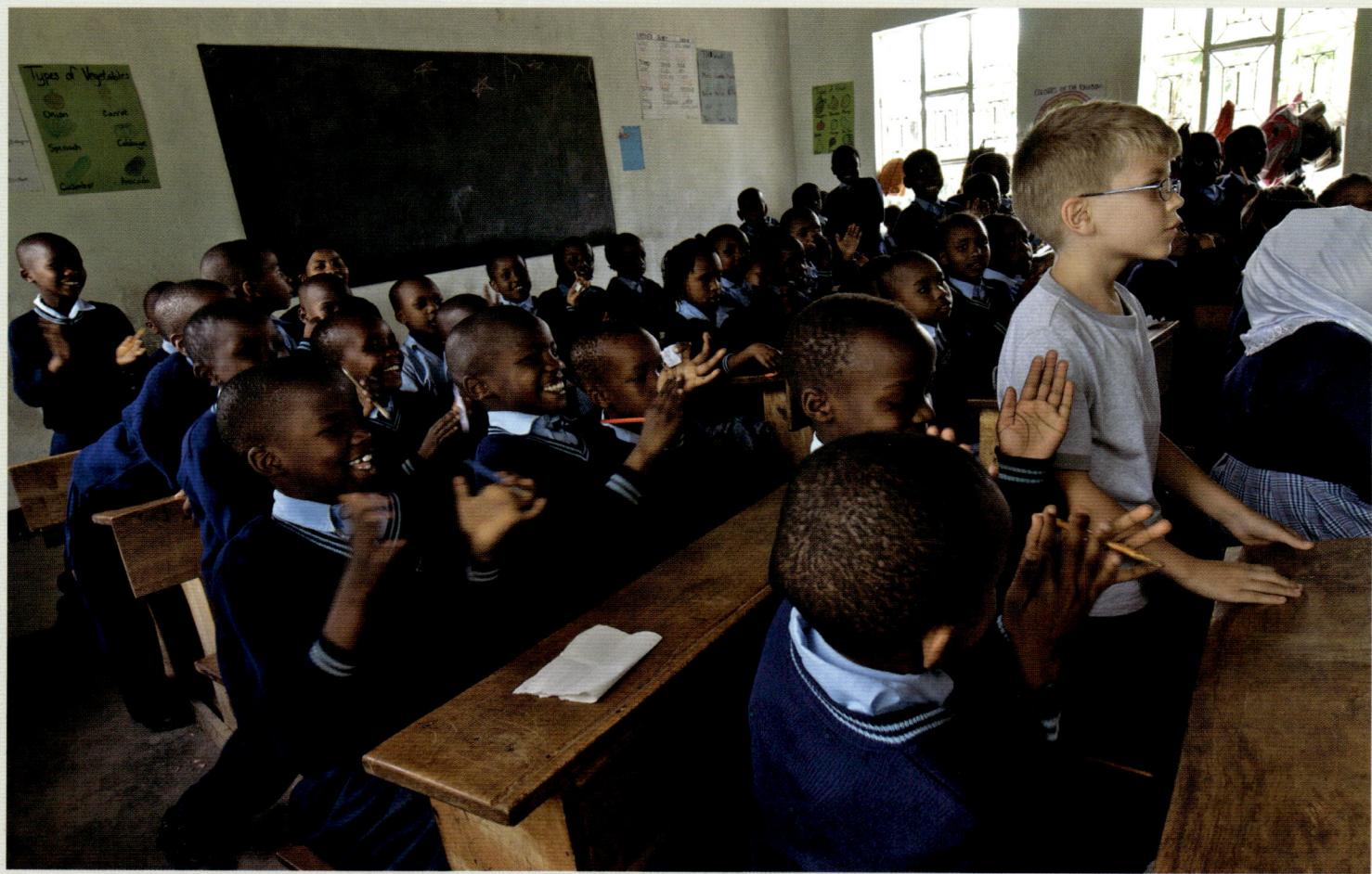

❂ What's happening in the image?

❂ Who are the characters and what do you assume about them?

❂ Where is the setting and why is it significant or insignificant?

❂ How does the image make you feel?

❂ What visual clues did you use to help craft your story?

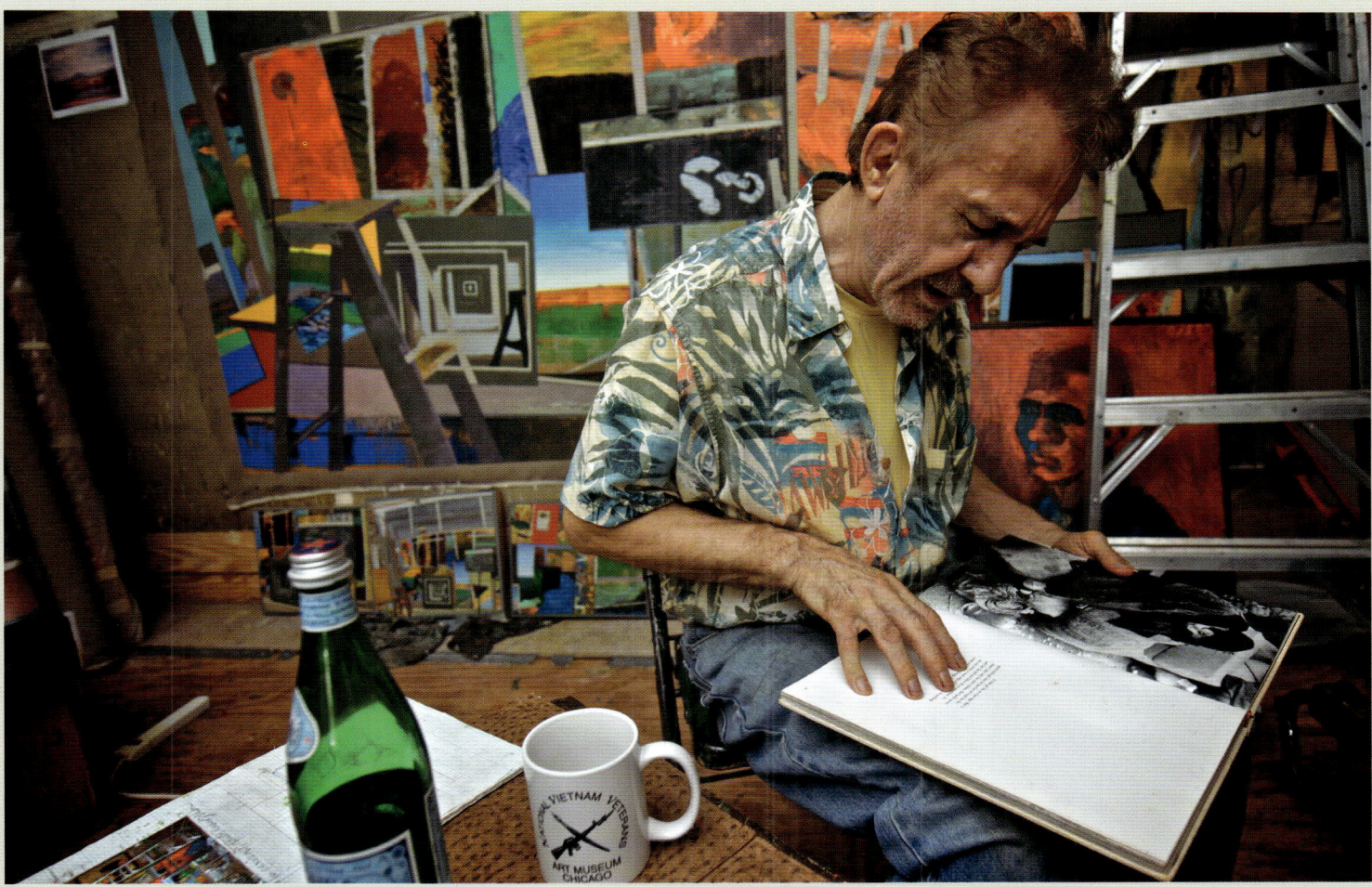

◉ What's happening in the image?

◉ Who are the characters and what do you assume about them?

◉ Where is the setting and why is it significant or insignificant?

◉ How does the image make you feel?

◉ What visual clues did you use to help craft your story?

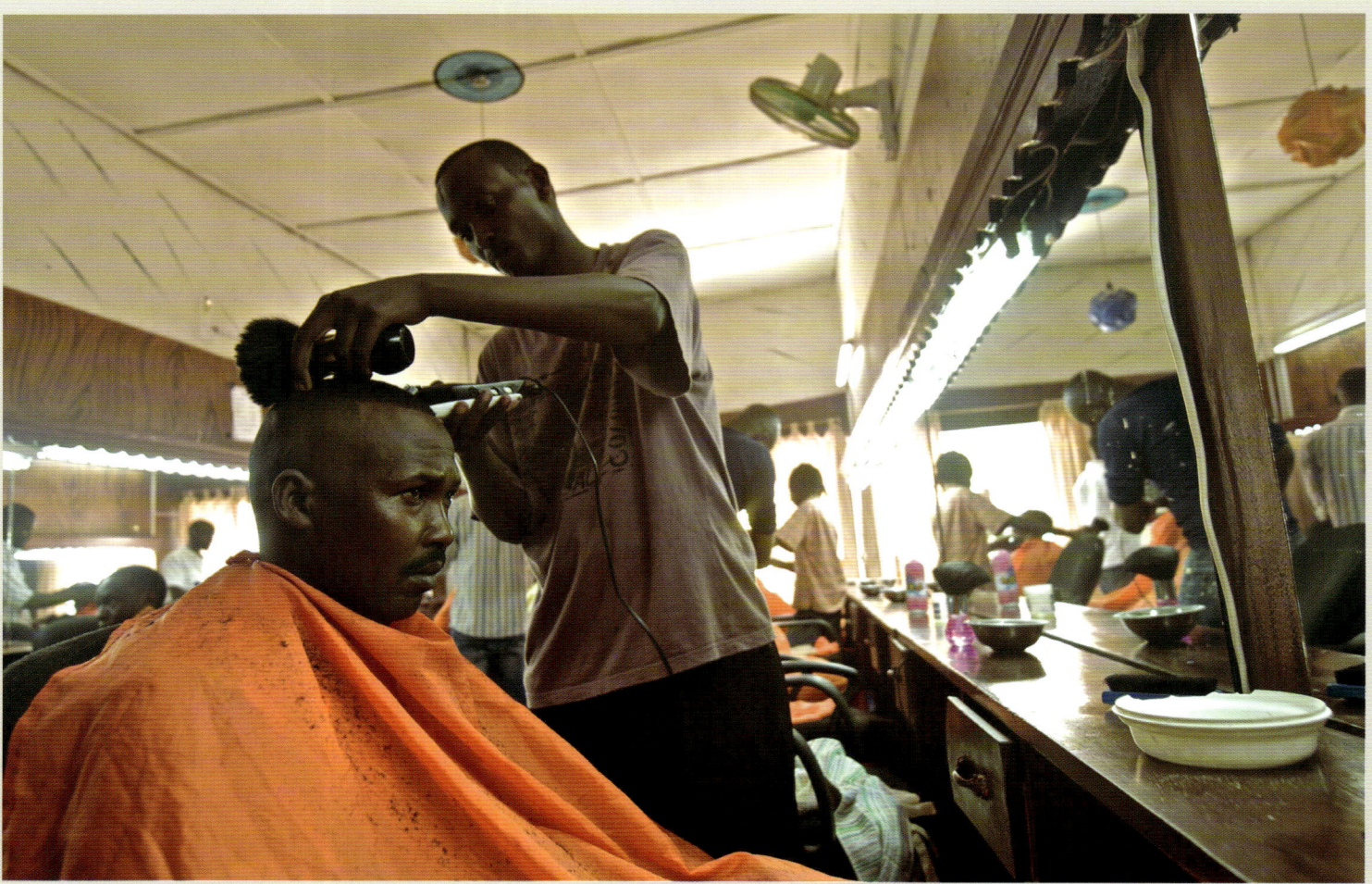

◉ What's happening in the image?

◉ Where is the setting and why is it significant or insignificant?

◉ How does the image make you feel?

◉ Who are the characters and what do you assume about them?

◉ What visual clues did you use to help craft your story?

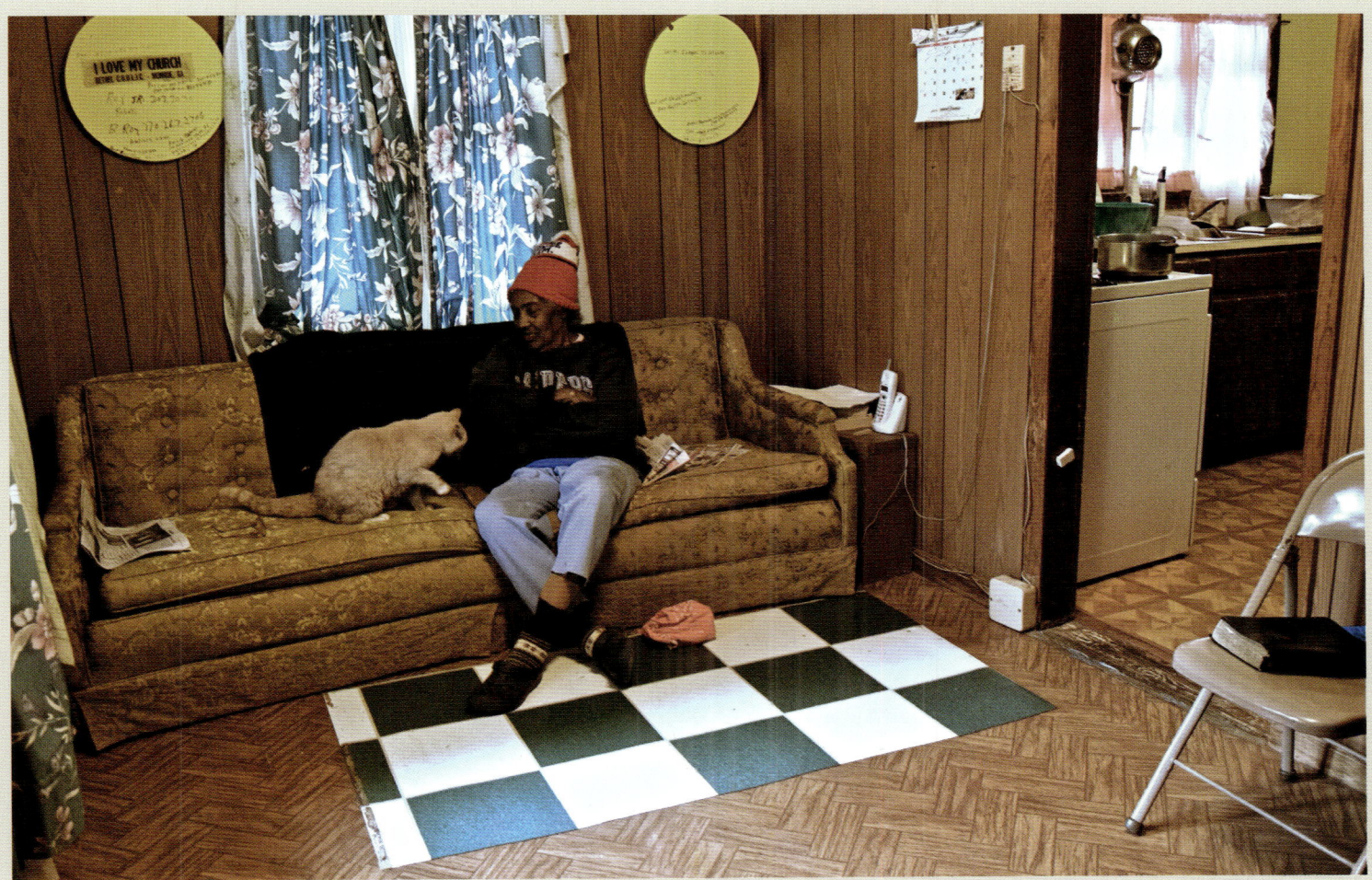

◉ What's happening in the image?

◉ Who are the characters and what do you assume about them?

◉ Where is the setting and why is it significant or insignificant?

◉ How does the image make you feel?

◉ What visual clues did you use to help craft your story?

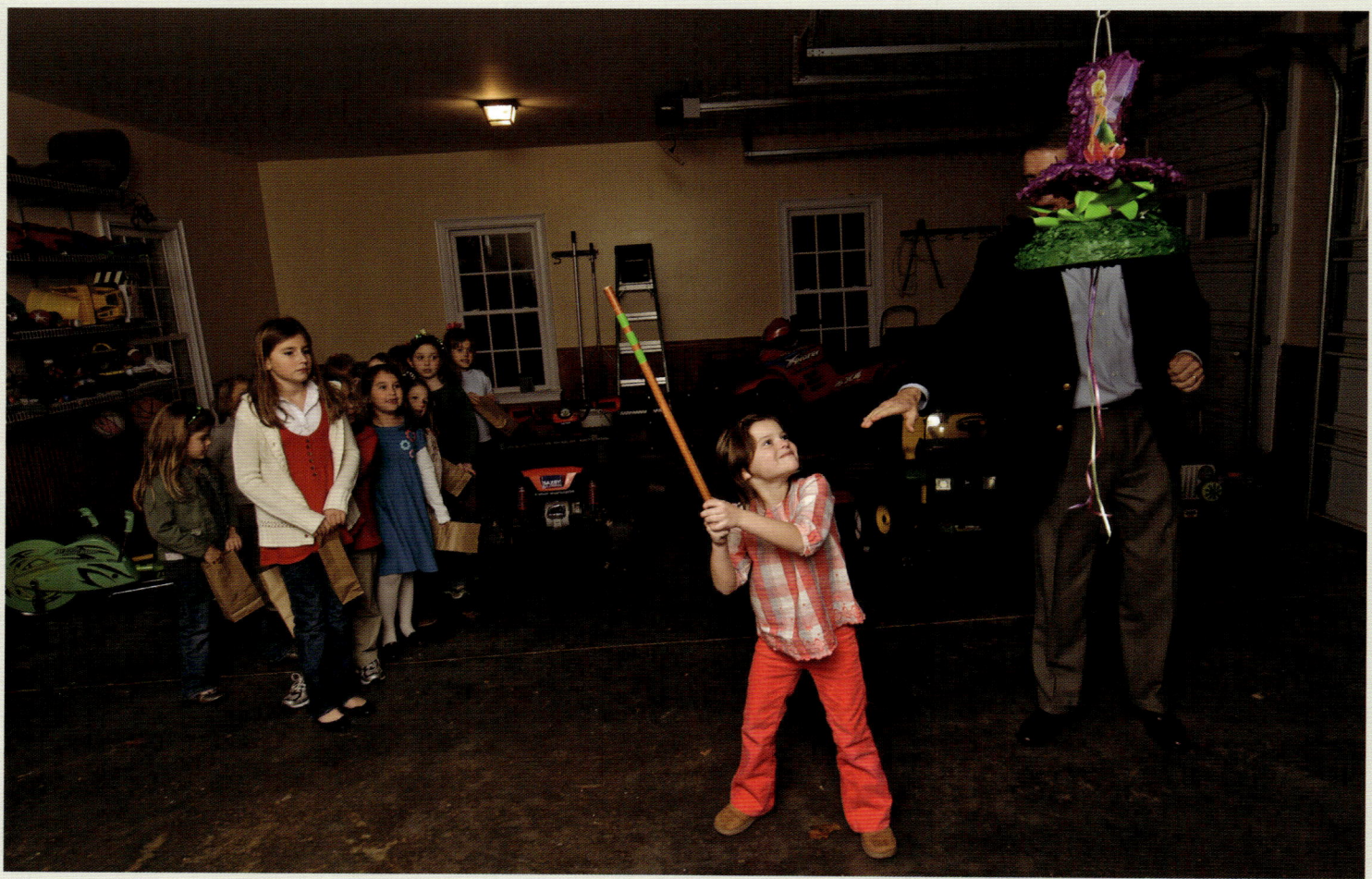

🔅 What's happening in the image?

🔅 Who are the characters and what do you assume about them?

🔅 Where is the setting and why is it significant or insignificant?

🔅 How does the image make you feel?

🔅 What visual clues did you use to help craft your story?

Hunt for Clues to Help Reveal Your Story

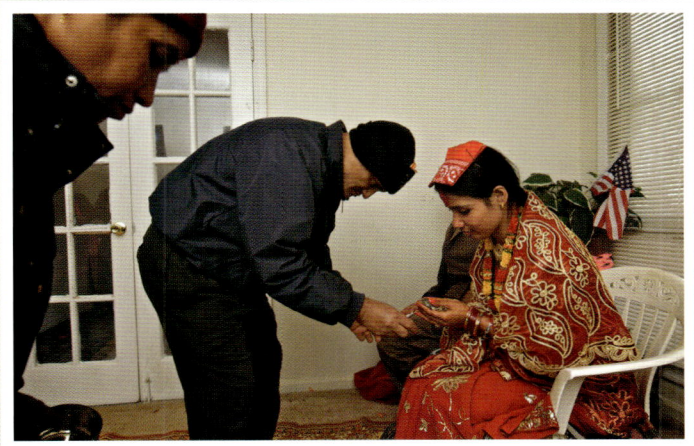

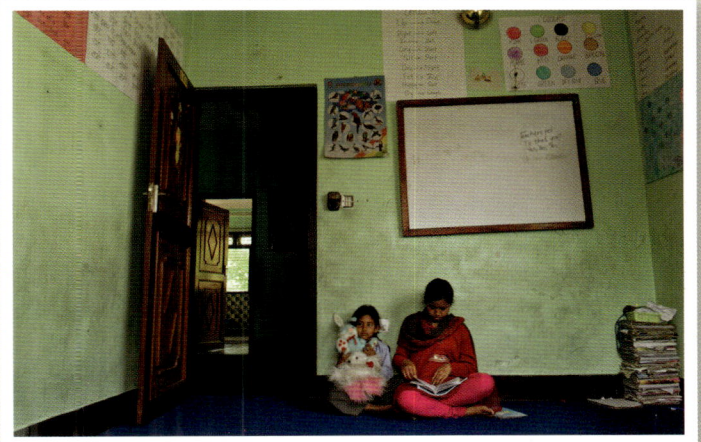

On a cold winter afternoon, a Bhutanese bride sits beside her groom (a young man she met for the first time that day, as their marriage had been arranged by their parents) in a modest, unheated apartment in Atlanta, Georgia—home to a growing community of Bhutanese refugees from Nepal rebuilding their lives in America. Here, the bride's father and mother offer their blessings, gifts, and a formal farewell to their daughter, as by Bhutanese custom she must leave them to live with her new husband and his family. Just minutes after this image was made, the bride and groom hopped up on the backs of two attendees (a Bhutanese wedding tradition) and left through the front door to begin their new life together.

Koseli School, founded by Renu Shah Bagaria, was created to provide a free education for children living in the slums of Kathmandu, Nepal. Most of these children's parents were unable to pay the modest tuition required by public schools. Following their morning lessons and a hearty lunch of dal-bhat, children have some free time to read and play before resuming their studies. Here, student Puja K.C. enjoys quiet time with a pet from the school's collection and her teacher, Smriti B.C.

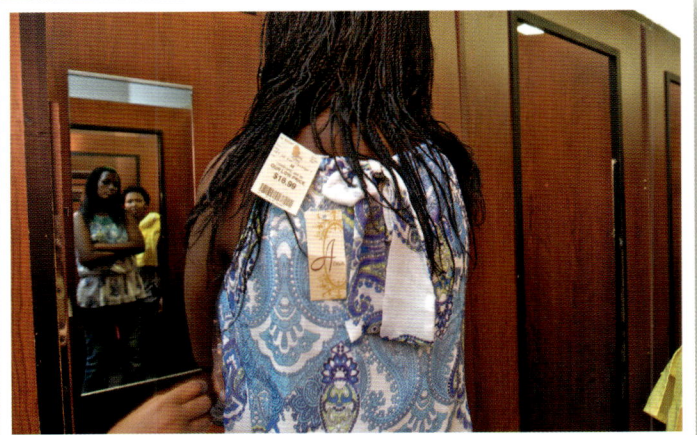

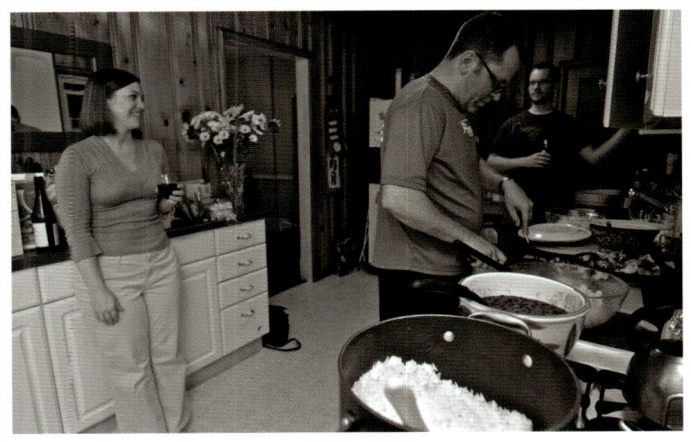

Fifteen-year-old Grace had just arrived to the United States from Rwanda to live with her mother, Odette, after four years of separation. A fashion-conscious Odette was eager to take a self-conscious Grace shopping for clothes, and led her through several budget department stores to scan racks of tops and dresses to craft her daughter's new wardrobe. Odette picked this one.

Dave Lemen did the majority of the cooking that night for a spontaneous gathering with close friends and neighbors in the Lemen house, affectionately known as "the commune." I had just learned that friends Jess and Nick had recently announced their engagement. You could feel their heat.

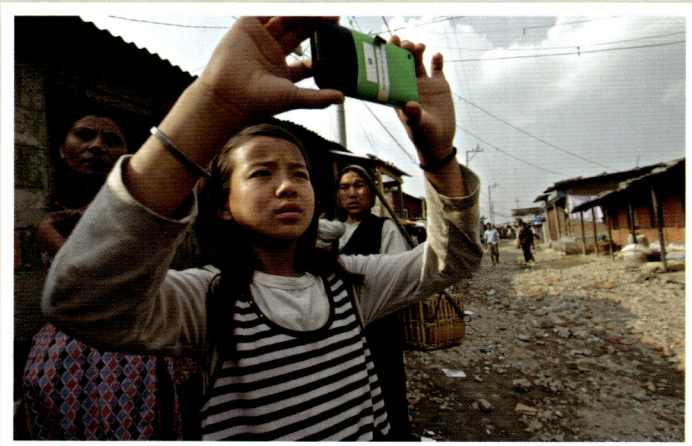

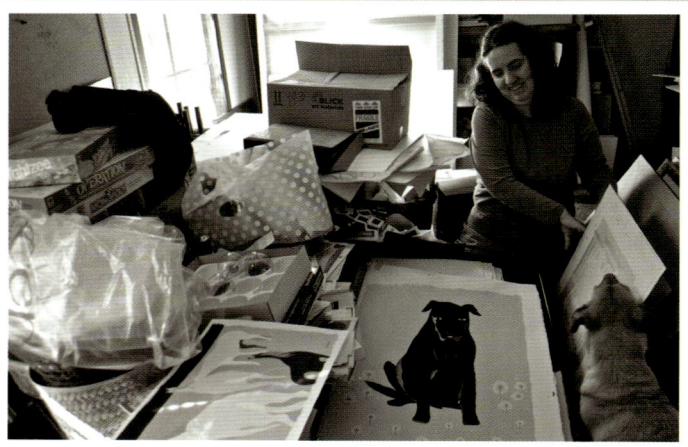

Pinky is a student at Koseli School in Kathmandu, Nepal and one of the first eight Lens on Life program participants. Here, using an iPhone camera donated by Lens on Life supporters, she documents an exterior view of her home in Jadibuti, while neighbors watch curiously.

Aside from being one of the most creative people I know, artist Melanie Eberhardt lives a colorful life in a small trailer on four acres of land at the end of the tire tracks, off a gravel road. She shares this space with an ever-growing collection of one-stray pets. Here, Mel reveals a painting she made of Alex, a dog she loved for many years, as his canine successor Lucky nudges his way toward his master. Mel rescued Lucky from an abandoned pen shortly after Alex's death. He rarely leaves her side.

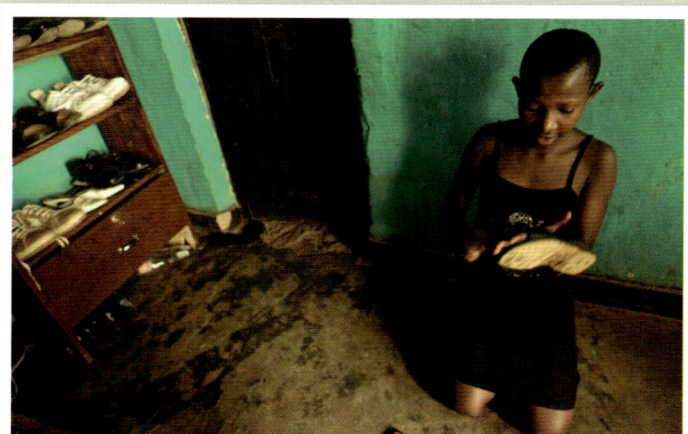

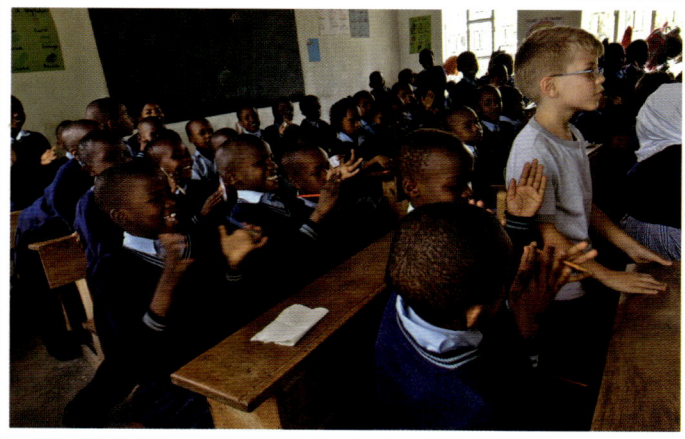

During a visit to Kigali, Rwanda, I spent the morning at my friend Innocent's home. After breakfast, his daughter, Muhawe, went to work to shine the family's shoes on the floor of their living room—a task that she did happily and without complaint.

My "Picture Hope" project partner, Jen Lemen, her two children, and I arrived at Shepherds Junior School in Arusha, Tanzania to document the students' first experience with computers and the Internet thanks to support from U.S.-based non-profit organization Epic Change. Jen's son, Carter, joined classmates his age in an English lesson on our second day of the visit. Carter observed the rhythm of the class for some time before raising his hand and standing to answer the teacher's question. A correct answer met with spontaneous applause from his new friends.

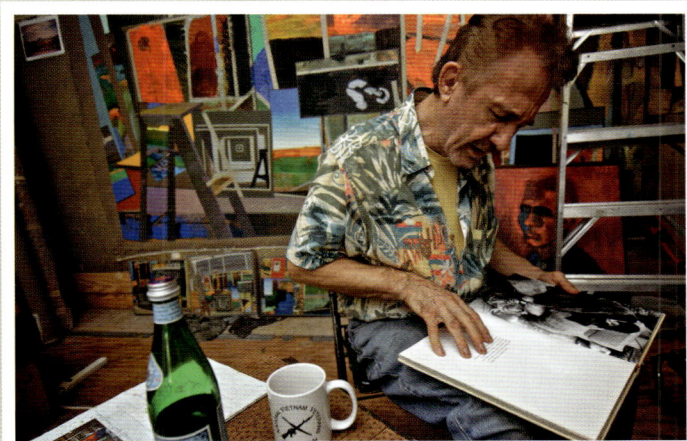

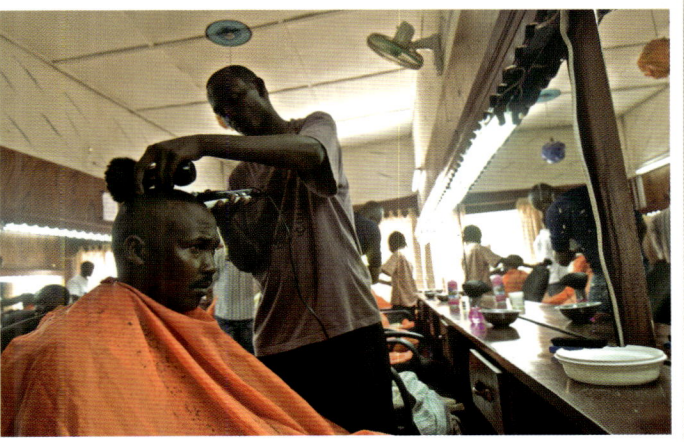

I sit in painter Richard Olsen's studio out behind his house and listen to his animated stories about flying planes during the Vietnam War, his escapades as a young painter and mixed media artist in Chicago, Illinois after the war, and the challenges he faced in funneling his creativity within the confines of a career as a university art professor in Athens, Georgia. Olsen (known affectionately as Ollie by his students, peers, and friends) shares his thoughts with intensity, punctuating them with animated hand gestures, expressions, and a booming laugh. Here, he pauses from his painting for a few moments to share his favorite quote from war photographer Robert Capa: "If your pictures aren't good enough, you aren't close enough." I leaned in.

I made this image of my friend Innocent at the barbershop in the bustling Remera district of Kigali, Rwanda. For several years, I've had a desire to create a series of images in barbershops across the American South—to capture this timeless experience shared by men of all ages, races, shapes, sizes, and statuses. While I anticipated that the visual details and clientele would vary in each barbershop, I felt certain that I would discover more of the same and less of the different. As I stood here making this image thousands of miles away from my home, I was convinced of it.

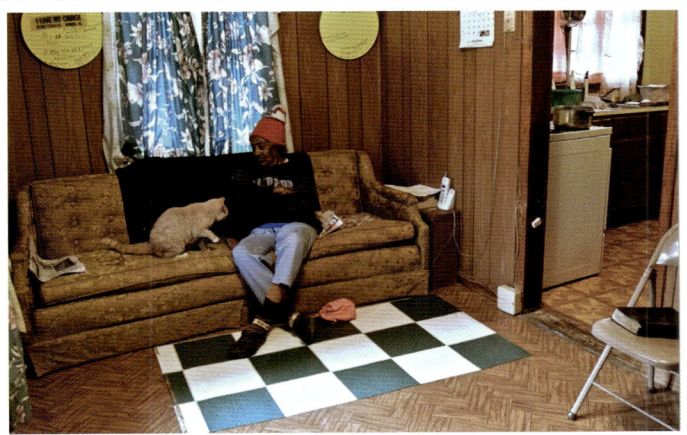

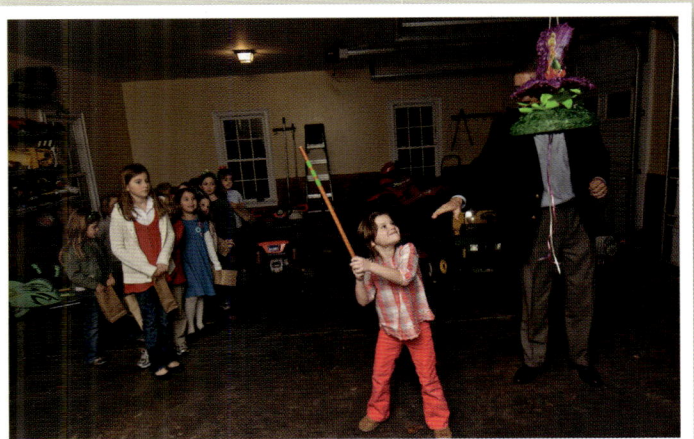

Imogene was a companion in my family's life for many years before she chose to leave the home she owned and move into a nursing home. She anchored the center of the kitchen at family holiday gatherings—cooking butter beans and cornbread, singing hymns as she washed the silver, and tending to the children. Imogene didn't have children of her own, but mothered many with so much love, including a wide array of stray dogs and cats that found a home in her yard. "It don't matter what color they are," she'd say.

For our birthday parties, my mom would plan a scavenger hunt in and around the house, and we'd play organized games like pin-the-tail-on-the-donkey and musical chairs. We'd eat homemade cake, open presents, and ultimately reach the climax of the party—the destruction of a colorful piñata with a broomstick. As children's birthday parties in the U.S. continue their trend toward extravagance, I've tried to stick to the homespun birthday experience. As far as eight-year-old fun goes for my daughter, some things never change.

Consider the Weight of Words in Framing Your Images

I sat on the concrete near the shallow end of the pool, taking pictures of my daughter jumping in the water with her seven-year-old cousin Lily Tate, who was visiting from South Africa. A very thoughtful and mature child, Lily Tate is not one to reveal her emotions. She defines boundaries, asks direct questions, states honest observations, reminds us of forgotten obligations, and makes succinct requests without hesitation.

"Take me," she said stepping into the viewfinder of my iPhone camera and leaning toward me. I clicked when she moved into place, and continued to make images of the girls performing. Later, as I flipped through the sequence of photographs, I kept coming back to the very still image of Lily Tate. Her subtle expression, awkward stance, and intense eye contact struck me. It was an honest portrayal of her, and my favorite image of the day. I processed the image in black and white using the Photo FX app to put visual emphasis on her form and expression, and sharpened it a bit. Satisfied with the result, I added a title (*"Take me," said Lily Tate of South Africa*) and published it in Instagram.

22 "likes" later, I noticed a comment appear below the image from a fellow iPhoneographer, Oliver Lange, known as "oggsie" on Instagram and Twitter. He wrote:

"I find this image and its title disturbing."

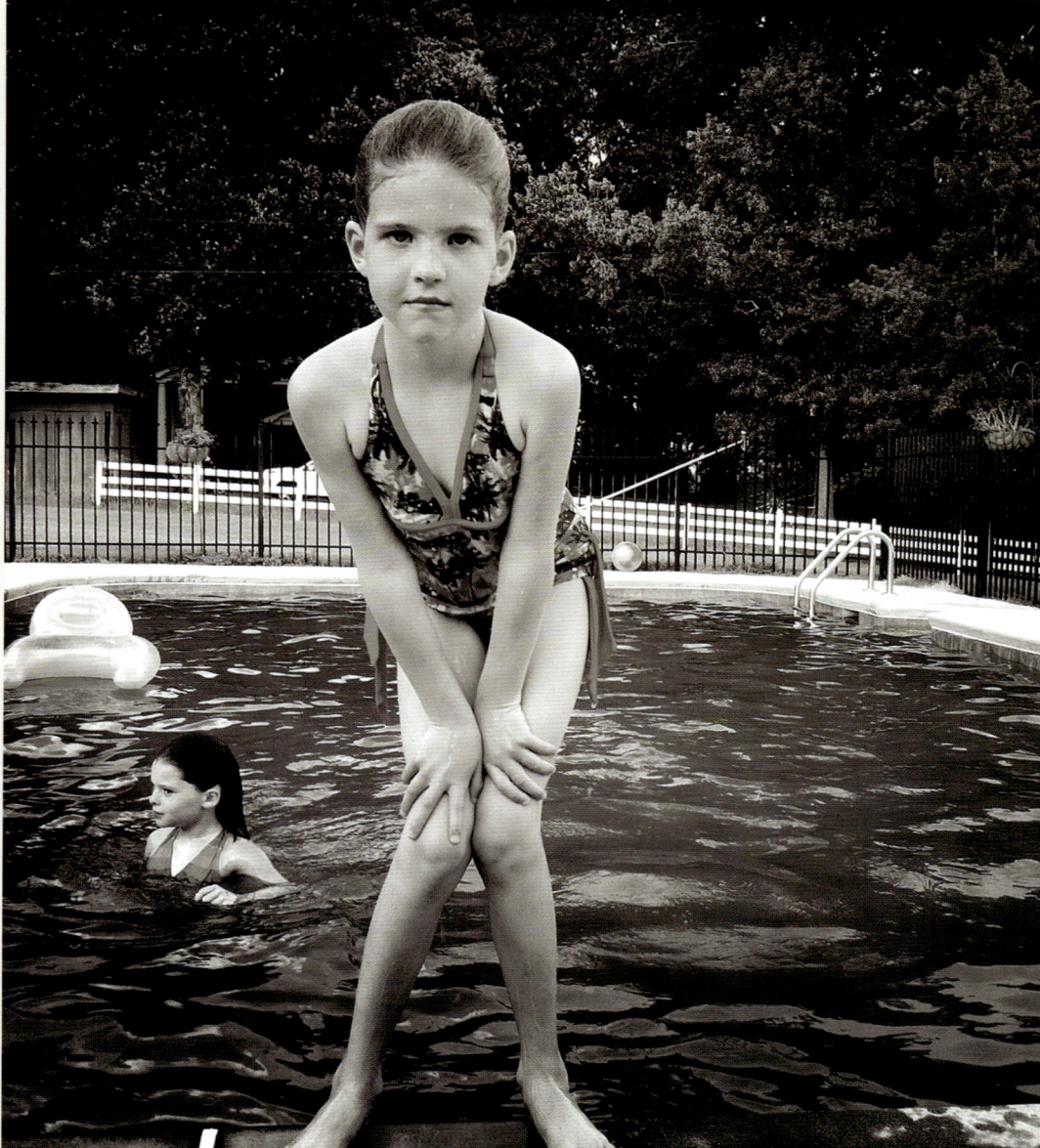

RIGHT: My niece posed before her jump into the pool.

"It's impossible to anticipate how each of your viewers will react to your images. They may not see what you see, or they may see something you don't see."

It was a record-scratch moment for me—the first time a viewer had ever shared a negative reaction to one of my images. I respect Oliver and the fact that he shared such an honest impression, so I detached the hurtful sting I felt from the words, unpublished the image, and made an attempt to step back and evaluate the image and its title without context. A viewer might wonder, "Who is this girl and why isn't she smiling? What could 'Take me' imply?" Stripping context from the image, Oliver's perspective came into focus.

It's impossible to anticipate how each of your viewers will react to your images. They may not see what you see, or they may see something you don't see. This doesn't mean that you should veer from your vision or hold back creatively from expressing yourself in an honest way; however, you should be sensitive to the fact that your images in connection with your words have the power to influence your viewers (intentionally or unintentionally) and their perception of your subject and you. Look for opportunities to engage with your viewers and encourage dialog around your images to broaden your perspective and sensitivities so you can make more conscious decisions in your work.

Thoughts from Photographer OLIVER LANG

"As someone who shoots street photography almost daily, I am aware of the potentially sensitive issues faced with children appearing in photographs. I will sometimes avoid taking shots when someone's child may be visible in an image to avoid exposing them." Oliver recommends that you provide context in the title or caption of your photographs as ". . . ambiguity will sometimes take you where you least expected or intended."

WEBSITE: www.mobilephotogroup.com/profile_lang.html
FLICKR: www.flickr.com/photos/oggsie
TWITTER: @oggsie
INSTAGRAM: @oggsie

Anticipate & Embrace the Energy of Motion

Unlike shooting cityscapes, landscapes, portraits, or still lifes, documenting fluid experiences of people in motion challenges you to be alert, move quickly, and anticipate the action of your subject so you can craft compositions on the fly. If you are interested in experimenting and playing with motion, focusing on children as your primary subject is a great place to start. It's nearly impossible for children not to move, regardless of the setting, and their movement is rarely inhibited by the presence of a camera.

When I first started making images of my subjects in motion, I remember feeling really frustrated. Everything seemed to move so fast, leaving me little time to adjust and readjust my settings and the positioning of my body to accommodate and retain a focus on my subject. But over time I began to appreciate the blur of motion using a slower speed to capture my images. I realized that what I lost in precision, I gained in a sense of energy in my photographs and increased my odds of capturing a spontaneous moment in a state of flux.

BELOW: Shooting with a mobile phone camera gives you no control over shutter speed and often exhibits slight hesitation on the timing of capture, so it's important to get in sync with your subjects and learn to anticipate their actions. In these images, I chose to shoot with the Hipstamatic app with Float film and the John S lens. After following my subjects' motion sequence to get a feel for the timing and placement of their throws, I actually pressed the shutter a split second before I thought the action would happen, to accommodate the delay of a sluggish shutter.

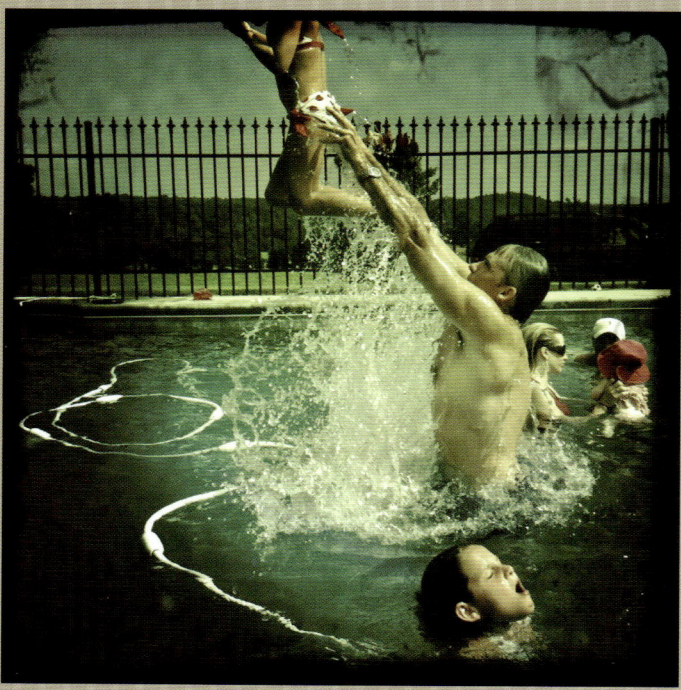
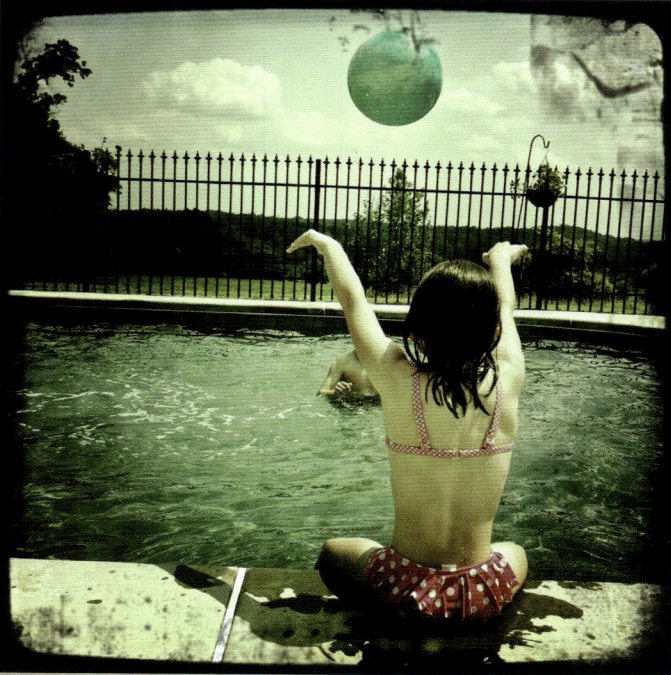

TO CAPTURE MOTION:

1. Study the location of your subject in the setting and watch their movement to get a feel for composition opportunities, light, and the speed and direction in which they are moving.

2. Place yourself in a location relative to your subjects under the best lighting conditions you can find. If your subjects are moving low to the ground within a limited space, you can get down on the ground and shift your body to follow the action. If they are moving within a broader area, stay on your feet and quickly assess what's around you so you're aware of hazards or obstructions including objects you might bump into or step on.

3. If you are shooting a sporting event or another motion experience that occurs for an extended period of time in roughly the same location, you might consider attaching a monopod to your camera to help stabilize it and take the weight off your hands. A monopod is more mobile than a tripod, making it easy for you to quickly lift the camera and reposition your location as needed.

4. Adjust your aperture setting for the desired depth of field of your subject, then adjust your ISO and white balance settings to accommodate your lighting conditions, keeping in mind that once you've selected your desired shutter speed, you may need to readjust these settings to accommodate for more or less light.

5. Think about how you want to convey the motion, and make a few test images while adjusting your shutter speed. If you want to freeze the action and show detail in your moving subject, increase your shutter speed.

If you want to soften and blur the action, giving the illusion of movement, decrease your shutter speed. As you increase your shutter speed, less light will enter the camera. As you decrease the shutter speed, more light will enter the camera.

6. Set your camera and lens (if necessary) to auto focus so you can quickly change your area of focus in the viewfinder while your subject is in motion. Frame your shot in the viewfinder, considering the background and other elements in the frame to optimize your focus on the action to frame your action, then remain alert and be patient as you follow the movement of your subject. If you are following more than one individual in motion, pick one as your primary focus and let that subject guide you through the action. When the elements align into a composition that connects with you, click.

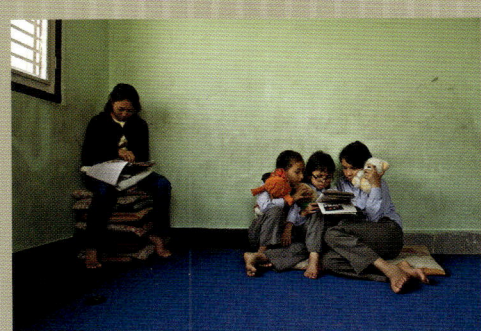
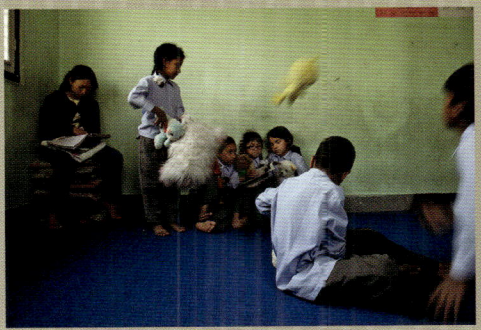
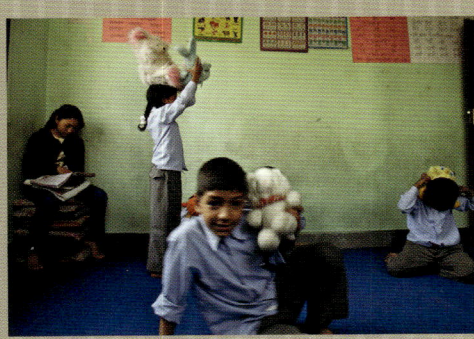
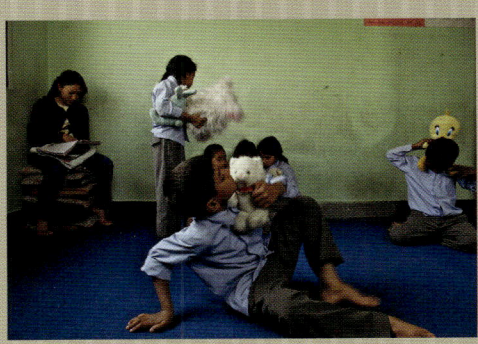
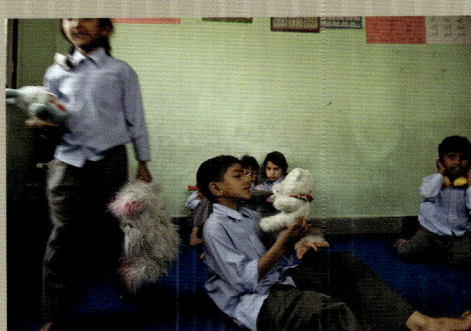

I made these image of young students enjoying their free time following lunch at Koseli School in Kathmandu, Nepal. As you can see from the sequence of images, what began as a quiet moment quickly evolved into a flurry of action. In this example, I feel that the blur of motion best portrays the essence of the moment.

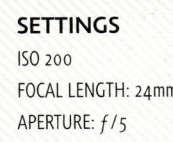

SETTINGS

ISO 200
FOCAL LENGTH: 24mm
APERTURE: ƒ/5
SHUTTER SPEED: 1/30

Minimize Color to Emphasize Expression & Gesture

My daughter had been on an indefinite hiatus from piano lessons until she unexpectedly expressed an interest in making music again. "I'm going to play in the recital!" she announced one morning after returning home from a sleepover at her grandmother (and piano teacher)'s house weeks before the annual holiday performance. And from that point forward, with no prompting from me, she practiced her "Christmas Waltz" each day to prepare for her moment in the spotlight.

It's a familiar cycle. The entrance, exit, and return of inspiration. The birth of a vision, and the decision to make it real. Acknowledging the need to practice and prepare for the moment when we're meant to stand in the spotlight. Assuming that courage will sustain us despite the presence of fear. I was so proud of her in this moment that I almost forgot to click.

When I process images, I often consider the potential strength and timeless appeal of an image in black and white, particularly if I want to place visual emphasis on an expression or gesture revealed in a spontaneous moment. What I don't typically consider is the use of sepia tone, but it can also be very successful in setting a mood. Using an image processing application on your desktop such as Aperture, or an app such as Photo fx on your iPhone, try varying the intensity of sepia tone to apply a light, warm color wash on your image. Light sepia toning works well when you want to minimize the distraction of color (the distracting red dresses in this example) and place visual emphasis on the action of your image. As an alternative to black and white, sepia offers a warm approach to achieve a similar timeless effect.

SETTINGS

ISO 200
FOCAL LENGTH: 24mm
APERTURE: *f*/5
SHUTTER SPEED: 1/30

RIGHT, OPPOSITE TOP, OPPOSITE BOTTOM: My daughter curtsies to an audience of family and friends following her piano recital performance at Villa Serena in Conyers, Georgia.

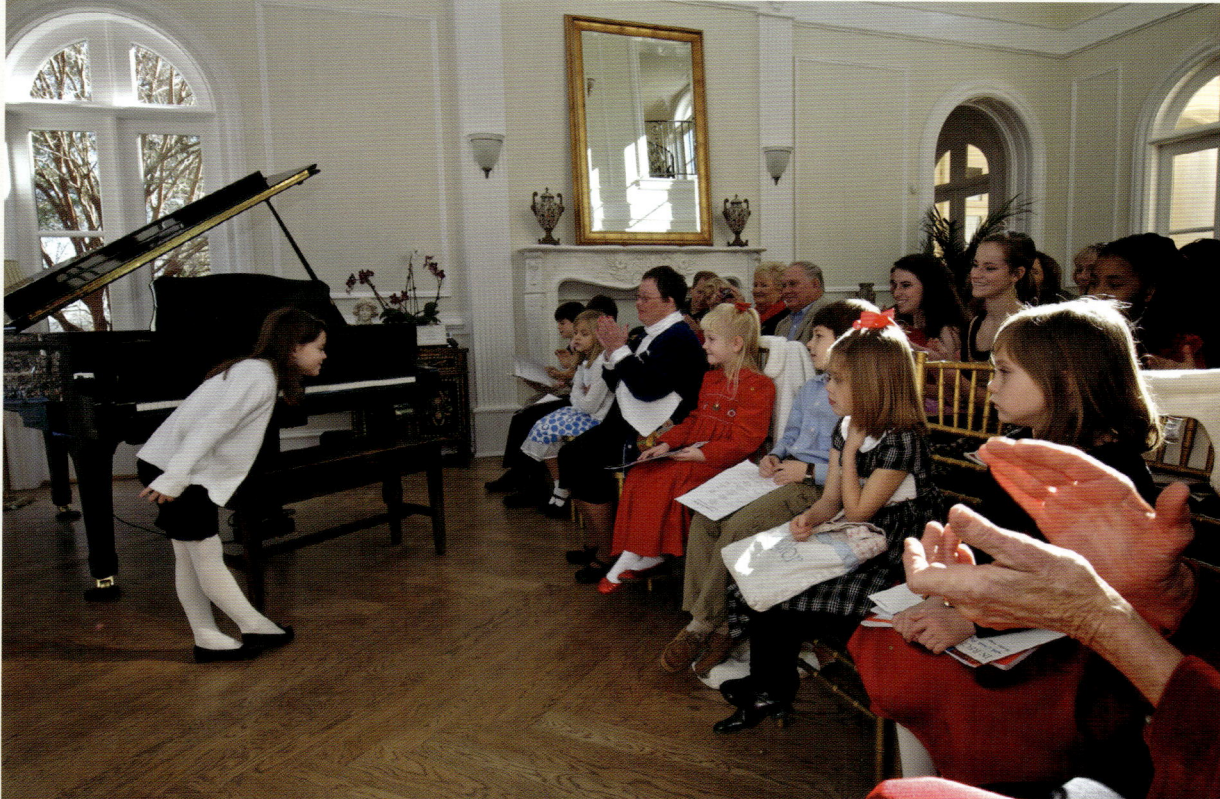

Original

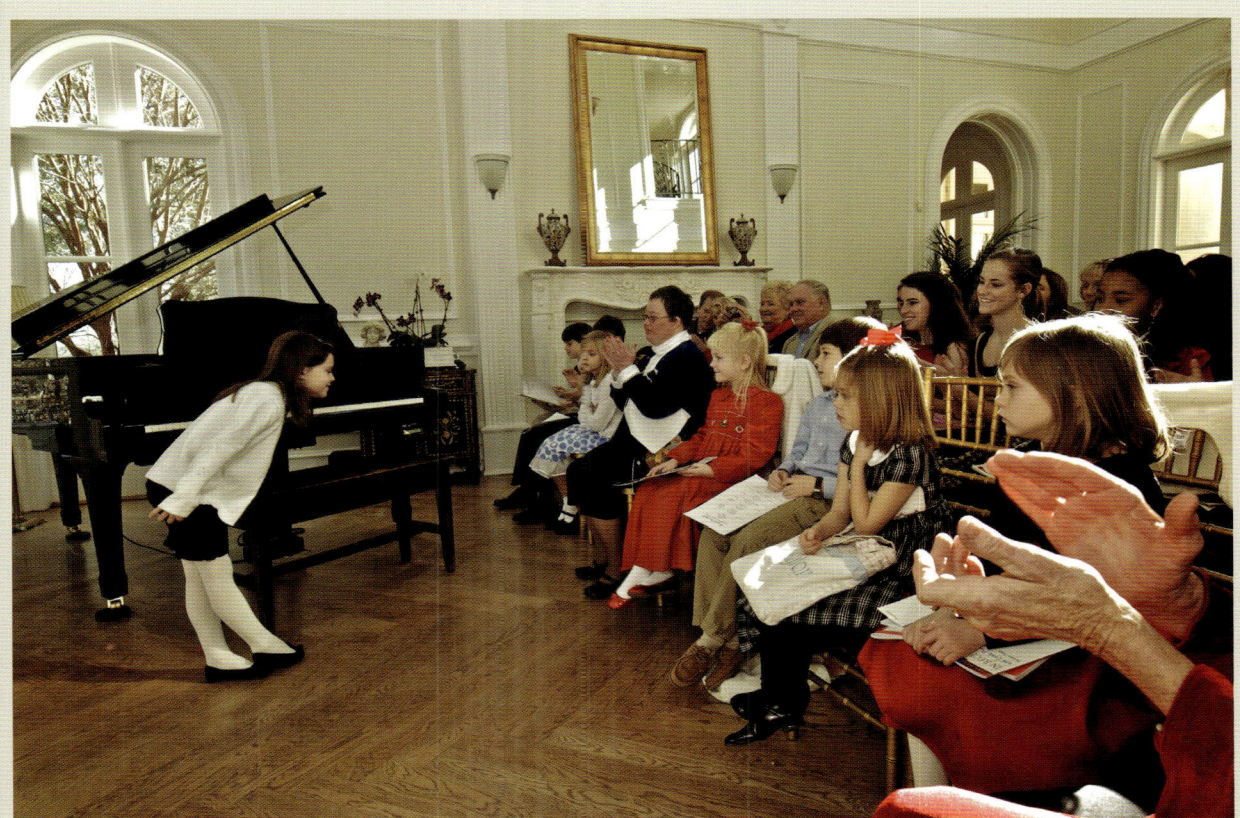

Sepia toned

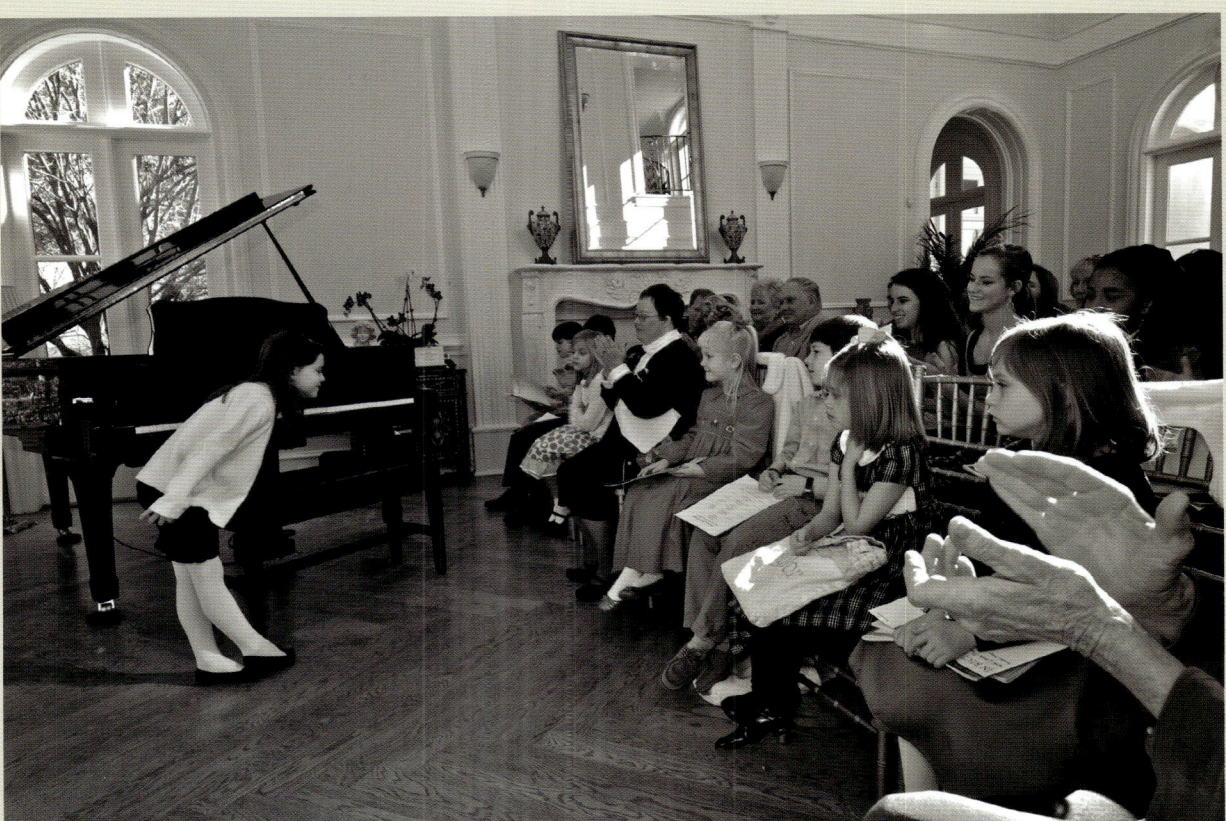

Black and white

Convey a Story Through Sequence

I sensed this baby would come that day. Not this baby specifically, but a baby. And he arrived on my birthday, July 29, 2010. Before arriving to Nepal during my flight from London to Delhi, I read a stapled stack of papers from my client detailing the goals, strategy, and activities defining CARE's CRADLE (Community Responsive Antenatal, Delivery and Life Essential Support for mothers and newborns in Nepal) Program. It outlined CARE's intent to help provide proper health facilities and

care to pregnant women and newborns in poor and remote communities in the Far West Region of Nepal in an effort to reduce neonatal and maternal mortality rates. Logically, it all made sense in the form of words on paper, but I couldn't help but think that if these women have been birthing and caring for their newborns in the privacy of their own homes for generations, how would they feel about having their babies in a health clinic? What would that look like?

"Wouldn't it be so great if we could see a mother connecting with her newborn for the first time in one of these health clinics?" I said to my friend and project partner, Jen Lemen, seated beside me. I had not yet seen our itinerary, nor had I spoken to my CARE Nepal contact about a wish as specific and unpredictable as this. But I said a silent little prayer that we'd see what needed to be seen, and that I would have the ability to document what needed to be shared.

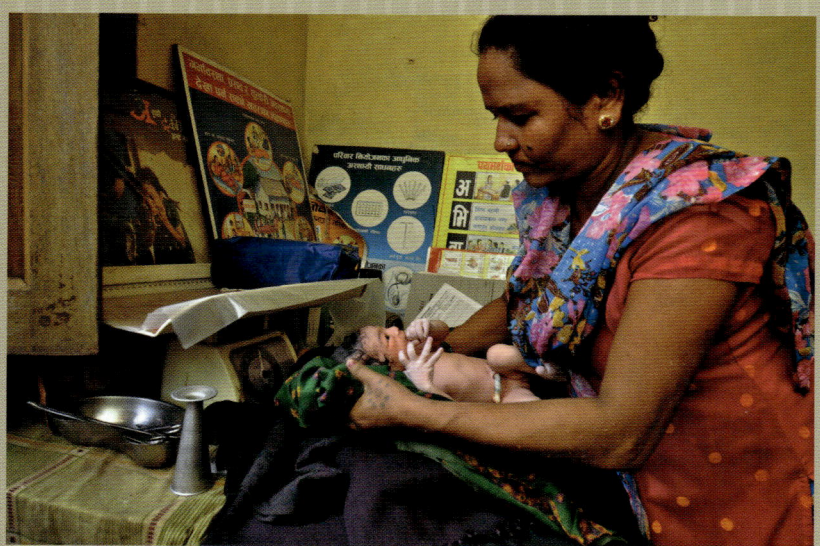 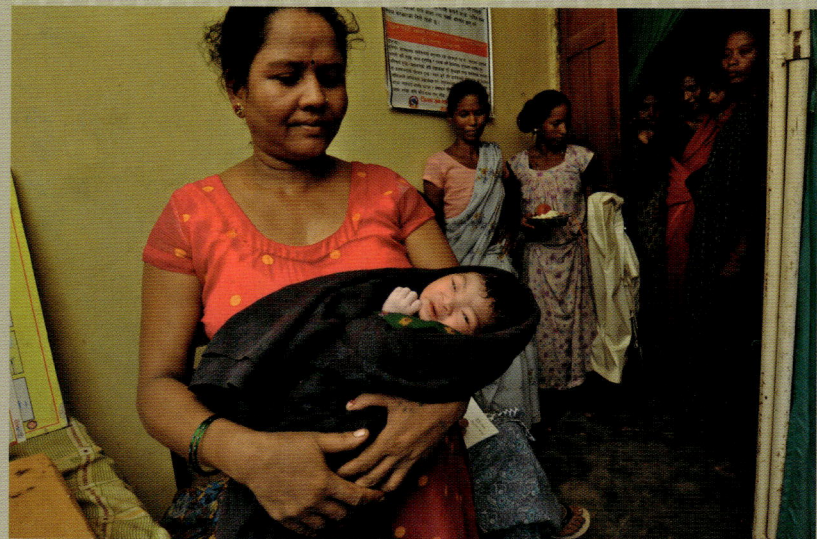

ABOVE, ABOVE RIGHT, OPPOSITE RIGHT, OPPOSITE LEFT:
Bindra Acharya, Maternal and Child Health Worker, cares for Ram Kumari Chaudhara and her newborn moments after delivery at the Health Facility in Hasuliya (Kailali District), Nepal. © Stephanie Calabrese Roberts/CARE.

Moments after we arrived to the modest Sub Health Post in Hasuliya (Kailali District), Bindra Acharya, the Maternal and Child Health Worker, rushed us through the open entrance of a simple building crowded with visitors to a small back room. I felt a surge of gratitude and excitement to find a brand new baby, born less than 15 minutes before our arrival, surrounded by caring women eager to share their support with new mother Ram Kumari Chaudhara.

I had very little time to prepare for the shoot in its very tight and dim setting, so I quickly chose my 14–24mm lens to give me the wide angle I needed to capture my primary subjects and the surrounding women. I wanted to retain a focus on the details within the setting, so I chose an $f/7.1$ aperture setting. I increased my ISO setting to 320 and fired an external mount flash (bouncing it off the wall behind me) to give me the extra light I needed without overwhelming my scene.

Portraying the experience of a newborn and mother learning to connect for the first time called for a concise sequence of images. I shot 91 images within 19 minutes (remaining sensitive to the comfort level of my subjects throughout our time together), but these four photographs sum up the story. When you are undertaking your own documentary work, challenge yourself to select the fewest number of images you need to share the essence of an experience.

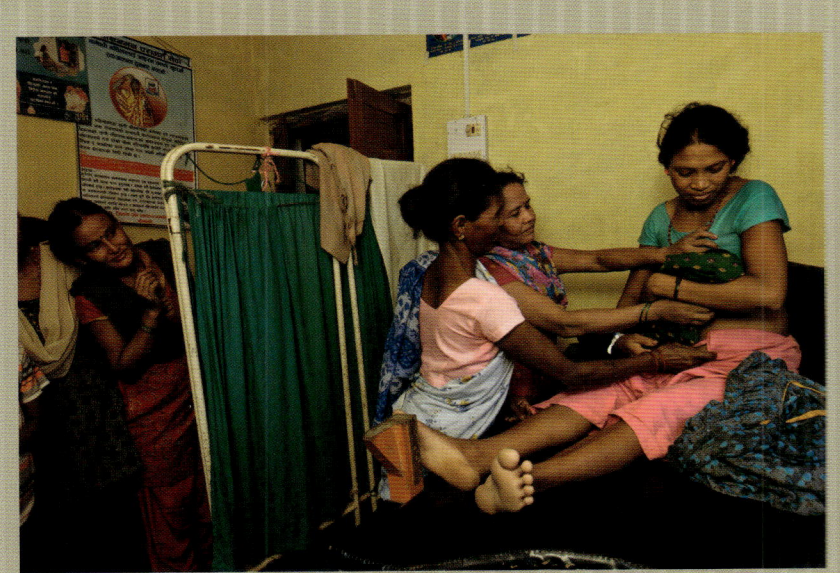
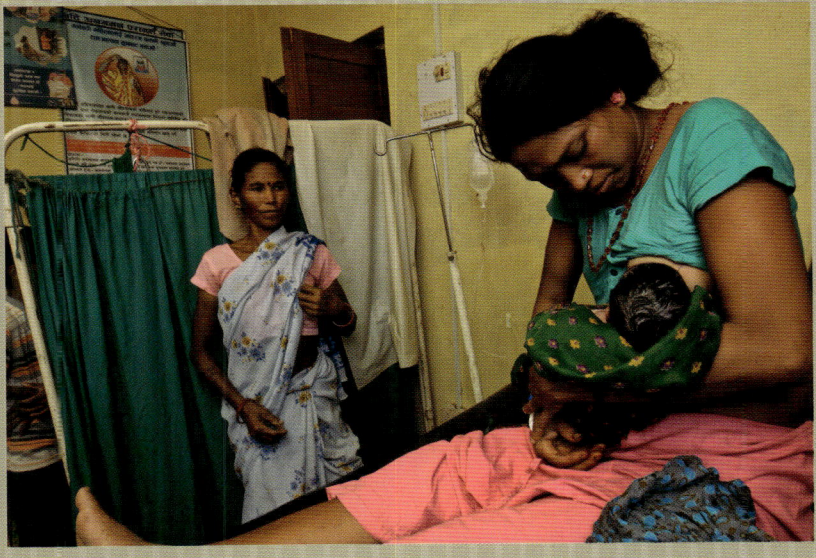

Settle on a Single Image to Convey the Moment

Dr. W. Robert Nix was my Photography 101 professor when I was at the University of Georgia. I didn't intend to pursue photography as a career at the time, but was intrigued enough to take the class as an elective *en route* to my BFA with a focus in scientific illustration. Dr. Nix taught me how to make a pinhole camera with balsa wood to emphasize the importance of learning to control light and craft compositions with the simplest of tools. He taught me how to develop film and make prints in the darkroom. But beyond all the technical stuff, he encouraged me. And hearing him say, "You've got a great eye" is, to this day, one of the best compliments I've ever received.

We reconnected a few years ago when I realized that he lived just 30 minutes from my door. Spending time with him and his wife in his home is such a gift for me. On February 19, 2010, the day I made these photographs, we talked about the start of his photography career as a photojournalist and the excitement of being called in the middle of the night to capture news in the making. "Have you ever seen an ol' 4 × 5?" he asked. I hadn't. And so my lesson began. Within minutes he returned to the sofa with a black box, pieced together his Crown Graphic 4 × 5 press camera (weighing in at a hefty 8 pounds), and demonstrated the very manual process of making images "on the

fly" back in 1953. And giving a sweet glance in the direction of his beautiful wife, he even told me about the time he had to change his film under a sorority girl's lengthy skirt.

I brought my camera with me to Dr. Nix's home that day, though I didn't know if I would make photographs or not. In fact, we talked for nearly two hours. I didn't see an image until I sensed his excitement when he returned to the sofa with a bulky gray camera box in his hand and a shooting hat on his head. As he carefully removed the camera pieces from the box, I quickly slid my camera out of my camera bag and attached my external mount flash to offset the backlight from the window behind him. I knew I didn't have much time to adjust settings as I didn't want to distract myself away from our conversation, so I quickly set my camera to aperture priority and auto-focus mode, and set the aperture narrowly enough to retain

some clarity for interesting elements in the background such as the painted woman and the doll, one of many in the home.

As he worked and spoke, I made a series of 24 images over the course of 25 minutes to document the experience. From that series, several caught awkward expressions and a few are out of focus and underexposed because the weakened batteries in my flash couldn't keep up with my clicks. From the series of 24, the three pictured here were best, but I settled on the more wide-angle view of Dr. Nix's fixed gaze to represent the experience. I liked the timeless feel of the photograph when I processed it in black and white. By stripping away the color, I focus less on the warmth of the environment and more on the sharp contrast between the soft humanity of the photographer and the harsh prominence of the man-made device intended to capture it.

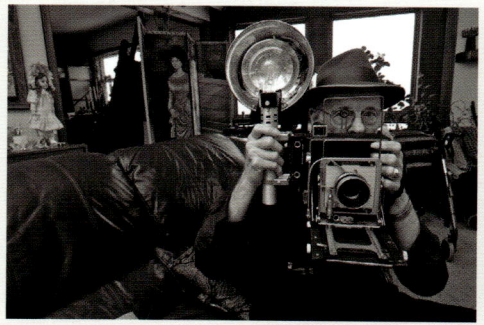 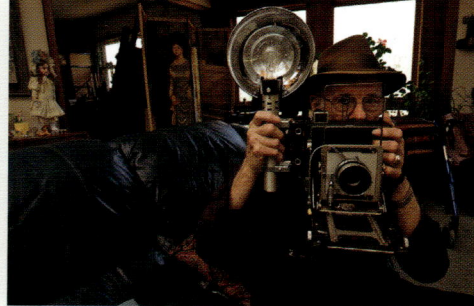

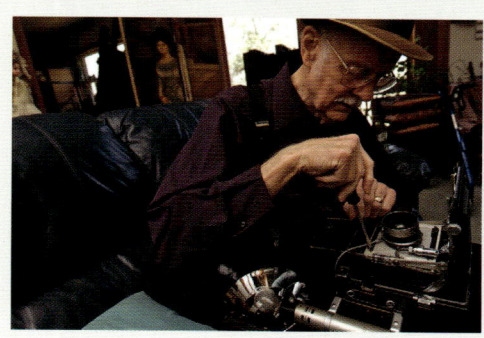 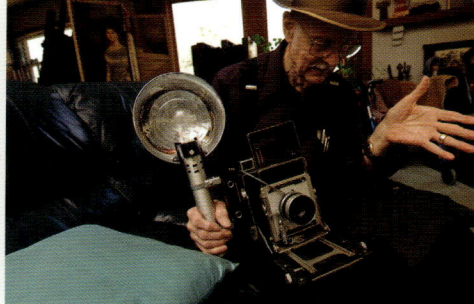

ABOVE LEFT, ABOVE RIGHT, BELOW LEFT, BELOW RIGHT:
Dr. W. Robert Nix, Emeritus Professor of Art Education/Photography from the University of Georgia, shares a view of his Crown Graphic 4 × 5 camera with me in his home.

SETTINGS
ISO 200
FOCAL LENGTH: 14mm
APERTURE: ƒ/6.3
SHUTTER SPEED: 1/60
FLASH: Fired

Adjusting Exposure

When using an external mount flash, keep an eye on your battery power. When battery power begins to wane, your flash may not fire when you intend it to. Here, you can see the natural lighting conditions for the room when my flash did not fire. Importing and processing the image in Aperture, a photo editing software application on my computer, I was able to increase exposure and reduce shadows and contrast to compensate for my underexposed image, resulting in a much clearer image (below).

SETTINGS

ISO 320
FOCAL LENGTH: 14mm
APERTURE: ƒ/10
SHUTTER SPEED: 1/60
FLASH: Not fired

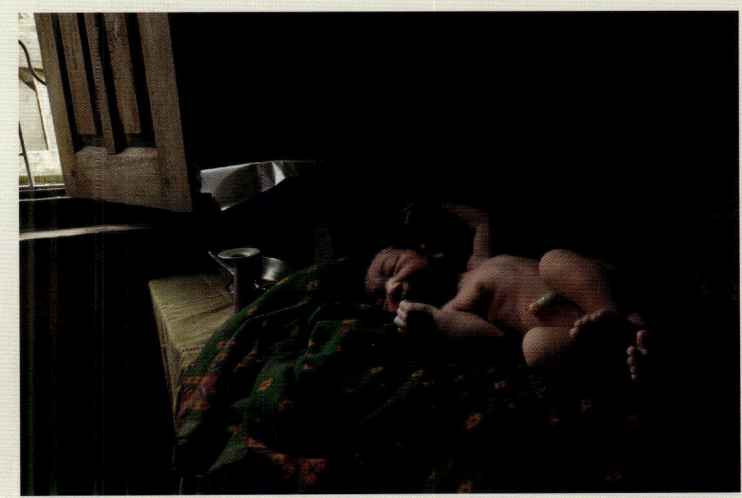

LEFT AND BELOW:
Ram Kumari Chaudhara's newborn moments after delivery at the Health Facility in Hasuliya, Nepal. © Stephanie Calabrese Roberts/CARE.

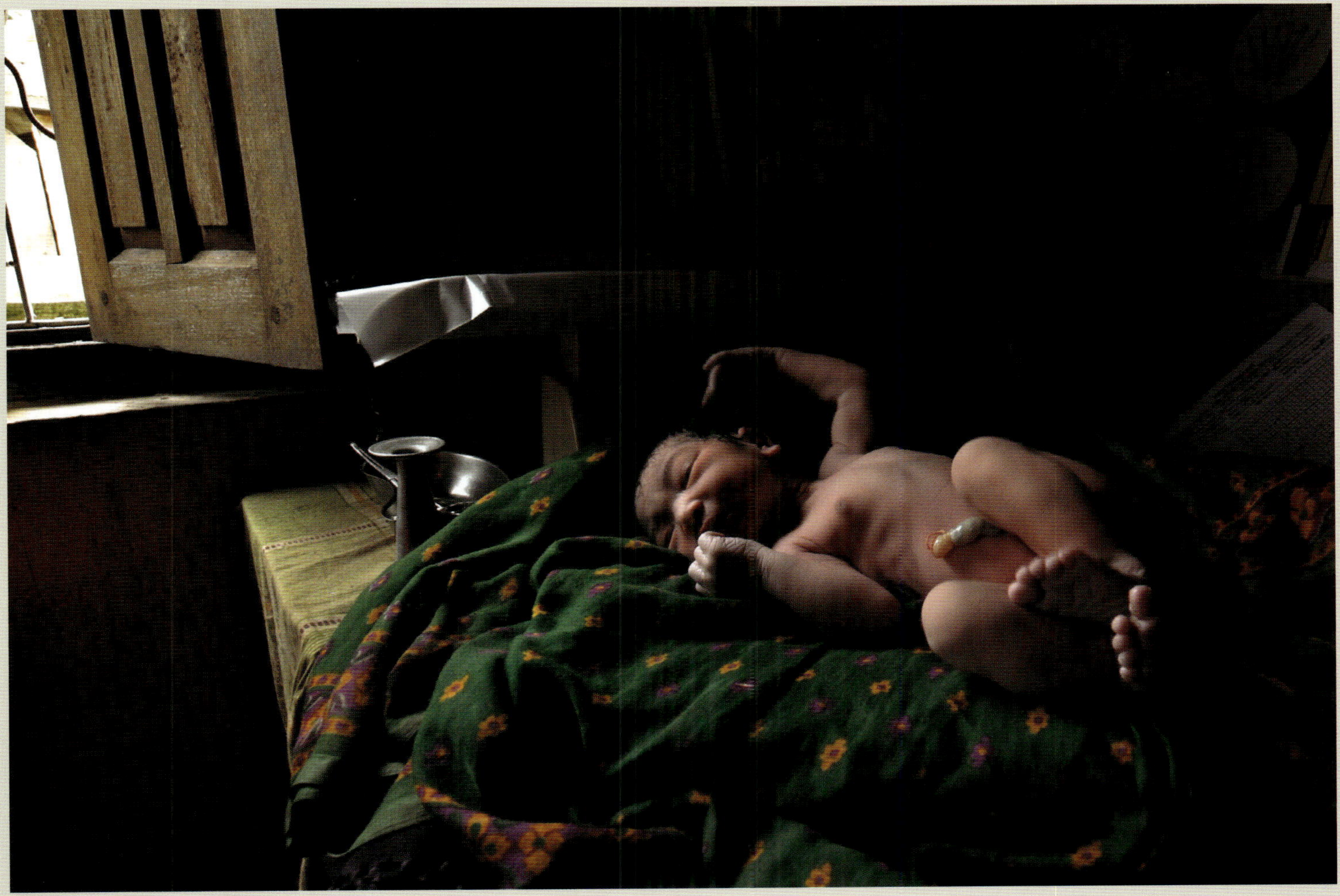

3

FIND YOUR FOCUS
& PLAN YOUR PROJECT

Cultivating a project-based approach to your documentary photography gives you an opportunity to explore a concept or subject in a deeper way, or use a series of photographs to share a story or an experience in a more comprehensive manner—something that couldn't have been conveyed in a single image. It's easy to shoot a lot of everything and a little of something because life is fascinating and there's so much to see and share, but I challenge you to find one or more areas of focus. Whether it's something as broad as dogs (one of Elliott Erwitt's favorites) or as specific as scenes behind the curtain of an Italian family circus (Beth Rooney's choice), find something that intrigues or excites you.

By defining one or more projects, and coming up with a set of guidelines for capturing and portraying a series of photographs, you can channel your creative energy toward a more defined area of focus. Just as a poet might feel more comfortable composing thoughts within

a specific form, or an artist might limit his or her raw materials and dimensions before beginning a sculpture, take some time to consider your subject matter, perspective, approach, equipment, processing style, and presentation options before you begin shooting. Ideally, your plans should help guide your creative process without putting unnecessary constraints on your creativity.

Finding your areas of focus, narrowing your subjects, and planning the execution of your documentary project can be challenging, particularly if your project takes you into unfamiliar territory. In this chapter, I'll share some exercises, thought processes, checklists, and a few secrets to get you started. I hope the information inspires you to start a project (or a few), and helps you gain confidence as you embark on your journey, whether you're traveling for the first time to a remote region in a faraway land, or just down the street.

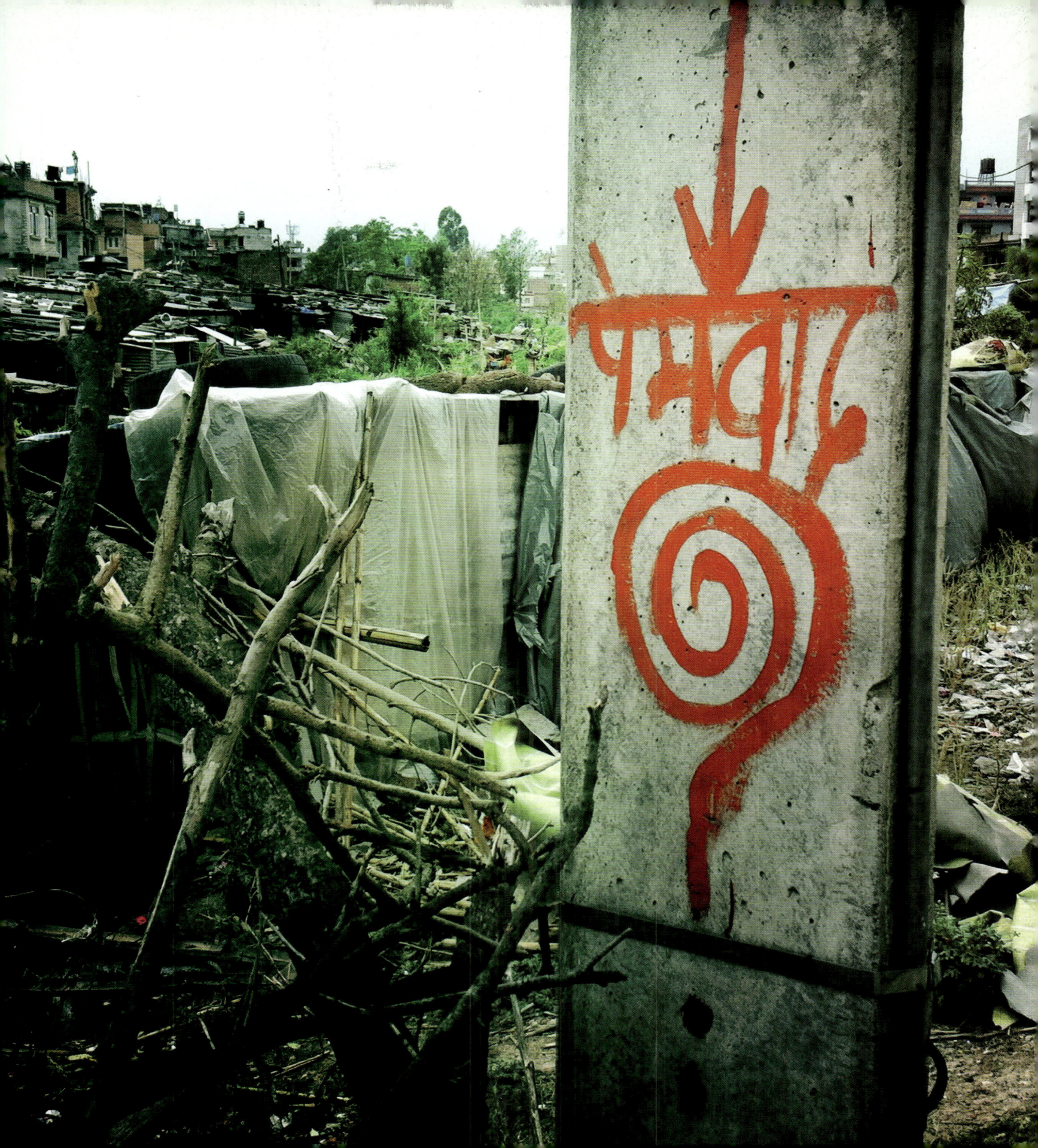

A Way to Conceptualize Personal Projects

Imagine your areas of focus (or potential projects) as a set of file folders—places to put your images when they reveal themselves to you. Now grab an imaginary pencil and write the title of your project on the outside of the folder. You can erase and rename the project folder at any time, as your areas of focus will undoubtedly evolve over time. Let your instincts guide how narrow your project title needs to be, and be conscious of what you are placing in each of these file folders. A folder you've initially titled "love" might later unexpectedly reveal images that portray compassion or a longing for love. Let your images guide further refinement of your projects. You might also find that two or more of your thin file folders begin to collect images that feel related in some way. Think about consolidating them into a single folder and renaming it with a broader title. Now apply this thought process to your actual digital image archive by creating project folders and placing your images within them, or define a set of tags to represent your projects and tag images that fall into one or more of your projects so you can find and review them with a quick search.

Often when I'm shooting a client assignment, I might serendipitously discover and capture an image that fits well within one of my ongoing projects. Because I've loosely defined my personal projects, I'm subconsciously aware when these images appear, so I shoot and collect them. I might not even acknowledge that the image fits within one of my personal projects until months after the shoot, but eventually I might move it into a project folder. When I find that a project folder holds a substantial collection of images, I can evaluate each of them, decide if they connect and complement each other, and determine if the project is complete. If I consider it complete, I might then curate the collection with a more critical eye, and seek out opportunities to share the project as a photo essay in an online or print publication, a live presentation, a self-published book, a gallery exhibition, or enter it in a photography competition.

AN ONGOING PROJECT
"Connect | Disconnect"

My ongoing "Connect | Disconnect" project explores ways in which individuals simultaneously connect and disconnect within the confines of a single frame. Nearly two years ago I began to notice that I was attracted to curious moments such as these. I wasn't able to articulate the essence of (or a title for) the project until I had collected and connected nearly ten of these images. In this ongoing project example, the images surfaced from my archive and dictated the title. I decided to make this a black-and-white series to put visual emphasis on expression and gesture—the basis for the point of connection and disconnection—and to visually relate images that have been captured in a wide variety of environments over an extended period of time.

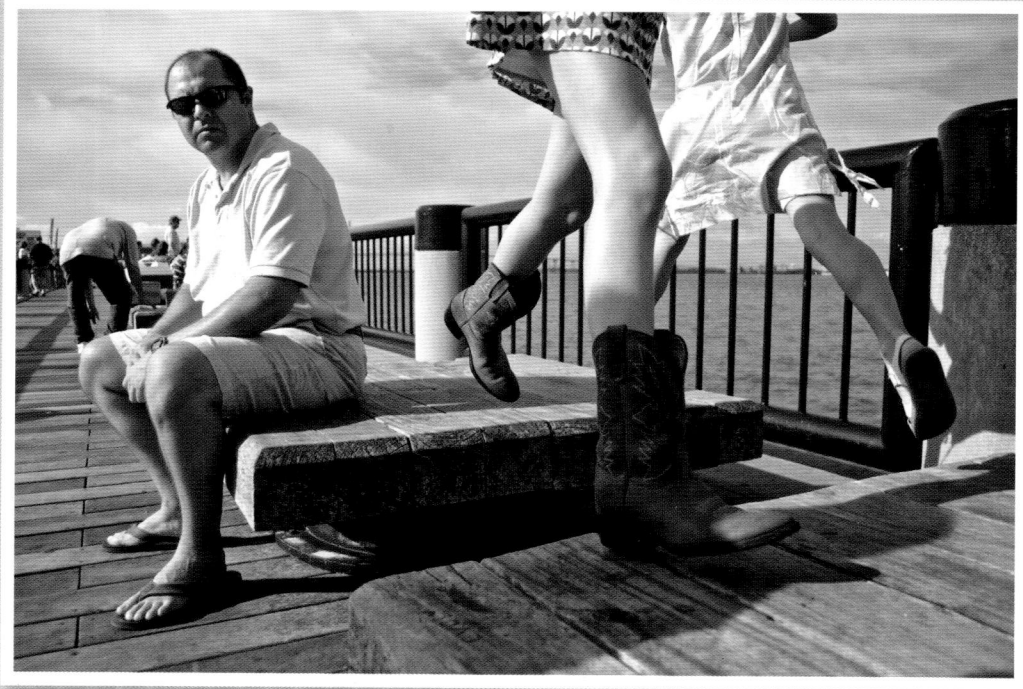

RIGHT: Jill and Todd attempt a stroll with son Wyatt through winter's first snowfall outside their home in Brooklyn, New York.

BELOW: Cousins Bo and Marshall find a moment to bond at the reception following their cousin's baptism in Atlanta, Georgia.

BELOW RIGHT: Artist Melanie Eberhardt shares a moment of love with her dog Lucky, while one of her many cats admires the connection.

OPPOSITE: My brother, Jeff, waits on the pier in Charleston, South Carolina while his daughter and niece leap between the benches.

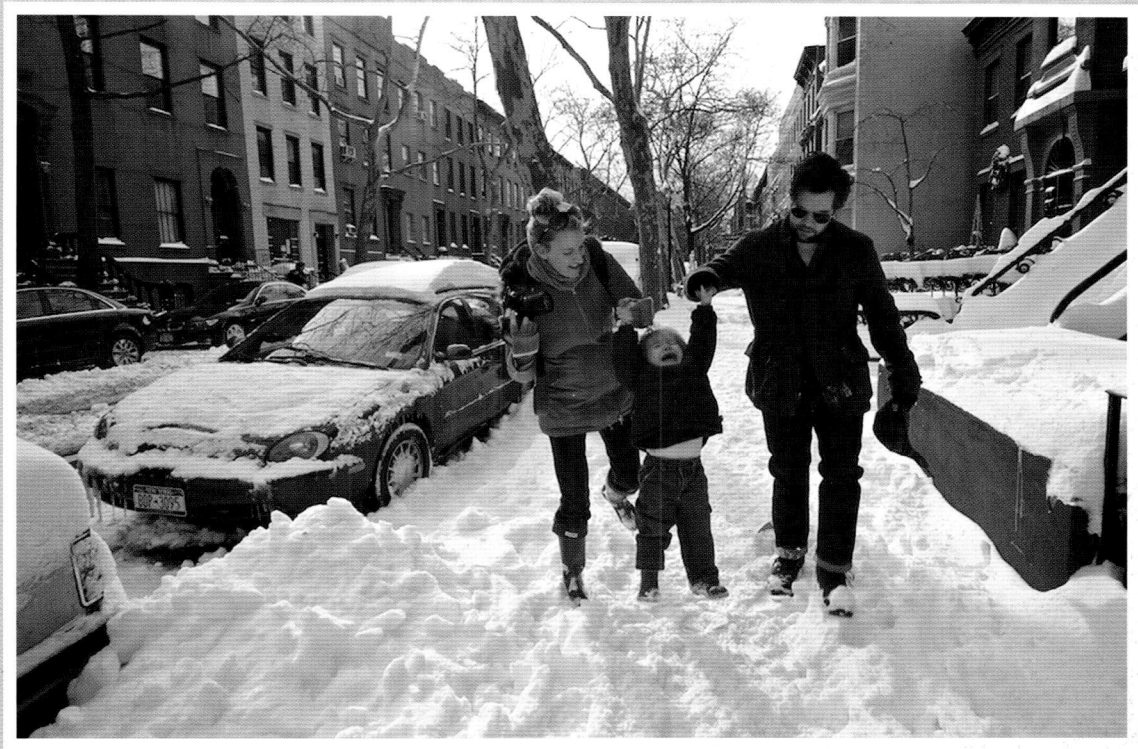

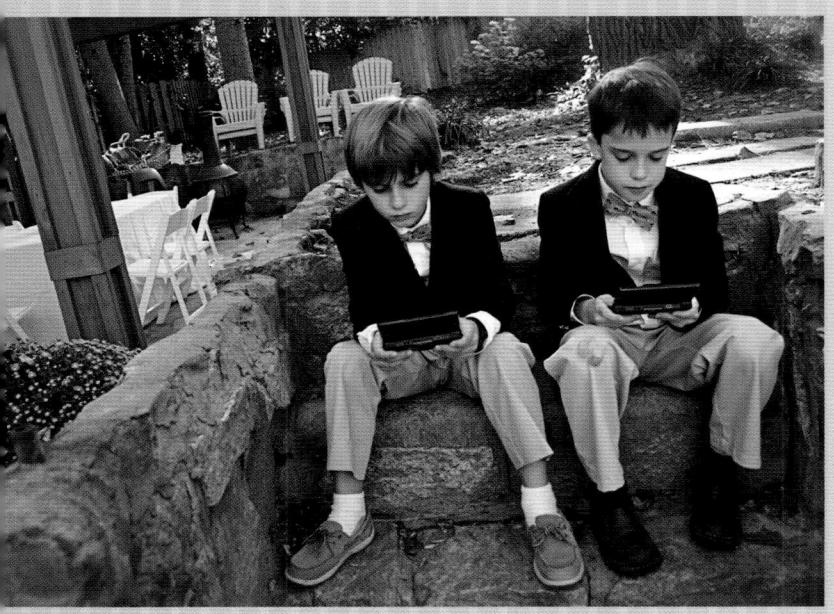

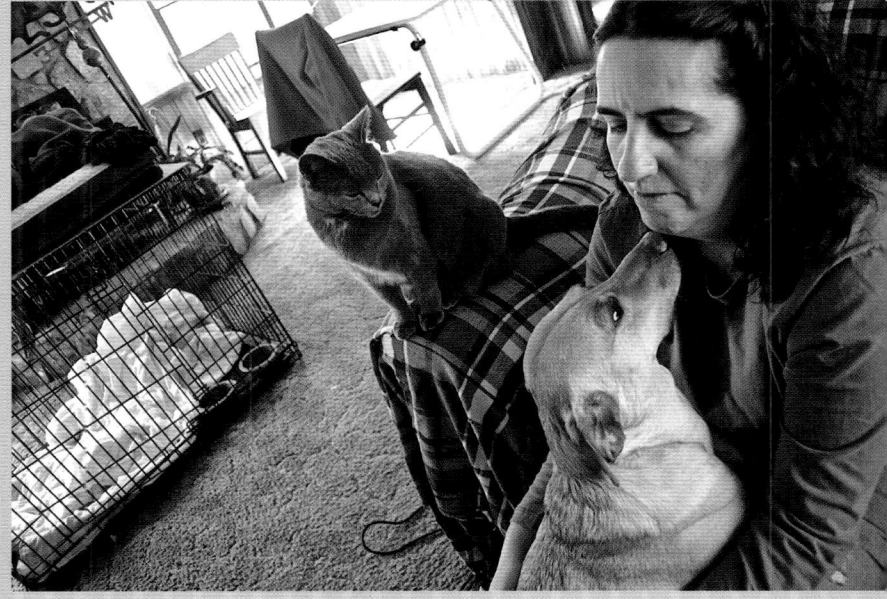

Deconstruct Your Interests to Identify Project Ideas

Working with the expansive landscape of life as your canvas, potential subjects are endless, and if you love looking at life through the viewfinder of your camera on a near daily basis, as I do, you might feel overwhelmed by the idea of identifying a single area of focus for a project. Think about books you read, movies you watch, places you like to go, and conversations that fulfill you. You might be thinking, "Where do I begin?" I've discovered two different methods that have worked for me. In this section, we'll deconstruct your interests to identify potential subjects. In the next section, we'll uncover project ideas hiding in your image archive.

Step 1. Clear your mind and think about broad areas of interest or concepts that intrigue you and write them down. Concepts might be as broad as people, art, animals, city life, racism, love, adventure, wealth, music, social justice, spirituality, or family. Let your mind wander and don't censor your thoughts at this stage of your creative process.

Step 2. Place a check mark beside five concepts that interest you most and sink into each broad concept more deeply. Write down ten subjects for potential projects that come to mind within each of these concept areas. Don't worry about how you might gain access to subjects, or find time or resources to execute the project at this time. When you grant yourself permission to define your dream projects over time, they often have a way of finding you.

If you wrote down "people," think about what types of people interest or intrigue you: teenage motocross racers, refugees, missionary Catholic nuns, dancers with disabilities, cattle ranchers, female CEOs, Cubans, survivors, suburban stay-at-home dads, day laborers, sailors, high school dropouts, or aging polka dancers.

If you wrote down "city life," consider what aspects of city life interest or intrigue you: homelessness, corner barbershops, dog walkers, graffiti art, street musicians, architecture, youth gangs, fashion trends, or urban farming.

If you wrote down "family," consider what aspect of family life is interesting or intriguing to you. You might want to compare and contrast the lives of adult twins, follow the life of a military family, or study the complex lives of foster families. Again, let your mind visualize subjects you'd like to explore and document.

CONCEPTS		CONCEPT		CONCEPT		CONCEPT		CONCEPT		CONCEPT	
_____	☐	SUBJECTS		SUBJECTS		SUBJECTS		SUBJECTS		SUBJECTS	
_____	☐	_____	☐	_____	☐	_____	☐	_____	☐	_____	☐
_____	☐	_____	☐	_____	☐	_____	☐	_____	☐	_____	☐
_____	☐	_____	☐	_____	☐	_____	☐	_____	☐	_____	☐
_____	☐	_____	☐	_____	☐	_____	☐	_____	☐	_____	☐
_____	☐	_____	☐	_____	☐	_____	☐	_____	☐	_____	☐
_____	☐	_____	☐	_____	☐	_____	☐	_____	☐	_____	☐
_____	☐	_____	☐	_____	☐	_____	☐	_____	☐	_____	☐
_____	☐	_____	☐	_____	☐	_____	☐	_____	☐	_____	☐
_____	☐	_____	☐	_____	☐	_____	☐	_____	☐	_____	☐
_____	☐	_____	☐	_____	☐	_____	☐	_____	☐	_____	☐

SUBJECT 1

What do you see?

Where are you?

Who is with you?

What actions define the moments?

How does the setting impact you?

SUBJECT 2

What do you see?

Where are you?

Who is with you?

What actions define the moments?

How does the setting impact you?

SUBJECT 3

What do you see?

Where are you?

Who is with you?

What actions define the moments?

How does the setting impact you?

SUBJECT 4

What do you see?

Where are you?

Who is with you?

What actions define the moments?

How does the setting impact you?

SUBJECT 5

What do you see?

Where are you?

Who is with you?

What actions define the moments?

How does the setting impact you?

Step 3. After you've written down 50 potential subjects, quickly put a check mark beside five subjects that you feel intuitively most passionate about—they might be visually stimulating, intellectually challenging, emotionally engaging, spiritually rewarding . . . don't think too much about why they may or may not work.

Step 4. Now, spend time daydreaming about each of these five subjects and begin to visualize what your images might look like using the questions below. Write down visuals that come to mind.

If you find that you can easily visualize images for a subject, this might be an indication that the subject is rich with potential and intuitively a good fit for you. If you find that you are unable to visualize images for a subject, it might indicate that you need more time to explore the subject matter before committing yourself to it—to talk with potential subjects and visit potential settings to get a feel for the visual possibilities.

For example, if you are intrigued by documenting the campaign trail of a political candidate, consider what you might photograph to make this project visually interesting. It wouldn't be enough to photograph him/her making speeches, shaking hands, participating in debates, talking on the phone, checking emails, and leading meetings at a conference table. We already know what this looks like. The challenge is to authentically reveal something about the candidate beyond the obvious. For example, it might be interesting to show the candidate in blue jeans assembling yard signs on the back porch with his young children, or to expose a glimpse of his wife gently smoothing out his hair before he steps out onto the floor of a televised debate. As you begin to daydream about interesting photographs, this will help you consider the visual potential for your documentary project and identify the breadth and depth of access you need to execute it.

Uncover Project Ideas Hiding in Your Image Archive

Did you know that the secret to a new project may be waiting in your image archive? If you shoot what moves you, a documentary project idea is likely to emerge when you least expect it. Be open to these spontaneous ideas and let them develop organically. One way to encourage this approach is to take time to study your image archive with a fresh perspective. When I do this, I often find that certain images stand out and connect in ways I didn't initially anticipate. Inserting time and space between image reviews can create just the right amount of distance you need for new ideas and patterns to emerge as your vision evolves.

As I studied the image archive of a friend's wedding weekend, I was intrigued by several images I made of people influenced by music. While the band remained the same, the songs inspired diverse reactions on the human body—stirring hearts, shaping expressions, and sending bodies leaping for joy. These images inspired me to seek out other images made under the influence of music in my "One Family at Home" series. There I found Lauren's soulful connection with her guitar to be in contrast with her son Jesse's focus on me. By reprocessing these images shot at different times and in different settings in a

similar way (for example, converting them to black and white), I realized a new visual connection between them, and was able to articulate an area of documentary interest to explore more fully over time—the power of music to influence human emotion.

While I didn't set out with the intent of starting a new documentary series, the images emerged. Now, as new experiences unfold over time, I can recognize and capture these moments to continue that area of focus.

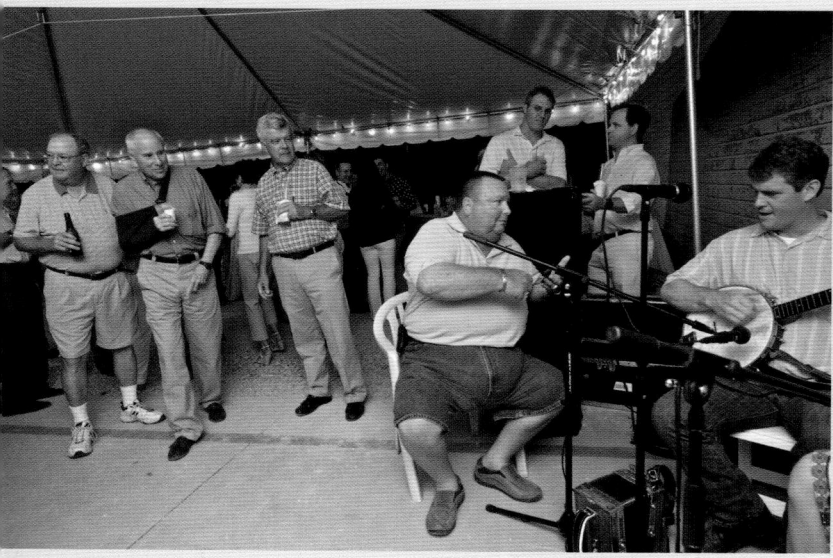

ABOVE: The owner of The Raw Bar in Indian Pass, Florida steps away from the kitchen to drop in on the band and play the spoons.

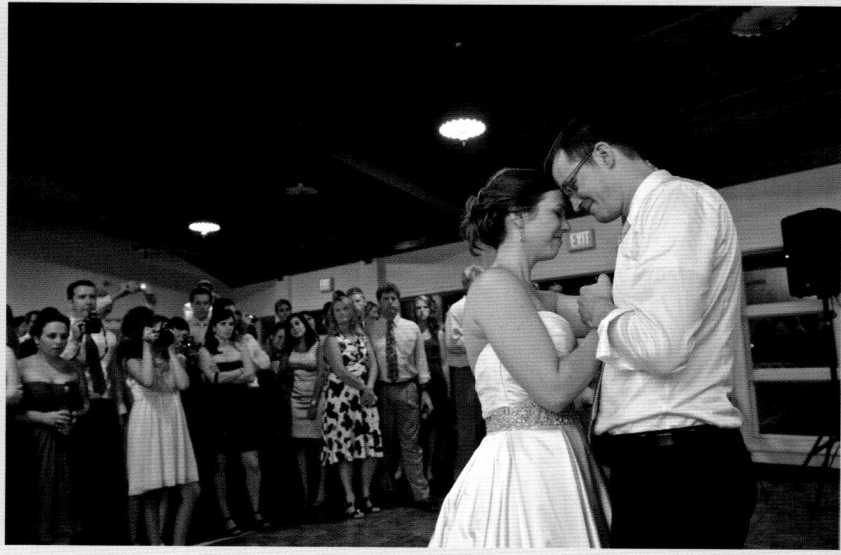

ABOVE: Music connects Jess and Nick Polt for their first dance as newlyweds in Maryland.

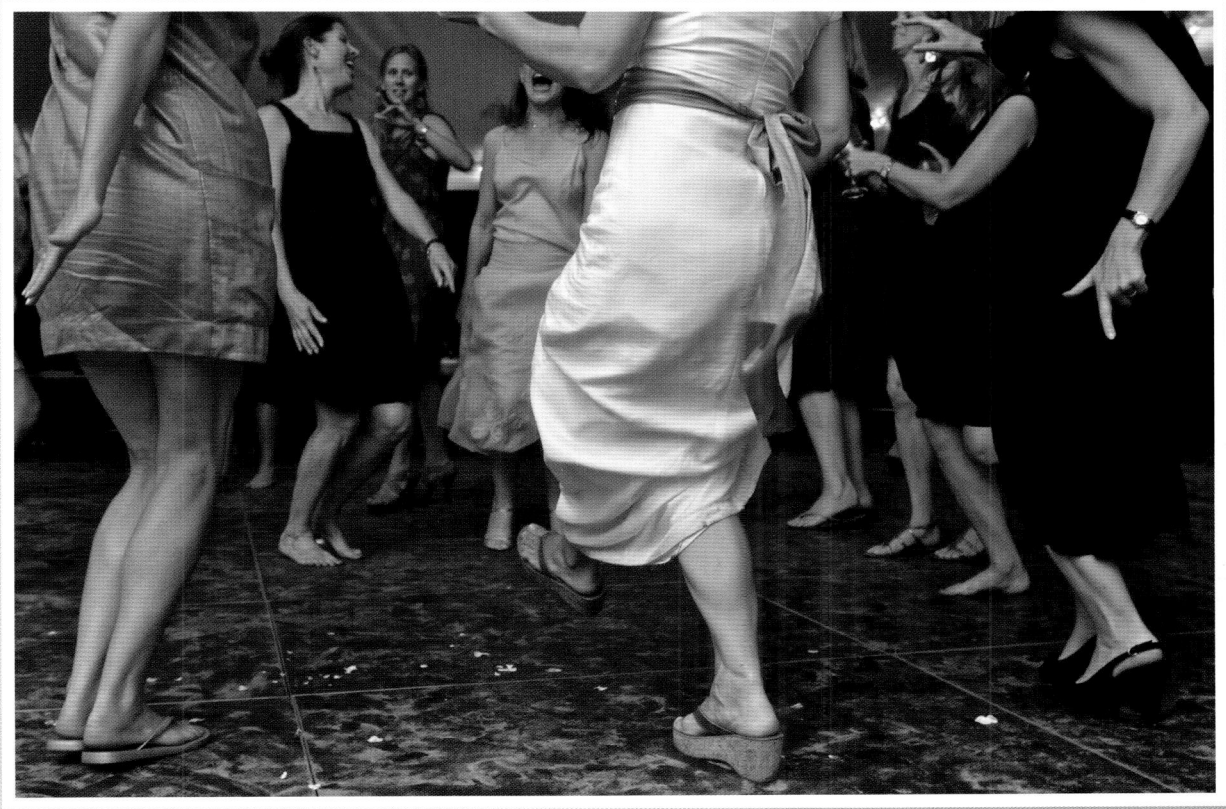

LEFT: Bride Sharon Webster Tate kicks up her heels with her bridesmaids at the reception in Apalachicola, Florida.

BELOW LEFT: A woman pauses to reflect on a song during the after party outside the Raw Bar in Indian Pass, Florida.

BELOW: Lauren beside son Jesse in their living room in Tate, Georgia.

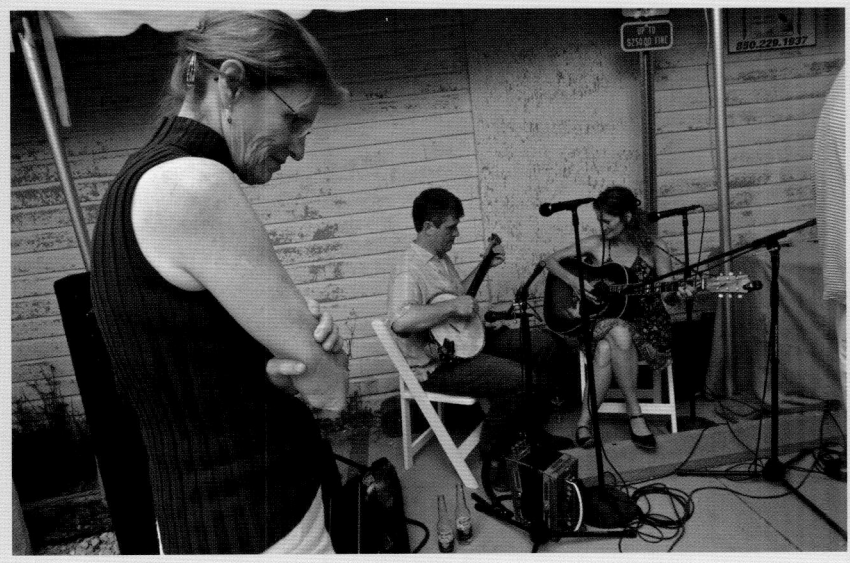

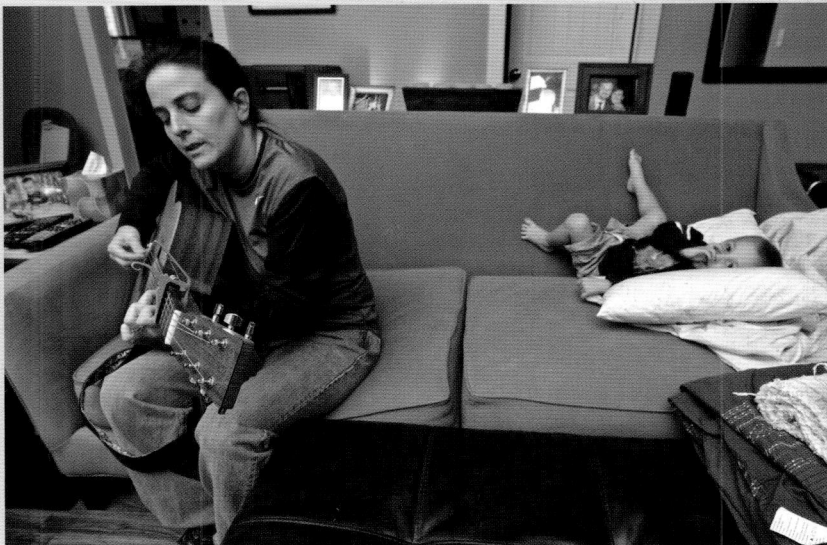

Establish Visual Guidelines

Establishing a set of flexible visual guidelines for your project can help ensure visual continuity for your series of photographs, whether your series spans five images or 500 and is shot over the course of five days or five years. Consider the desired end result and let that guide your visual parameters for the project before you begin shooting. Guidelines for visually connecting the images in your series might include one or more of the following considerations:

EQUIPMENT

To retain continuity among images shot in a variety of settings at different times, consider working on the project with a single camera so the quality and aspect ratio of your photographs are consistent. If you want to create large-format prints to display on a wall, ensure that you are using a camera that can generate the image size you need without compromising the quality of the print.

You might also consider limiting your lens choice. Shooting an entire set of images with a 35mm and 50mm fixed lens still gives you broad creative freedom, yet visually connects your images when shown as a single set (and lightens the load of your camera bag while you're working on your project). For example, if you are shooting 100 portraits of strangers in a consistent way, you might want to use a single lens set at a common aperture setting.

PROCESSING STYLE

Shooting with a digital camera gives you the flexibility of capturing color images that can be processed in unlimited ways. Experimenting with digital processing, whether you're making finely tuned color adjustments using Adobe Photoshop on a desktop computer or applying filters and/or adding borders using photography apps on an iPhone, can help you craft a very specific visual style for your images.

Defining a consistent processing approach is valuable in that it can visually connect images you've shot in a variety of settings and at different times. For example, by processing color images in black and white, you minimize color distractions and connect images. It's easier to connect images in a series when you minimize or soften differences among them. Let the differences be conveyed in the subject matter—the moment, the message, the environment—not in the presentation of it.

BELOW LEFT:
This graffiti, known as Lovism, can be found painted in red throughout Kathmandu, Nepal.

BELOW: Koseli School student uniforms dry in the sun on the roof of the school's building.

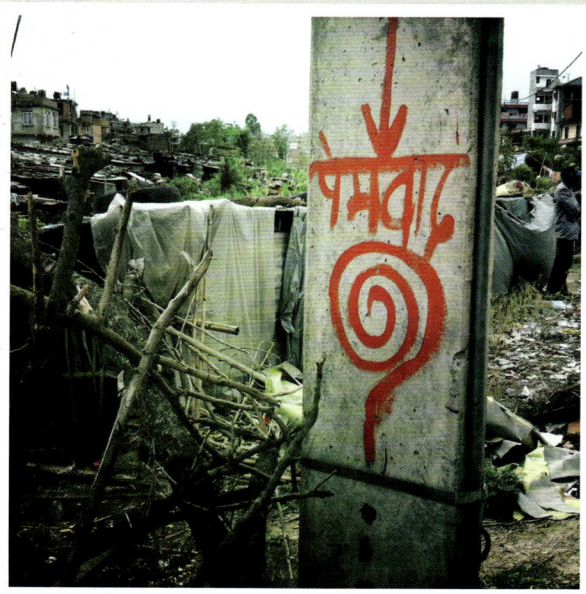

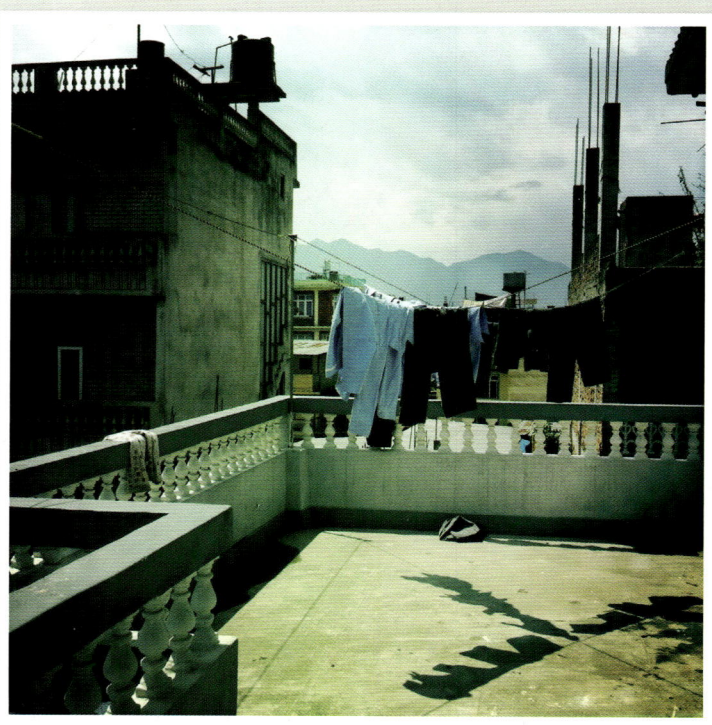

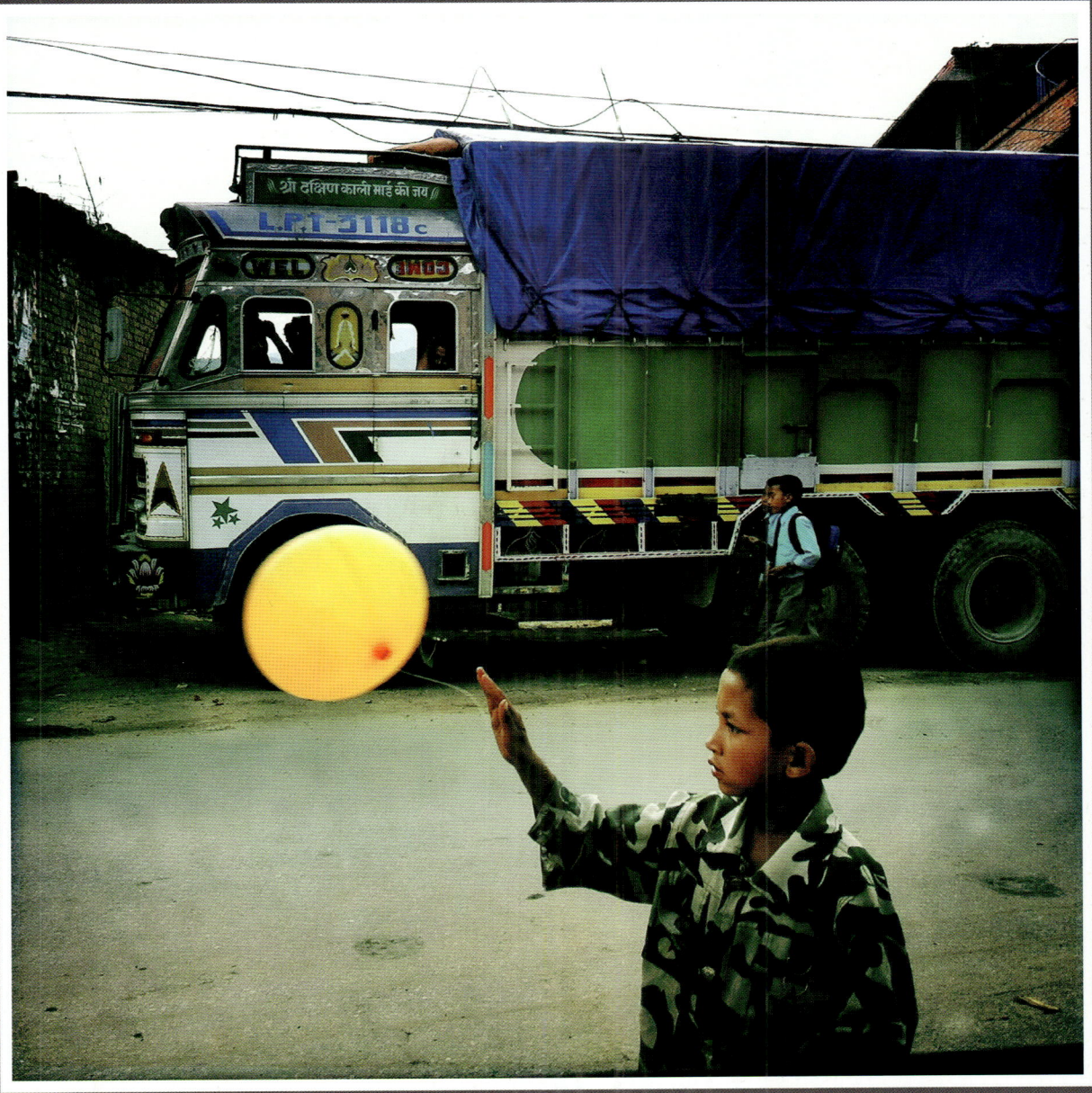

ABOVE: The streets of this community had been shut down in Kathmandu, Nepal due to a local festival and impending parade. My driver had to stop the car less than a mile from my destination. As I waited for my escort to meet me at the car, this young boy walked up and began to bounce his balloon. I waited for the balloon to align with the front tire of the truck parked across the street.

Establish Visual Guidelines

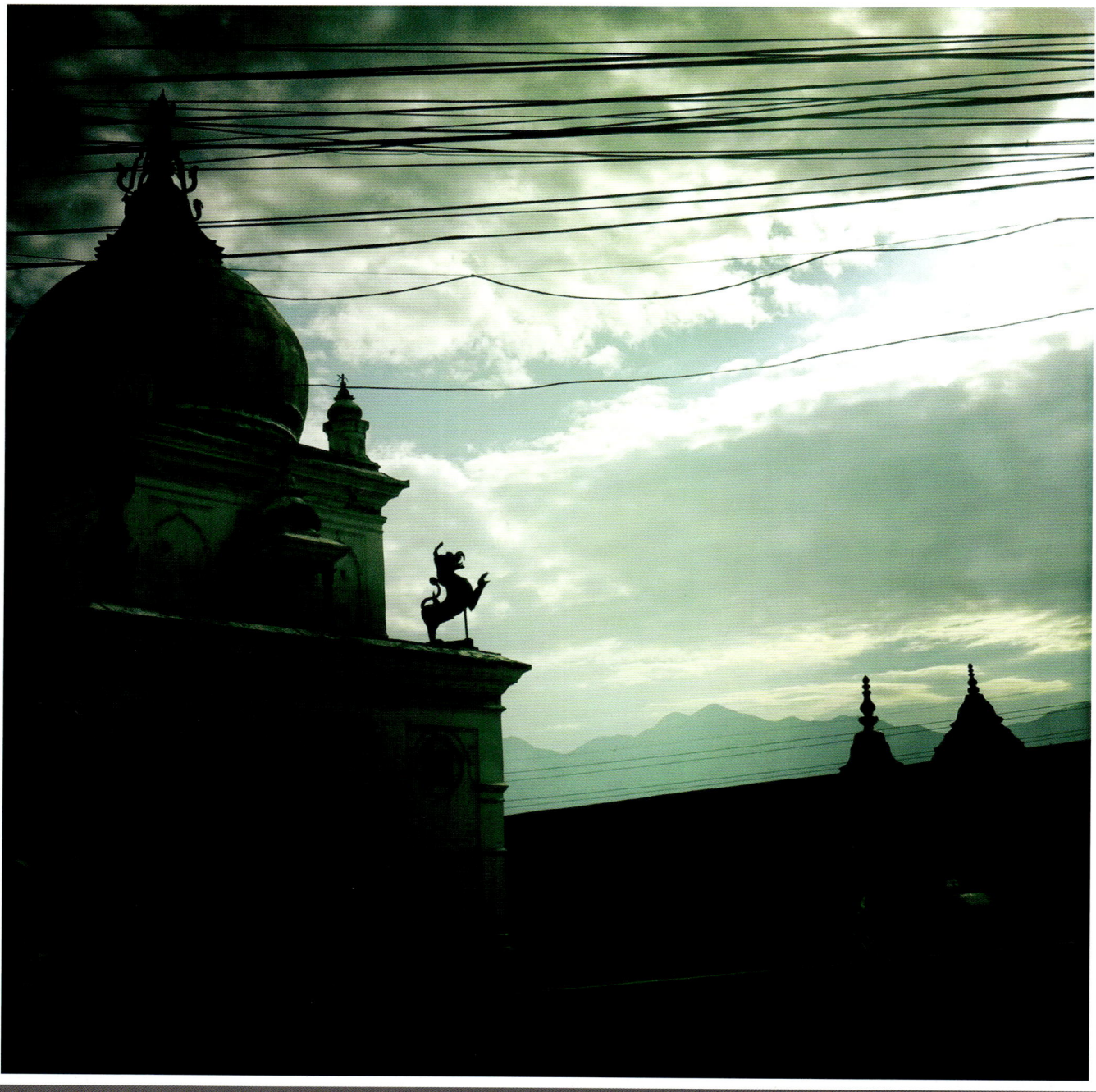

ABOVE: Overhead electrical wires line the streets of Kathmandu, Nepal. The city is punctuated by ornate temples and surrounded by soft hills in the distance.

PRESENTATION

While you may not be able to define the final form or destination for your project, think through your presentation options and consider how that might impact visual guidelines and plans for your project:

- If you intend to use your photographs in a multimedia presentation, consider the need to capture audio narration, sound effects, and/or video. If you intend to mix still photographs with video in a seamless way, you should limit your photographs to horizontal format, as vertical format images could visually disrupt what is typically a horizontal experience.
- If you intend to publish your photographs in a book or make prints for wall display, consider minimum size requirements for your photographs. Shoot on the highest quality setting your camera offers, or as Raw image files (like digital negatives) for minimal loss of information obtained by the camera sensor and maximum processing and printing flexibility.
- If you intend to share your digital images with captions or camera settings with publishers and/or clients, plan to auto-capture as much metadata (i.e., EXIF information including accurate date and time, GPS, your contact information and copyright, key words, etc.) as you can as you shoot and when you import images into your library. Plan to embed your captions within the metadata of your images and find out if the publisher or client has specific requirements for content and/or style.

TRY MAKING A PROCESSING DECISION BEFORE YOU SHOOT

I created this series of images portraying the texture of Kathmandu, Nepal using the Hipstamatic app on my iPhone to give them a consistent look and feel. When I'm traveling, I like to focus my time on seeing, shooting, and sharing images (versus processing them) with my followers on Twitter and Instagram in real time. Using the Hipstamatic app, I chose to make my processing decision upfront, and chose to shoot with a square-format viewfinder, a single lens (John S), and a single "film" (Blanko) throughout the trip. I didn't want to waste time thinking about what app to use each time

I grabbed my iPhone to make an image, so I made the decision to use just one that would create photographs with a look that would be very different from the more pure images I would make with my digital SLR camera.

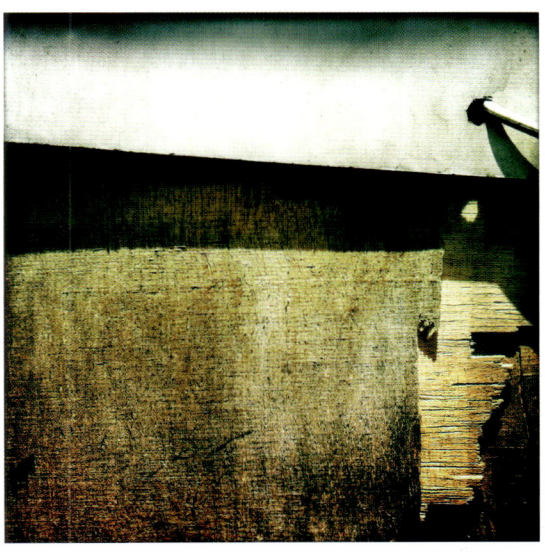

RIGHT: I'm often lured into the abstraction possibilities of texture on city streets. It's a way for me to experiment with the composition of inanimate objects. I discovered this in Thamel in Kathmandu.

BELOW: This small parking lot was filled with old and rusted Volkswagen buses.

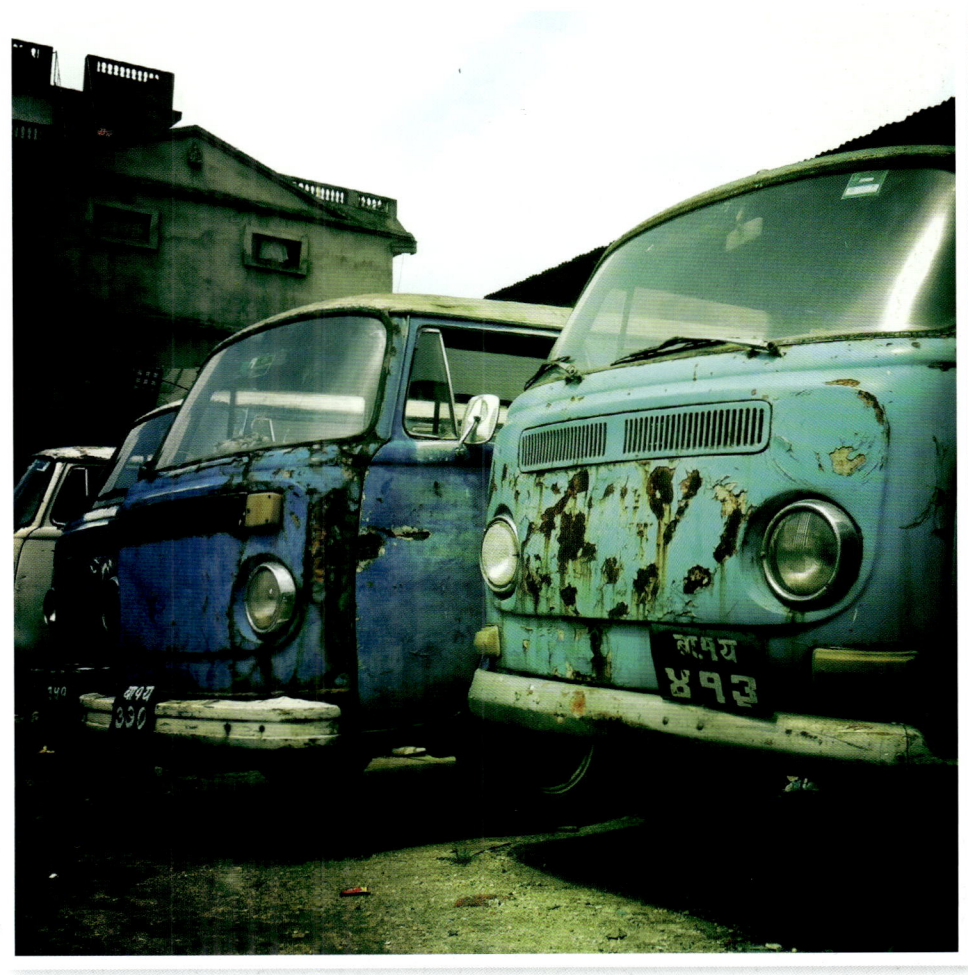

Narrow Your Subject

As you consider potential subjects for your next documentary project, consider the fact that a comprehensive portrayal of a broad subject will likely require more time and effort to produce than a narrow subject. That said, a narrow subject studied in depth or over an extended period of time could require as much (if not more) time and effort than a more surface-level study of a broader subject.

If you intend to share your project—online, in a gallery or a presentation, or in a print publication—it's important that your documentary project title and summary clearly define the scope of your work to avoid misrepresentation of your subject. For example, if I documented the introduction of technology to students at Shepherds Junior School in Arusha, Tanzania, my project title and/or summary should clearly communicate this narrow focus. I would not title the project "Technology and Education in Tanzania," because images from my single experience at one private school in Arusha would not accurately portray the breadth implied by this title.

Let's think through the process of narrowing an imaginary subject—a process that, for me, is part analytical and part serendipitous. If my broad concept is "dogs," I might narrow my area of focus to "show dogs in America." As I muse on this subject, I might discover that what I'm truly interested in documenting is the bond between show dogs and their masters, so I might stretch the subject to "show dogs and their masters in America." Because I'm interested in revealing a relationship, I would recognize that this would require a more intimate study of my subjects engaged in a variety of activities and settings. Photographing dogs and their masters in a competition setting would not be enough, so I might decide that several visits would be required with each subject. For that reason, I might decide to limit my travel to one location. In thinking about the location, I would first consider what might yield interesting visual results, and then consider the time and budget required to reach my subject's location. I might choose Manhattan because showing a dog on a busy city street seems to have good visual potential, because I enjoy the city and feel comfortable there, and because LaGuardia Airport is an inexpensive, two-hour flight from my hometown of Atlanta and a quick commute to my cousin's apartment in Astoria. So now, I've narrowed my project to "show dogs and their masters in Manhattan." In order to portray the breadth of show dogs, I would need to document several different types of dogs with their masters in Manhattan, but time and budget might push me to limit my study to one type of dog. In that case, I might narrow my subject to "Great Dane show dogs and their masters in Manhattan." I might choose Great Danes because I like the visual contrast of showing a very large dog in a small apartment. At this stage in my thought process, I might attend a statewide dog show in New York and study the Great Dane contestants to seek out my subjects. During that experience, I might discover a very petite woman working with her Great Dane, so I might introduce myself and ask her a few questions about her dog. We might connect fabulously, and suddenly, I've narrowed and locked in on my subject: "One Great Dane and His Petite Master."

PERSONAL PROJECT

As you narrow your subject for a personal project, consider these questions to help guide your decision-making process:

- What will yield interesting visual results?
- How will you gain access to your subject?
- How much travel is required to photograph your subject?
- How much time do you need to spend with your subject?
- How soon do you want to complete and/or share your project?

RIGHT: Koseli School students and Lens on Life program participants Manoj and his sister Manju photograph fellow student (and program participant) Rajesh and his mother in their home in Kathmandu, Nepal.

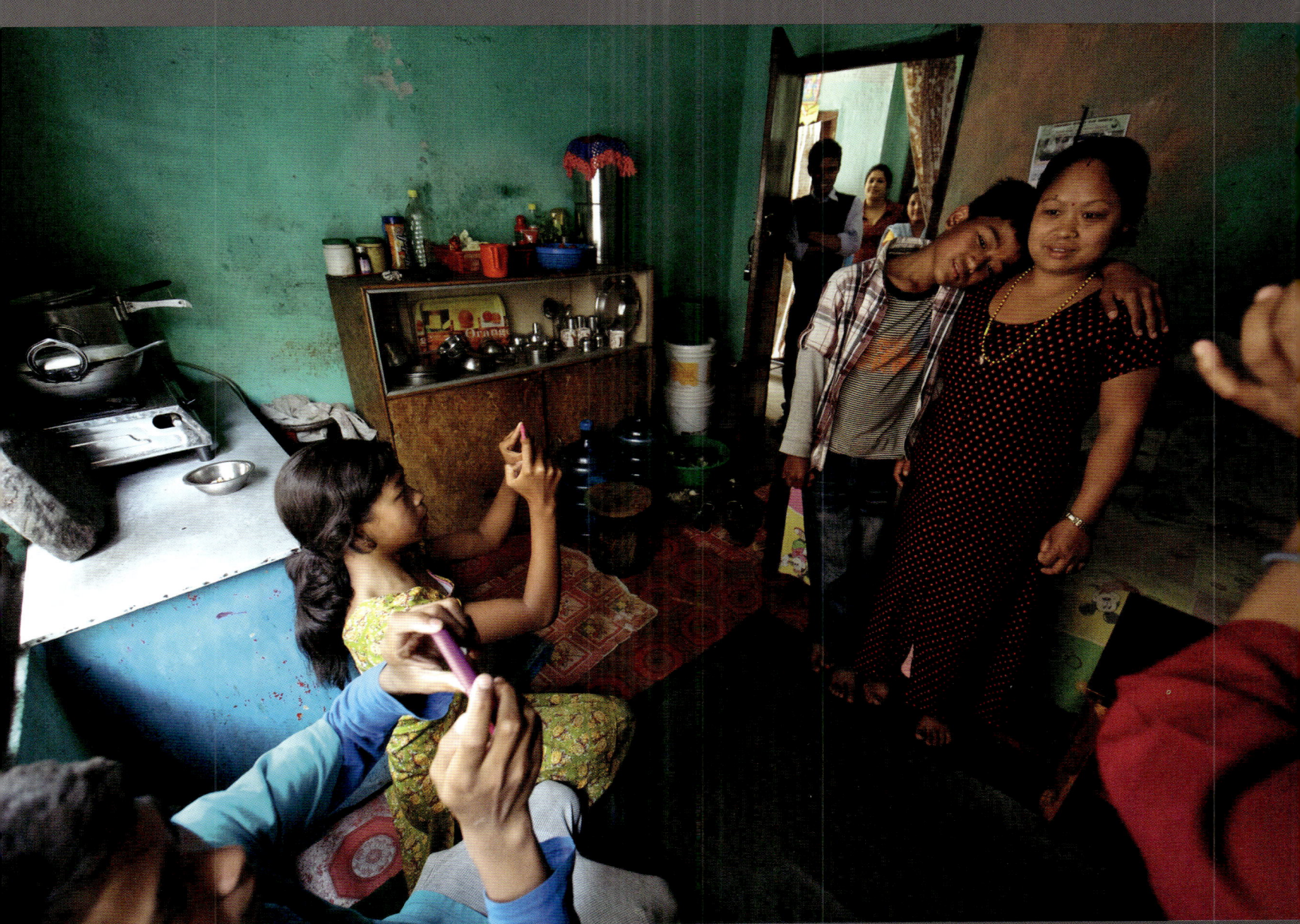

Narrow Your Subject

Because I've narrowed my subject to one Great Dane and his petite master in New York City, I can now expand my project within the confines of my specific subject to provide an in-depth view of their relationship. I can spend more time with the woman and her dog engaged in a variety of activities in a variety of settings. I might plan to capture the woman walking, grooming, training, feeding, carrying, loving, reprimanding, and shaking hands with her dog. On one of my visits, I might catch her dancing with the dog, watch her signal for him to press the buttons in the elevator, or learn that he sleeps with a stuffed animal at the foot of her bed every night. Narrowing my area of focus gives me the ability to visualize more detailed potential photographs for my story and to more clearly define a schedule, target completion date, and budget for the project, leaving enough space around these guidelines to let the project evolve in an organic way.

If I wanted to keep a fairly broad area of focus on "Show Dogs in America," but put clear limits on my investment of time and effort, I might narrow the boundaries of the project with a subtitle: "Show Dogs in America: Three on the Path to Best of Breed." By narrowing the focus on three dogs competing for a specific title in a single competition, I can define a target end date for my project (the competition date), select three different dogs (maybe a Great Dane, a collie, and a Chihuahua for visual interest) ideally in three different environments (maybe an apartment in the city, a suburban home, and a trailer on some acreage), and provide a more in-depth view of what it takes to prepare these three dogs to compete for the best of breed competition. Once I secured my subjects, I'd schedule one extended visit or two shorter visits with each subject to document them engaged in a variety of activities, and I'd plan to capture all three

of my subjects onsite at the National Dog Show before, during, and after the event. In this example, my photographs would likely portray more breadth (similarities and differences among show dogs and their masters) and less depth than a single relationship.

An area of focus might be partially defined or honed over time by the reality of your current limitations such as time, access, budget, language, and/or geography. You might need to balance a project that would place heavy demands in one or more of these areas with a project (or projects) that might be more in sync with your current situation. For example, I might define an area of focus to be the experience of teaching photography and documenting Koseli School students in Kathmandu, Nepal. As a mother of two children running a full-time business with a limited travel budget, it's difficult for me to travel internationally on a personal project more than once or twice a year, and then not for more than two weeks at a time. At this moment in my life, it's not possible for me to work on this kind of project more than once each year. While I'm unable to teach and document the experiences of my subjects throughout the year, I can document more dramatic shifts in their development on an annual basis. For that reason, I consider this one of my long-term projects that will steadily expand over the course of several years. As you define the scope of your project, consider ways to make it fit within your current reality or recognize that your project may require you to stretch some boundaries.

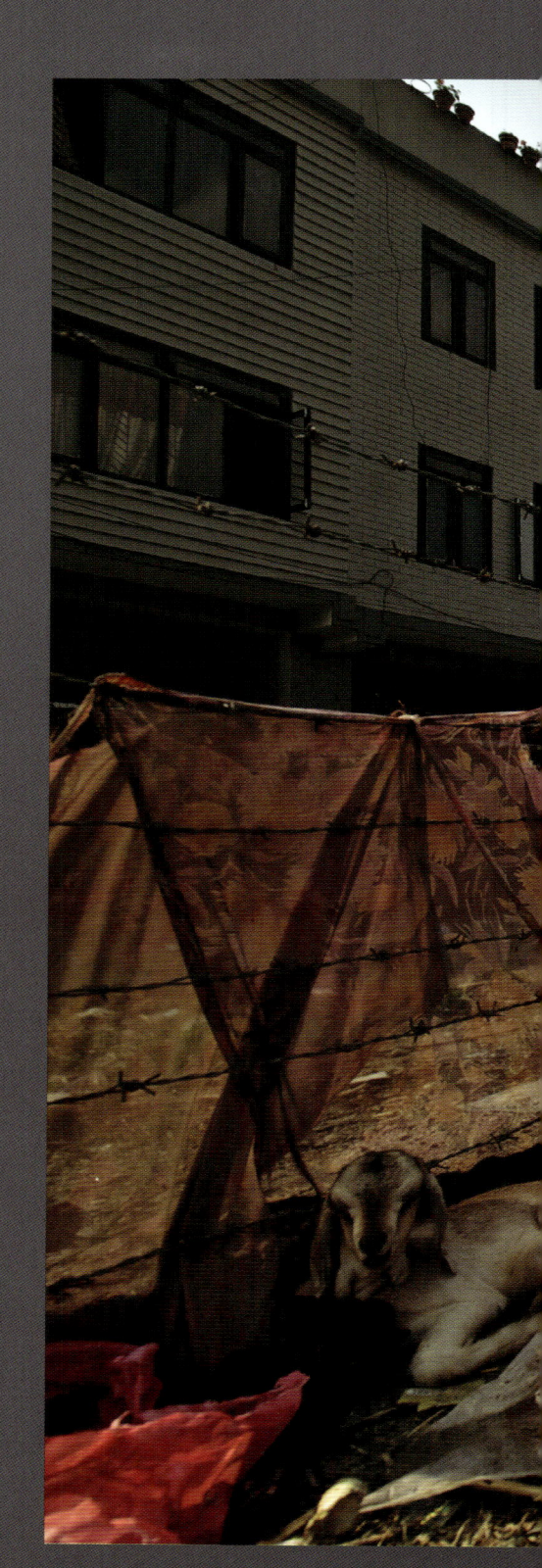

RIGHT: Koseli School students and Lens on Life program participants Srijana, Manju, Rajesh, and Manoj photograph goats with iPhone cameras in Bagmati area of Kathmandu, Nepal.

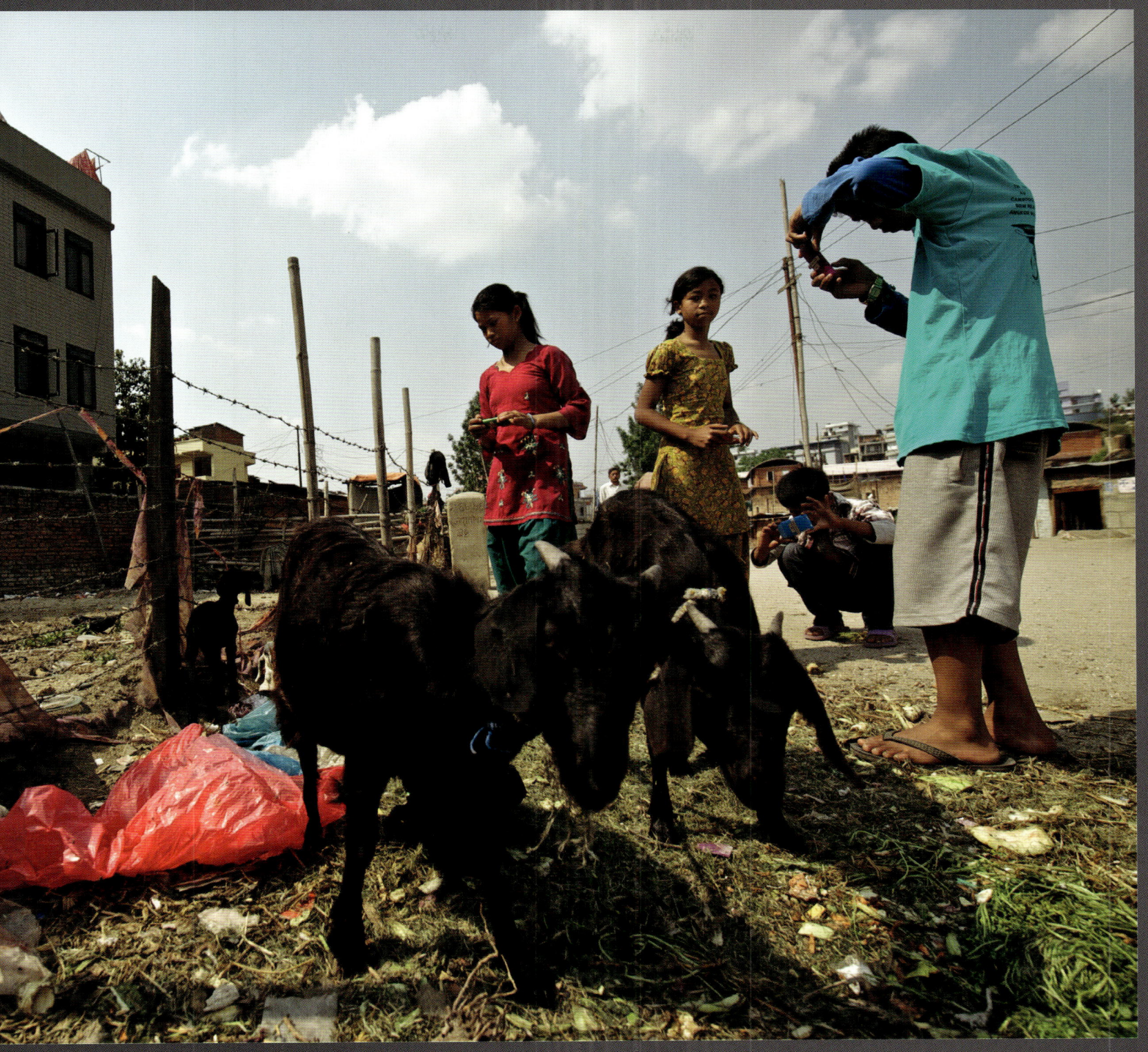

Capture & Craft Captions to Support Your Images

One of the most challenging tasks of a documentary project is to capture and retain detailed information about your subjects and setting to craft informative and accurate captions. There's no question that captions add value to your photographs and to the overall story you wish to share, but how can you master the art of capturing source material for captions when all you really want to do is shoot?

SIX TIPS TO GUIDE YOU

1. Learn as much as you can about the story, your subjects, and the location before you arrive. Ask your client to provide you with written details about the project or conduct your own research to build a knowledge base to guide image-making. Ask questions. Consult and print maps. The more information you understand before you arrive, the more informed questions you will ask during the assignment. Be sensitive to not waste your guide's or subjects' time by asking for information you could have obtained on your own with the help of online resources. On arrival, you can ask your hosts or guides to help you understand and annotate maps with onsite details.

2. Curb your curiosity enough to ask questions focused on your assignment. We photographers are curious beings. I could easily explore many aspects of a situation when I'm embedded within it, but it's important to focus on the assignment and to ask questions that relate to your telling of the story to use your time most wisely. The more information you capture, the more time you'll need to sort and filter information following the shoot. Ask yourself, "Will the answer to this question enhance the story portrayed in the images?" If the answer is yes, ask. If not, hold back and save the question for later, if time allows.

3. Don't rely on your memory; record conversations. I travel with a handheld professional audio recorder (and an ample supply of batteries, as electricity is not always accessible or within the reach of my power cord) to capture my conversations with client contacts and my subjects throughout an assignment. Always ask permission to record the conversation, and start the recording before you ask the first question. I often record my own verbal notes about the setting and the subject preceding each conversation to help connect voices with individuals I'm shooting. I typically record the entire conversation on the highest audio quality setting in the event I want to edit and integrate portions of the audio in a multimedia presentation. While this could produce a lengthy and very large audio file, it ensures that you won't forget to turn the device on and off between questions.

4. Type names of your subjects and location details into a portable device or write notes in a journal. I've used the Notes app on my iPhone for this, but if you have questionable access to electricity, bring a journal and several pens. In the throes of a documentary assignment, you are often pressed for time, and this can lead to less-than-legible handwriting. I've made the mistake of having someone write down names for me while I'm shooting, only to find that I had difficulty reading her handwriting long after the shoot. If you must obtain handwritten names (e.g., print photo release forms), print the names in your own handwriting or ensure you can read the handwriting of your assistant. Beside each name, write a physical description (e.g., clothing details) to help connect the names with your images.

If you are shooting a variety of subjects in a single session, consider writing the subjects' names on index cards and shooting a quick headshot of your subject holding the index card with their name to easily connect faces with names.

5. Photograph signs and physical markers. Because you want to devote more of your time to shooting and less to writing down details, at times it might be easier to photograph signs, badges, or physical markers (e.g., scientific names for flora in a botanical garden) to record locations or subject matter information for later use in caption writing. Assuming your digital camera is set to capture EXIF data, the date and time of image capture will automatically be associated with those pictures, giving you an easy method of backtracking your sequence of events.

6. Transcribe the audio to make it easy to copy and paste details into your captions and/or written story. While you can take on the task of transcribing your audio recordings (as I have), be aware that it can be a very time-consuming and tedious task. Your time might be better spent on other tasks, so consider paying a transcription service to perform the task for you. A quick online search will yield services offering a variety of options, based on your turnaround needs and budget. Plan for this time and expense in your budget.

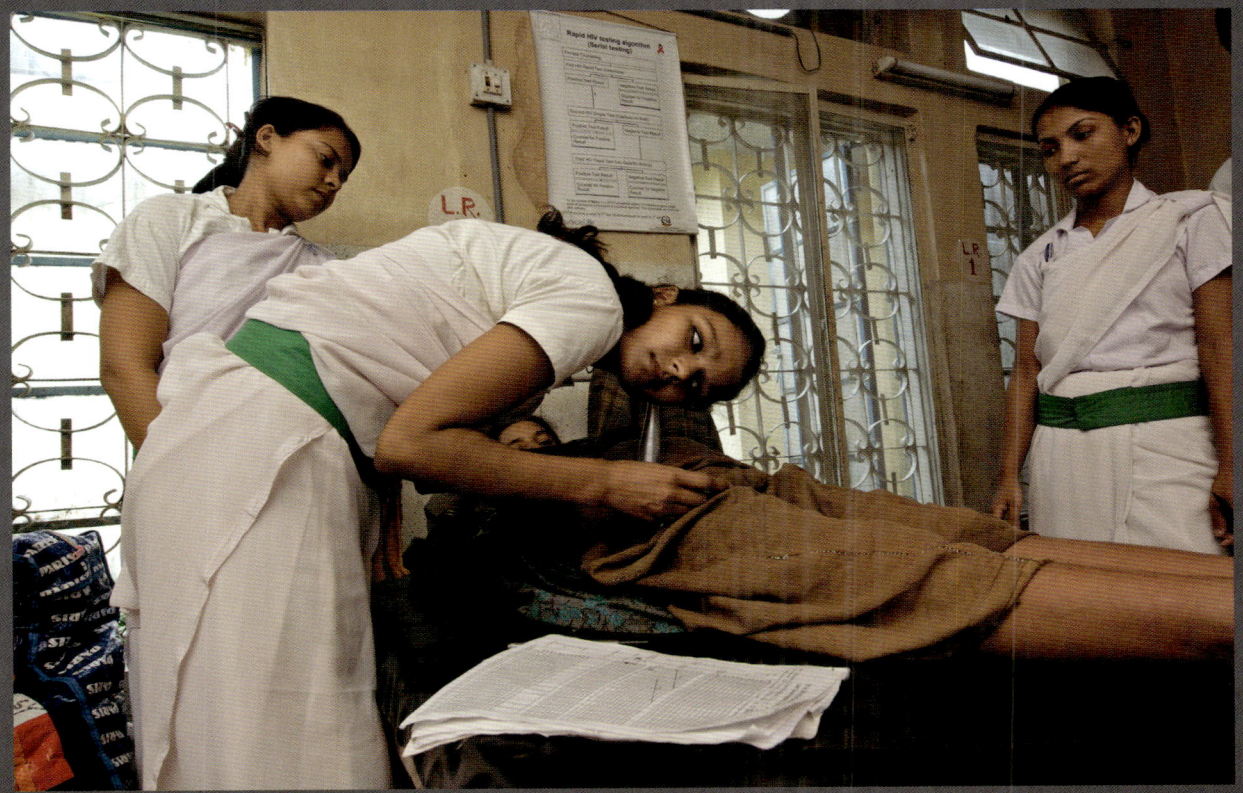

LEFT: Student nurse Sheadha Paril checks a baby's heartbeat in the delivery room at Seti Zonal Hospital in Dhangadhi Municipality (Kailali District, Nepal). Expectant mothers (like Lalmati Kathariya, pictured here) wait in this room prior to their delivery. Funding from CARE, a leading humanitarian organization fighting global poverty, provides lighting, delivery beds and equipment, and toilet facilities for expectant mothers. © Stephanie Calabrese Roberts/CARE.

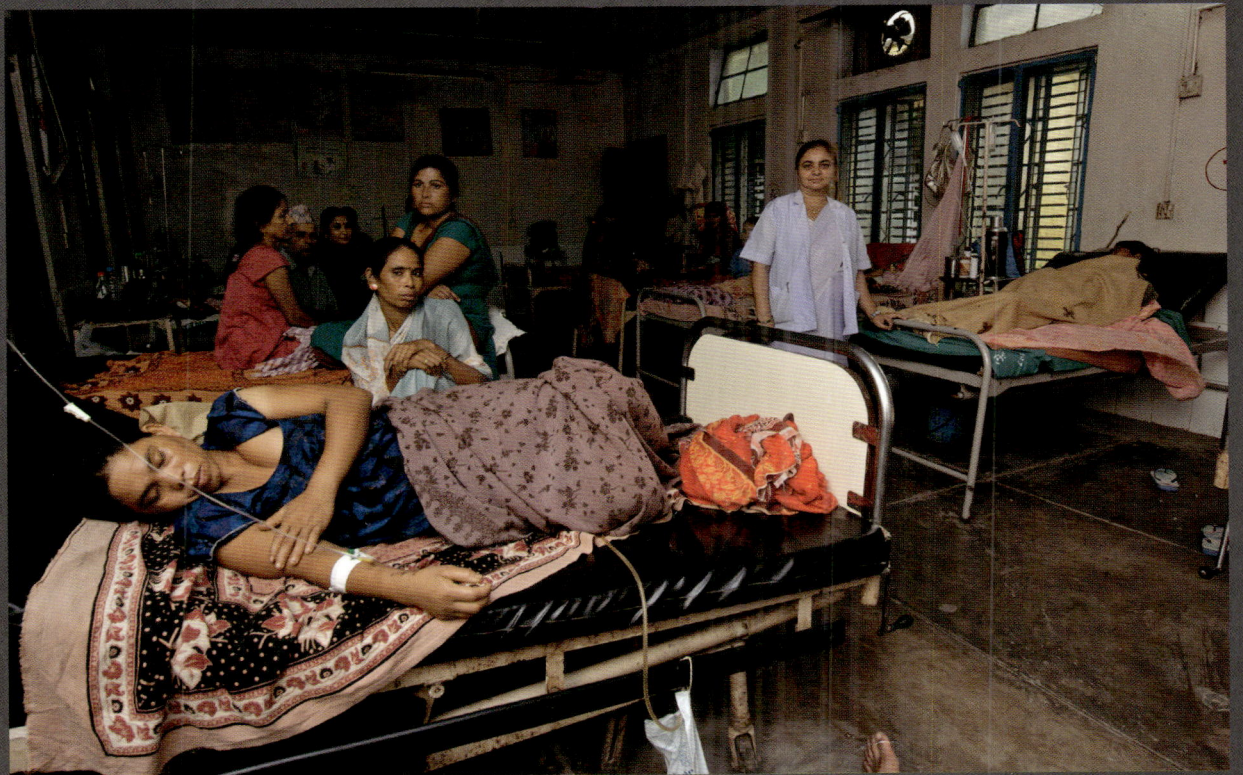

LEFT: Manju (standing to right, dressed in blue) has been the head matron of the Gynecology Ward at Seti Zonal Hospital in Kailali District for the past seven years. She manages 16 nurses who provide pre- and post-operative delivery care, help with breastfeeding, and hygiene care for new mothers. Recently-delivered mothers stay here at the hospital under her care for six hours following a vaginal delivery and a week to ten days following a Caesarean section delivery. © Stephanie Calabrese Roberts/CARE.

Visualize the Actions & Settings for Your Subject

Now that you've spent time thinking through your subject, considering your subject's actions and the settings in which these actions might occur is an important aspect of the project. First, have a conversation or spend time with your subject so you can get a feel for his/her natural routine. You want to understand where, when, and how your subject does what he or she does so you can begin to visualize how you might document your subject in the most unobtrusive and organic way. This initial conversation or experience gives you a way of conceptualizing the project in advance of your arrival and helps you plan your schedule. If your subject wakes up at 5:00 a.m. to begin his day with a morning prayer in an outdoor temple down the street, and you've deemed this a routine you want to document, then you will need to be prepared and ready to begin shooting by 5:00 a.m. (potentially by candlelight).

Having a good understanding of your subject's actions and settings in advance also gives you a way of visualizing the execution of your shoot. While the intended actions of your subject likely won't occur exactly as you've discussed or visualized them in your own mind, going through this exercise helps you think about the visual rhythm of your image series and the equipment you might need to execute each "scene." There's no need to haul your entire lens collection with you on all of your shoots if you can clearly define or preview the setting where the action will take place. If you're unsure how close you'll be able to get to your subject, pack a 24–70mm or 24–105mm lens to give you a good range of width and reach.

LIMITED SETTINGS

If you find that your subject's actions are likely to occur within a single setting, think about ways to add visual interest in the actions

or individuals you can reveal to convey the story. For example, if you are photographing "A Day in the Life of High-Security Prisoners" in a U.S. jail, recognize the fact that all of the prisoners will be dressed alike and that your setting will be confined to one destination with limited visual interest. For that reason, your challenge will be to reveal visual interest in the emotion (using expressions, gestures, body language) and actions of the prisoners, use of repeating lines and the integration of interior elements, interesting spaces, slices of light, and negative space in your compositions. In this example, because you might expect the setting to be fairly simple with hard edges and clean lines, it gives you an opportunity to focus on the softer edges of humanity portrayed in your photographs.

The benefit to a project within a limited setting is that it gives you a higher level of predictability with color and light, minimizing

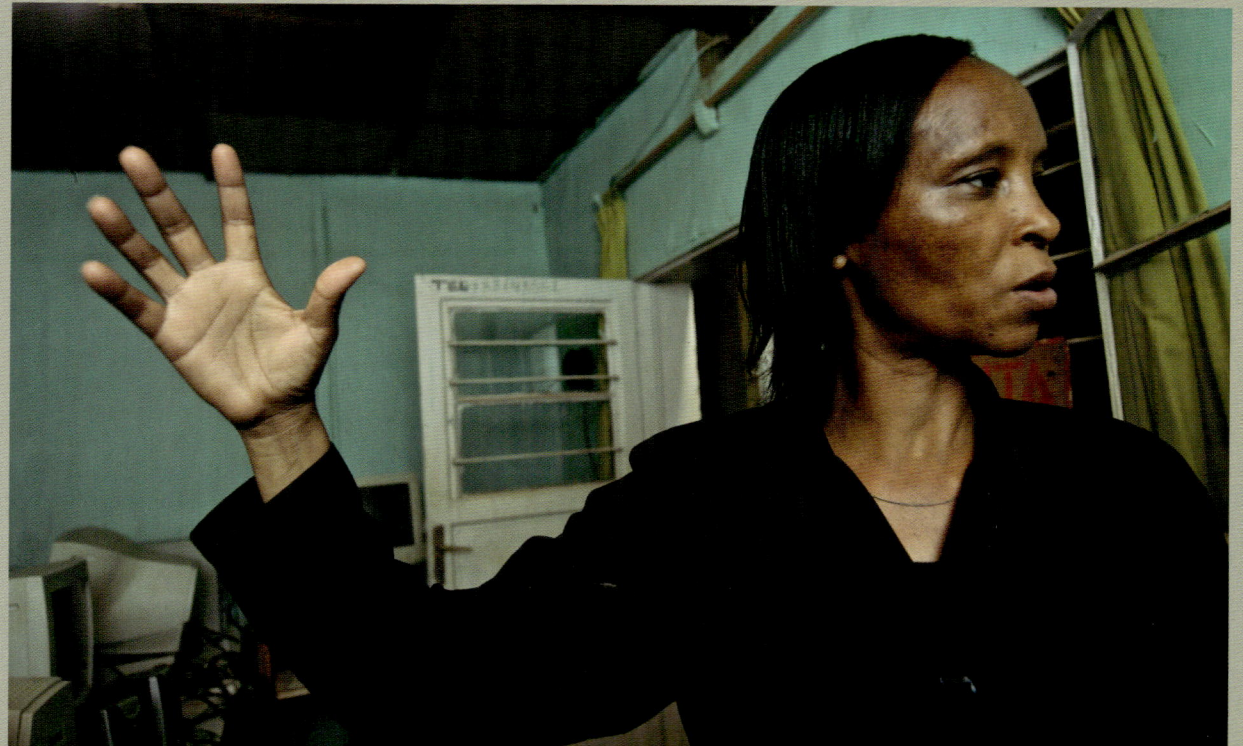

SETTING
ISO 640
FOCAL LENGTH: 14mm
APERTURE: f/2.8
SHUTTER SPEED: 1/60
FLASH: Fired

LEFT AND OPPOSITE: The computer center in Kigali, Rwanda, owned by female entrepreneur Dativa, offers training in and access to word processing and spreadsheet applications despite common electricity outages in the area.

your need to adjust camera settings for white balance and exposure, giving you the ability to focus more on your subjects and less on your camera. Color photographs would likely yield visual continuity throughout your series of images because a limited interior setting would yield a consistent color palette throughout the setting (e.g., wall and door colors, flooring, uniforms, furniture).

VARIED SETTINGS

If you've selected a subject that needs to be portrayed in a variety of settings to convey the range of their activities, such as "A Day in the Life of a Broadway Cast Member," you can plan to shoot your subject engaged in a variety of actions in various "behind the scenes" settings— settings that viewers might not otherwise have access to. In this example, your settings can add significant value to the weight of the visual story, and might attract viewers intrigued with

a behind-the-scenes view, regardless of the "star quality" of your performer.

For example, you might photograph him doing yoga on the living room floor of his studio apartment; walking his Eskimo dog on Broadway *en route* to a vocal lesson; applying his own makeup in the mirror within his dressing room; clowning around with his fellow performers backstage before the show; tugging on his sparkly silver boots with a grimace; waiting anxiously behind the curtain for his cue; bowing modestly to a standing ovation; embracing his fiancée backstage after the show; signing autographs for eager fans outside the stage door; and quietly strolling home beneath the sizzle of Times Square lights.

The broader your setting, the more time you need to consider visual continuity in terms of light and color. For example, if eight of your ten best photographs were shot in dim interior settings that exposed rich color and deep

shadows, and two were shot in bright sunlight, you might consider omitting those bright light images to minimize the jarring change in lighting conditions within your sequence. Alternatively, you could expand your image series to include a broader range of lighting conditions to balance the visual impact of light throughout the series.

UNKNOWN SETTINGS

While you may enjoy the freedom and ability to plan your personal documentary assignments and identify the settings in which they occur, your client assignments may place you in settings and situations with little advance notice. I like going into a new setting with fresh eyes and limited prior knowledge as it challenges me to think fast and follow my instincts. You likely won't have the ability to "scout" a location in advance of an assigned shoot, but you might have an opportunity to

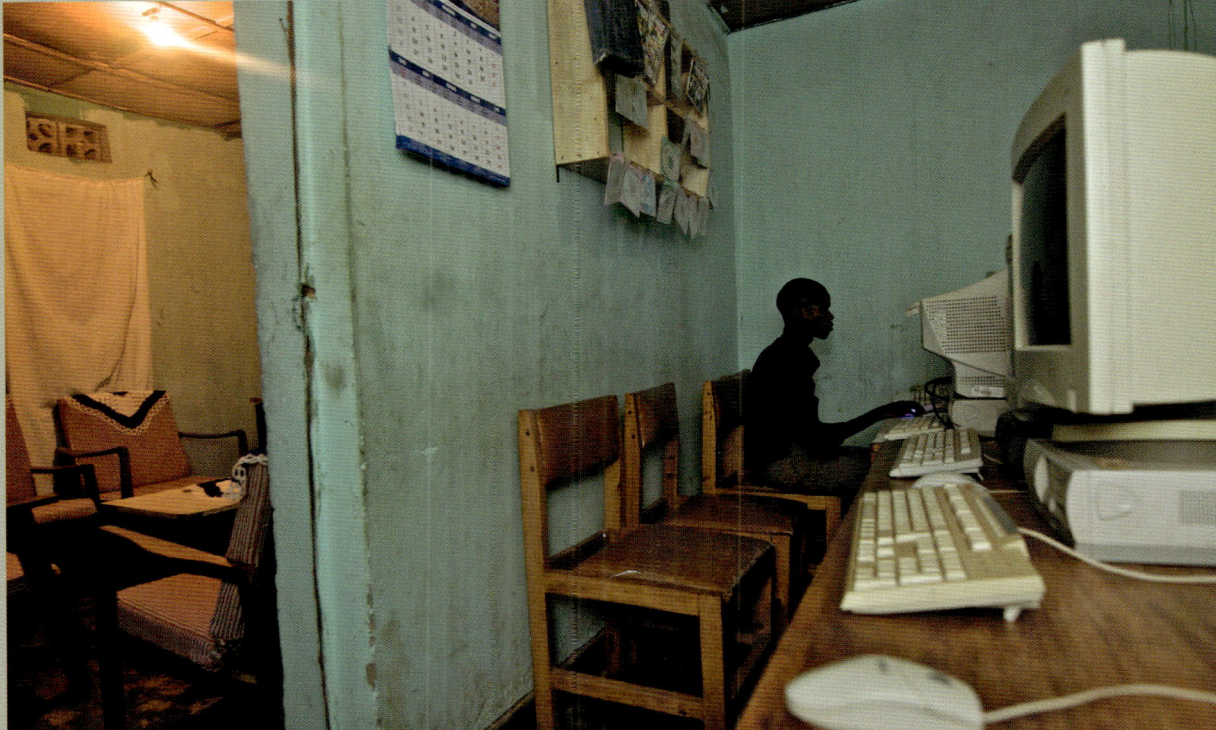

SETTING
ISO 640
FOCAL LENGTH: 14mm
APERTURE: ƒ/2.8
SHUTTER SPEED: 1/60
FLASH: Fired

Visualize the Actions & Settings for Your Subject

arrive a few minutes early to a location before the action occurs. Use this time to assess the light, color, and background elements that might influence where you choose to stand and shoot.

If you expect a group of children to come running out of a door when the bell rings at 10:00 a.m., show up at 9:50 a.m. Figure out which way the door will open, notice any details you'd like to include in the setting, and stand in a place that will yield what you perceive to be the most interesting vantage point. Showing up early gives you time to make your lens choice and click a few test images to ensure you are satisfied with your camera settings.

REMOTE SETTINGS

Shooting in remote settings and/or in developing countries is an exciting challenge, but requires you to plan in different ways.

Electricity may not always be available or reliable. In some areas, the flow of electricity might be limited, yet fairly predictable. Find out if there are anticipated blackout hours so you can plan to charge your gear when electricity is available.

Bring the appropriate travel voltage converter to charge your gear as voltage and electrical outlet plug holes vary in size and shape throughout the world.

Bring backup camera batteries so you don't have to rely on electricity to keep you charged through your shoot. In your camera bag, devise

a way to clearly separate dead batteries from new batteries so you can quickly and easily access them without confusion while you're focused on your shoot.

Bring two flashlights. Keep one in your camera bag and one in your luggage. And remember that after the sun sets, it's difficult to find your flashlight in the dark.

You can bring rechargeable batteries for your flash, but realize that you will be reliant upon access to electricity to keep them charged. I always bring more batteries than I think I'll need. But be aware that batteries add weight to your bags. Pack as many as you can in your luggage and carry on only what's necessary to get you through your initial day or two of shooting in your camera bag.

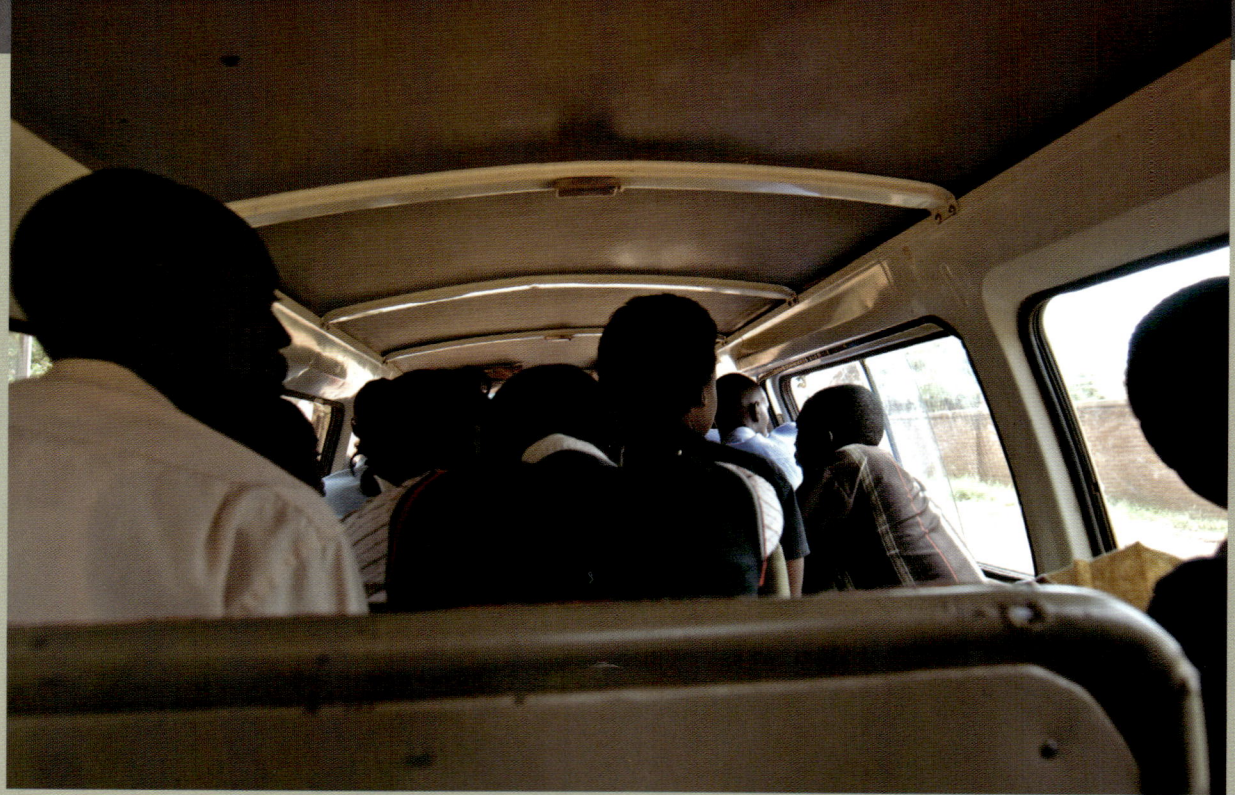

SETTING
ISO 500
FOCAL LENGTH: 14mm
APERTURE: ƒ/2.8
SHUTTER SPEED: 1/500
FLASH: Not fired

LEFT: My view from the back seat of a public transportation vehicle in Kigali, Rwanda. Two passengers sat beside me.

Transit can be cramped and time-consuming. If you intend to use public transportation such as buses or taxis, assume that space in the vehicle will be limited and that public transportation vehicles may or may not run on schedule. Leave time to accommodate travel delays. Whether you are using public transportation or a hired driver, you might also experience delays *en route* to a remote setting during inclement weather (especially during rainy seasons), as a significant portion of your journey may not occur on paved roads. Rainy season travel through mountainous or lowland regions could make travel treacherous due to mudslides or floods, so be sure to consult local contacts as you plan the timing of your shoot. Because public transportation is a primary mode of travel for many local residents, vehicles are often packed tightly. Your camera bag will most often be sitting (and jostling) on your lap. For this reason, I like traveling with the least amount of gear I might need and carrying it in a fairly compact sling bag so I can quickly and easily swing the bag around from my back to my front.

LOW-LIGHT SHOOTING SCENARIOS

If you are shooting in homes in remote regions, many of them may be constructed of mud, natural materials, cardboard, and sheets of metal, and may have few windows. If electricity is present in the home, it's likely that the light emitted from a single low-wattage light bulb overhead will be your only source of light. For this reason, I shoot with a camera body and lenses that perform well in low-light situations, and I bring an external mount flash to provide a dose of light when I need it. When I'm walking through slums or in a remote village out under a bright daylight sun, I keep the flash mounted on my camera so I can quickly turn it on when I step into small dark interiors requiring a dose of light. If I'm shooting in low-light scenarios and feel that artificial light might desensitize the mood or emotion of the moment, I shoot on a very low aperture setting to let as much light into the camera as possible and might substantially increase my ISO setting.

SETTING
ISO 3200
FOCAL LENGTH: 14mm
APERTURE: *f*/2.8
SHUTTER SPEED: 1/200
FLASH: Not fired

RIGHT: Koseli School student and Lens on Life program participant Manisha makes a self-portrait in her bedroom with an iPhone camera in Kathmandu, Nepal.

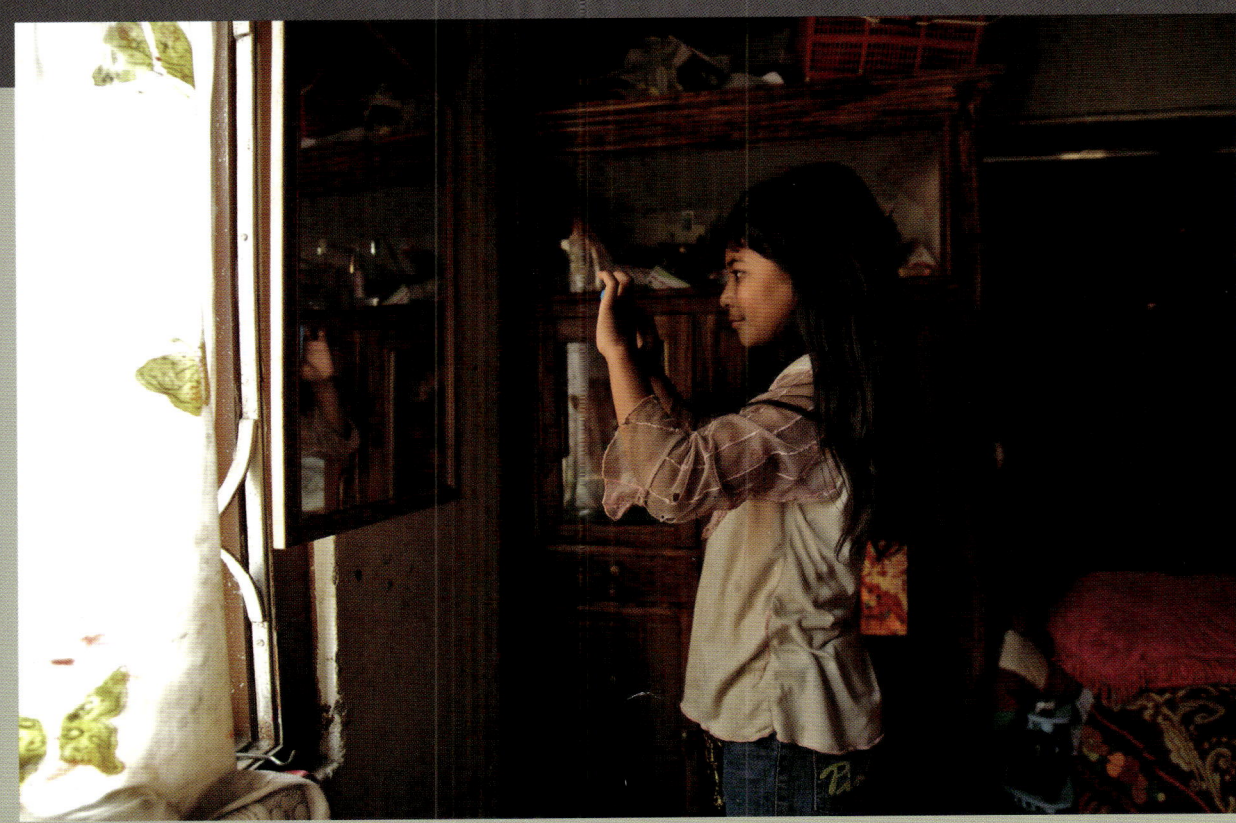

Plan an Assignment in a Faraway Land

INTRODUCTION

Are you eager to experience and document life in faraway places? Maybe you remember what it felt like to explore thin paths in the woods as a child or venture down streets in a city where you've never been—a sense of wonder for uncharted territory and a delight in the unfamiliar. Maybe you've long felt the tug in your heart to explore the unknown and push yourself past the familiar boundaries of your day-to-day life. Or maybe you've remained comfortably within the lines of a predictable path up until this moment because you've been a little bit fearful of the unknown, yet still envious of modern-day explorers in your midst.

I know that feeling. When I was ten years old, I remember my parents giving me a great deal of freedom to explore and express my independence as long as I was home in time for dinner at 5:30 p.m. I walked to and from elementary school and the public library with my younger brother and friends, and rode my bike all over town on the weekends. I enjoyed convincing my friends to explore the Jewish cemetery at the end of our street and beyond it into the woods around our neighborhood. We built forts and hunted for interesting "clues" found on bottle caps, faded newspapers, and torn magazines. I remembered feeling confined in my backyard. There just wasn't enough to see.

Occasionally, I still feel that need to experience the unfamiliar. Travel fulfills me in this way, but less in a way that's like a relaxing vacation and more like a transformative life experience. While I admire the natural beauty of sunsets, a snow-capped mountain range, and the infinite ripples of the sea, I don't feel moved to photograph these things regardless of where they are in the world. For me, the draw of documenting life in a faraway land is connected with humanity, particularly when I have the opportunity to shine a light on people in challenging circumstances in places where very few people want to go. Through my photographs, I attempt to connect diverse people divided by cultural, socioeconomic, and geographic boundaries.

Your first documentary assignment to a remote region in the world will likely expose you to a very different way of life and change you in a profound way. As you begin planning potential destinations and target timeframes for your first adventure—whether it's a paid assignment for a client, a volunteer project for a non-profit organization, or a personal project, preparing for your first photography-based trip to a developing country can be intimidating. I remember feeling this way when my "Picture Hope" documentary project partner, Jen Lemen, and I began making plans to travel to Rwanda during the summer of 2009. Though Jen had visited Rwanda, developed relationships with our hosting families, and shared advice with me on how to prepare for our first trip, I still possessed a hearty dose of fear of the unknown. Since then, Jen and I have successfully traveled and completed documentary photography assignments together in several remote destinations in developing countries. I highly recommend traveling with a partner you trust and enjoy—someone who complements you.

I'm certain there is no one right way to prepare for and plan an assignment in a remote region, but in this section, I'll share what I've learned and what's worked well for me. Consider it one woman's perspective. I hope it gives you enough confidence to plan your own adventure.

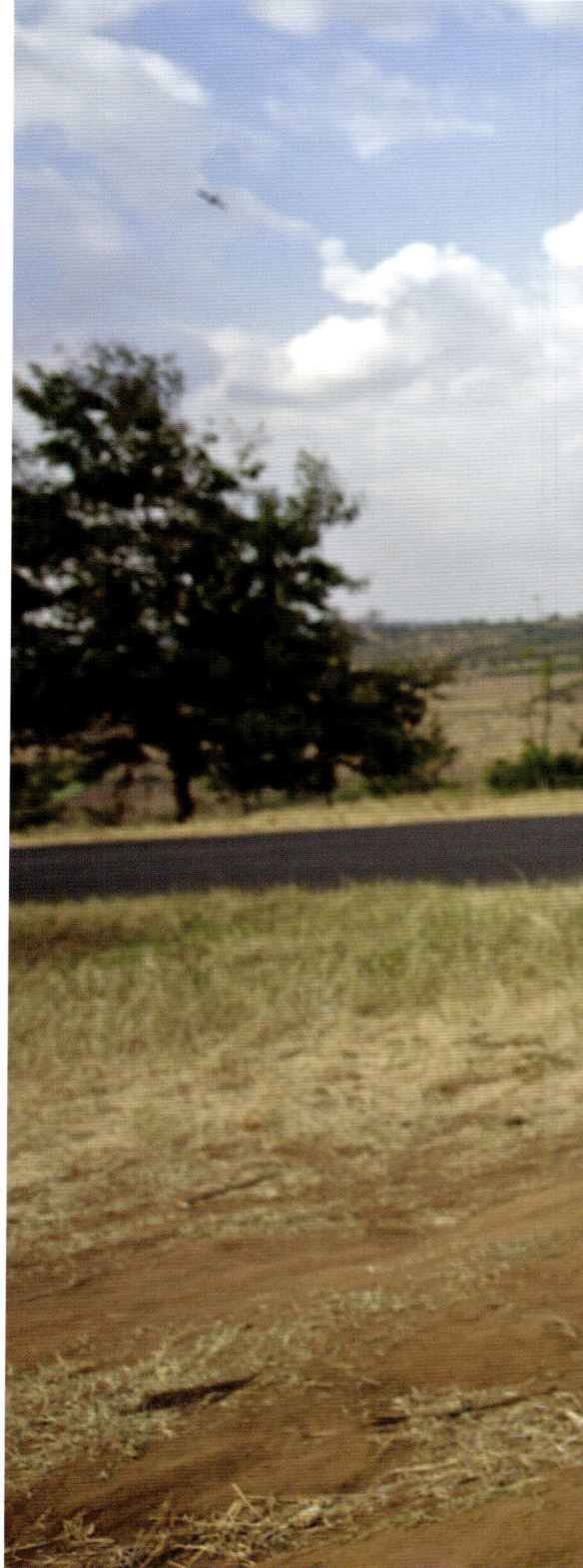

RIGHT: Our friend Innocent and his siblings hosted Jen and me throughout our visit in Rwanda. Here, he and Jen hop on a rented motorcycle in the village of Kizarakome, where his mother resides.

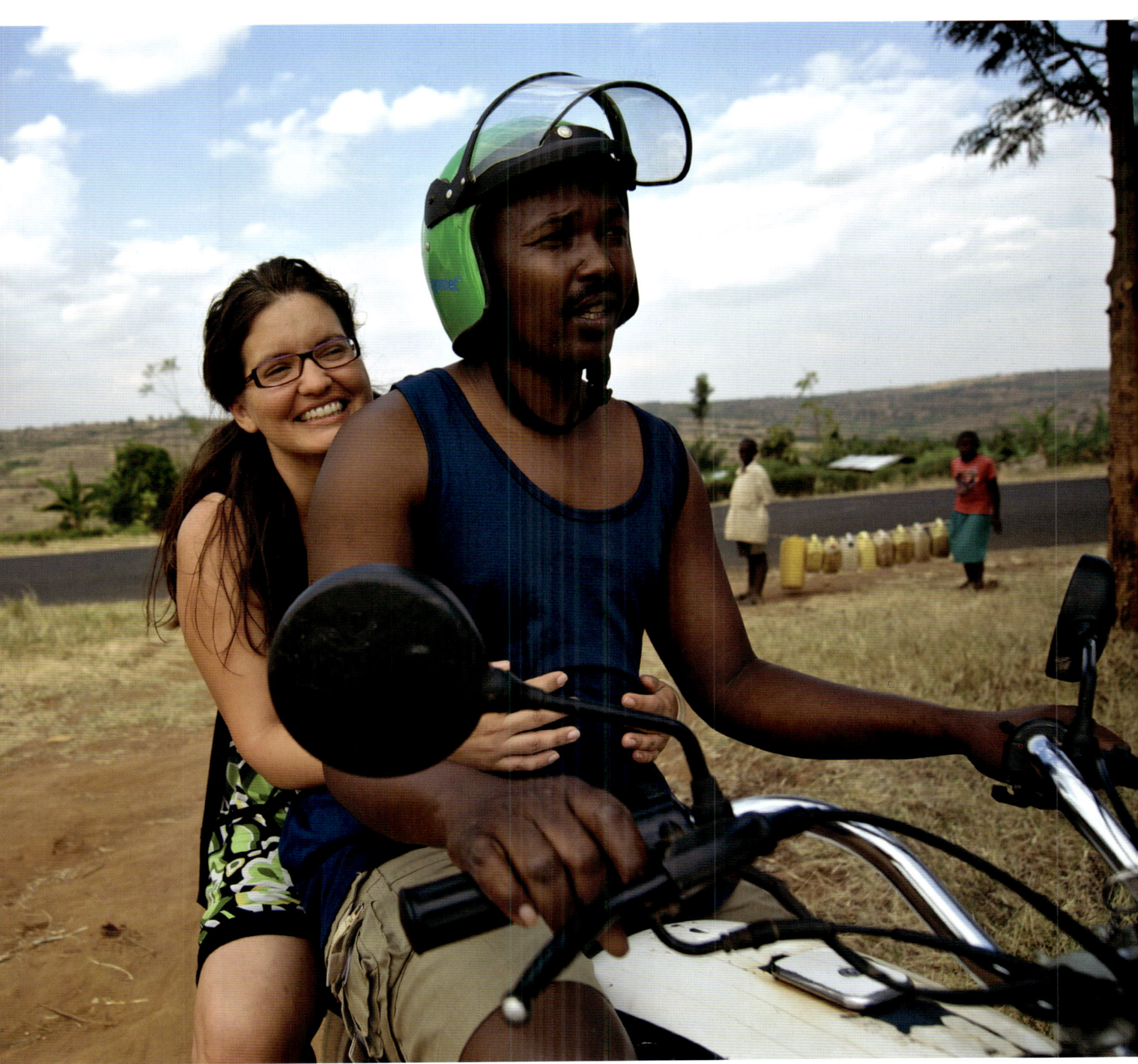

Before You Book Your Flight

Identify a trusted local contact to guide you. When I've traveled to developing countries, thus far, I've only traveled with a partner and we've always had more than one local contact (who, more often than not, has been a friend) to serve as our primary guide.

A LOCAL GUIDE

I highly recommend this approach for several obvious reasons:

- A local contact knows the country, the people, the culture, the language, the food, the transit system, the climate, the geography, the holidays, the customs, and the currency, and can help you develop relationships with other trusted local contacts.
- A local contact can connect you with people, experiences, and settings that are authentic to the region, moving you off the tourist track and onto the path less traveled by foreigners.
- A local contact can more swiftly and effectively translate conversations, negotiate options and decisions, offer perspective, and help navigate sensitive situations on your behalf. For example, if you are interested in taking photographs of individuals in a remote village, you may require permission to gain access into the village by the village leader and offer advice on what you might offer as a gift of thanks if this is appropriate. Or, if you want to make photographs during a religious ceremony, seeking direction on when to shoot and when not to shoot is important to ensure respect and avoid disrupting the experience.

DO YOUR HOMEWORK

Learn as much as you can about your subject—the people, the experience, event, or situation, and the location. Get a perspective on any historical, political, religious, economic, cultural, and social undercurrents, as these factors will undoubtedly influence what you will see and how you might portray your subject or story. Find out if other photographers have focused on the same (or similar) subject or story and review their work. Think about ways you can offer your own unique perspective.

DISCUSS THE INTENT OF YOUR PROJECT

And collaborate with your client, host(s), and/or subject(s) in advance of your trip If you are working through an organization such as a local school or NGO, start with those contacts and they can help you identify your subjects and plan your visit, as well as orchestrate introductions when you arrive on site. Rely on your contacts' counsel for the best way to work with local groups and individuals. Be open and share as much information about your intent and plans for your project. If you are not certain if, when, or how the images may be published, be honest about that, but share your intent. Explain any specific support requests you have in advance such as recommendations for transit, itinerary plans, your need for a translator and/or guide, and access to any specific events or locations.

Consult with your local contacts, your client, host(s), and/or subject(s) well in advance of your trip so you can give them ample time to coordinate plans and offer support prior to your arrival. Keep in mind that Internet access in remote regions of developing countries is not always accessible or convenient, so responses may take time. Encourage your hosts to share any expectations they have of you, and respond to their questions or requests as quickly as you can. The last thing you want to do is inconvenience your contacts or set unrealistic expectations. Be gracious and express your appreciation for their support.

CHECK THE CLIMATE AND HOLIDAY SCHEDULE FOR YOUR DESTINATION

Avoid rainy seasons (unless this is a requirement for your project) or allow for extra time in your schedule to accommodate rain delays and/or transit-related delays due to weather issues such as floods and mudslides, particularly in mountainous regions. In very remote regions, most in-country flights could be cancelled due to limited visibility. Keep in mind that local holidays and/or religious events may influence your plans. Be respectful of your subjects' local customs and existing commitments.

BE AWARE OF ANY TRAVEL WARNINGS

Before you plan your destination, check the safety and stability of the country you intend to visit by reviewing any travel warnings your local government may have shared with citizens of your country. United States citizens can check the U.S. Department of State website for up-to-date travel warnings and tips for international travel. This website also provides information about passport applications and renewals and guidance on what to do if your passport gets lost or stolen while you're out of the country. www.travel.state.gov.

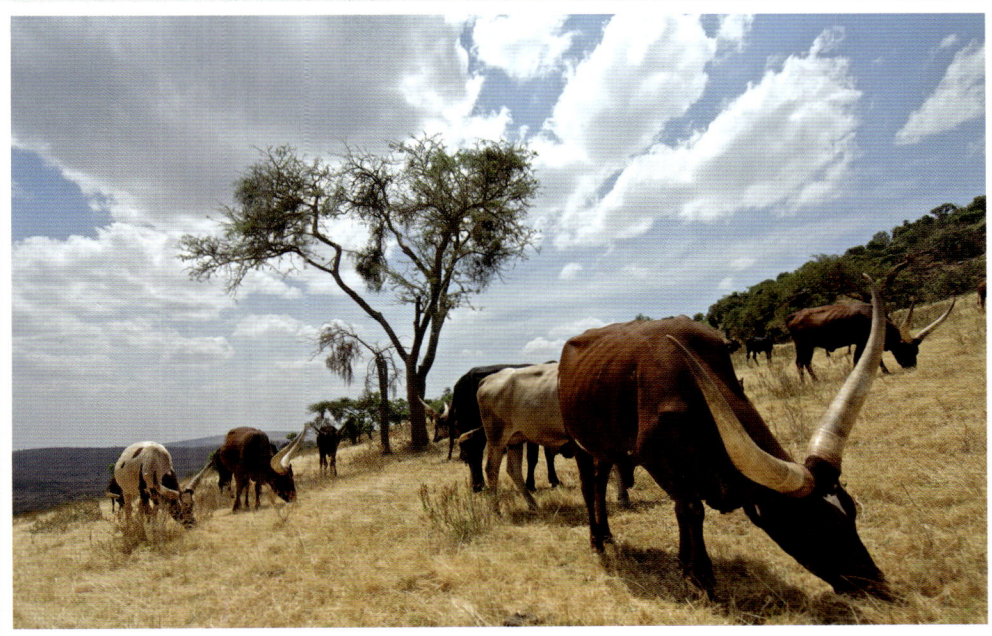

RIGHT: I asked my friend and motorcycle driver, Mupenzi, to stop for a moment so I could document these cows grazing on the mountain where his brother (and my friend) Innocent goes to pray in Kizarakome, Rwanda. grazing on the prayer mountain in Kizarakome, Rwanda.

CHECK THE EXPIRATION DATE ON YOUR PASSPORT

Make sure your passport is up to date and not expiring soon. Getting your passport renewed can take several weeks, so checking this well in advance of the date of your trip is critical. Make three photocopies of your passport data page: one to put in your camera bag, one to put in your luggage, and one to leave at home with a family member or friend. Then, while traveling, keep your actual passport in a small purse or pouch and keep it on your person at all times. In the event your passport is misplaced or stolen, having a copy of it (in your camera bag and in your luggage) will help simplify the process of replacing it.

GET YOUR VACCINATIONS AND TRAVEL MEDICATIONS

Set up an appointment with a healthcare provider four to six weeks prior to your departure date to find out what vaccinations are routine, recommended, and required, and to identify any travel medications you might need. For example, if you are traveling to a region where malaria might be a threat, your healthcare provider may prescribe antimalarial medication.

KEEP IN MIND

- If you've already received vaccinations for the country you plan to visit, check to ensure they are up-to-date.
- Most vaccines take time to become effective in your body, and some vaccines must be given in a series over a period of days or sometimes weeks.
- For some destinations, such as countries in Africa and South America, you will be required to present proof (a yellow certificate) that you have received the yellow fever vaccine upon entry to the country. Keep this yellow card paper-clipped inside your passport.
- Immunizations are typically not covered by United States health insurance plans, so be aware that immunizations can be costly.

FIND OUT IF YOU NEED TO OBTAIN A TRAVEL VISA FOR YOUR DESTINATION

Well in advance of our trip (ideally four to six weeks before your departure date), find out if the country you plan to enter requires you to obtain a travel visa to enter and exit the country within a specific period of time. Requirements and application procedures vary. Some countries may require you to apply for and obtain a travel visa in advance of your arrival, while other countries allow you to obtain a travel visa upon arrival. If you are traveling through a country *en route* to your destination and you intend to leave the airport during your layover, keep in mind that you may need a visa in order to leave the airport. If you don't have a visa, you will likely be required to remain in a restricted area of the airport. For this reason, it's a good idea to check your bags all the way through to your destination country. A good place to begin to research visa requirements for your international trip is the U.S. Department of State.

After You Book Your Flight

IDENTIFY WHAT TYPE OF ELECTRICITY ADAPTOR(S) YOU'LL NEED AT YOUR DESTINATION

I recently invested in an all-in-one adaptor, which is particularly useful if you are traveling to (or have layovers in) more than one country on a single trip. Pack two or three of these, as you will undoubtedly leave one plugged into an outlet somewhere in the world.

INVEST IN A GOOD TRAVEL PILLOW

You can use your travel pillow for comfort on the flight, at an airport if you've got an extended layover, as well as on your bed at your destination. Accommodations in remote regions may not be as comfortable as you expect them to be, so traveling with your own pillow can aid your ability to sleep. Find a pillow with a hook mechanism so you can attach it to the outside of your camera bag for hands-free transport.

CLEAR MORE MEMORY CARDS THAN YOU THINK YOU'LL NEED

Assume you will not be able to purchase memory cards for your camera if you are traveling to a remote region. Have more memory on hand than you think you might need. I typically don't bring my laptop as I don't like hauling the extra weight and usually don't have time to download images from my camera to a computer. The last thing I want to do is spend time processing images when I could be shooting, so I keep my photographs on memory cards until I return home. After a day of shooting, I'll review my images and delete some obvious images, but not many. It's a good idea to hold back on deleting until you can take the time to evaluate your images properly on a computer screen.

PRINT YOUR TRAVEL ITINERARY

Make three copies of your travel itinerary: one to put in our camera bag, one to put in your luggage, and one to leave at home with a family member or friend. Beyond transportation (e.g., flight numbers, departure and arrival times and dates) and the addresses of my destinations, I write down my in-country contacts' names and mobile phone numbers (plus any special dialing instructions) on the itinerary I leave at home in the event someone needs to reach me. You will be asked to provide a primary address for your in-country destination when you enter a country, so have the hotel or your host's address readily available with your passport. Because electricity is not dependable in most remote regions, don't rely on having access to an electronic version of your itinerary on your computer or mobile device.

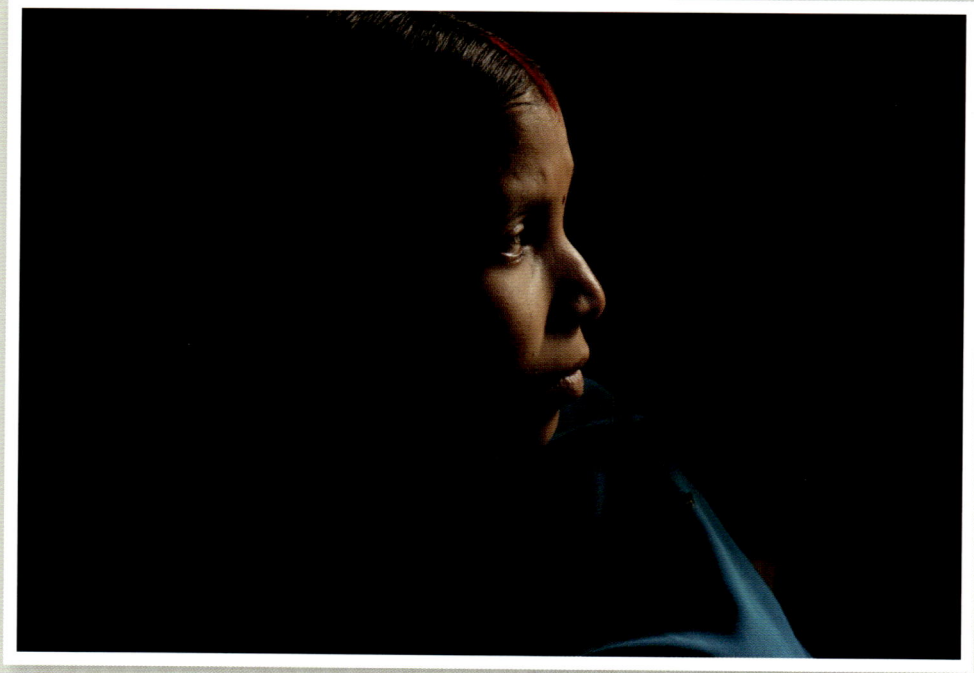

RIGHT: Sahahara Mothers' Group member attends monthly meeting in hills of Doti District, Nepal. Community women attend this meeting, supported in part by the CARE CRADLE Project, to learn about maternal and newborn care and to provide general ongoing support for one another. © Stephanie Calabrese Roberts/CARE.

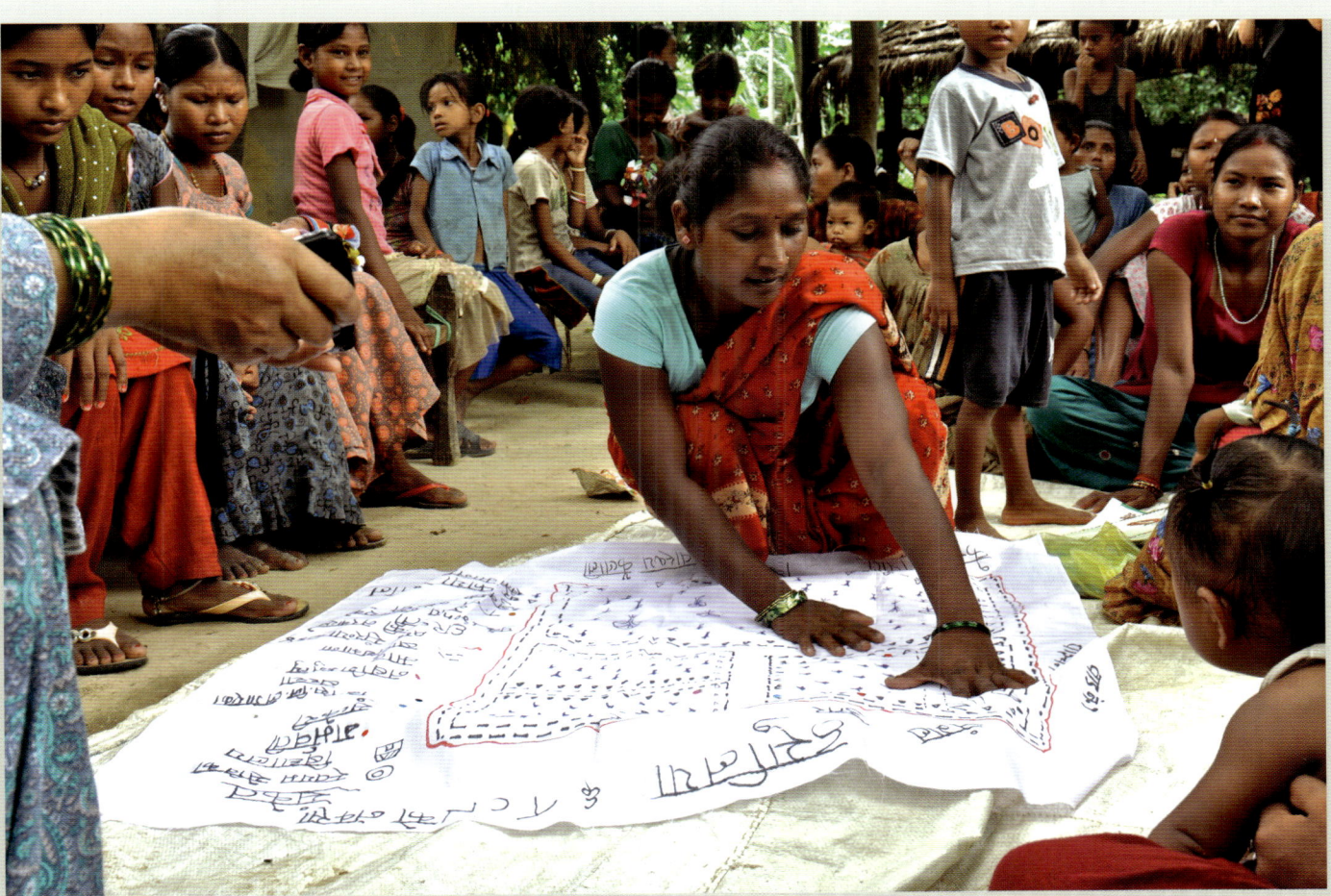

PREPARE ANY MODEL AND PROPERTY RELEASES NEEDED

It's ideal to obtain a signed model release from any recognizable individual you photograph and a property release from the owner of private property featured in your image, unless you are sure that you will not use the images for anything other than editorial purposes. A signed release says that the person being photographed has given consent to have their picture taken and gives you permission to use the images you make. Use a release that is clear, concise and easy to understand as a translator may need to be able to efficiently communicate these words to your subjects. If you are shooting on assignment for a client, consult with your client regarding their requirements for releases.

ABOVE: Female Community Health Volunteer Kamala Chaudhary leads the monthly Mothers' Group meeting in Hasuliya (Kailali District), Nepal where she provides maternal and newborn education to women in her community with support from CARE. Here Kamala displays a visual record documenting locations of pregnant and recently-delivered women in the community. © Stephanie Calabrese Roberts/CARE.

What to Wear

Research wardrobe customs of the place to which you are traveling, as well as the anticipated climate during the time of your trip, and use that information as your primary guide for what clothing to pack. Wardrobe customs tend to be more restrictive for women, particularly in remote regions where few tourists venture. For example, in certain parts of Africa, it's considered inappropriate for women to wear sleeveless tops and shorts or skirts above the knee. When thinking through your wardrobe options, be yourself, but be sensitive to the fact that as a documentary photographer, you want to blend in with the people around you as much as possible.

Bring comfortable clothes that can be layered and mixed and matched for maximum flexibility (think elements versus outfits). Because most remote regions tend to get very dusty, opt for darker colors to hide dust as you will likely recycle items in your wardrobe several times. When I travel, I generally shoot in moderate to hot daytime climates with cool evening climates.

CLOTHING FOR YOUR DESTINATION

Here is what I typically pack and wear:

- Athletic or travel pants designed for hiking or outdoor exploring. When I'm shooting, jeans tend to feel heavy and less flexible on my body, so I prefer to shoot in pants that are lightweight and made of a more breathable and stretchy fabric. I also like pants with lots of pockets so I can quickly stuff a handful of batteries or a lens cap inside. Consider pants that can be easily rolled up and secured above the ankles. This keeps the hem of your pants off the ground in unsanitary environments, which is particularly appealing when you are wearing the same pair again and again. Avoid wearing belts with metal buckles on your travel days so you don't have to take them off going through airport security. Keep in mind that shorts are considered inappropriate attire in some regions around the world.

- Lightweight shirts with a mix of short, three-quarter, or long sleeves for layering and modest coverage. Avoid camisoles or sleeveless shirts unless you intend to wear a jacket or sweater layer over them, as bare shoulders are considered inappropriate in some regions around the world.

- Travel dresses and skirts are comfortable and you have the option of dressing them up or down, depending on the setting. Ensure that the hem sits below your knee to give you modest coverage (a requirement for certain regions) and consider the fact that you might find yourself lying on the ground to get your shot. Pack a dressier (yet comfortable) pair of shoes to wear in case you need a more formal option for an event or dinner. I usually bring a few pieces of fun jewelry.

- Scarves give you extra warmth, coverage (for modesty), and a shot of visual energy when you need it. They're easy to roll up and store in your camera bag as the day heats up and they offer an easy way to spice up your wardrobe as you recycle your clothes day after day.

- Undergarments for each day, if you don't want to hand wash.

- Lightweight pajamas or loungewear with more rather than less coverage is best if malaria is a cause for concern in the region, particularly if you may not be sleeping under a mosquito net. If you will be sleeping under a mosquito net, be aware that it gets warm under them, so choose lightweight fabrics that can be layered.

- A lightweight sweater, a warm pullover or jacket, and a hooded waterproof rain jacket—one that covers your hips, as you never know where you might need to sit. Coverage is important in the evenings, particularly if you're in a region where malaria might be a concern.

- Comfortable, waterproof, closed-toe trekking shoes or sandals are best because you'll likely be walking on dirt roads, stepping in mud and over trash, broken bricks, and jagged rocks, and maybe even hiking some hills or mountains. Find a shoe or sandal that you can slip on and off easily as you will likely leave your shoes at the door before you enter a home. Slip-ons are best, as you don't want to worry about shoelaces dragging on the ground, particularly in unsanitary areas.

- A couple of pairs of socks to wear to bed and/or with your shoes or sandals during the day, evening if the weather is cool, or if you are traveling in remote environments where leeches might be common.

- Inexpensive flip-flops or slip-on sandals to wear inside your hotel room, guest house, or in your host's home. These will be your clean indoor shoes. If the home doesn't have running water, you might also wear these flip-flips in the outdoor bath house.

What to Pack

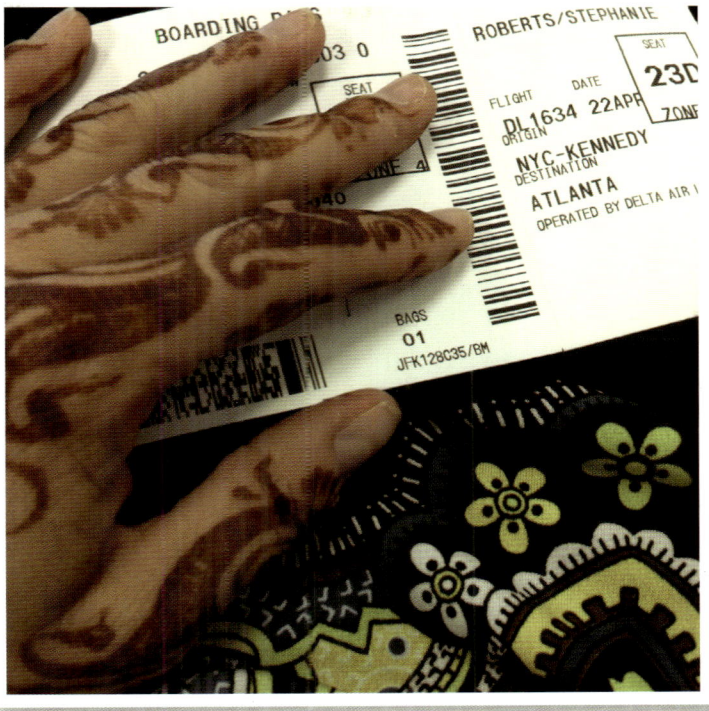

While I don't consider myself an avid international traveler, I have had the wonderful opportunity to take photographs in several very remote destinations in developing countries. On each of these 10–14-day trips, I've packed essentially the same items and felt that I've had everything I needed to be comfortable and capable of making photographs throughout my experience. Customize this list to meet your specific requirements.

A WORD ABOUT WEIGHT AND CARRY-ON LIMITS

Check carry-on and luggage weight limits for each of the airlines you will fly with to reach your destination and weigh each of your bags well in advance of leaving for the airport. If your bag is even one kilogram or pound over the limit, take something out of your bag before you leave home. You won't want to have to reconsolidate the items in your bags under duress at the ticket counter.

Flights restrict you to two carry-on items, so I typically travel with my current camera bag, a LowePro Slingshot (that I stuff in the overhead bin during my flight(s)) and a medium size pocketbook within hand's reach to quickly access carry-on items I'll need throughout the journey to my final destination.

LEFT: Double- and triple-check that you have your tickets—the last thing you want is a last-minute problem at the gate.

IN THE CAMERA BAG

Find a camera bag that comes with a detachable water-resistant cover to protect your gear in the rain, or invest in one that's waterproof if you intend to camp or spend a lot of time outdoors in wet conditions.

DOCUMENTARY EQUIPMENT

- Camera body with two clear memory cards.
- External mount flash with a filter.
- Three to four lenses: 14–24mm $f/2.8$, 24–70mm $f/2.8$, 50mm $f/1.4$, and/or 85mm $f/1.8$.
- Two camera batteries* powered up and ready to go.
- Two microfiber lens cloths.
- Portable digital audio recorder loaded with a clear memory card and required batteries.
- Stereo lavaliere microphones with two clips
- One refill of batteries for flash and digital audio recorder.
- Extra memory cards for camera.
- Extra memory cards for digital audio recorder.
- Pack your camera battery charger in your checked suitcase.

If you are not 100 percent comfortable with any of your gear, pack the user manual or troubleshooting guide.

PERSONAL ITEMS

- Travel itinerary.
- Small LED flashlight (It could be dark when you arrive at your destination).
- Two travel-size packs of tissues.
- Handful of packets of wet wipes.
- Black permanent markers, extra fine point.
- Mobile phone and/or tablet device charger.
- Multi-country electric adaptor.
- Ziplock or small enclosable bag of toiletries for the flight, containing contact lens solution, contact case, and an extra set of disposable contacts, if you wear contacts; a small mirror; toothbrush and toothpaste; makeup; facial cleansing wipes; and deodorant.
- Travel pillow (I clip mine to the outside of my camera bag).

What to Pack

IN YOUR PERSONAL CARRY-ON BAG

- Travel itinerary.
- Passport (if your destination requires proof of your yellow fever immunization, paperclip the yellow card inside your passport, as you'll need to share it upon entry to the country).
- Cash. Check the currency exchange rate for your destination and keep in mind that it's better to have more than less. You can convert your currency once you arrive to your destination. When traveling to remote regions, you will need to use local currency for most of your expenses (hotel, transit, food, in-country flights) as many local businesses will not accept credit cards. You can likely convert a portion of your money on arrival at the airport. If your flight arrives to your destination late at night or very early in the morning, consider converting a small amount of foreign currency before you leave home to pay for local transit or incidentals in the event that the currency exchange counter at your destination is not open for business. Keep in mind that you may need to pay unexpected fees at your destination's airport ticket counter on your return flight, so ensure that you have local currency with you at all times.
- Credit card. I've only used my credit card in airports and in major cities.
- Multi-country electric adaptor.
- Mobile phone and headphones or earbuds. My iPhone serves as my communication device, camera, map, alarm clock, notepad, and source of music. Aside from those primary uses, there are many apps you can download to help you with currency conversion and language translation. I typically sign up for a month of international texting from my service provider so I can send and receive a limited amount of text messages at a reduced rate. While I don't use my iPhone for voice or data roaming outside the United States, I do use the Skype app on my iPhone to make voice calls when wifi is available.
- Tablet device or lightweight laptop. I use my iPad primarily as my entertainment device (loaded up with several books and videos for the long flight) and my presentation tool. Before I leave home, I load my iPad up with my latest work (and some family photos) so I can share my photographs and videos with my contacts and subjects.
- Mobile device charger(s).
- Small journal. While I often type notes in the notepad app on my iPhone, having a written method of jotting down questions, contact information, and notes is important as I can't always rely on having a charged phone. Before I leave home, I write my international contacts' information, the address of my hotel or the home where I will be staying (you'll need to provide this information at immigration), my itinerary, as well as notes, tasks, observations, and questions related to my project or the experience.
- Two pens.
- Small bottle of hand sanitizer.
- Pack of tissues.
- Portable packets of wet wipes.
- Lip balm.
- Breath mints.
- Portable snacks.
- Medications: Dramamine, any sleep aids, headache medicine, and anti-malaria prescription (if traveling to regions that require it).

IN YOUR CHECKED SUITCASE

Beyond clothing, here's a list of items I typically pack in my checked suitcase. As you're packing your suitcase, be sure to take everything you intend to bring out of its original packaging, and dispose of all plastic and cardboard containers at home. Avoid disposing of trash at your destination..

- Portable tripod, monopod, or camera stabilizing device. If you are planning to shoot video, this is a must for stabilization.
- Snacks such as granola or protein bars. If you're unsure when and where you might be able to eat, having snacks from home on hand is a smart idea. I typically put one in my camera bag before I head out to shoot for the day.
- First-aid kit. It's best to assume that you will have limited access to medical care, so be prepared to provide self-care for basic issues. It's a good idea to pack: Immodium or similar treatment for traveler's diarrhea; sanitary wipes, Neosporin (or other antibiotic ointment), and a variety of Band-Aids (or adhesive bandages); blister cushions (particularly if you're hiking); sleep aids to help your body adjust to the daytime/nighttime cycle for your destination; ibuprofen or acetaminophen to treat headaches and/or aches and pains; topical hydrocortisone to treat insect bites, allergic reactions, or rashes; and tweezers or a needle for splinter removal.
- A few small gifts for special people you will meet. Consider packing some small, lightweight gifts to share as tokens of thanks for special people. For children, consider gifts such as glow sticks, colorful/sparkly pencils, markers, or nice pens, small colorful notepads or journals, small stuffed animals, colorful rubber balls, jump ropes, small bottles of bubbles, keychain flashlights with extra batteries, and books. For adults, consider jewelry, scarves, journals, and nice pens or books.

- Portable umbrella.
- Small purse or passport pouch. I pack a small purse to hold my passport, cash, tissues, wet wipes, hand sanitizer, and my iPhone with me at all times while I'm shooting. If you are traveling with a partner or a trusted guide, it's helpful to be able to leave your camera bag with one of them or secure it inside the car, so you can step into a very confined toilet with just a small purse.
- Resealable package of wet wipes. In many developing regions, running water is not always accessible, so having wet wipes on hand to wipe off your body, especially dusty feet and hands before you get in bed, is a must. In many remote regions, you may be eating with your hands, so pack a number of travel-size wet wipe packets in your suitcase so you can drop a handful of them into your camera bag before heading out for the day.
- Bathing supplies. If your destination doesn't have access to running water, you may likely bathe in a small room outside of your dwelling using a bucket filled with as little as a few inches of cold water. Well water is challenging to obtain, and thus used judiciously. Bring a towel, a washcloth, soap, and a plastic cup so you can easily scoop up water in the bucket and pour it over your head and body. Because the bath house might be a walk away, pack a small travel bag to store and transport your toiletries to and from the bath house.
- Toiletries. Beyond what you've stored in your carry-on bag, don't forget to pack: shampoo, conditioner, extra set of contacts (if you wear them), lotion, sunscreen, feminine products, brush or comb, deodorant, and hair bands and/or barrettes. I've also found that dry shampoo is a good option for absorbing excess oils in your hair if you're unable to wash it as often as you'd like.
- Fabric refresher. You may not have the ability to wash clothes, so having a small fabric refresher spray such as Febreze is great for freshening up clothes you've worn again and again.
- Large resealable bags. Have a couple of large resealable bags in your luggage so you can separate and contain dirty clothes and/or shoes. Consider packing one outfit in a large resealable bag and keeping it aside in your suitcase for your trip home. Having one fresh outfit for the long flight home can be a simple luxury.

BELOW: Theresia, a female entrepreneur supported by local non-profit organization BEST (Business and Entrepreneurship Support Tanzania) and her children outside their home in Magadini Village, Tanzania.

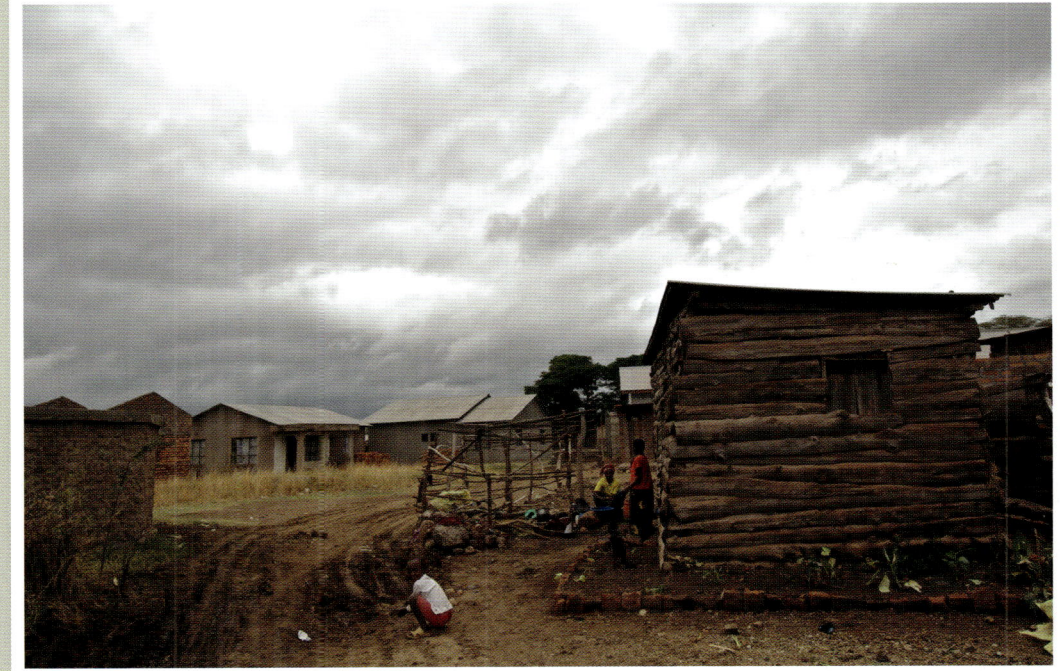

4
PUSH THROUGH BOUNDARIES
& LET YOUR SUBJECT GUIDE YOU

One of the most challenging aspects of documentary photography is learning to push through the invisible boundaries that stand between you and your subject, whether you are studying the agitated gestures of a stranger on the subway or following a subtle expression of love between your child and her pet. What's important to keep in mind is that these boundaries are just permeable dotted lines, and they exist only in your mind. Learning to move through these boundaries respectfully and in sync with your subject will help you portray your subject in an authentic and more intimate way.

The legendary documentary photographer Robert Capa once said, "If your pictures aren't good enough, you aren't close enough." It's true. And it's not just about the positioning of your feet or the reach of your lens. It's about tightening the distance between you and your subject— opening your mind and minimizing the boundaries. The best way to improve your documentary photography skills is to focus first (and frequently) on the people closest to you, because they trust you and feel at ease in your presence. The boundaries between you are minimal, or at least more permeable. Set your zoom lens aside, and try creeping in close with a wide-angle lens until you bump into that invisible barrier of discomfort—of getting too close—and then just click. There's no need to hold yourself back, unless your subject requests that you do.

As you begin to follow and photograph people you may not know, you must first push through the invisible boundary surrounding yourself by being open. Deflate your ego, assumptions, personal beliefs, and misconceptions, and let your curiosity guide you. Move toward your subject with questions and a genuine desire to learn, making it clear that you are following his or her lead through the experience. If your subject is seated on the ground beside chickens or standing knee-deep in a rice field, drop your inhibitions and meet them where they are. Make no judgments. Be kind and respectful. Trust your subject, and your subject will begin to trust you.

Another way to get comfortable pushing through invisible boundaries is to make images of diverse people with a mobile camera on a daily basis. Whether we like it or not, our cameras serve as physical obstructions— a visible barrier between the photographer and subject. Minimizing the size and weight of your camera or lens makes you more agile and less intimidating to your subject, particularly in the eyes of people you don't know well, or strangers (if you're experimenting with street photography, for example). Get comfortable holding your camera and taking pictures in a variety of unfamiliar environments. Introduce yourself to someone you'd like to photograph, ask questions, and build a rapport to establish a connection with your subject before you even think about lifting the camera to your eye. Let yourself be open and get comfortable feeling vulnerable. The more you push yourself through your own personal boundary, the closer you get to your subject.

In this chapter, I'll share a handful of personal documentary project experiences. I hope they reveal the vulnerability, curiosity, and awe I often feel in the presence of my subjects, and I hope they inspire you to trust your intuition and to be courageous in revealing stories that need to be seen.

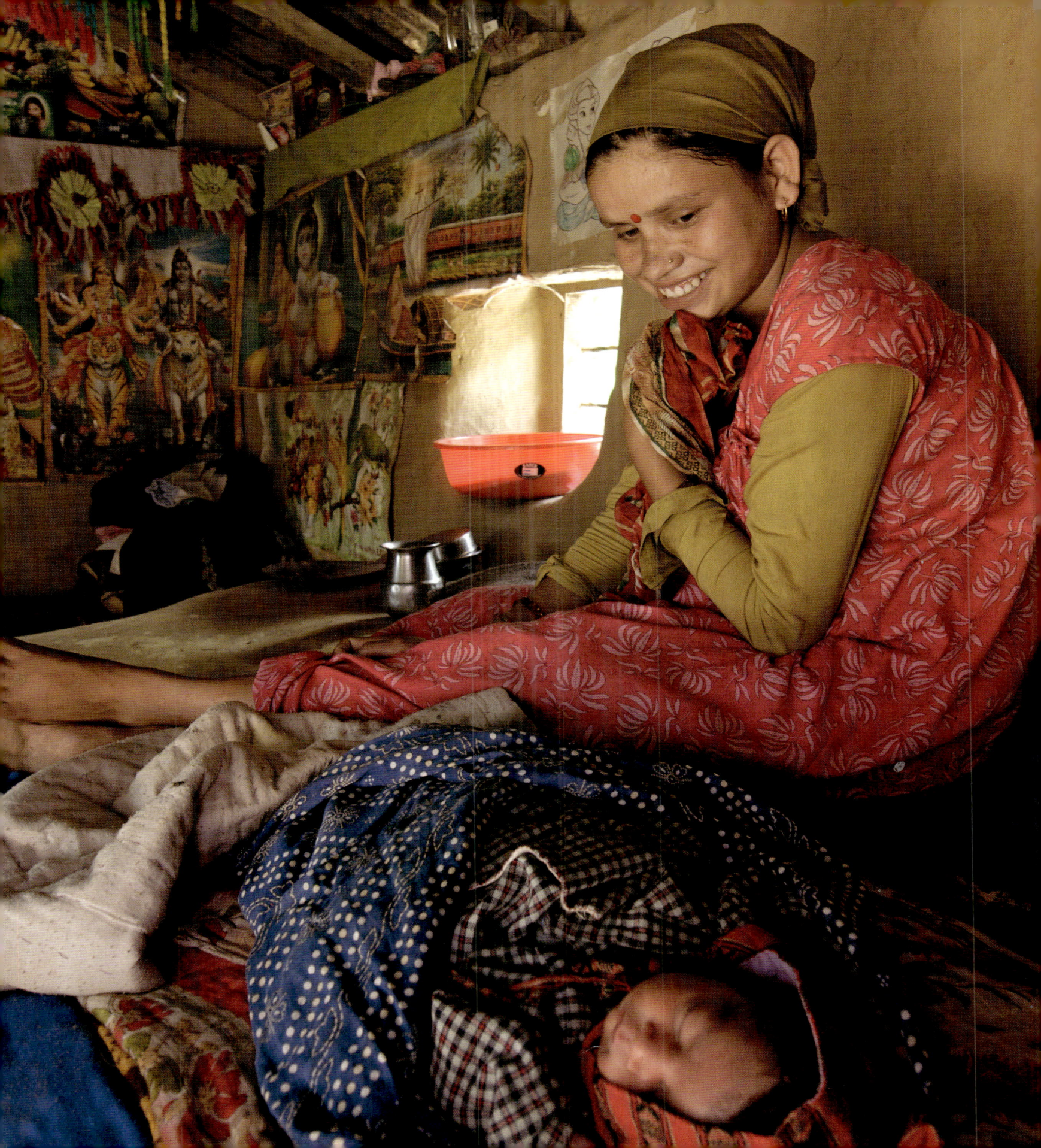

Connect with People You Respect & Admire

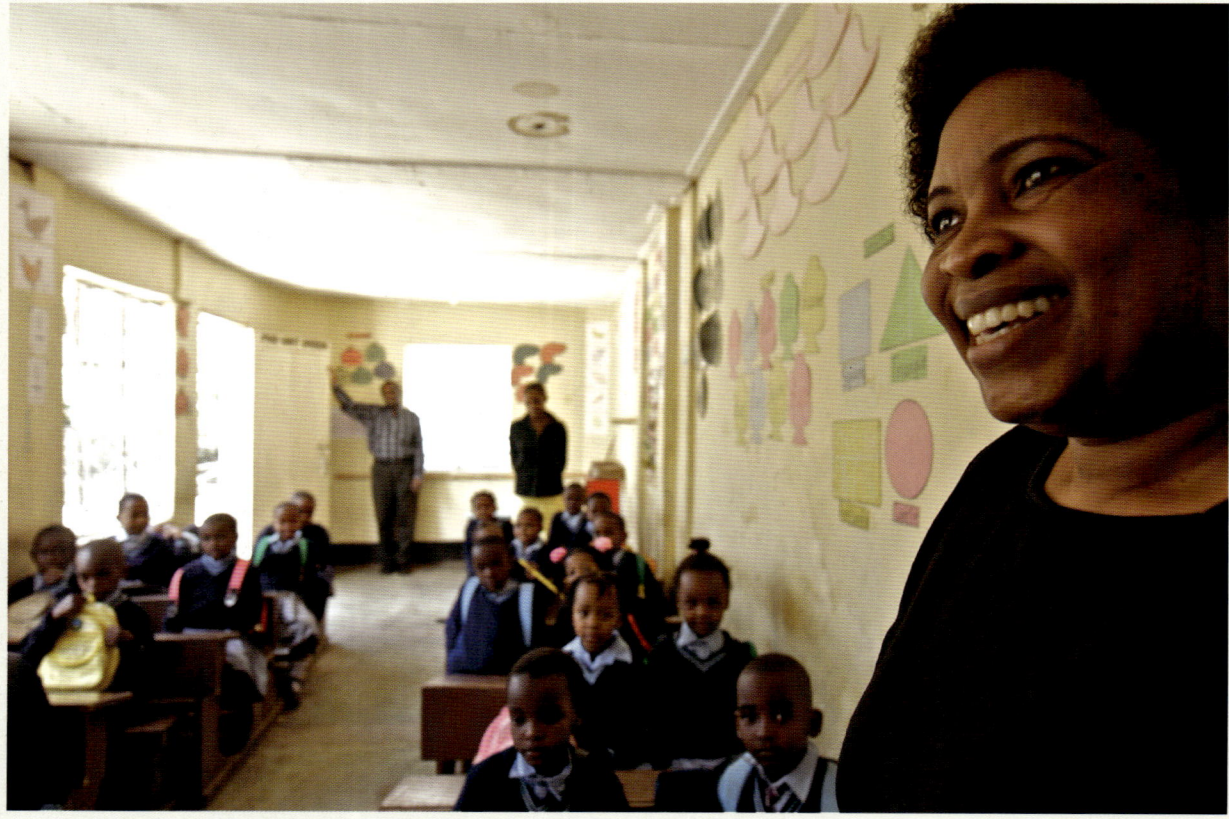

LEFT: Mama Lucy Kamptoni, founder of Shepherds Junior School, stands before a nursery school class housed in a room behind her home in Arusha, Tanzania. She started Shepherds Junior School in this chicken-coop-turned-classroom with money she saved from her small poultry business.

I find that most of my favorite photographs have been made in situations when I showed up simply because I believed in the goodness of my subjects and the positive impact of their actions. This is the work I assign myself. Your ability to document and share an experience in a visually compelling way through your photographs is a gift. Think about ways in which you can use that gift to shine a light on and garner support for people you respect and admire and who are doing inspiring work. Volunteer your time and photography skills to individuals or non-profit organizations doing work you find moving and fulfilling. The photography that comes of this, the work of your heart, may eventually attract publishers and an audience beyond your reach,

which in turn can help advance awareness and support for your subjects.

On April 24, 2009, my friend and project partner Jen Lemen and I were named the grand prize winners of the Name Your Dream Assignment photography competition sponsored by Lenovo and Microsoft—a competition that attracted more than 2,500 submissions from photographers across the United States—for our "Picture Hope" submission. We traveled to Rwanda, Tanzania, and Nepal to shine a light on icons of hope— genocide survivors, courageous change makers, old visionaries, and new immigrants.

Following are select images from two photo essays from my "Picture Hope" assignment,

inspired by two women I respect and admire: Mama Lucy Kamptoni, founder of Shepherds Junior School in Arusha, Tanzania, and Renu Bagaria, founder of Koseli School in Kathmandu, Nepal. Both women followed their passion to provide education to impoverished children in their communities, children who might not have otherwise had an opportunity to go to school. I challenge you to find and focus your lens on someone you respect and admire, and shine a light on the impact of their good work.

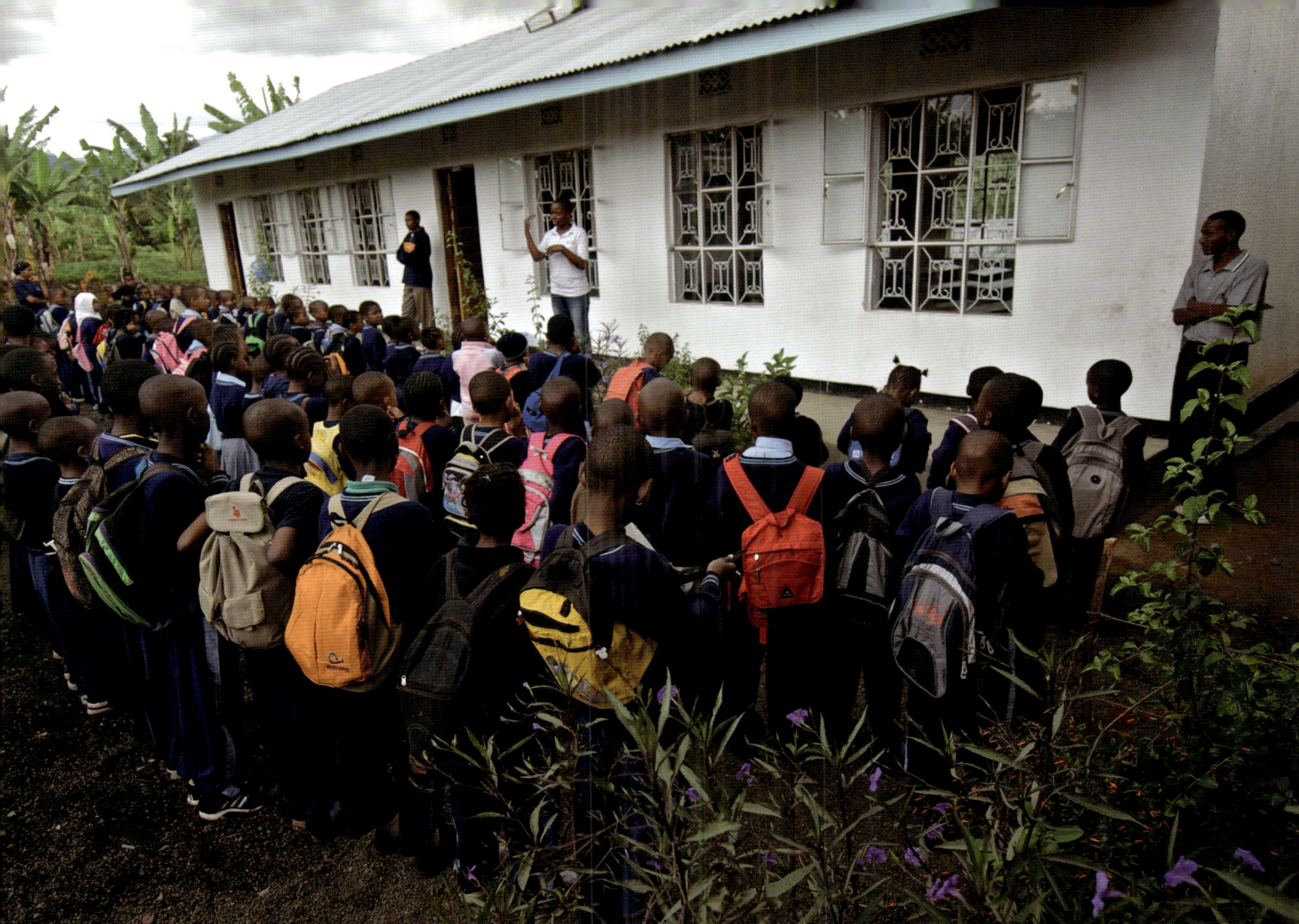

SHEPHERDS JUNIOR SCHOOL, ARUSHA, TANZANIA

Shepherds Junior School in Arusha, Tanzania began as a seed of hope in the heart of its founder, Mama Lucy Kamptoni, in 2003. Using what few resources she had—income from her modest poultry business, rented land beside her home, a chicken coop she converted into a classroom, and a strong dose of faith—Mama Lucy grew that seed of hope, with support from non-profit organization Epic Change, into a primary school that now educates hundreds of students and provides many children a caring place to call home.

Thanks to Epic Change, co-founded by Stacey Monk and Sanjay Patel, and their innovative use of social media tools such as Twitter to inspire social change, supporters from around the world contributed funds to help introduce technology and establish Internet connectivity for Shepherds Junior School. During a month-long visit to the school in October 2009, Epic Change, with support from volunteers AJ and Melissa Leon, implemented a social media curriculum and worked with eager teachers and fifth-grade students to establish online communications and information sharing using blogs, email, and Twitter. Since that experience, teachers and students have continued to cultivate relationships with supporters from around the world.

ABOVE: Students from first through fifth grade at Shepherds Junior School gather in the campus courtyard at the end of each day to hear final announcements, share songs, and say farewell before boarding the buses to return to their homes throughout the Kimandolu area of Arusha, Tanzania.

CONNECT

Learn more:
Shepherds Junior School: www.shepherdsjr.com
Epic Change: www.EpicChange.org

Connect with People You Respect & Admire

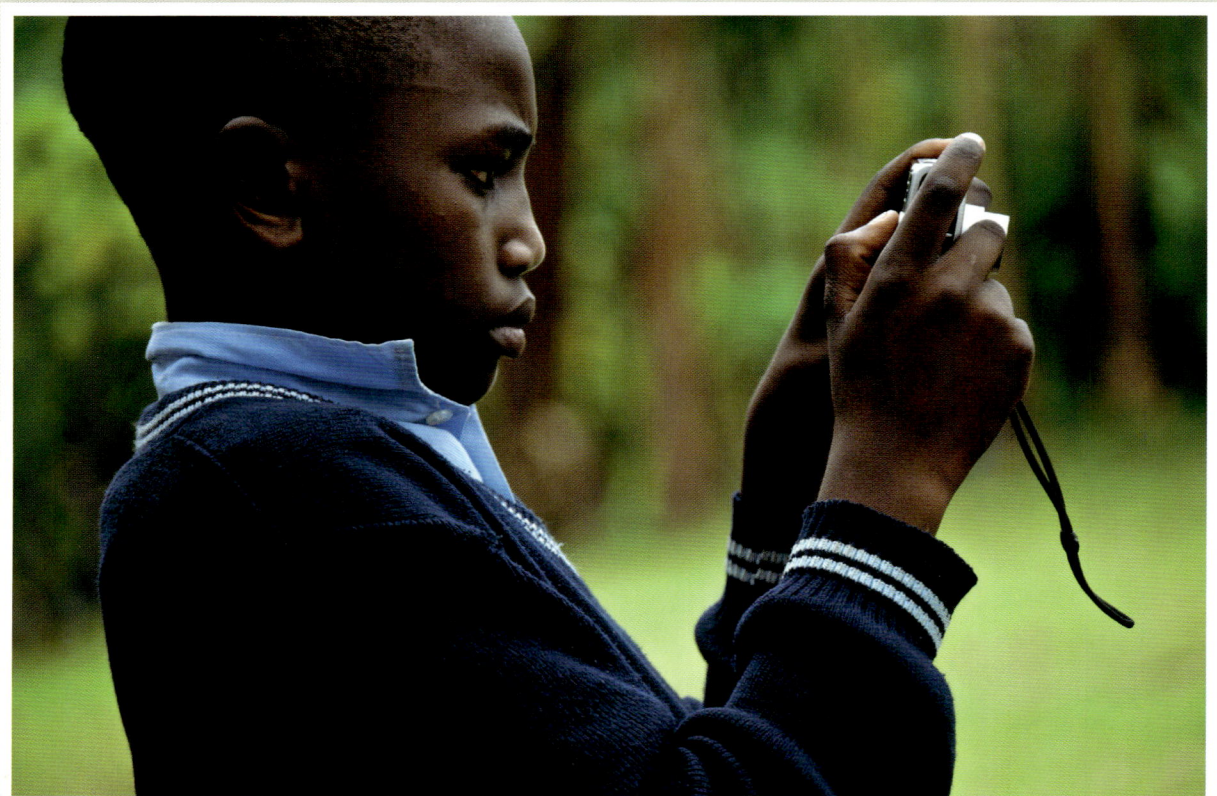

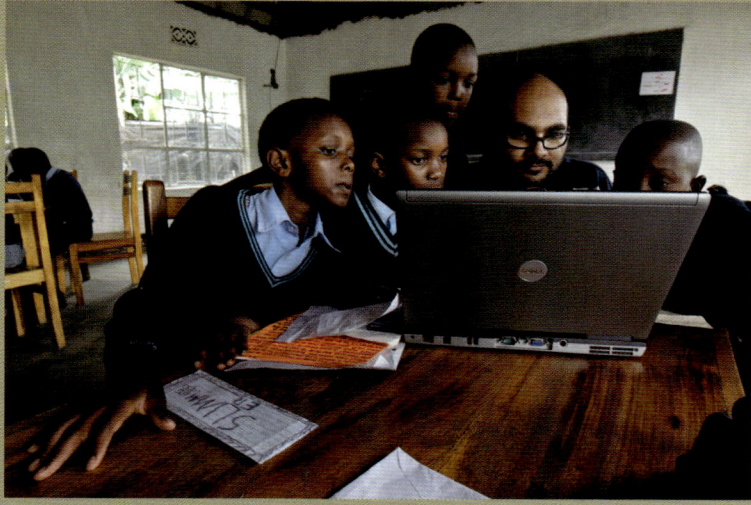

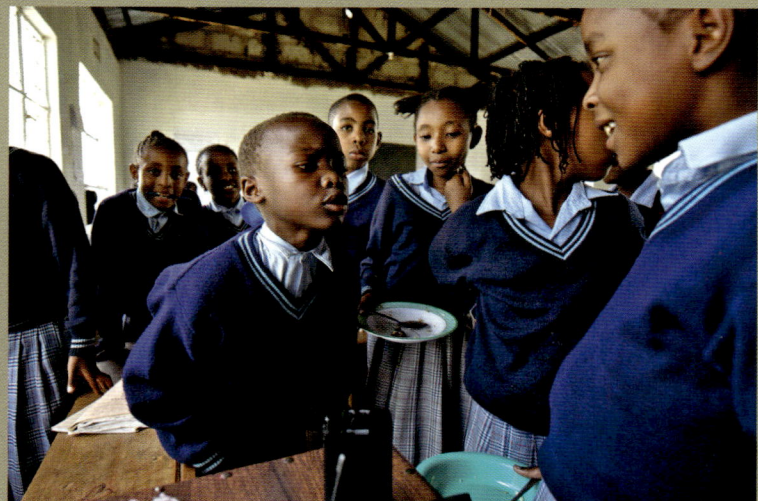

LEFT: A curious young student at Shepherds Junior School in Arusha, Tanzania makes his first images with a digital camera.

BELOW LEFT: Sanjay Patel, chairman and co-founder of Epic Change, introduces fifth-grade students to the concept of email on one of the school's new laptops.

BELOW: Luther exercises his interview skills with fellow classmates using a digital audio recorder during his lunch break between lessons.

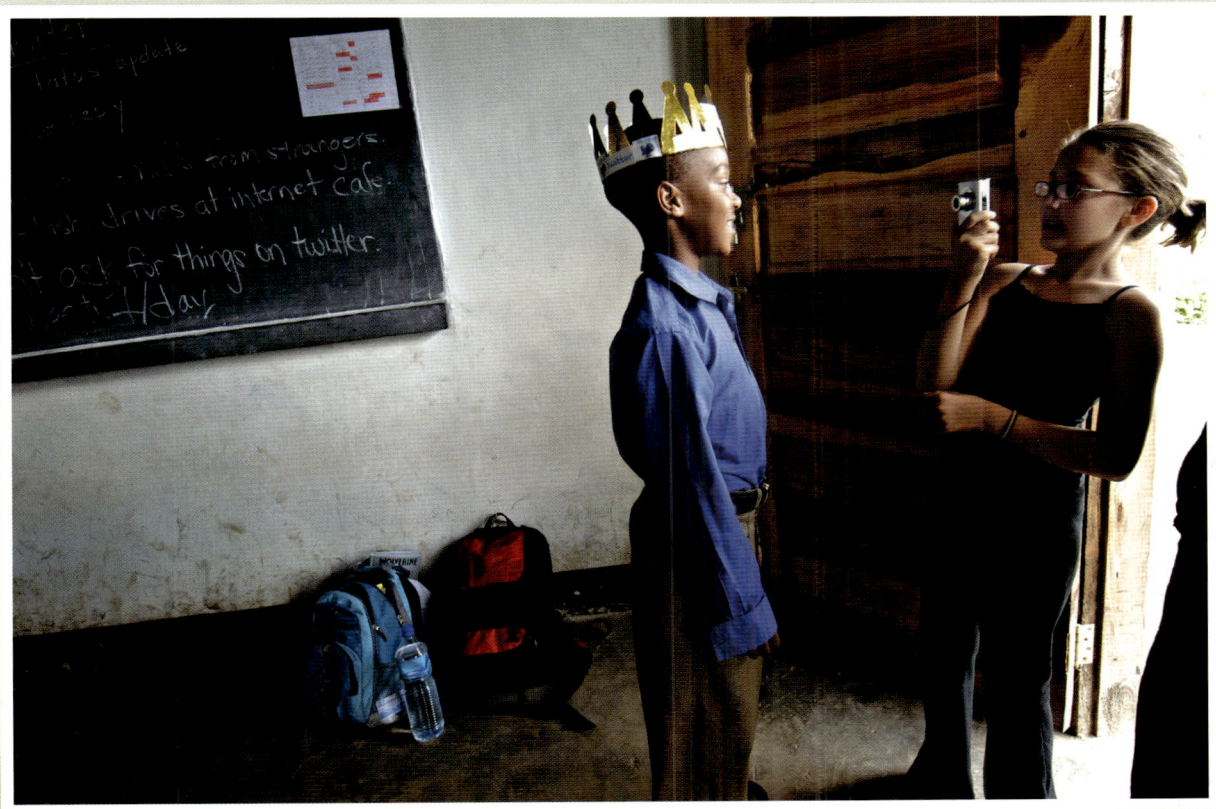

LEFT: Fifth-grade student Rodgers stands proudly before visitor Madeleine Lemen to have his picture made in recognition of completing his technology introduction class. Having successfully set up his Twitter account and unleashed his first set of tweets, he bears a paper crown with the Twitter logo.

BELOW LEFT: Teacher Sylvester carefully taps out his first blog post on one of fourteen laptop computers donated to Shepherds Junior School by Epic Change.

BELOW: Headmaster Sylvano Nanyaro and a student welcome visitors in the school's administrative office.

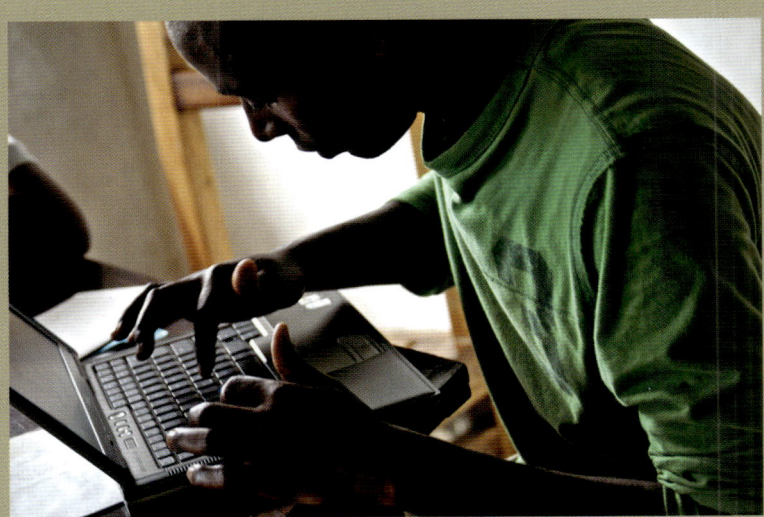

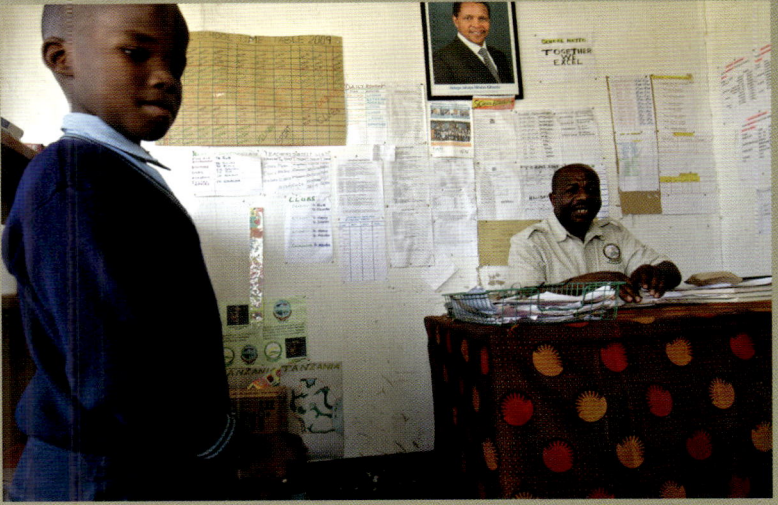

Connect with People You Respect & Admire

KOSELI SCHOOL, KATHMANDU, NEPAL

Hundreds of thousands of children are not attending school in Nepal. Many of these children are working as domestic help and in adult establishments as a means of survival. On the streets of Kathmandu, you will find children gambling and begging for money, as their families cannot afford to send them to school. Education is beyond their reach as they struggle to provide the basics of food, shelter, and clothing.

Though poverty and lack of access to primary education is a massive problem for Nepal, Renu Bagaria felt moved to do something, so she started small by gathering five of her friends in 1997 to collectively send five children from the slums to school, and supported them for ten years. Inspired by the performance of those five children and their ability to enter mainstream society as well-educated young adults, Renu was moved to do more. In 2007, she founded a free evening school for 22 students, but soon realized that the needs of the children exceeded what she could provide. Many of the children were still gambling on the streets during the day, and few had eaten before they arrived to school in the evenings.

Within just three years, Renu increased her network of donors and expanded her efforts to open the doors of Koseli School, a free, comprehensive day school providing academic studies; exposure to the arts including crafts, photography, drama, and dance; healthy meals; and basic medical support for the poorest of the poor children living in Kathmandu's largest slums.

Reliant upon financial donations, Koseli School has steadily grown to support more than 100 children, increasing its admissions to keep up with the demands that consistently exceed available resources. Following an onsite interview at the school, they visit each child's home to assess the family's level of need, and get a sense for the parent or guardian's commitment to send the child to school each day. Because demand always exceeds what the school can accommodate, Koseli may only be able to accept one child from a family with several children, offering hope that that one child will become empowered and inspired to find a career path and help support his or her family in the future. Renu says there is so much more that needs to be done. But she believes Koseli is a hopeful place to start.

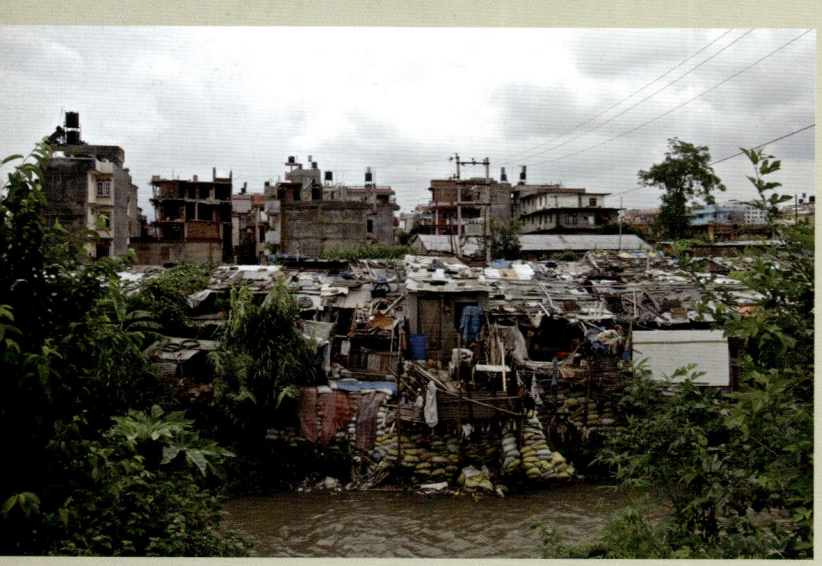

CONNECT

Learn more about Koseli School
www.nepalkoseli.blogspot.com

RIGHT: Renu Bagaria, founder of Koseli School, visits student Upendra at his home in Jadibuti area of Kathmandu.

LEFT AND RIGHT: A view of Bagmati area in Kathmandu, home to numerous Koseli School students. During the rainy season, the river pictured floods many homes, making it difficult for children to walk to school.

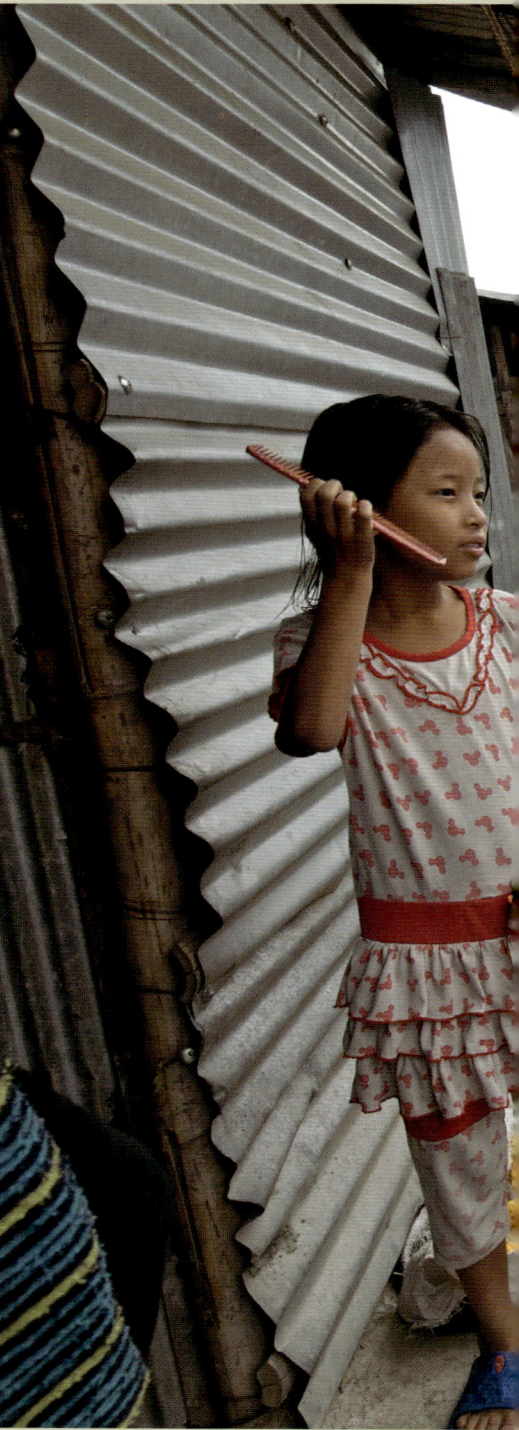

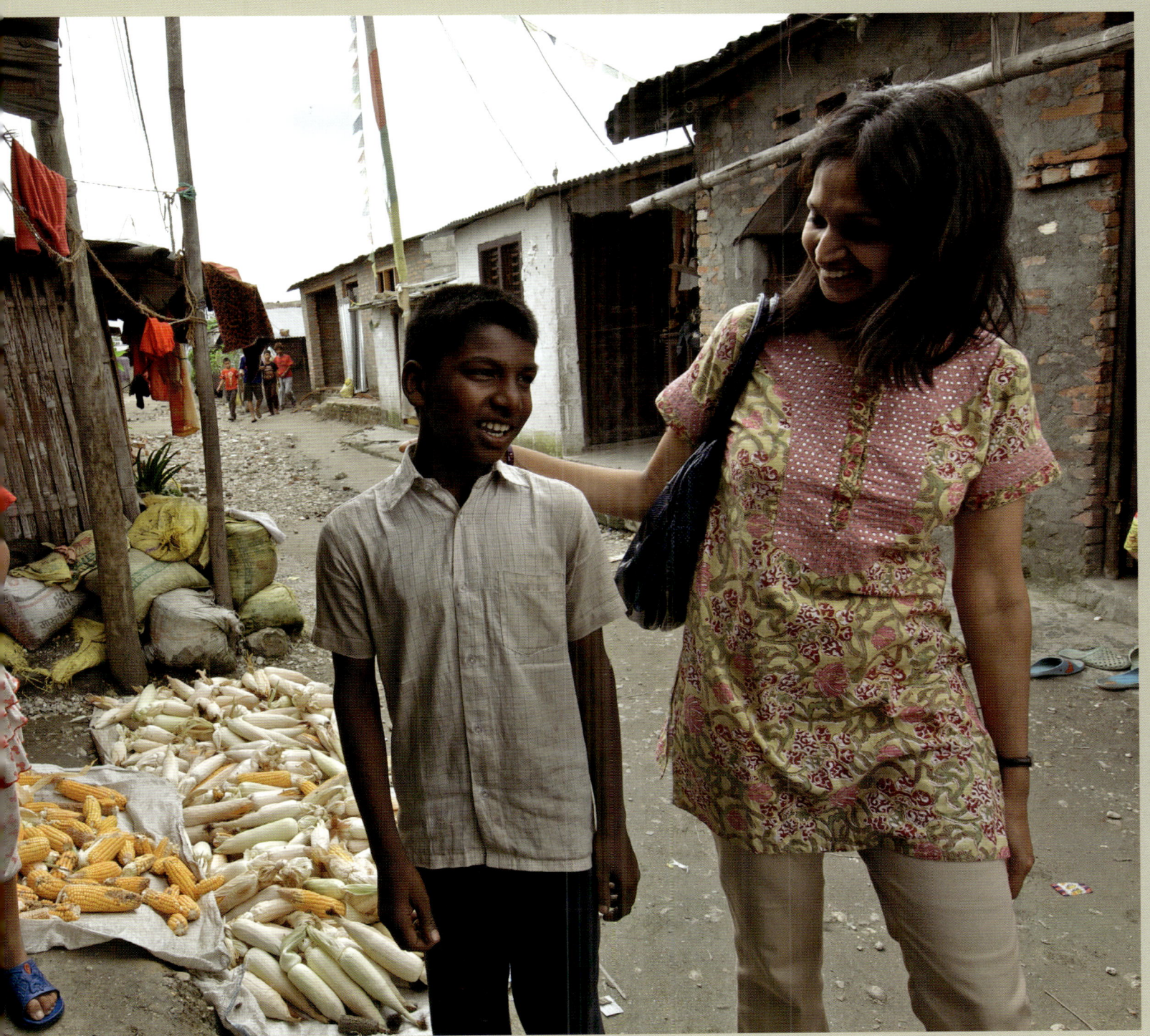

Connect with People You Respect & Admire

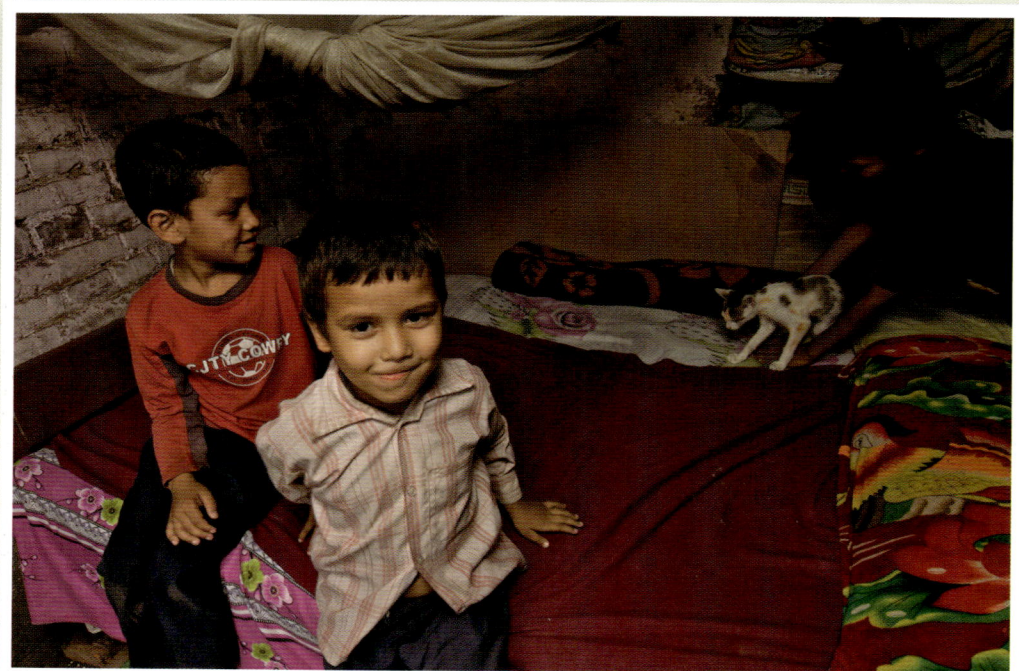

LEFT: Koseli School students and brothers Sanjeev and Sudip and friend Hari enjoy playing with a kitten on the family bed in their one-room home.

BELOW LEFT: Koseli School students and close friends Manju, Srijana, and Manisha show off their henna designs while on a field trip to the Central Zoo in Kathmandu.

BELOW: A young Koseli School student admires teacher Sapana.

RIGHT: Koseli School student Manisha washes her hair outside her home in the Jadibuti area of Kathmandu.

BELOW RIGHT: Teacher Nabeena, also a dancer and choreographer, shares a lesson with eager young students.

BELOW FAR RIGHT: Teacher Krishna (left) guides students as they tour the Central Zoo in Kathmandu.

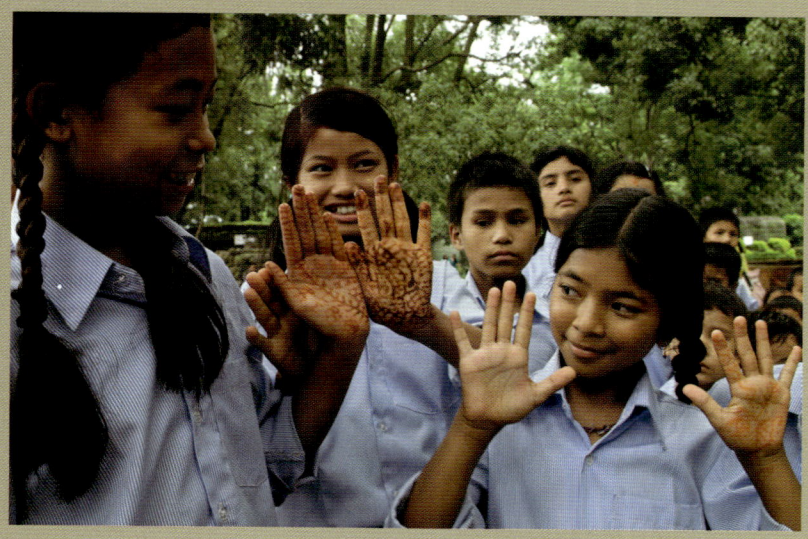

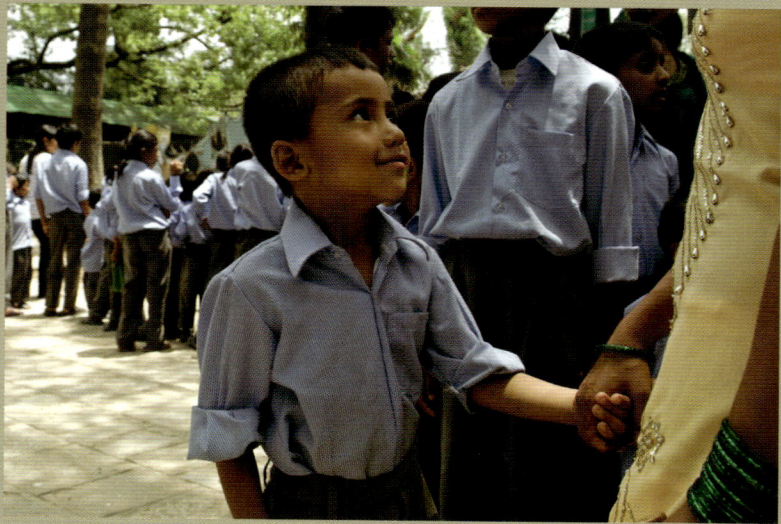

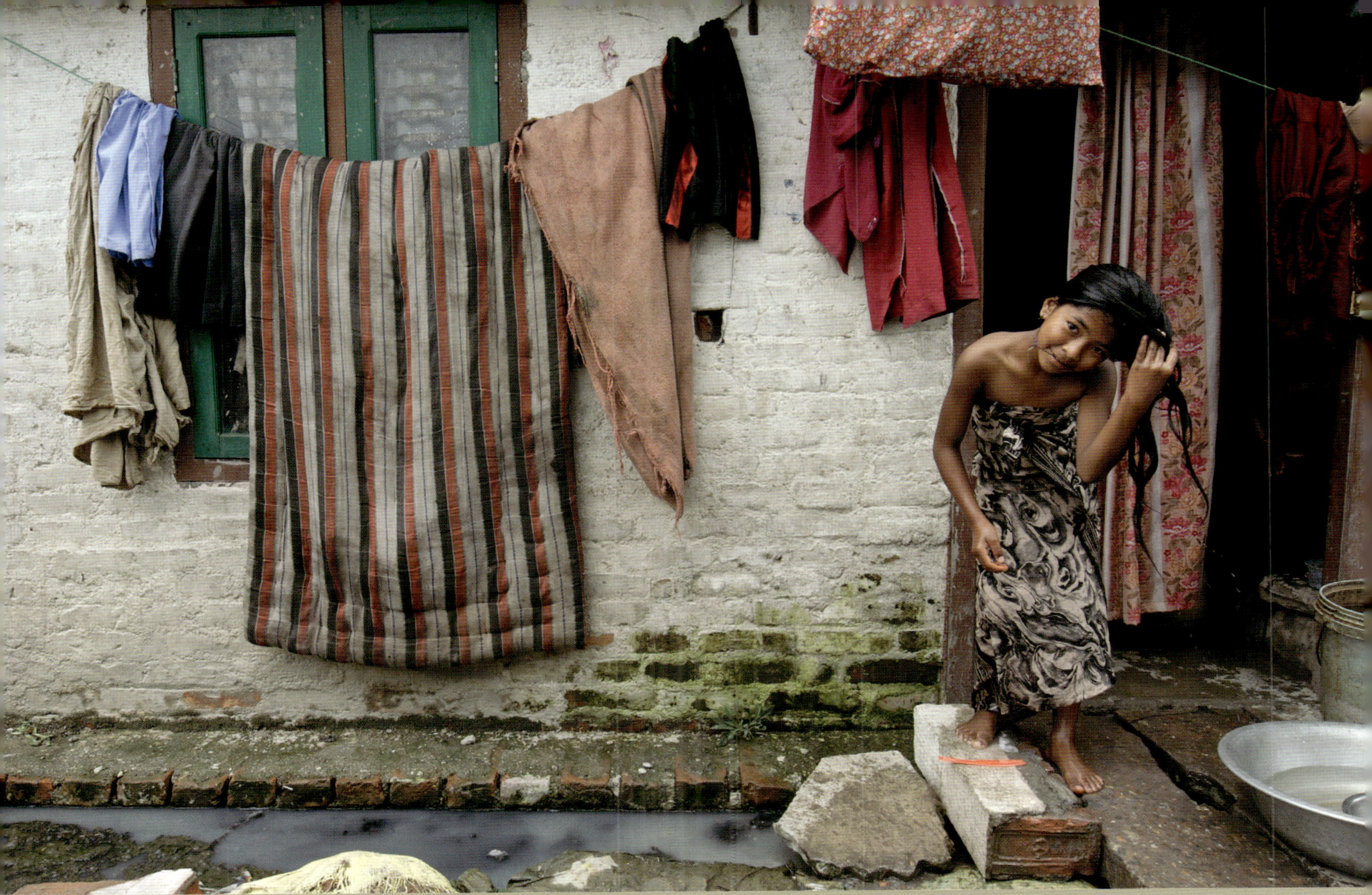

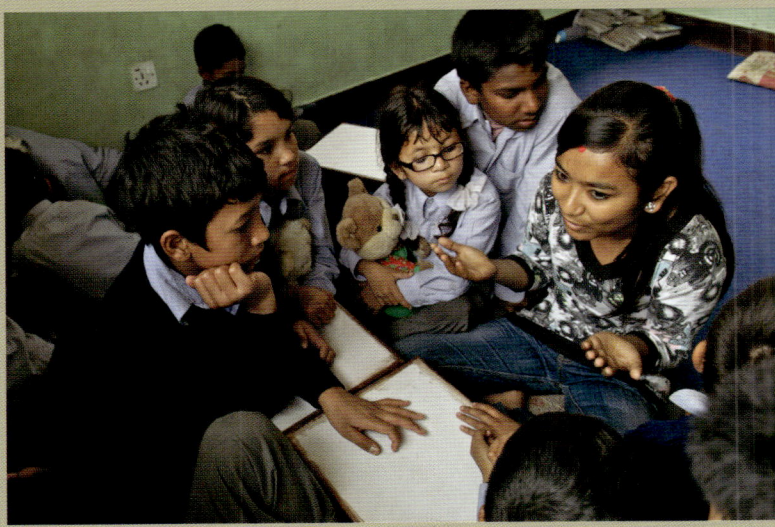
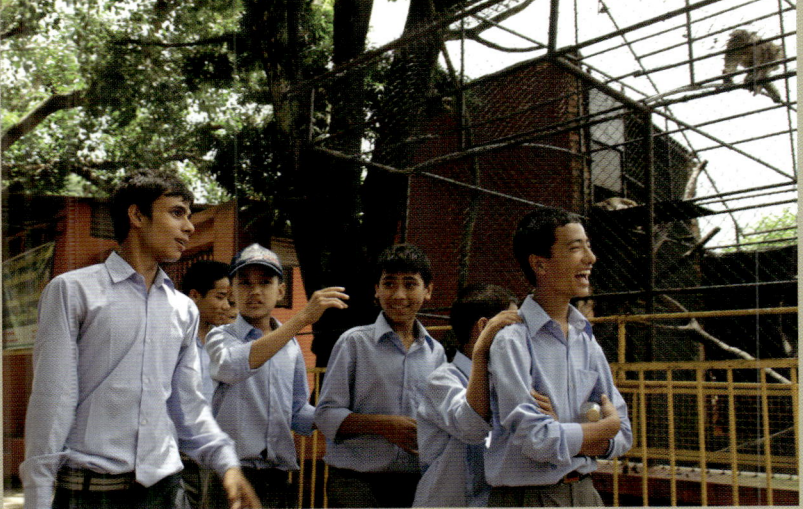

Follow Your Intuition & Trust Your Instincts

Documentary photography requires you to follow your intuition and trust your instincts, because life moves by the second. During the shooting process alone, you will make rapid decisions about what to shoot, where to stand, how to expose, where to focus, and what to reveal in each image you make, and if you're truly focused on the moment, as you should be, an analytical thought process won't have the capacity to keep up. Loosen your grip, and let your intuition guide you. Trusting your instincts about your subject, the setting, and the situation forces you to be open and vulnerable and to take risks. You could move in too close. You could make your subject uncomfortable. You could step on something. You could miss a non-verbal cue. You could cross a boundary. But you likely won't have time to stop and think about these things or wait for permission. Just follow your intuition and trust your instincts. If you take a risk and make a mistake, apologize and seek forgiveness.

Following my intuition has never come easily for me, though I've recognized the quiet voice inside urging me in various directions. I often silenced it because logic or an analytical thought process served me well for so many years. I could talk myself out of actions that might result in an unsuccessful outcome. I limited my risks to minimize the need for me to trust my intuition, drawing an invisible line around "the knowns" in my life, and stayed comfortably within that boundary for many years.

But, particularly over the past several years, I'm finding that the more often I cross that boundary and follow my intuition, my requirements for trust increase. I have to trust that the person who took my passport will give it back to me. I have to trust that the driver will take me to a destination I can't pronounce or find on a map. I have to trust that the people I meet and photograph will accept me with open arms. I have to trust that my children are safe when I'm far from home.

But most importantly, I've learned that I have to trust myself—to trust my intuition, well ahead of anything that my mind might process and direct. I've learned that I don't need a lot of evidence or extensive analysis to guide me. Naturally, there are times when I feel weak and wonder if my intuition is worthy of such trust, when the calculations of my mind don't equal that of my heart. But I can't recall a time when my intuition has failed me. Even when it's led me to a place I've never been.

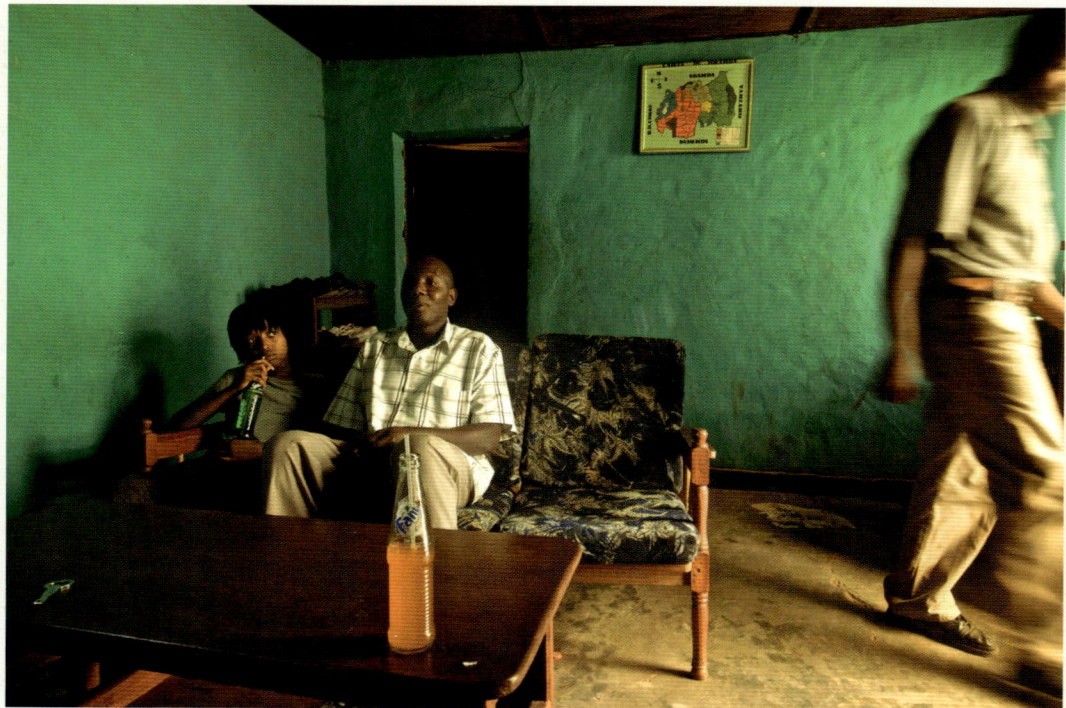

LEFT: Mutoni sits beside family friend William after breakfast. William talks about life as a Rwandan refugee in Uganda and his return to his father's homeland with his mother and 19 brothers and sisters in 1995 following the genocide. Neighbors enter and exit through the open door.

RIGHT: New mother Jai Dhara BK and her baby attend a Sahahara Mothers' Group monthly meeting, supported in part by the CARE CRADLE program, high in the hills of Doti District in the far west region of Nepal. Women from the community gather to learn about maternal and newborn care and to provide cooperative financial support for one another. © Stephanie Calabrese Roberts/CARE.

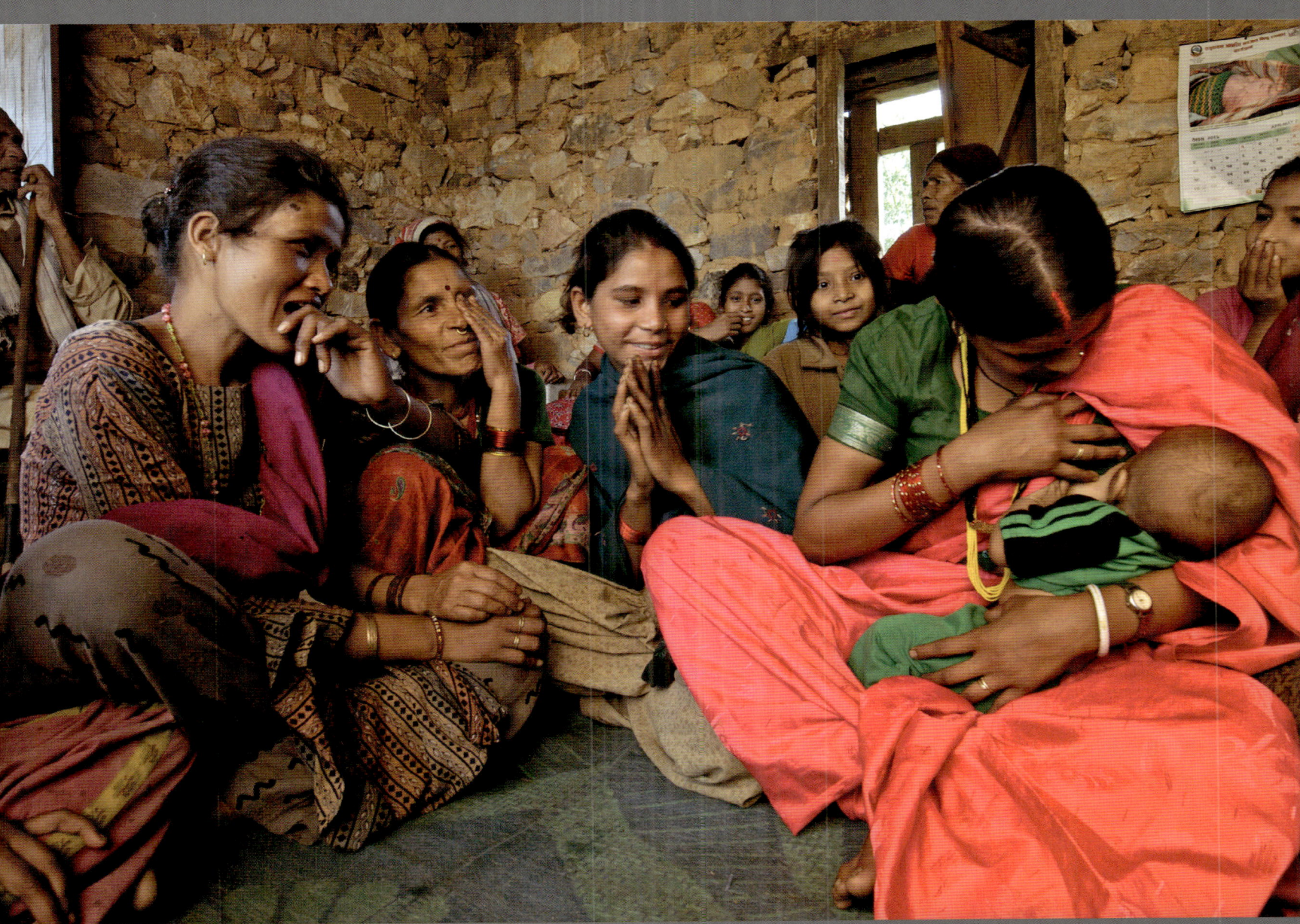

Be Kind, Respectful, & Aware of Your Presence

Working on the first day of my assignment for CARE in the far west region of Nepal on July 28, 2010, I was asked to document their CRADLE Support Project focused on mothers and newborns. Four of us climbed up a wooden ladder to reach a new mother and her six-day old baby, tucked away in the loft of the Nagri family's dried-clay home high in the hills of Chhatiwan (Doti District). When I saw young Dharma, age 17, sitting quietly beside her newborn swaddled snugly in layers of colorful wraps, I felt so humbled and grateful to have been invited into such an intimate space. "Namaste," I said softly, looking into Dharma's eyes.

Quickly taking in her presence and the vivid colors and details of the space, I adjusted my ISO setting to accommodate for the dim setting (with just one stream of harsh light through a small window), pointed my external mount flash to fire at the wall behind me to bounce and soften the light, and chose a moderate aperture setting to let in as much light as possible while retaining some focus on the detailed background elements. I was sensitive to the fact that Dharma and her baby were seated comfortably on layers of blankets, so I positioned myself to find the right perspective.

As I began to make my first few images, I sensed that Dharma was shy and hesitant to move. The baby was sleeping, so there was little for her to do but focus on the four of us and the sounds of my clicks. Conscious of my presence and eager to minimize it, I turned on my digital audio recorder and asked my partner Jen to interview Dharma about her birth experience. I needed conversation in the space to draw the focus away from my camera. When Dharma began to answer questions in Nepali, I could see that she was beginning to feel more at ease with us, but I didn't feel that I could accurately portray the loving emotion I knew she felt for her sleeping newborn. "Can you ask her to pick up the baby?" I asked Mukesh, my primary CARE host. At this, Dharma smiled toward her sleeping son and reached down to lift him with such tenderness. I quickly got down on the dirt floor and inched in close with my 14–24mm lens. Following her carefully, I clicked, on instinct, at the moment when her eyes met mine. It was a connection.

As much as I want to blend in with my surroundings and photograph people unaware of my presence, this 22-minute experience reminds me that my presence does influence the photographs I make, and whether I like it or not, I am seen. The way in which I connect with my subject through my words, actions, expressions, and gestures will influence the photographs I make and the way in which I am able to portray my subject.

> "Saturate yourself with your subject and the camera will all but take you by the hand."
>
> MARGARET BOURKE-WHITE, PHOTOGRAPHER

RIGHT: Mother Dharma Nagri, age 17, cradles her six-day-old son in her home where she lives with her husband and 16 other family members high in the hills of Chhatiwan (Doti District) in Nepal.

ABOUT THE PHOTOGRAPHS

It is customary for a young married woman such as Dharma to live with her husband (a marriage arranged by their parents) and his immediate family and to share in the responsibility of caring for her mother-in-law, while Dharma's husband and brothers-in-law leave the home for extended periods of time to work and earn money for the family. Dharma and her sisters-in-law remain home to farm, prepare food, manage domestic chores, and care for the children.

Dharma delivered her first child here in her home, with help from her sister-in-law who used a clean, new razor blade to cut the umbilical cord and helped the new mother to breastfeed her baby within 30 minutes of the birth. What's significant about this experience is that it's an innovative approach to in-home delivery and newborn care for this remote region of Nepal. Dharma's sister-in-law learned about the importance of umbilical cord hygiene and the nutritional benefits of colostrum (early breast milk) for newborns by attending monthly Mothers' Group meetings in their village. Historically, it has been customary in this region for women to purge the colostrum, as Dharma's ancestors believed that early breast milk was unclean.

While the Public Health Department of Nepal, with support from CARE, is making great strides to improve maternal health and education in an effort to decrease the infant mortality rate, women in the Doti District rarely have access to health facilities and medical care during labor as transit can be time-consuming and treacherous (particularly during rainy seasons when mudslides are common), and most remote health facilities are not staffed during the night due to lack of resources. Images © Stephanie Calabrese Roberts/CARE.

CONNECT

Learn more about CARE
www.care.org

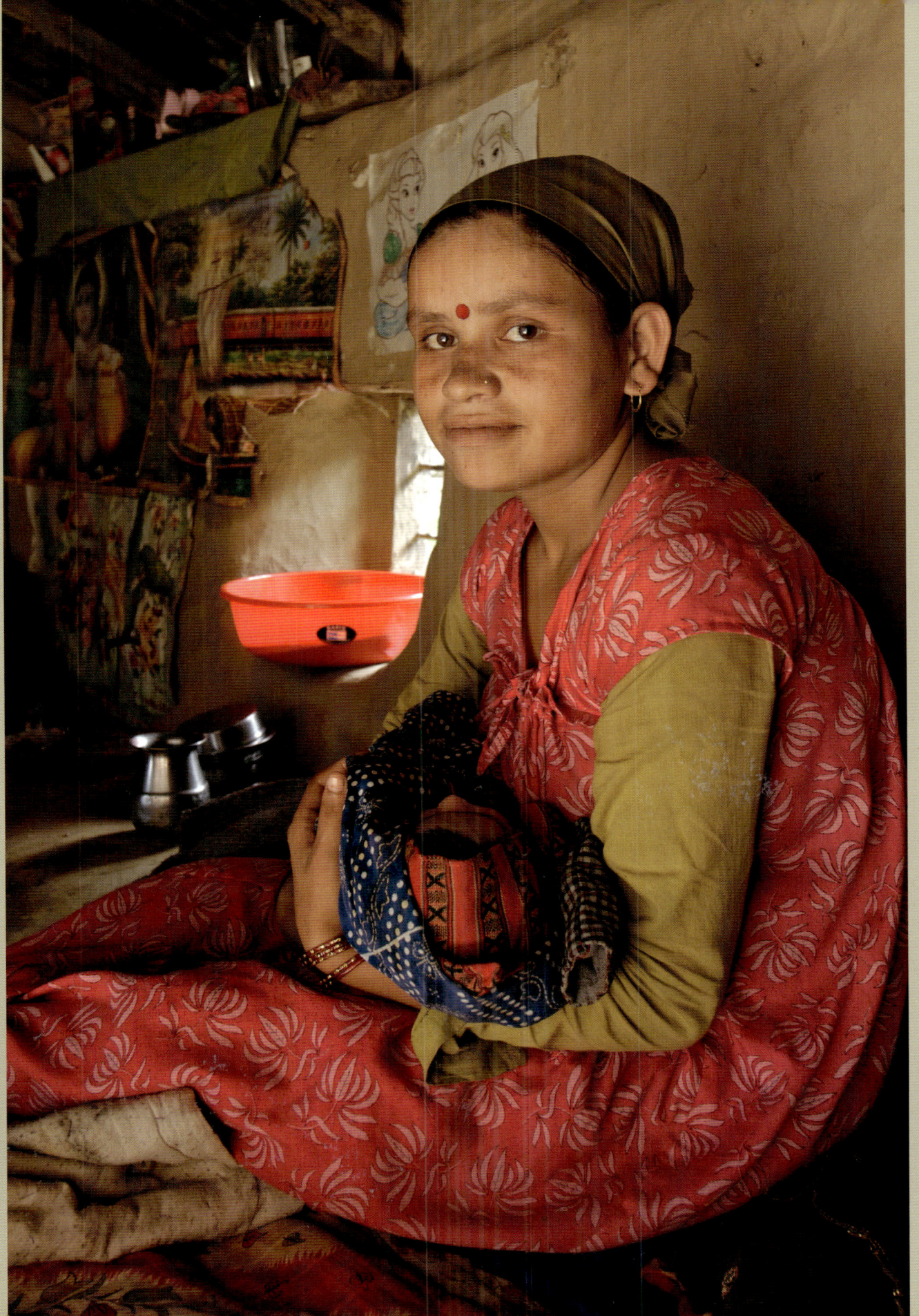

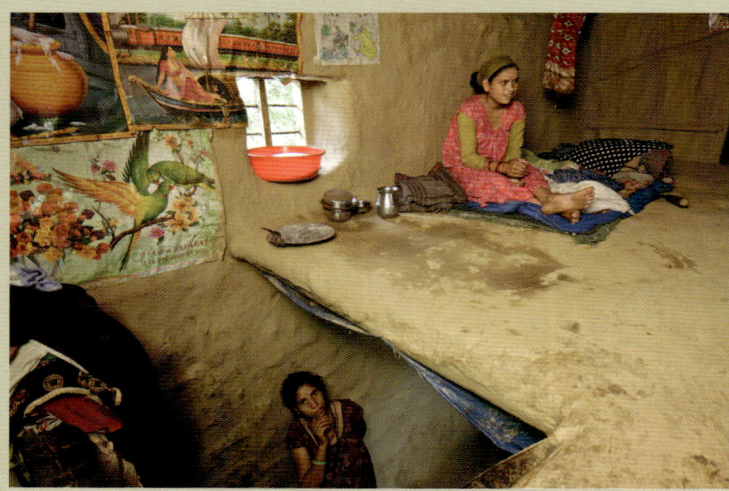
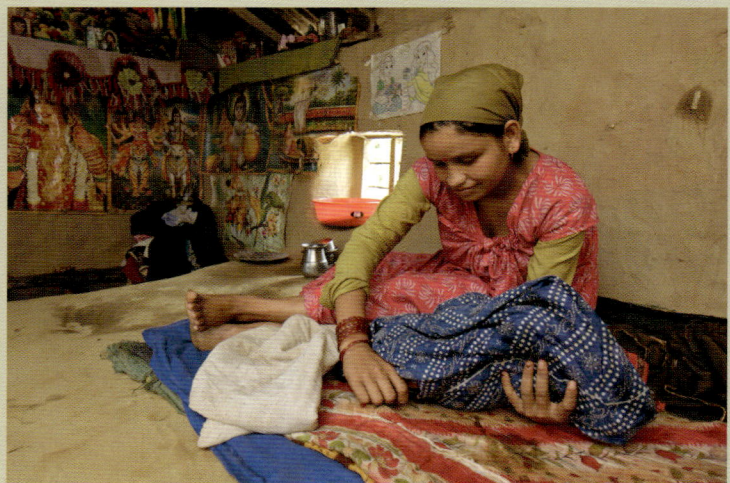

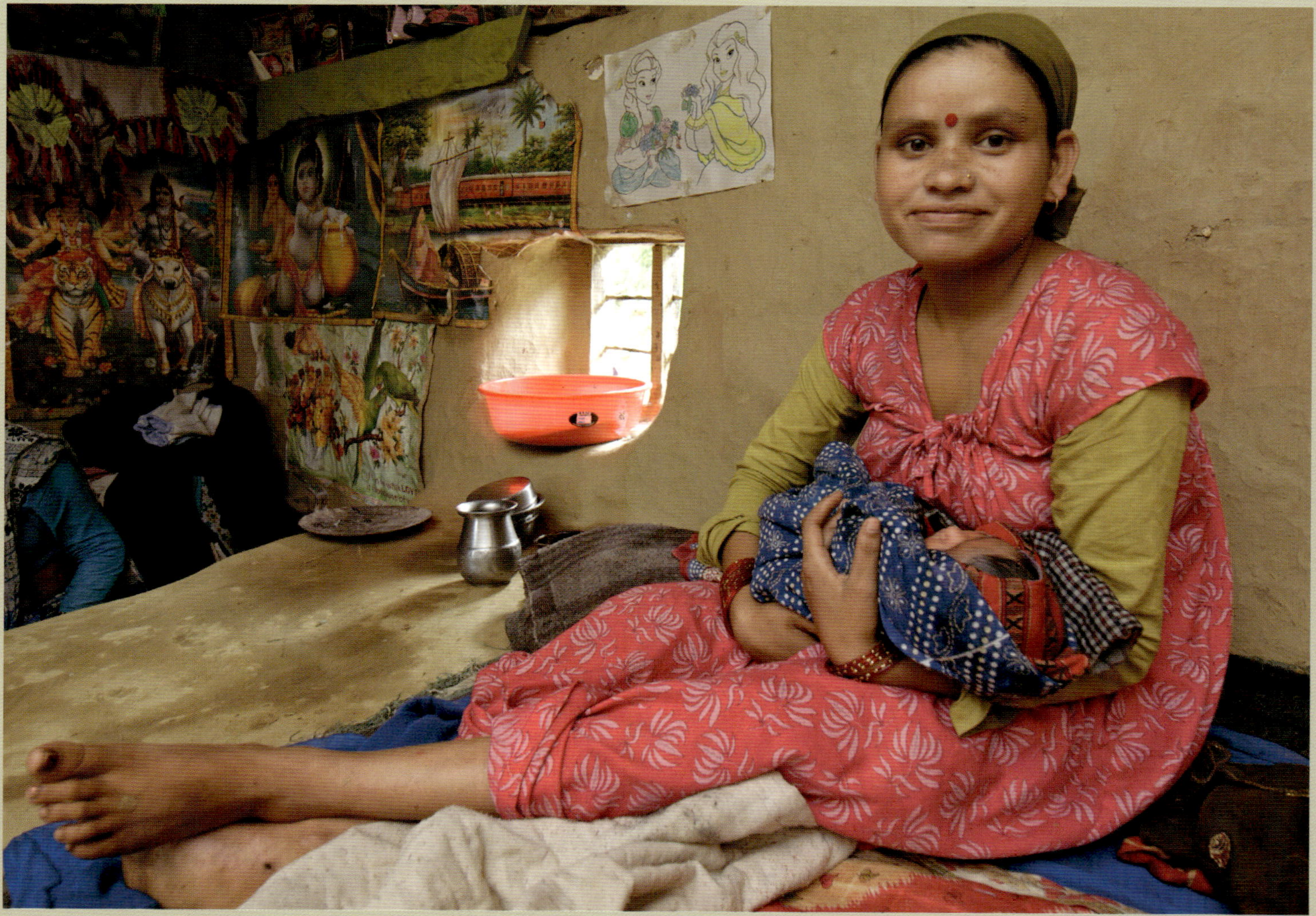

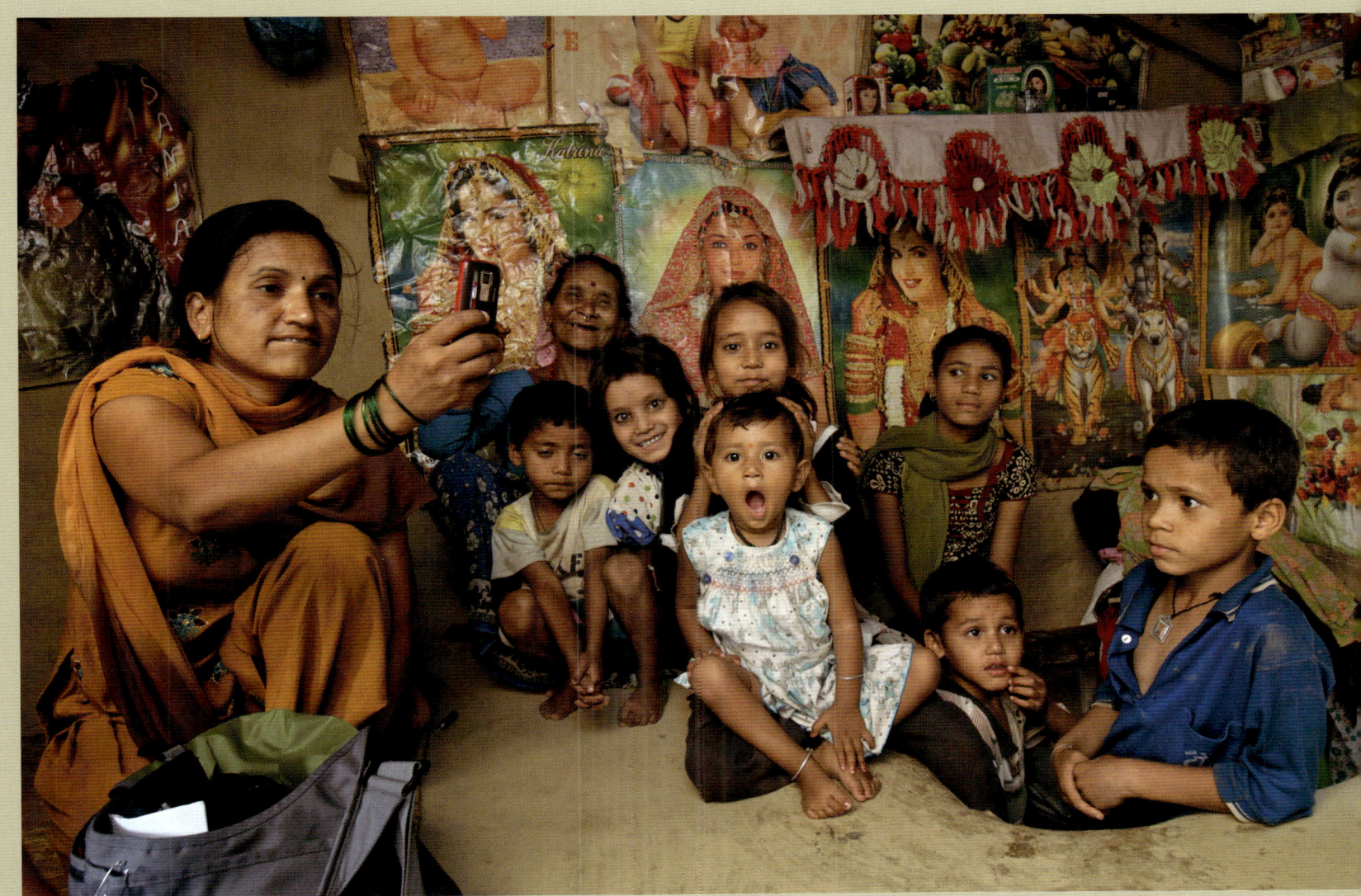

ABOVE: Eight of the nineteen Nagri family members (Dharma's mother-in-law and seven nieces and nephews) living in this home gather beside CARE Senior Field Mobilizer Induka Karki as she focuses her mobile phone camera on Dharma and her newborn.

OPPOSITE: Dharma Nagri with her newborn in her home high in the hills of Chhatiwan (Doti District) in Nepal.

Focus on Family, Friends, & the Familiar

It's not necessary to travel to faraway lands or to seek out unfamiliar subjects to practice documentary photography. In fact, you can find a lifetime of documentary material just by turning your lens on your own life—the people closest to you, in settings that feel most familiar. Finding a level of comfort in documenting people as they are can come more easily if you photograph people who know and trust you and are comfortable in your presence.

When I photograph friends, I often do this while I'm staying in their home for one or more nights, giving us plenty of time to connect and enjoy each other. If I'm shooting an experience for a friend, such as a wedding, I'll make time to linger between significant moments to reveal unexpected moments throughout the experience—the bride's father chewing nervously on his fingernails before the ceremony, a goodnight kiss, or the comical expression on a young boy's face just before he was love-tackled by an older cousin. This stretch of time often opens up unique opportunities to photograph my subjects doing things that come naturally for them, revealing a glimpse of their authentic selves. The longer I am present with my camera, the less significant I become, putting my subjects more at ease.

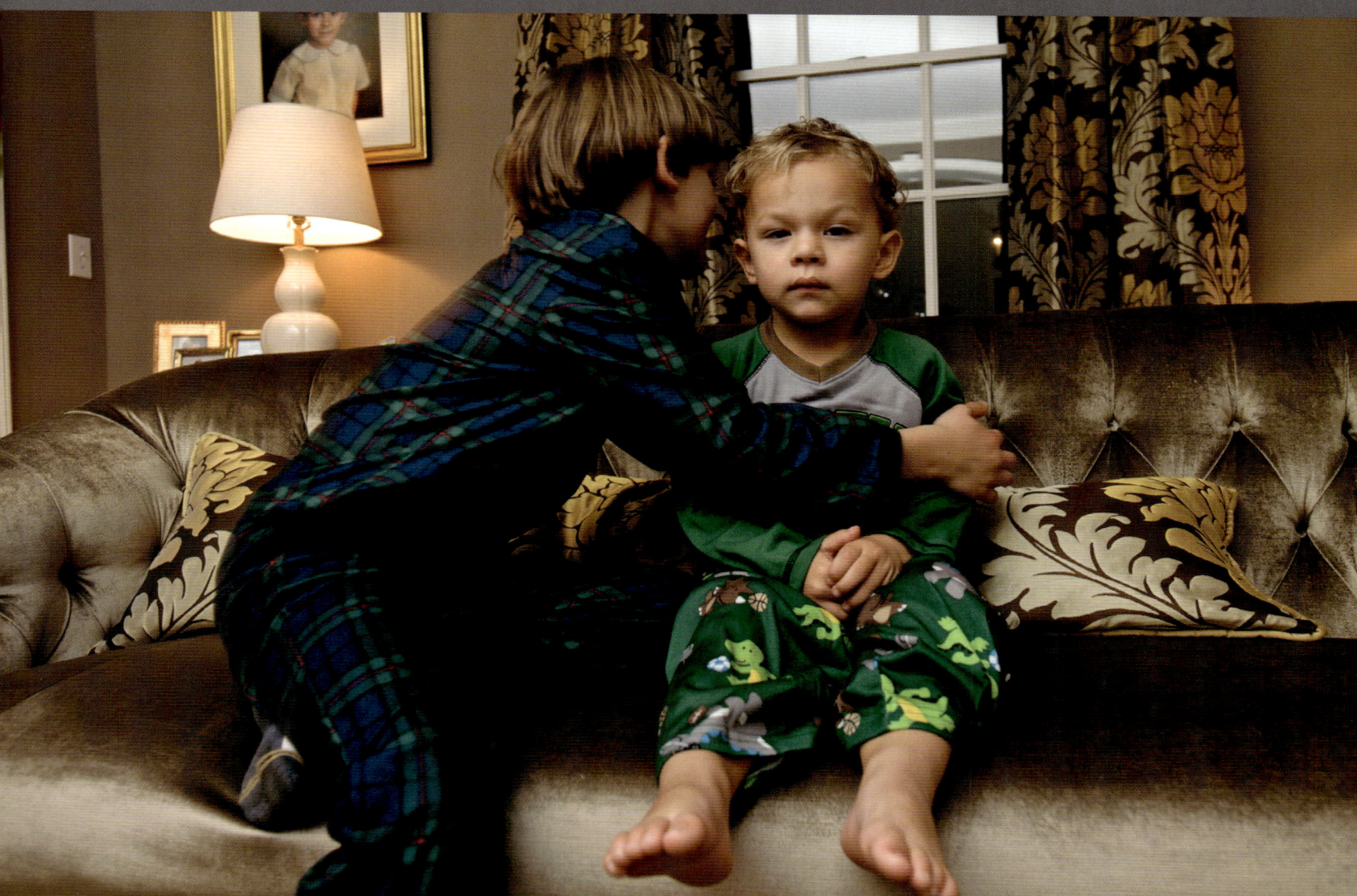

LEFT: Zack anticipates a tackle hug from his cousin Lawson.

BELOW: Expectant mother Jill offers support to son Wyatt and his pepper grinder in the kitchen.

When I pick up my camera in a personal setting, I can't help but distance myself from the experience. I become less involved in the action and dialog, and more in tune with following the visual of the experience. I'm thinking about light, making decisions about what to include in the frame of my viewfinder, and anticipating what might happen next. I can't remain in this zone throughout our entire time together, as I'd miss the opportunity for a personal connection with my subjects, so I find it critically important to put my camera down and be fully present with my subjects at other times.

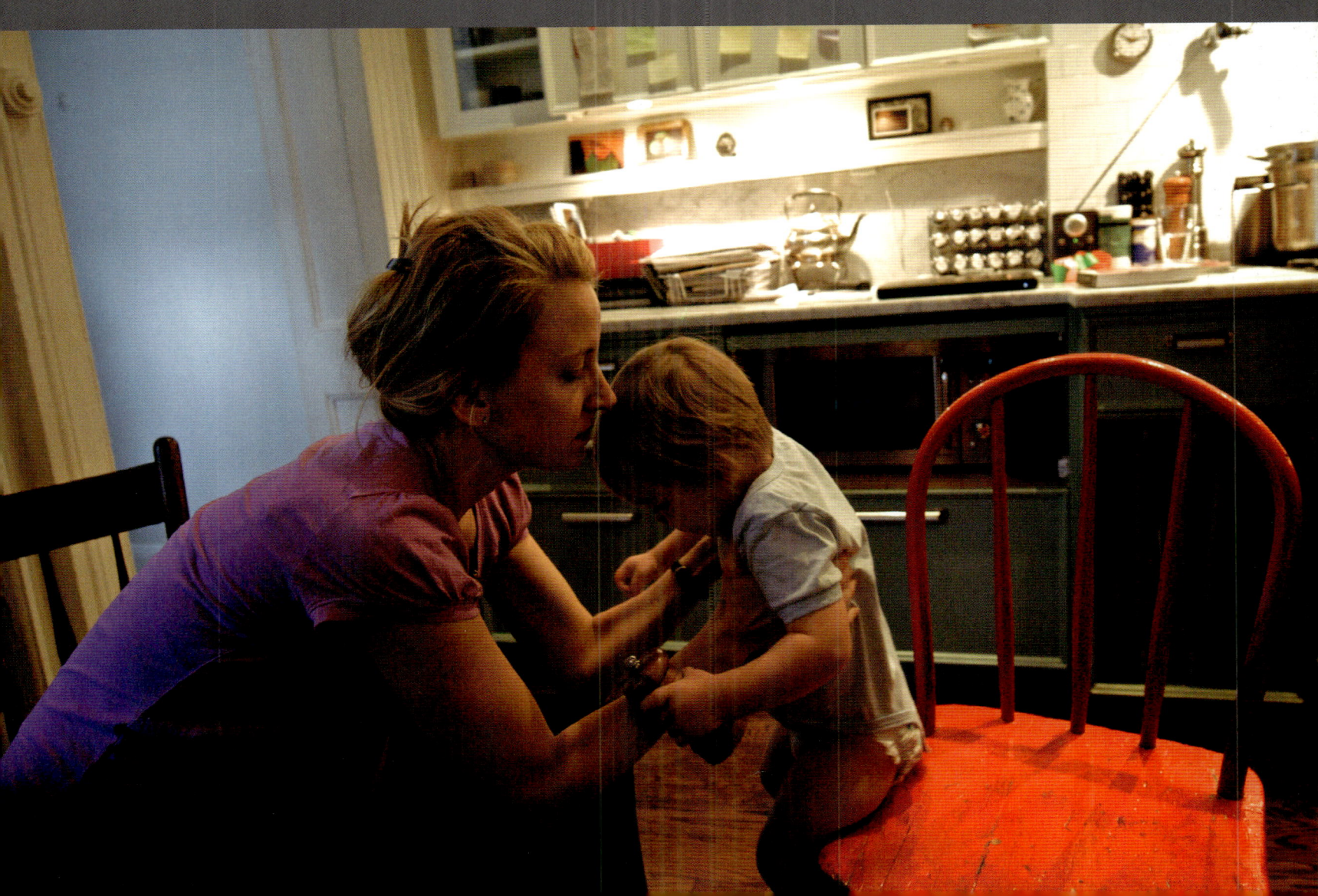

Focus on Family, Friends, & the Familiar

When photographing family and friends in their homes or private settings, discuss your desire to photograph them authentically throughout your visit to ensure they are comfortable with your focus on them. If you hope to share the photographs in a public way at some point in the future, share your intent and gain their consent. If your subject expresses a desire to see the photographs before you share them publicly (particularly if you are photographing sensitive experiences), honor this request and follow through by sharing your images with your subject(s) in a private online environment or in person, and obtain permission before you share your images in a public way. Give your best digital photographs to your subject(s) or make prints as an expression of thanks if they are interested in having the photographs for their personal use.

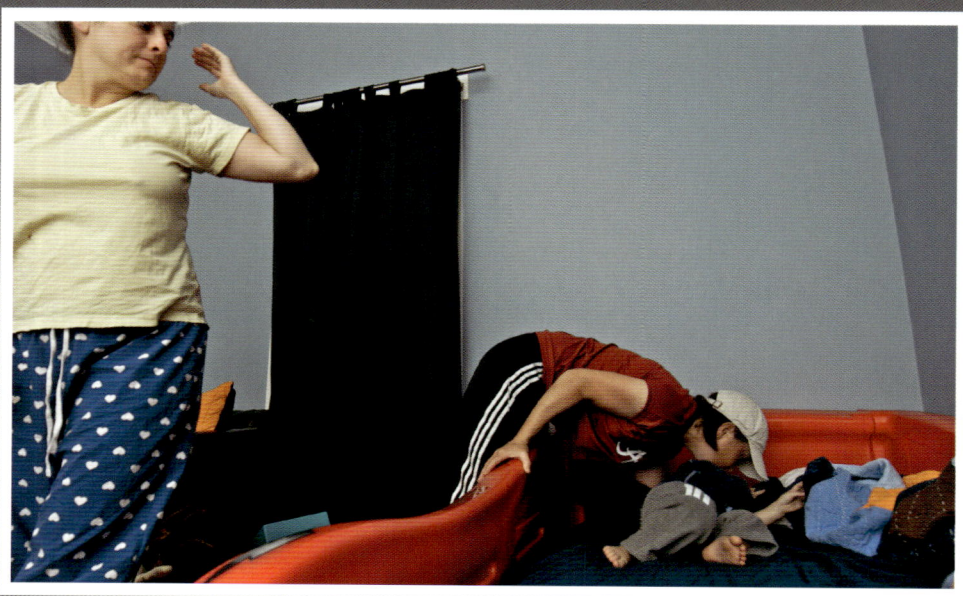

ABOVE: Mothers Lauren and Paige kiss their son Jesse goodnight.

RIGHT: Nieces (and bridesmaids) of the bride grow tired of the wedding rehearsal.

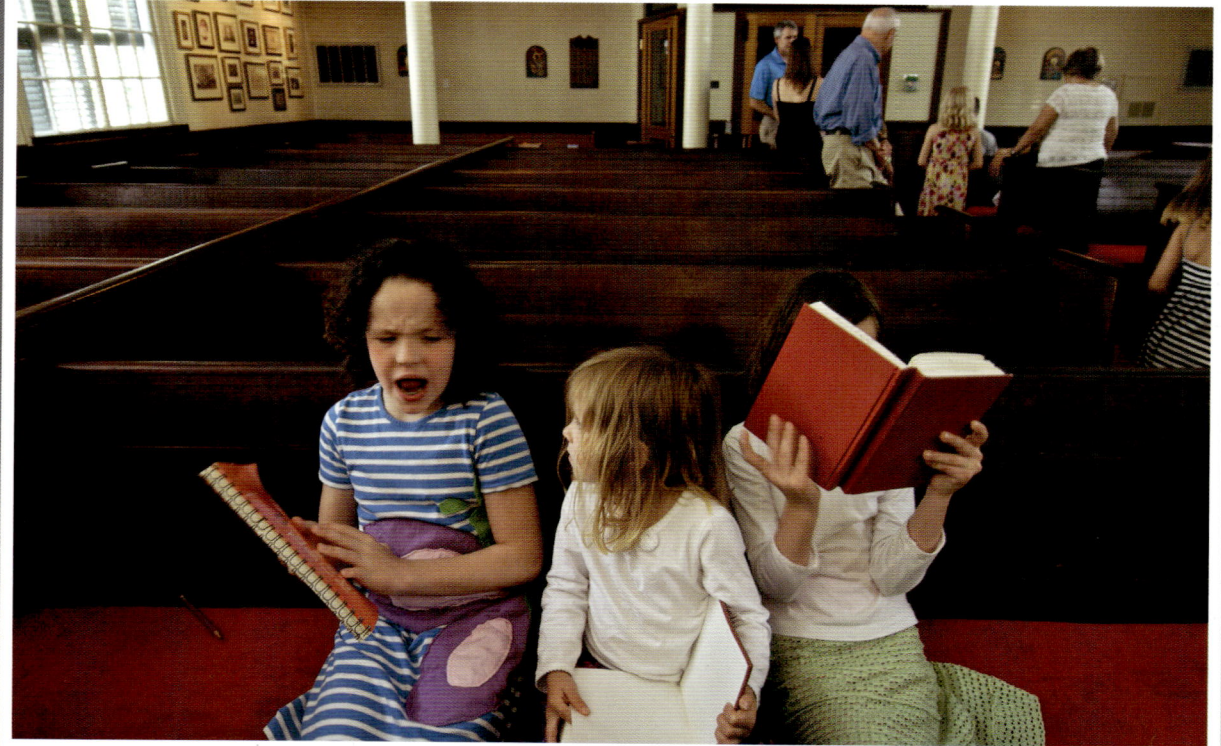

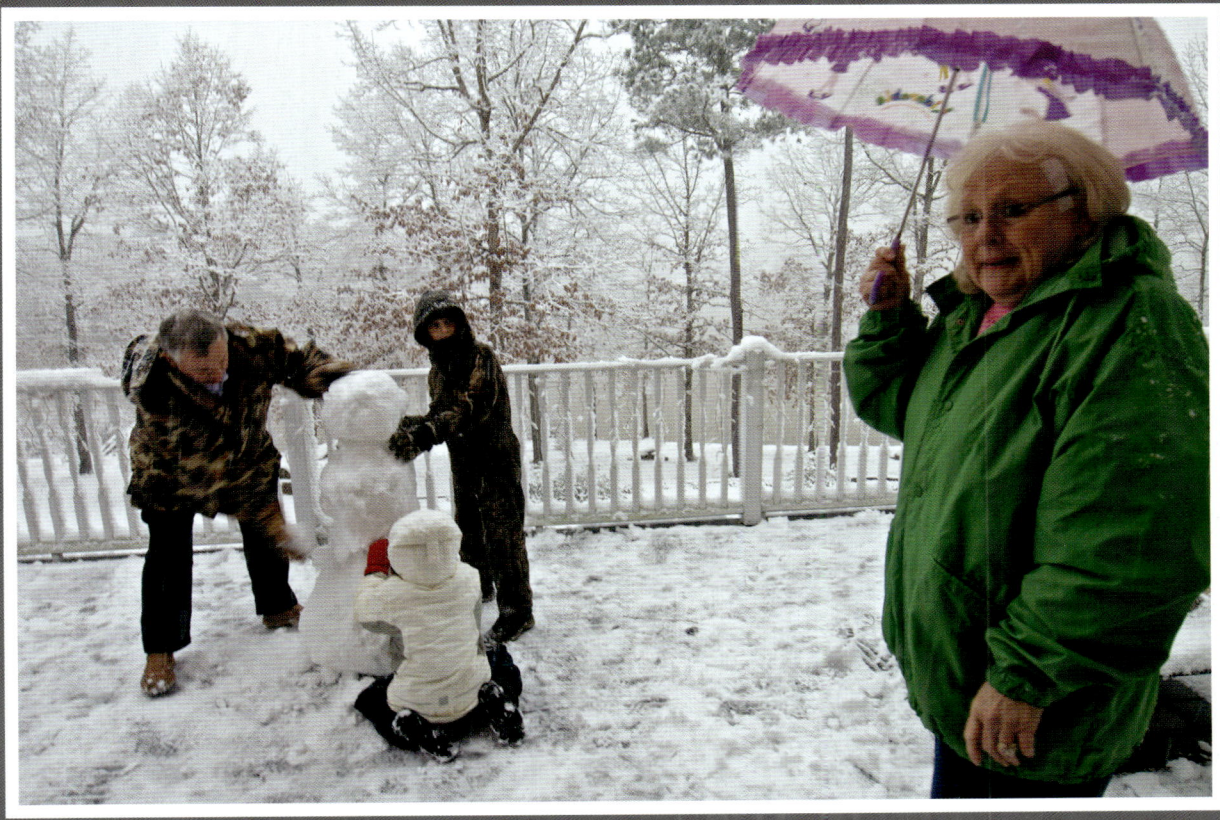

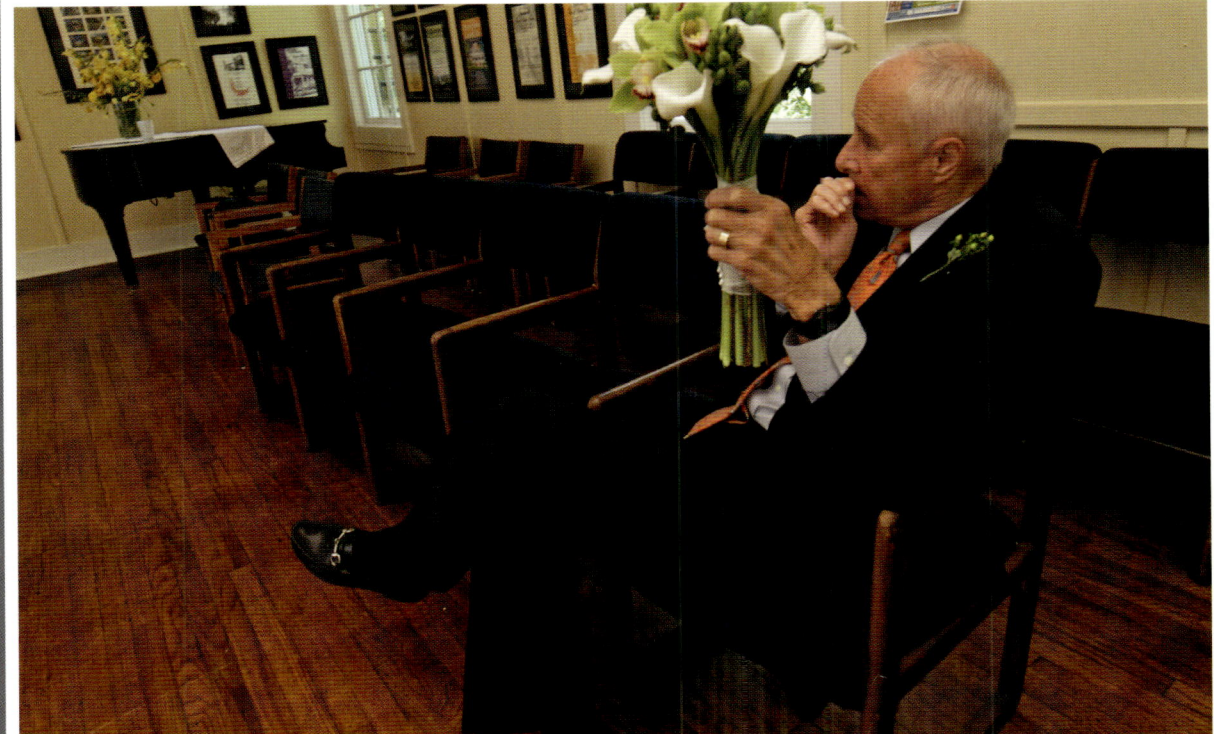

ABOVE: Papa helps grandchildren Bov and Mary Elise craft a snowman on the back porch while Mimi shivers in the foreground.

LEFT: Bucky, father of the bride, waits.

Focus on Family, Friends, & the Familiar

Use a Mobile Phone Camera for Spontaneous Documentary

I capture most of my favorite spontaneous moments of my children, my favorite (and most frequent) subjects, on a near daily basis using my iPhone camera and a variety of photography apps, quite simply because the iPhone is always with me and because it's so unobtrusive. I can easily shoot, process, and share a quick photograph without detaching myself from the experience. The mobile experience of processing my personal photographs in real time, titling them in intriguing ways, and sharing them with my viewers in Instagram and Twitter on my iPhone has become almost as appealing as the act of shooting. Sharing my personal documentary regularly online has been a way for me to gradually open myself up and experiment with photography as a form of expression—to learn what it feels like to expose who I am, what I see, and how I feel. It's helped me gain perspective on what it feels like to be the subject of a documentary study—a practice of letting my guard down and getting comfortable with a certain amount of exposure and vulnerability. Consequently, it's helped me gain a new level of appreciation and sensitivity for my subjects, and keeps me focused in the present moment.

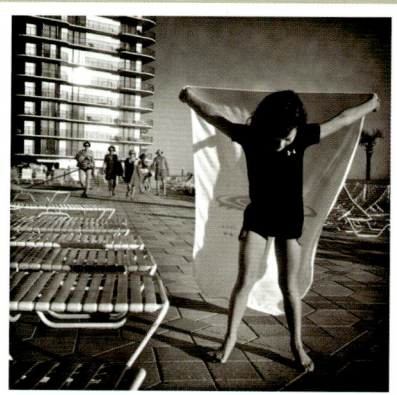

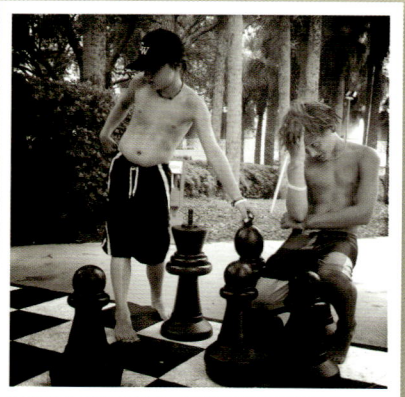

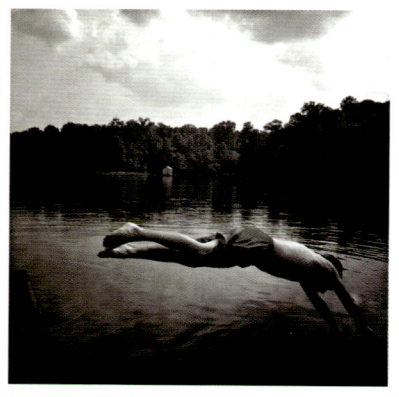

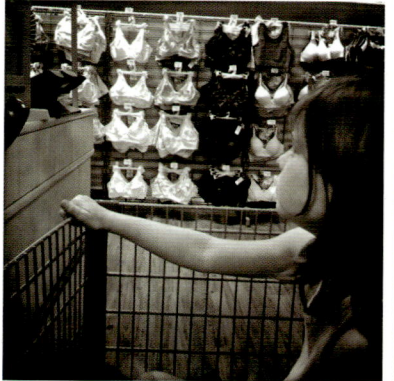

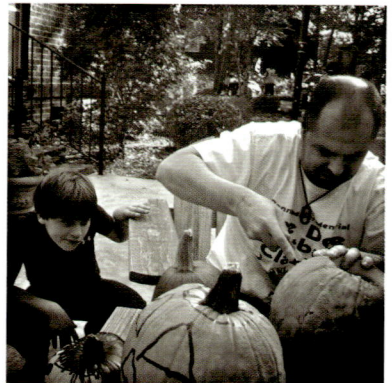

ABOVE: My son dives off the dock built by his father in the backyard. I shot this image while seated on the pontoon boat beside the dock, known as "ye old barge."

RIGHT: My daughter blows bubbles while I pump gasoline into our vehicle

ABOVE FAR LEFT: My daughter dons her superhero cape before racing along the edge of the pool with her fellow gymnasts in Panama City Beach, Florida.

FAR LEFT: My daughter takes a quick glance at the future (in a variety of shapes and sizes) from the confines of a shopping cart.

ABOVE LEFT: My son plans his next move on the poolside chess set at the Westin Hotel on Hilton Head Island, South Carolina, while his cousin questions the result.

LEFT: My son watches my brother carve the pumpkin to his exacting design specifications.

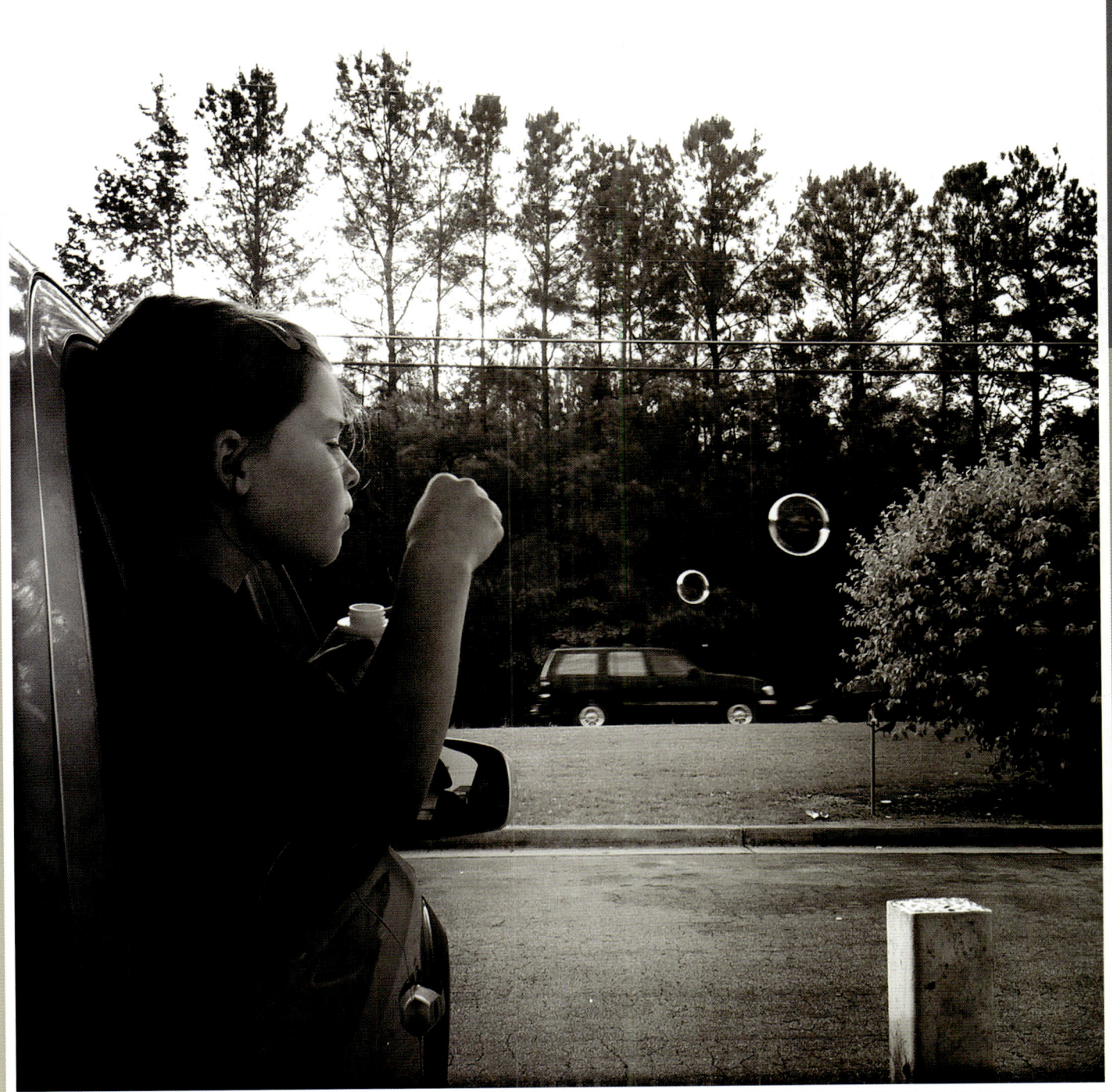

Raise Questions & Help Seek Solutions

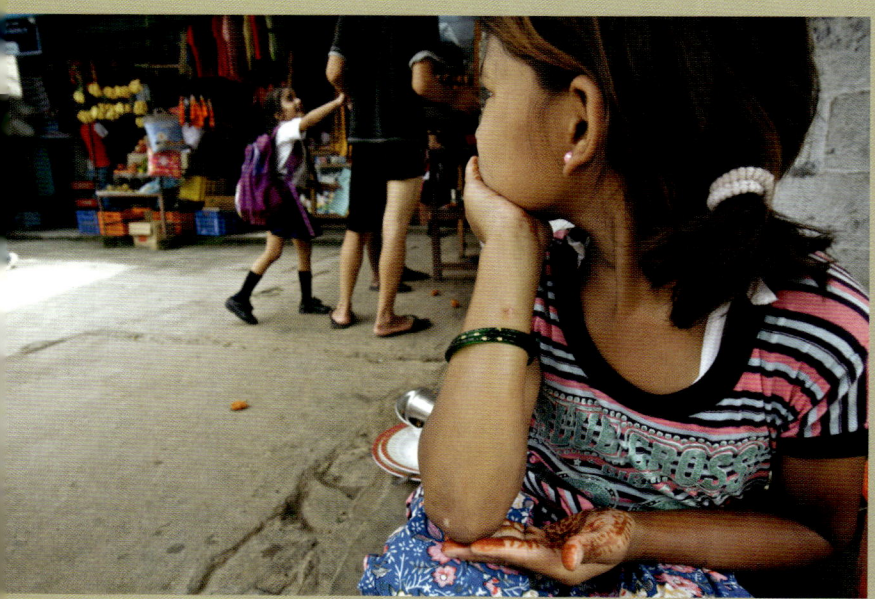
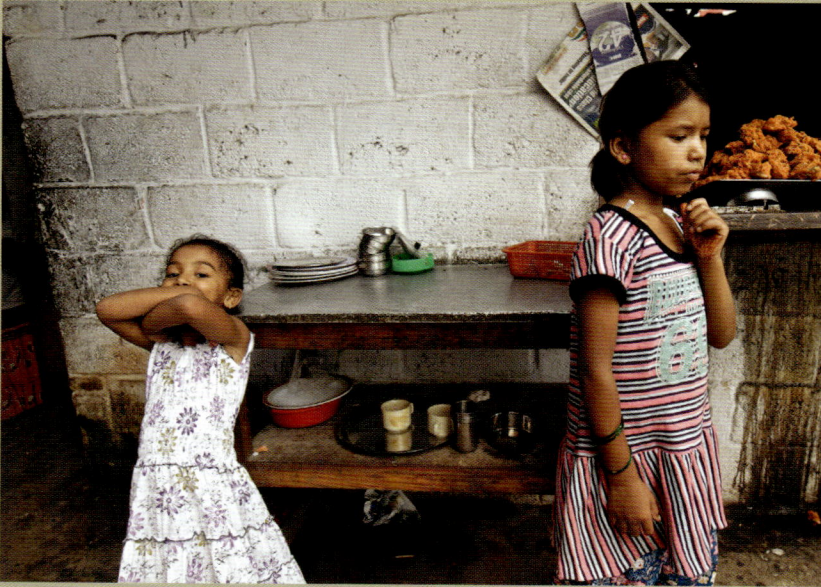

Documentary portraiture carries the weight of making a statement, raising a question, or revealing the truth on behalf of your subject. Shortly after I arrived in Pokhara, Nepal, a friend introduced us to several children known as "street kids" who lived and worked in the hotel downstairs. As I watched the young girls washing dishes with a hose and a bucket outside the restaurant, they seemed content on first glance. Intrigued with my interest and big camera, they giggled and exposed henna designs on the palms of their hands. I was relieved to see them smile because it helped me convince myself that they were okay, but had I only made images of these girls smiling, it would not have revealed the truth of their challenging existence.

My Nepali friend explained that these children had been sent away from their homes to work at the hotel—to earn a place to live, food to eat, and money that would be saved on their behalf when the time came for them to go out on their own. She explained that some street kids are sent to school. Others are not. It moved me very deeply to learn about this way of life, to witness it and document it with my own eyes. As I stood there studying the girls, I wondered what it might feel like to be far from home and to have to accept what's been given to you without question, to be vulnerable, to have a job at age ten, to appreciate what little you have, and to wish you had been given the chance to wear a school uniform.

Following my brief encounter with these children, my initial instinct was to return home and figure out a way to rally my family and friends to raise money for these children, but my Nepali friend stopped me. It would have been a short-term Western fix to a Nepali problem requiring a more long-term, sustainable solution. The real solution to the problem rests in the inspired hearts and minds of the local change makers in Nepal, individuals like my friend Renu Bagaria, founder of Koseli School. Our resources and support can be channeled to support these local change makers in a way they deem most valuable and in sync with their own culture and environment.

As a documentary photographer, it can be challenging (and perhaps impossible) to reveal harsh truths in life from an objective perspective—to provide answers, support, and/or solutions to your subjects' challenges. Life is complex. Learn to get comfortable with the questions, and use your talent responsibly as a documentary photographer to broaden perspectives, challenge norms, build empathy, and expose the truth in ways that might create awareness for ssues unseen or ignored and generate thoughts that could result in potential solutions. I challenge you (and myself) to find ways to use our talent as photographers and storytellers to not only document, but find a way to benefit the lives of our subjects.

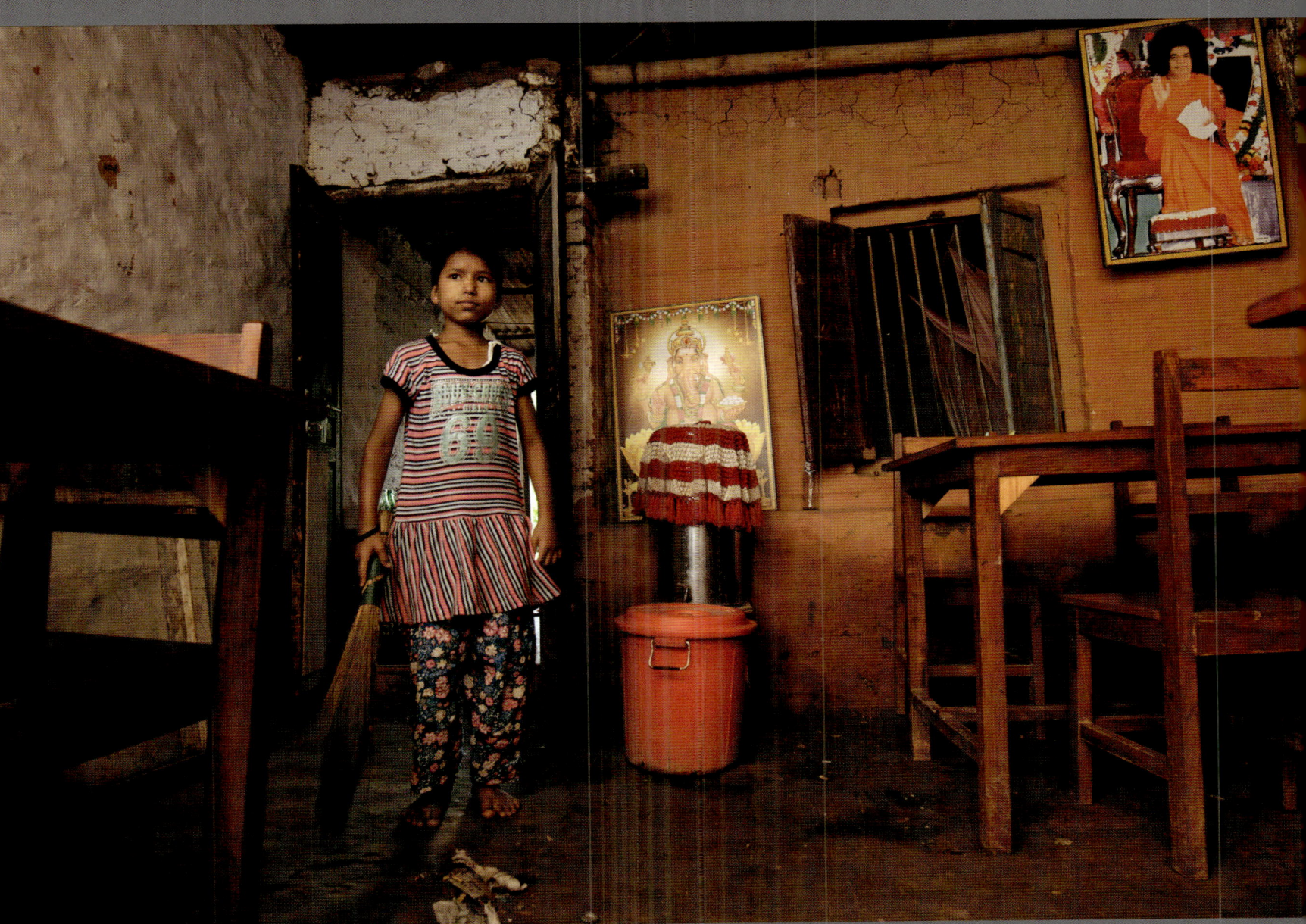

ABOVE, OPPOSITE LEFT, OPPOSITE RIGHT:
A young Nepali girl lives and works in
a restaurant/hotel situated in an area that
attracts tourists visiting and trekking in Nepal.
She admires her friend in the school uniform.

REFERENCE

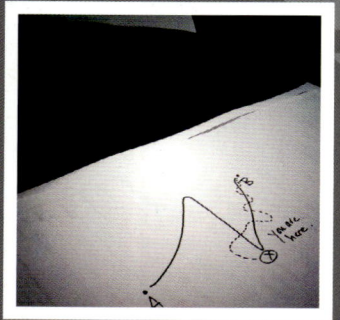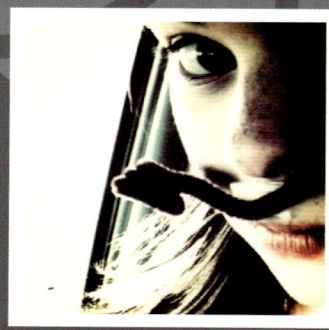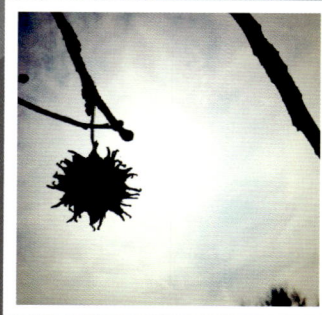

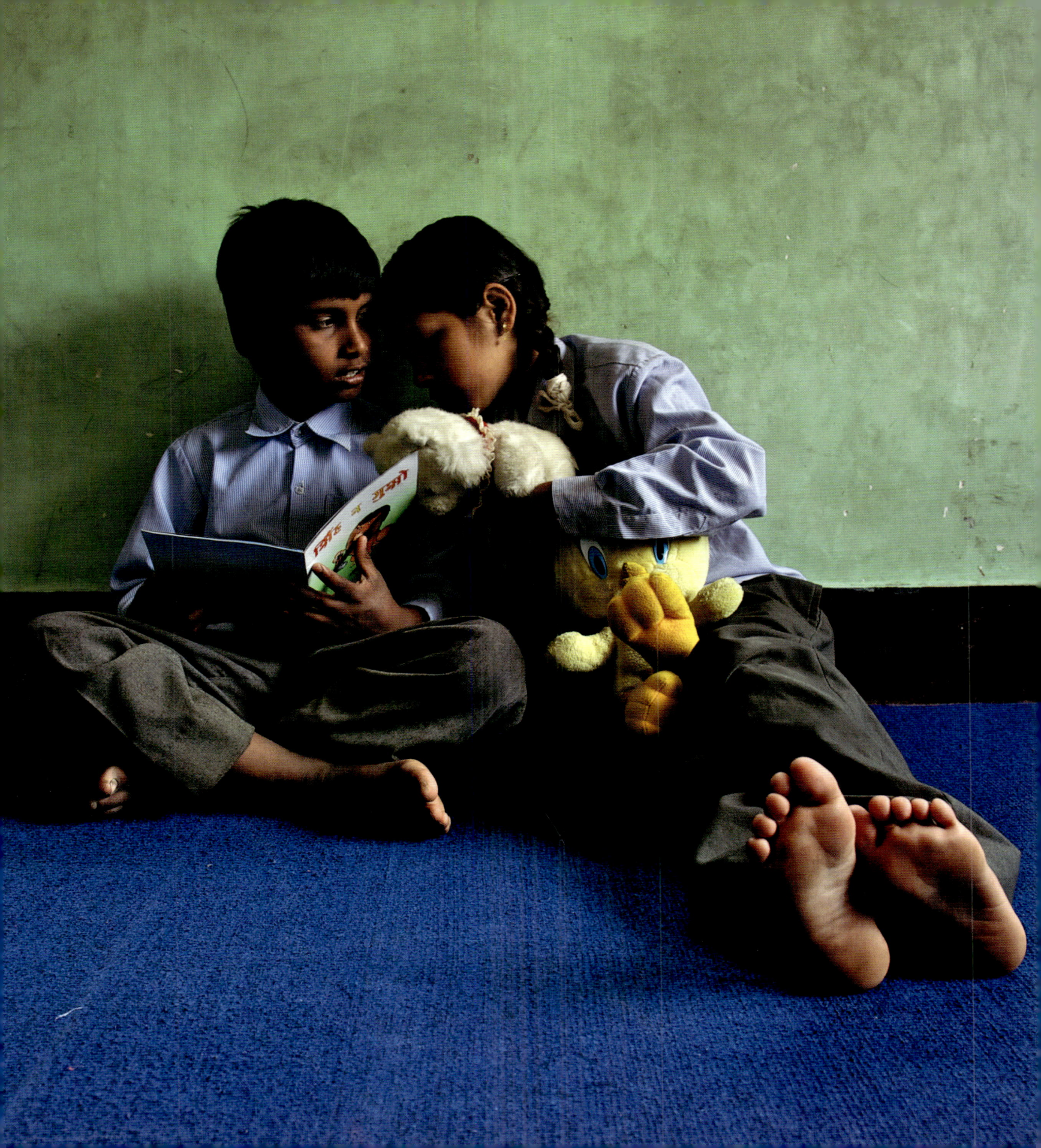

Thoughts on Fair Content

ABOUT FAIR CONTENT

The Fair Content concept was inspired and conceived by the contributions of Stacey Monk and Sanjay Patel of Epic Change, Jen Lemen of Hopeful World, and Samuel Suraphel of Beta Bahil, all in the United States, and Lucy Kamptoni of Shepherds Junior School in Arusha, Tanzania. This description of Fair Content is adapted from FairContent.org, an initiative of U.S. nonprofit Epic Change.

WHAT IF THE GREATEST ASSETS WE OWN ARE THE STORIES WE LIVE?

Stories educate, entertain, inspire, spread hope, share wisdom, and help us learn about the world in which we live. Stories have the capacity to generate or increase income when they take the form of products, communications, and/or marketing tools and campaigns for individuals, organizations, and businesses. As such, stories (delivered in a myriad of physical forms including photographs, essays, articles, books, marketing campaigns, and advertisements) are valuable assets.

Often, due to complex inequalities of wealth and power, storytellers, writers, photographers, filmmakers, nonprofit organizations, corporations, publishers, and others benefit financially by sharing stories without fairly compensating or providing editorial input to the individuals who have lived the stories they portray. Ironically, this may be especially true in telling stories related to issues of social justice, social change, and social innovation, and in situations where content providers live in material poverty or in marginalized communities. While in many cases, stories and imagery may be used in ways that benefit content providers, too frequently these stories are told in ways that evoke pity, exploit or denigrate their subjects, manipulate audiences, perpetuate negative stereotypes, and convey an implicit sense of inequality.

Fair Content is a movement and collaborative effort to encourage creative communicators, non-profit organizations, corporations, and publishers to provide fair compensation and editorial input to their subjects. Supporters of Fair Content believe people who share personal stories about their own lives have the right to determine how, to whom, and for what purposes their stories may be shared; to validate that their stories are portrayed in an honest and authentic way; and, particularly when their stories are shared in ways that generate income, to receive fair payment, not as a form of charity, but as compensation for a valuable asset.

FAIR CONTENT IN THIS BOOK

In the spirit of Fair Content, Lucy Kamptoni of Shepherds Junior School in Arusha, Tanzania proposed that she and I craft a Fair Content agreement so that Shepherds Junior School might benefit financially in part from any proceeds I receive from the creation and sale of this book. We worked collaboratively to craft and finalize a Fair Content agreement. Using our initial agreement as a model, I then proposed a Fair Content agreement with Renu Bagaria of Koseli School in Kathmandu, Nepal, so that Koseli School might share proceeds with me in the same way. As you consider starting or developing your documentary project ideas and find that you may have an opportunity to generate income from your portrayal of your subject's story, I encourage you to work collaboratively with your subject(s) to craft a Fair Content agreement.

CONNECT
Learn more about Fair Content:
www.faircontent.org

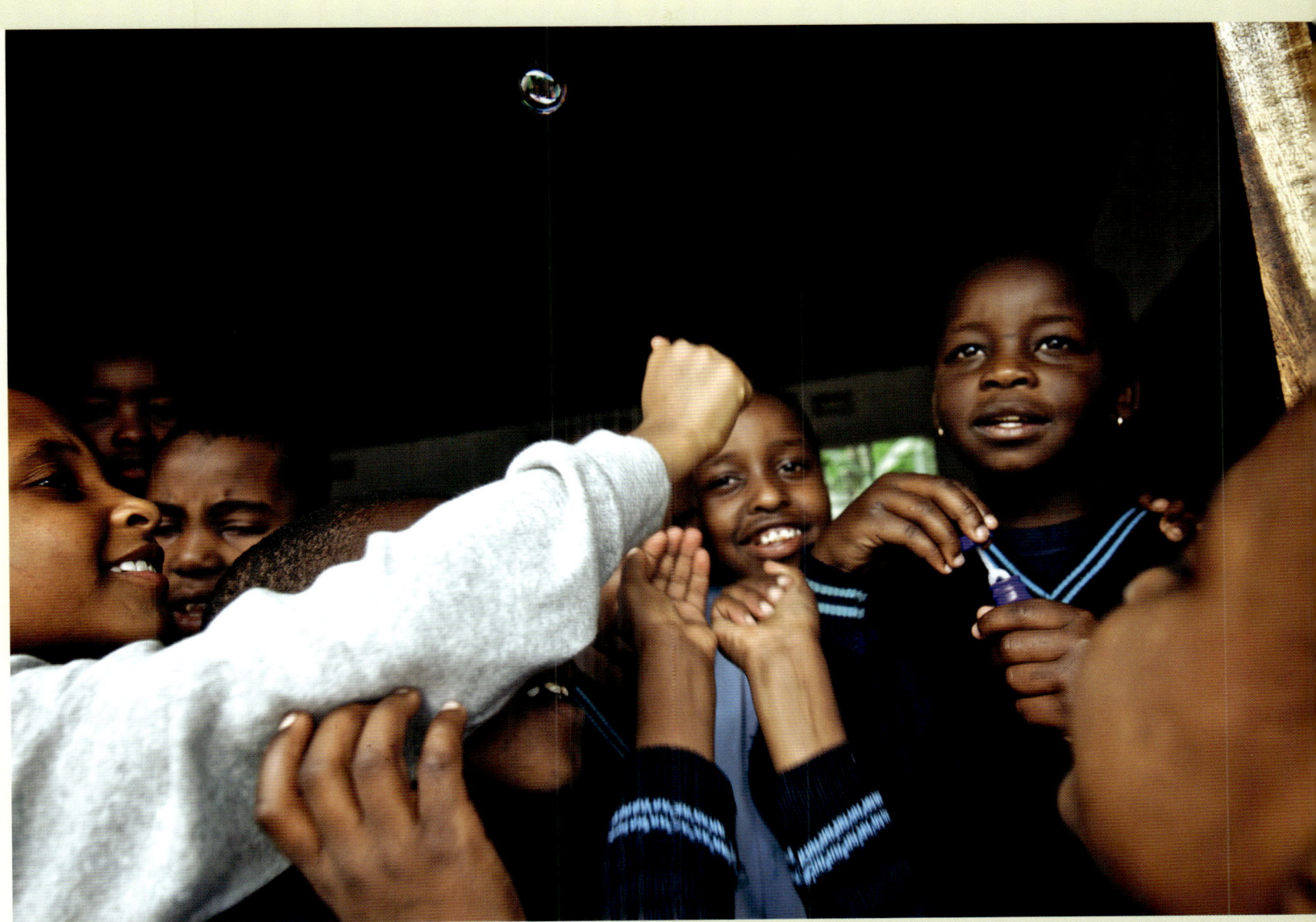

ABOVE: Students at Shepherds Junior School in Arusha, Tanzania.Learn more about the school on page 162 in Chapter 4: Push Through Boundaries and Let Your Subject Guide You.

Index

About the Author

Stephanie Calabrese Roberts is an award-winning documentary photographer, writer, and the creator of LittlePurpleCow Productions. Stephanie is the author of The Art of iPhoneography: A Guide to Mobile Creativity, and co-author of Expressive Photography: A Shutter Sisters Guide to Shooting from the Heart. Both books are available in numerous languages and distributed throughout the world. Her photography and writing have been published on www.life.com, www.forbes.com, Digital Photo magazine, Photographer's i magazine, and ASMP Bulletin, the publication of the American Society of Media Photographers. Stephanie is also a regular contributor to Shutter Sisters, the most popular online women's photography community.

In 2009, Stephanie (in partnership with fellow Shutter Sister Jen Lemen) won the "Name Your Dream Assignment" global photography competition sponsored by Microsoft and Lenovo. This award sent her on a journey to remote regions of Rwanda, Tanzania, and Nepal to capture and share images and stories of hope from wise and courageous changemakers, genocide survivors, and refugees. Following her Picture Hope project experience, she founded non-profit organization Lens on Life, Inc. in January 2011 with a vision to extend documentary photography education and resources to children and young adults living in material poverty around the world.

A social media and technology enthusiast, Stephanie is among the early leaders in the mobile photography movement and documents her own life through the lens of her iPhone on a near daily basis. She is mostly adventurous, always curious, and the proud mother of two fascinating children.

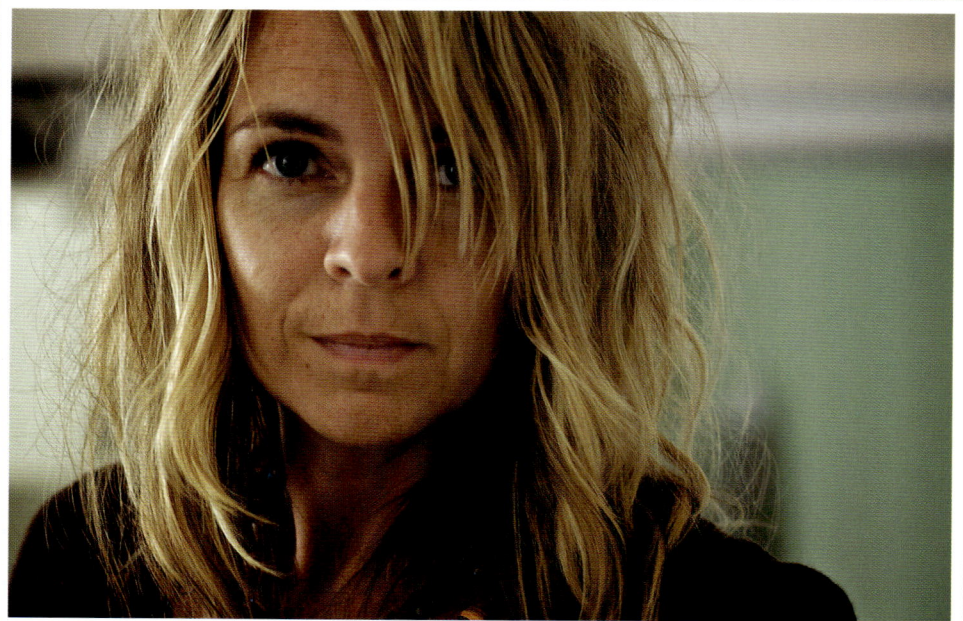

CONNECT AND FOLLOW
Stephanie Calabrese Roberts
BOOK: www.lensonlifebook.com
ORGANIZATION: www.lensonlife.org
TWITTER: @littlepurplecow
INSTAGRAM: @littlepurplecow

LEFT: Self-portrait of Stephanie Calabrese Roberts moments after returning home from a ten-day documentary shooting experience in Rwanda, August 2009.

About Lens On Life, The Non-Profit Organization

Lens on Life, a 501(c)(3) non-profit organization based in the United States, reveals and illuminates a visual voice for the unseen, particularly children and young adults living in material poverty around the world. The organization inspires creativity and cultivates photography skills in its participants through the lens of connecting diverse people across cultural, socioeconomic, and geographic boundaries. Lens on Life provides education, resources, community, and the sale and promotion of participants' photographic creations to help support the continuing education of its hopeful young photographers. Lens on Life partners with local schools and organizations around the world to host programs led by a volunteer community of seasoned photographers. Program workshops include instruction on camera and photography basics; study and discussion of photographs by seasoned photographers; journaling and story planning; creative exercises to engage students in shooting, processing, and captioning their photographs; and group critiques of students' work.

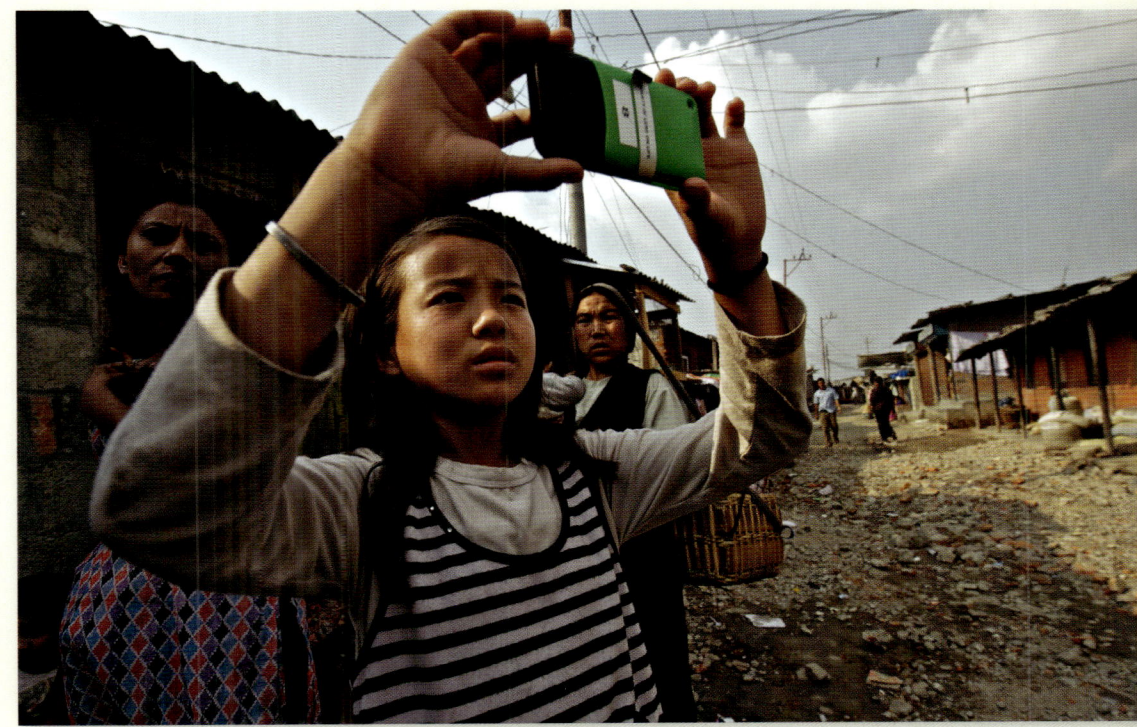

ABOVE: Koseli School student and Lens on Life program participant, Pinky, makes images of her home in Kathmandu, Nepal using an iPhone camera. Learn more about Koseli School on page 166 in Chapter 4: Push Through Boundaries and Let Your Subject Guide You.

Acknowledgments

AUTHORS ACKNOWLEDGMENTS

This book bears my name on its cover, yet it was created by the hearts and hands of many. I find great fascination, joy, and fulfillment in studying and photographing the lives of others and I feel blessed to have this opportunity to share my view with you. My sincere appreciation goes to:

My Picture Hope partner and friend, Jen Lemen, and our gracious hosts in Rwanda, Tanzania, and Nepal for guiding and supporting me through experiences that have deeply enriched my life, and for making me feel most welcome: (Rwanda) Innocent, Mupenzi, William, Betty, Frank, Alex, Goreth, Esteria, Odette, Mutoni, and Grace; (Tanzania) Mama Lucy and the staff and students at Shepherds Junior School, Stacey, Sanjay, and Praise and the staff at BEST; (Nepal) Nirmala, Mukesh, Induka, Shanti, Arun, Upama, Subhash, Sabi, Renu, Anand, Tanuj, and and the staff and students at Koseli School, especially Krishna, Mukesh, Manju, Rajesh, Raj, Manisha, Manoj, Namrata, Srijana, and Pinky.

Lucy Kamptoni, Stacey Monk, Sanjay Patel, Samuel Suraphel, and Jen Lemen for introducing me to the fair content initiative and for collaborating with me as I continue to explore and define my role and responsibilities as a documentarian.

My editor, Carey Jones, for sharing thoughtful, comprehensive, and timely feedback, questions, suggestions, and encouragement to me. Working with you is always a pleasure.

Adam Juniper, Natalia Price-Cabrera, Tara Gallagher, Zara Larcombe, and the Ilex Press design team for embracing, designing, editing, managing, producing, marketing, and guiding this book out into the world.

Elliott Erwitt, Elizabeth Fleming, Sion Fullana, Ed Kashi, Jen Lemen, John Loengard, Beth Rooney, and Rick Smolan for sharing your experiences, perspectives, and photographs in this book. You inspire me.

My subjects, many of whom are family and friends I love, and especially to my children, Bo and Mary Elise, for being interesting, open, trusting, patient, and generous with me.

God for continuing to inspire, challenge, and support me on my journey.